HPBooks®

Pro Techniques of

Beauty & Glamour PHOTOGRAPHY

Gary Bernstein

Published by HPBooks, A Division of HPBooks, Inc.
P.O. Box 5367, Tucson, AZ 85703 (602) 888-2150
ISBN:0-89586-364-2 Library of Congress Catalog No. 85-60457
 Printed in U.S.A.
3rd Printing

Publisher: Rick Bailey
Executive Editor: Randy Summerlin
Senior Editor: Vernon Gorter
Art Director: Don Burton
Book Design & Drawings: Kathleen Koopman
Production Coordinator: Cindy J. Coatsworth
Typography: Michelle Carter
Director of Manufacturing: Anthony B. Narducci

THANKS

I'm sincerely grateful for the generous help given by many individuals and companies.
Special thanks to:
Thomas Slatky (represented by Lee + Lou of Los Angeles)—for his sure hand and quality retouching;
A & I Labs., Inc. Hollywood, California—for fine transparency duplicating services;
Alfa Color Labs, Inc., Gardena, California—for color printing services;
Kay Sutton York—for her creative contribution

DEDICATION

For Iris

FOREWORD

One feels deeply honored when asked to do something that bears a great deal of responsibility. It is especially meaningful if that responsibility is to a friend.

During the past 22 years I have looked at a lot of lenses. Fortunately, most of them were on movie cameras. I always felt comfortable. However, I never felt relaxed in front of a still camera—maybe because it captured "moments," many of which were private. The photos usually ended up in one of our notorious tabloids or movie magazines, with some silly caption.

Having a simple photograph shot for GQ magazine in 1979 sounded easy enough. For most, it would have been. For me, it was like going to the dentist! I arrived feeling uneasy, expecting the worst. Being basically a shy and introverted person didn't help.

As soon as I met the photographer, I felt a little more comfortable. We began to shoot—and we talked football, hunting, fishing and about the business we're both involved in. From pictures of personalities he had photographed in the past, I could tell that he was fantastic at what he does.

I left the studio feeling good about the session. A few days later I saw the results. I have never used another photographer since then. That was six years ago. I recommend this photographer to everyone who asks me who's the best.

He's Gary Bernstein—now my friend!

Lee Majors

Donna Mills
by Gary Bernstein
for Jean-Paul
Germain, Ltd.

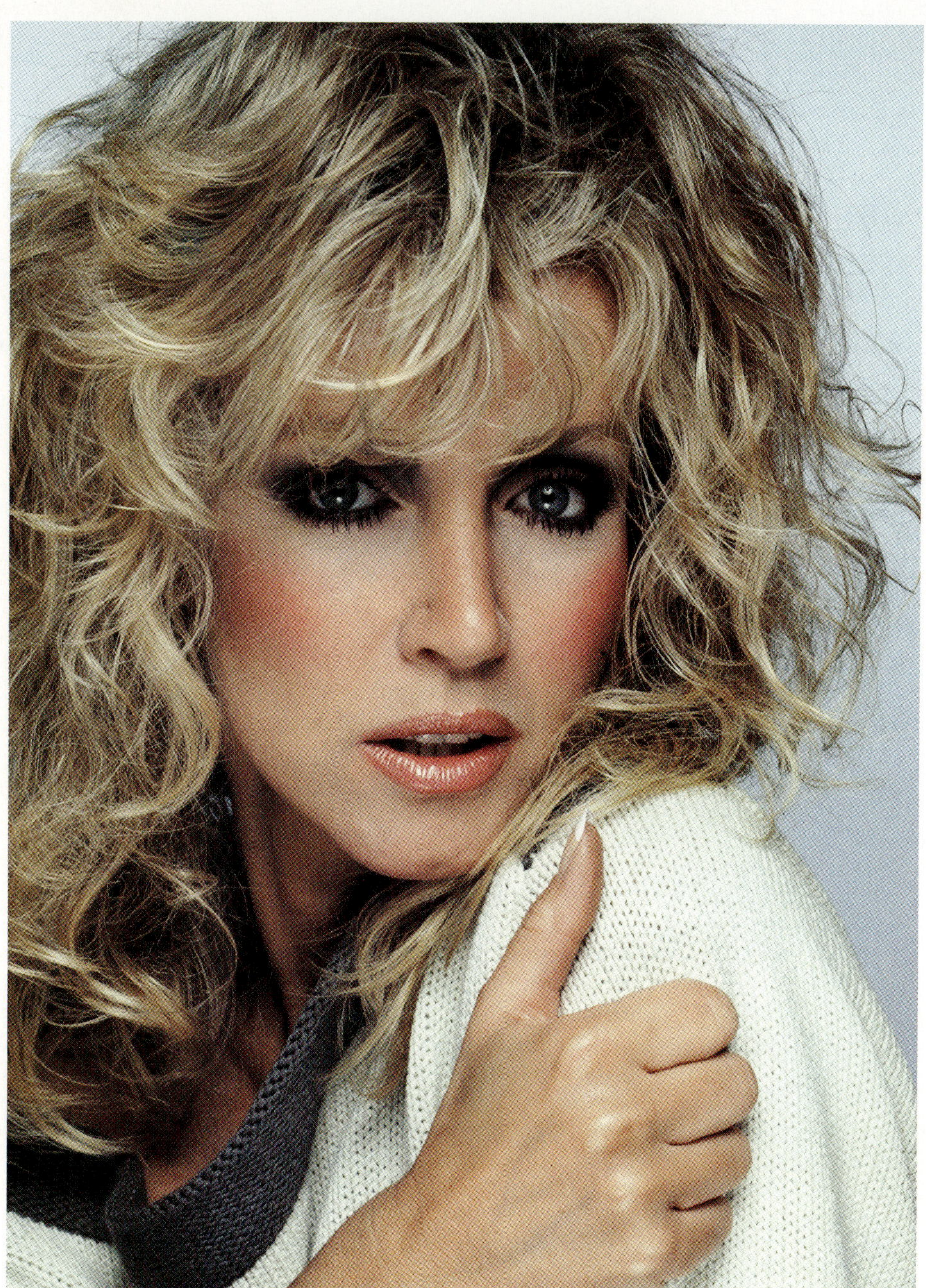

Contents

Introduction

Photography, like life, is composed of those who merely fantasize about doing and those who go out and do. This book is directed at, and dedicated to, the doers—the photographers with a passion for self-expression. It is intended for those of you who want to move a step beyond the crowd in terms of photographic technique and pictorial quality.

Completion of my first book for HPBooks, *Pro Techniques of People Photography,* gave me a great feeling of accomplishment. This was accompanied, however, by at least a little disappointment. It seemed that there was still so much more to say.

In *Pro Techniques of Beauty & Glamour Photography,* I'll give you a detailed look at a variety of photo techniques in practical application. As with the first volume, a rich portfolio section depicts noteworthy examples from assignments produced for some of the world's top companies and celebrities. The portfolio affords you a unique look at photographic principles in practice.

This book describes a variety of lighting and metering techniques and applications. Some of the accompanying instructional photos I took specifically for this purpose. I've discussed makeup and hairstyling in a way I think will be informative and stimulating. I've also included special advice for those aiming to pursue photography as a career.

Dogmatically imposed constraints serve little purpose in artistic endeavors. Therefore, I'm not going to impose rules on you. I'm simply going to tell you what has worked, and does work, for me. If what I tell you proves thought-provoking, the purpose of the book will be fulfilled. Remember, however, that viewpoints and opinions are living entities and always subject to change.

What's contained in this book represents what I believe today—at this moment in my development and career. While it's all valid, it is also subject to subtle changes as I proceed through life.

Don't stagnate! You, too, should not be afraid to change when change is appropriate. The essence of art—as of life—is change and growth.

It is my aim to provide through this book a stimulant that will lead to better and more imaginative photography. However, the ultimate success of the book is largely dependent on you alone.

You can't produce high-quality photographs as long as you are only a spectator—or reader. You must be a *doer!* When all is said and done, your success will be mainly dependent on your own motivation and dedication.

I wish you success! □

1

Planning the Photo Session

Good photography is much more dependent on *mind* than on *matter.* What you do, how you do it and—perhaps most essentially—why you do it, are much more important than the equipment you do it with.

The psychology behind advertisements for cameras is often based on the assumption that serious amateur photographers like to think of themselves as being on an equal level with professionals. The domain of the professional beauty and glamour photographer is perceived as being filled with excitement. And, indeed, it often is. However, the most important characteristic of a professional photographer is his commitment to quality and dependability.

The professional must display a dedication and desire to fulfill his personal esthetic goals while at the same time satisfying the client's needs. Furthermore, not only must the professional aim to produce quality—he is expected to do so consistently.

Different photographers approach their subjects in different ways. The photographer of still-lifes, scenics and products, for example, deals with inanimate materials and scenes. He can generally work at his own pace and without the need to interact. His only concern is the finished photograph. His attitude and mode of operation are relatively inconsequential because they don't affect the subject. His photos may often elicit emotion, but his subject matter is totally unresponsive.

It's very different with the people photographer, who must interact favorably with other human beings to get the pictures he wants.

ESTABLISH THE PURPOSE OF YOUR PHOTOGRAPHY

As a photographer of people, you must carefully define your reasons for making photographs. If your aim is to beautify people—which is the purpose of most people photography—your results will depend on significant emotional involvement with the subject. You must have a logical plan for achieving the goal. The plan must be tempered with the awareness that all subjects are sensitive and none are exactly alike. Consistent success in photographing people depends on a harmonious interrelationship with each and every subject.

It is you, the photographer, who must be the leader. Behind the camera, you are the director. Regardless of whether you're shooting for fun or hired to produce a photograph, harmonious communication between you and your subject is imperative.

What is the specific purpose of the photography session? Is your subject a client who needs a business portrait suitable for a newspaper or publicity release? If so, select a suitable location for the photography. The subject's office may be the best place. If he prefers the privacy of your studio, prepare appropriate backgrounds and props. You may need to rent an oak desk or perhaps some shelves filled with books. It may be necessary to panel part of a studio wall. Do whatever is necessary to create the right environment for the session.

Satisfy the Subject—The public is used to seeing contemporary editorial and advertising photographs in large quantities. Many of my female subjects look for informality in photos depicting them. Some like an image that's ethereal. Women frequently indicate their desires by showing me pages torn from magazines. "I love the way the model looks in this ad," expressed one of my clients, adding "Can you make me look like that?"

If the model in the example I'm shown was photographed in soft focus on a fur rug, I prepare for the session by getting a diffuser and a selection of fur rugs. My foremost desire is to please the client. To do this, I must be prepared before the session starts.

When taking portraits, determine the subject's esthetic likes and dislikes prior to the photography session. You can help to do this by also showing photographs. Show your subject a variety of pictures—they need not all be your own work. Which photographs appeal to the subject? And why? Discuss the pose, location, clothing, props and background with the subject.

Remember, appealing people photographs are rarely produced by the photographer alone. A joint effort creates a more enjoyable, productive shooting experience for both of you.

Your creative possibilities are almost unlimited. There is not a *right* or *wrong* way to take a photograph. An infinite number of visual effects are at your command. Use the best means you can find to ensure the subject's satisfaction.

EMOTIONAL NEEDS OF SUBJECT

The volumes of self-help books on the market indicate the basic insecurity of the public in many areas of personal endeavor. To be successful in your photography, you must be capable of putting your subjects totally at ease. Very few individuals are confident at the start of a photo session. Almost all need encouragement—some of them every step of the way.

Each subject has one common goal: To be photographed in the most pleasing and flattering way. Consequently, confident but relaxed *direction* is the key to all good beauty and glamour photography.

Try to establish *immediate* rapport with your subjects. I flatter them from the moment they enter my studio. And, I continue to build their confidence throughout the photo session. Even if my earliest images are less than I had hoped to achieve, I continue to give encouragement.

Subject Sensitivity—Be sensitive to the fact that you are much easier to please than the subject—and with good reason. As photographer, your view of the subject is objective. Your main concern tends to be with eyes, facial features and skin texture. However, your subjects see themselves in a very subjective way. They have preconceived ideas about the way the world sees them. The image you produce may be totally contrary to the way a subject has learned to see himself over a lifetime.

A photo session is not an everyday occurrence for most people. Upon viewing the results of a session, a subject will be concerned about the effect your photographs will have on others—friends, family members and business associates. A first look at photos sometimes comes as a shock to a subject—even if he eventually comes to like the images.

Photography lends itself to great creativity and manipulation. I'm enthralled with the different aspects of a personality that can be derived from a single individual. Because I don't know most of my subjects well prior to photography, I don't have a preconceived idea of their character or personality, as I would have with close friends. Therefore, I can shoot with minimal inhibitions. However, I must be sensitive to the fact that the subject's self-image is very subjective.

Communicate—Often, the gap between our different viewpoints can be largely bridged by sympathetic discussion before a session. I can then *direct* the subject in a manner most likely to produce images that bring satisfaction to us both. Giving your photo session direction isn't a negative constraint. It is an aid that you can push aside whenever you feel like it.

The commercial photographer, who must suit the needs of a specific client, has relatively little flexibility. However, when you're shooting portraits for a subject, don't be afraid to shoot spontaneously. This sometimes leads to the best pictures of all.

When people *feel* good, they generally *look* good. The sheer power of encouragement can work visual wonders on a face and body.

SPEED AND EFFICIENCY

The professional photographer's success depends largely on speed and efficiency of operation. This is necessary to avoid subject boredom, not merely to handle a possibly excessive workload. Your subjects require constant encouragement and attention. You may lose their cooperation if you're preoccupied with technicalities.

You can retain a subject's attention and enthusiasm in two major ways—with constant verbal encouragement and with efficiency in your operations. Don't keep the subject waiting while you fidget with lights, reflectors and camera. If you do, the subject will soon fidget, too—and the chance of the session being a success will be slight.

Photography has few unbreakable rules. Those that exist do so only because of photography's dependence on certain laws of physics. Know those laws and how they affect the photographic process. Beyond that, your own creativity is the lifeblood of your work. It is your individuality alone that separates your photographs from those made by others.

The examples in this text are not meant to indicate *right* from *wrong.* Quite to the contrary, they represent only one photographer's vision. For you, they can serve as a "starting block" from which to grow and expand.

Most subjects haven't the slightest knowledge of photographic principles and technique. However, everyone can sense instinctively when incompetence or sloppiness is present. Setting up and moving lights, placement of reflectors and adjustment of exposure should come as naturally as taking the next breath. Most of your conscious energy should be devoted to your communication with the subject and the creative process.

When You Work Alone—If you don't have the luxury of an assistant, as will often be the case, be extra sure to be fully prepared for a smoothly operating session. To minimize interruptions in your shooting, load the longest rolls of film obtainable. For example, use 36-exposure 35mm film rather than 20-exposure film. An added advantage is the lower cost per image.

If you own two or more camera bodies, load them all—and attach a lens of different focal length to each. This enables you to shoot for an extended period without having to take a break. Basically, it's a good idea to always have more of everything than you think you'll need.

Plan Your Lighting—If you have an opportunity to meet the subject before the session, determine in advance the lighting you consider most suitable. However, be prepared for last-minute changes. For example, you may determine that your subject should be photographed by soft window light. Check the available light a day before the shooting at the time of day scheduled for photography. If you make test exposure readings on an overcast day, be sure that direct sunshine won't enter the window if the sun should shine during the session.

Make allowances for the need for a film of different speed or exposure variations under different lighting conditions. In an extreme situation, you may have to use artificial light to simulate window light. Be prepared for all eventualities!

EQUIPMENT YOU NEED

Just as a good cook wouldn't be caught without salt and pepper, you should be sure to have the photographic staples essential to operational effectiveness and efficiency. Let's evaluate some of them:

Tripod With Pan-and-Tilt Head— The specific photographic situation dictates whether a tripod is needed. I use a Gitzo tripod with pan-and-tilt head when I have to adhere to a specific layout where the model must occupy a specified part of the composition. The object is usually to leave a predetermined area clear for headlines and body copy. With my camera on a tripod, I can position the critical compositional elements at the start of the session and then concentrate my attention on the model.

Image sharpness and clarity is a prime requirement in most of my assignments. Consequently, I select slow, fine-grain transparency film for most of my work. Generally, I use Kodachrome 25. Such slow film often requires a relatively slow shutter speed during natural-light beauty assignments. Rather than use a faster film, I'll use a tripod whenever the light level and lens aperture demand a shutter speed of 1/125 second or slower.

Many advertising assignments require sequential photography. This means a series of shots must all have the same basic composition and lighting characteristics. A tripod ensures this consistency—particularly when I'm using multiple light sources of varying intensities.

Photography of groups of people often involves intricate posing and precise cropping. Here, too, the use of a tripod allows me to set the composition at the start of the session. Then I'm free to concentrate on my subjects—all the more essential because I have to deal with several people at once.

A pan-and-tilt head, or a ball head, is essential. It enables me to make minor adjustments in cropping—rapidly and accurately.

Reflectors—Reflectors are as important as your light sources. As you'll see throughout this book, a great variety of photographic effects can be produced by them.

Reflectors can have a matte white or a shiny silver surface. They can even be black, to *remove* light from specific areas. With reflectors, contrast can be reduced or enhanced without a change in the main-light position. When positioned properly, a reflector can add sparkle to a subject's eyes or soften lines and skin blemishes that might otherwise require extensive retouching.

Outdoors, a reflector can redirect midday sunlight so it strikes the subject from a lower, more flattering, angle. A reflector can also create shade on a sunny day or produce a controllable source of fill light.

When on location, I've even used large reflectors to shield subject and camera from rain. I've also used large reflectors to build a makeshift dressing room on location. As in your actual photography, *inventiveness* is the key word!

Filters—A skylight filter and a diffusion attachment should be part of your permanent equipment arsenal. Open shade is an ideal source of soft, natural light. It is flattering to most faces. However, a large area of blue or overcast sky gives the subject and other elements in the scene a bluish cast. A *skylight filter* removes much of the unwanted blue and renders skin tones, as well as the other colors in the scene, normally.

An image can be softened with the use of a good *diffusion attachment.* In my beauty and glamour photography, the subject or client frequently prefers a soft-focus version. The diffusion can take place when the camera exposure is made, or later. I generally prefer softening my images at the printing or duplicating stage. It enables me to control the degree of diffusion and leaves me with the undiffused original. If I were to diffuse an image in the camera, I would have only the diffused image. If a client specifically requests a diffused original slide, I'll shoot it without diffuser also.

There are many excellent commercial diffusers on the market. However, I've achieved wonderful results with diffusers I made myself. As base, I use glass ultraviolet (UV) filters or sheets of acetate. On this base I spray commercial fixative in varying densities, depending on the degree of softening I want.

A glass base has a distinct advantage: If you want to reduce the diffusion effect, it's easy to remove spray fixative with a lacquer thinner.

Light Meter—The quality and accuracy of modern through-the-lens (TTL) metering systems leave little to be desired. However, a good separate handheld meter provides far greater flexibility in use. Most handheld meters can be used in both the incident-light and reflected-light modes. Many allow for selective angles of acceptance and multiple exposure readings, too. And, at the very least, the handheld meter provides you with a valuable "second opinion."

How accurate must your light meter be? I consider reliability and consistency to be far more important than accuracy. When a meter performs consistently, you can easily calibrate it for your own purposes. However, a meter that's accurate—but only some of the time—is of little use.

Too much emphasis is often placed on obtaining critically accurate exposures. However, in practice the best a light meter can do is provide an approximation of "best" exposure. That's because there are too many variables in the typical situation. They include film-speed variances, camera-performance variances, subject-contrast conditions and your own visual preferences.

Fortunately, most films have adequate exposure range to allow for minor exposure errors without much harm. By habitually bracketing exposures, you can generally eliminate the effect of undesirable variables.

Color-transparency films require the greatest exposure accuracy, because no corrections can be made once the film is processed. If you're aware of exposure errors at the time of shooting, and you're using films such as Ektachrome—which lend themselves to processing manipulation—you can compensate to some extent by an adjustment in the processing. However, Kodachromes generally don't allow for processing variations, so that compensation for inaccurate exposure cannot be made.

Even when I know that the lighting conditions have changed during a session, I won't stop to make further meter readings. Doing so would endanger the continuity and mood of the session—and I can't risk that. Consequently, I bracket my exposures liberally. When we reach a "natural" break in the shooting, I'll check my meter readings. If my calculation were way off, I'll adjust the exposure and shoot some more.

Electric Fan—One of my non-photographic staples is a small, portable electric fan. I often use it to blow a subject's hair, to add a little motion or "life" to a photograph. A fan can also have a noticeable relaxing effect on a subject. Its gentle sound and the moving air tend to have a calming effect on nervous subjects.

You'll put a lot of thought and energy into your photo sessions. Don't deprive yourself of the best possible results by not having some relatively small, but very important, piece of equipment. You owe it to both yourself and your subject.

CREATIVE VARIETY

There isn't an *ideal* time of day for photography, nor is there an *ideal* aperture, lens, camera angle, filter, film or lighting effect. There is not one *ideal* view of the face. And, as explained earlier, there isn't even an *ideal* exposure. Because each subject is unique, and because each photographer has his own special vision and sensitivity, inflexible rules are inappropriate.

So what *is* the measure of photographic success? I consider a successful photograph to be one in which I like the results because they are precisely how I had previsualized them. I also consider a photo to be a success when the subject is totally pleased with the result.

Only *you* know the direction you want your photography to take. Only *you* envision the finished photograph prior to its appearance on film or paper. An essential part of your preparation for photography is the mental, technical and creative process of previsualizing. The next logical step is the execution of your intentions.

You don't want unpleasant surprises when viewing your efforts. The results should be as you had anticipated them. This requires you to be consistent in your work. As I've indicated in this essay several times, one essential way of ensuring consistency is to be totally prepared. In addition to having the necessary equipment, you must be prepared with technical know-how and creative ideas.

Many photographers don't give free rein to their potential creativity. Don't be afraid to vary your technique and its application. Try something new. If it doesn't work, throw the result away. At the very least, you'll learn something from the experience.

Adapt your technique to the specific needs and characteristics of your subject. And, always strive to satisfy the specific desires of the subject.

FIND THE BEST IN PEOPLE

What of those individuals who, by our society's standards, are less than beautiful? Look for their special features—eyes that smile, wonderful hair, a finely chiseled nose or jawline. Try shooting extreme close-ups of such subjects, emphasizing their best features. Employ a wide variety of lighting techniques and camera angles. Alter perspective through the use of different shooting distances —and lenses of accordingly shorter or longer focal lengths.

On a recent portrait assignment, I was confronted by an unusually insecure subject. She was concerned over her weight and poor skin. She had always wanted to be photographed like a magazine model or celebrity. However, she thought that she had always looked unattractive in previous photographic results.

As we spoke, I noticed the size and beautiful color of her eyes. I always look at eyes first. They are, after all, the portals of the soul. The eyes reveal the subject's mood and rapport with the photographer the moment the exposure is made.

I knew my subject could be photographed in a way she would find appealing and I told her so. In fact, I *convinced* her of it. Remember, you must give emotional energy and support to your subject. Elevate the subject's spirit. Believe in the subject's characteristics as you do in your own capabilities. It will be reflected in your photographic results.

I decided to use a coarse-grain color film for the session. The film minimizes apparent skin problems, creating a softer rendition of the subject. It allowed the shape of her eyes and facial contours to appear without distraction. During the course of the photo session, I used a variety of cardboard scraps and boxes to create carefully located shadows on her face. I was able to emphasize certain areas—such as her eyes—while subduing elements she considered unappealing.

I was able to further emphasize the size of her eyes by using two large, silver reflectors below and to the side of her face. The eyes sparkled in the finished photographs. She loved the results!

You'll be surprised at what you can create with a concerted effort. *Everyone* is beautiful. It begins with *your* recognition of it!

Plan to meet all eventualities. To be successful in *all* your people photography, you must have both adequate equipment and know-how. □

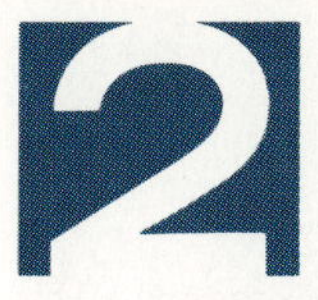

Lighting and Metering Applications

Photography enables us to preserve a moment in time. Through a unique combination of science and art, we can depict a three-dimensional object or scene on a two-dimensional surface.

Lighting has a lot to do with creating the illusion of depth in space on flat film. For example, light areas in a photo tend to project forward while darker tones recede to the distance. Consequently, proper rendition of highlight to shadow is often critical for pictorial impact.

The novice photographer is often eager to live by a collection of inflexible rules governing the use of light. Basic guidelines do exist, but only the experienced and dedicated photographer realizes the need for thought beyond the rules. He manipulates light to suit the individual subject. It is the thought process alone that can make a photographer's work a personal statement.

As contemporary photographers, we have a great advantage over the early pioneers. Modern technology has provided us with instruments capable of accurate and consistent control and measurement of light.

In photography, light and its metering are inseparable. Throughout the text, I'll discuss them jointly.

Each photographic subject is unique in personal characteristics such as age, physical appearance and attitude. A lighting application that enhances the look of one individual may be inappropriate for the next. It's important to develop an extensive understanding of lighting principles so you command a variety of applications and effects. When used wisely, light can enhance the beauty of the human face and form.

The photographic examples in this essay represent only a few of the many possible lighting variations. There is not a formula for creativity. It is composed of too many personal, often intangible, factors to be reduced to a formula. The examples, however, provide a starting block—a foundation from which to experiment, analyze and expand.

Throughout the book, you'll see a variety of flattering glamour lighting applications. Through them, I'm trying to show you the diversity and power of lighting—its creative, manipulative and corrective uses in the photography of people.

I made most of the photos in this essay in my Los Angeles studio with state-of-the-art lighting equipment. However, you can produce the same lighting variations in your own home with significantly less expensive gear.

The main advantage of large studio lighting units is their power. It facilitates the use of smaller apertures for increased depth of field. It enables you to use slower films with finer grain and better image resolution. Professional lighting systems also tend to be more dependable and consistent.

EQUIPMENT

The equipment used for the production of the photos in this essay included the following essential items:

Light Meters—I regularly use a Gossen Ultra-Pro and a Minolta Auto-Flash III Meter. I use each in the studio for electronic flash exposures and outside for available-light photography. The meters are relatively expensive but well worth the cost in terms of their remarkable accuracy and reliability. Each may be used in incident- or reflected-light mode.

Electronic Flash—My studio is equipped with Photogenic Versatron 800 flash units and flash heads. I consider it to be among the finest flash equipment made.

Because the Versatron 800 is relatively expensive for the amateur photographer, I suggest using the Porta-Master 400 instead. It is a self-contained system designed for portability and is available at a significantly lower price. The Porta-Master 400 has special safety circuits, to prevent the possibility of an overload.

The power pack of the Porta-Master 400 is approximately the size of a vacuum cleaner. It comes with a flash head incorporating a proportional modeling light. It is also provided with a light stand. A second stand and a clamp are also included as standard equipment.

Reflector Panels—I use Sibern Rocaflectors and reflectors made by Photogenic. A quality photo reflector must provide uniform illumination that is free from hot spots. A silvered reflector should reflect approximately 95% of the light striking its surface. Reflectors should be portable so they can be used on location as easily as in the studio.

Halos—Since the introduction of umbrella lighting many years ago, there has been little development of new light modifiers. However, recently Photogenic Machine Company, of Youngstown, Ohio, introduced the *Halo*—the most versatile light modifier I've used to date. Because you'll see the Halo mentioned several times in the Portfolio section, I want to say a little about it here.

The Halo is a combination of silvered and translucent umbrellas, as

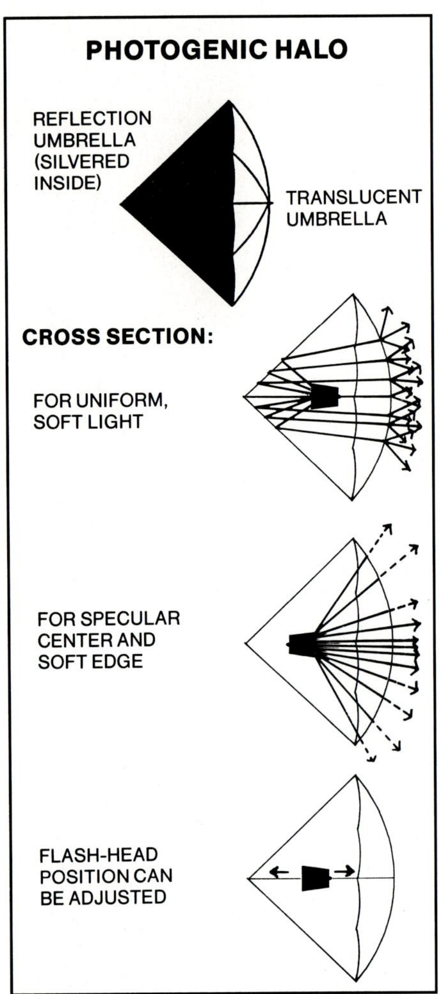

the accompanying sketches show. It mounts easily to lights and light stands and folds like an umbrella. The Halo comes in diameters of 32 inches, 45 inches and 54 inches. What's new and special about the Halo is the quality of light produced.

The Halo gives a soft to medium-contrast light especially suitable for portraiture. By changing the direction in which the flash head faces, and adjusting the lamp position within the Halo, you can achieve a wide variety of effects, as shown in the accompanying sketches.

In addition to subject illumination, the Halo is excellent for producing evenly lit backgrounds.

Cameras and Lenses—I make nearly all of my photographs on 35mm film. For me, that means Nikon cameras. I learned many years ago that you get what you pay for. With Nikon, I have durability and reliability in what I consider the ultimate system camera.

At the end of the book, you'll find a listing of products I've used in the production of the photos for this book, together with the suppliers.

Beauty and Glamour: Lighting the Woman

The subject for this section is pretty, 22-year-old Jana Kay Moore of Dallas, Texas. She's a talented dancer, not a model. She hasn't spent more time in front of a camera than the average person. These pictures, taken specifically for this book, were the first I had made of her.

Jana was nervous when we began. Her own evaluation was that she "never takes a good picture." Doesn't that sound familiar? However, there was an interesting transition in her attitude as the session progressed. I think you can see it in the photos. She seemed to become more relaxed and confident as we went along. However, she was also changed by the lighting I used.

The Weight of Light—Controlled lighting can change a person's appearance. Light has *weight.* This was first pointed out to me many years ago, when I began my career in fashion photography in New York City. It's significant to me that I learned most of my early lighting techniques from experienced professional models rather than photographers.

In one of the "lessons," a top model asked me to stand in front of the camera and lights. She returned to the camera position. I watched as she raised the main light higher than seemed appropriate. "Do you feel the light on your face?" she asked. I responded that I did. "Do you feel the light in your eyes?" she continued. I wasn't sure. Then she lowered the main light and asked me again. There was no question that I could feel when the light struck the surface of my eye, producing a catchlight.

"That's the point," she concluded, "light has real substance—or *weight.*" The more time you spend in front of the camera, the more attuned you become to how light models a face.

I make a point of making a subject aware of this phenomenon. It helps her to *feel* when the light on her is right, just as she intuitively *knows* how the photo session is going, based on her rapport with the photographer.

Now, let's evaluate the photos I made of Jana.

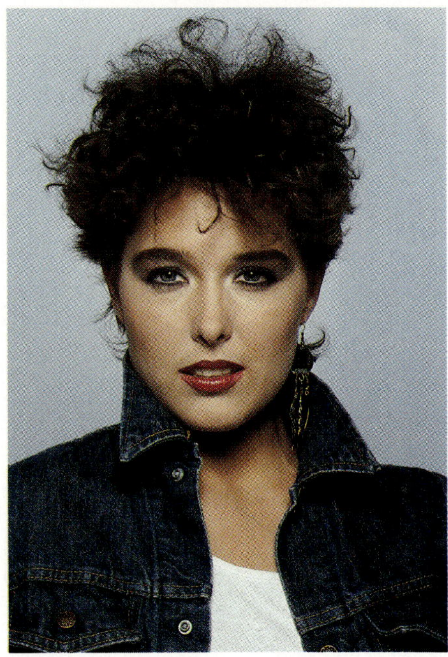

2-1

PHOTO 2-1

This represents the most basic approach to glamour lighting. Jana was positioned about 10 feet from a white seamless background. She was seated on a small cube. I positioned a single Versatron 800 flash head four feet in front of Jana, bouncing the light from a 52-inch umbrella. The single light produced about a two-step falloff between subject and background. This accounts for the medium-gray reproduction of the white background.

The required relative distances between main light, subject and background to produce a specific background falloff varies in different studios. Ceiling height, room dimensions, wall surfaces, light sources and color of background and walls are some of the factors that affect the results. Test and evaluate each new setup before you photograph an important session.

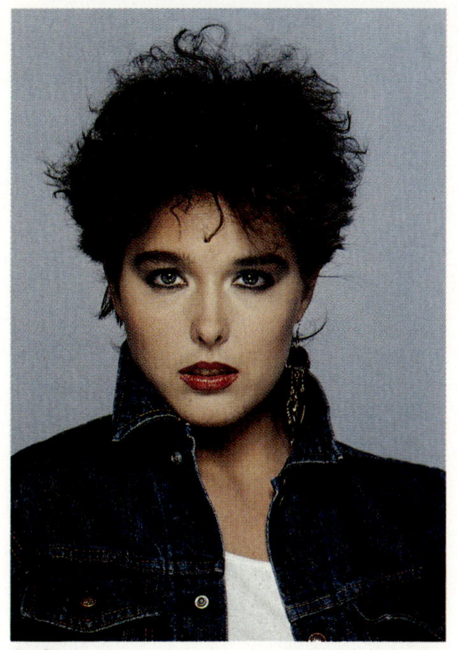

2-2

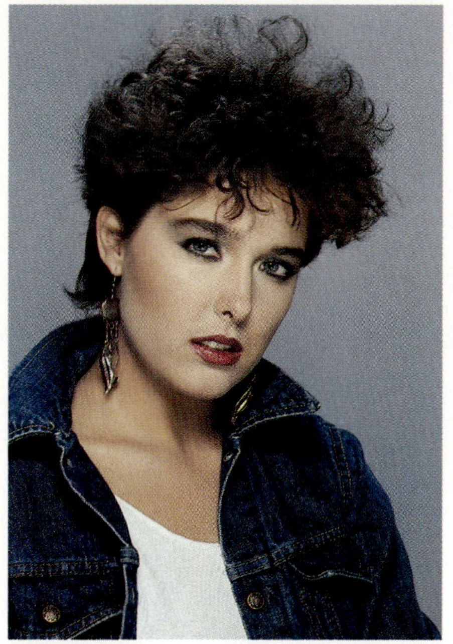

2-3

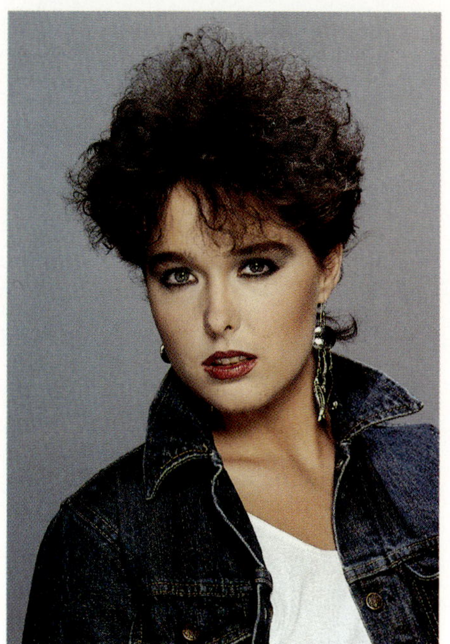

2-4

PHOTO 2-2

I made only one change for this photo, placing a 27-inch silver reflector beneath Jana's face. It was about a foot in front of her and just below the camera's view.

The addition of the reflector reduced contrast. It also bounced light into the subject's eyes from a low angle, filling the slight shadow created on the surface of the eye by the long eyelashes. As a result, the whites of the eyes appear clearer.

The most significant change is in the iris of each eye. It is lighter, brighter and reflects a second catchlight from the silver reflector. The extra sparkle is immediately apparent. However, the face looks a little too wide. The next step will correct that.

PHOTOS 2-3, 2-4 & 2-5

The basic lighting for these three photos is identical to that used for photo 2-2. However, I placed a seven-foot *black* Sibern Rocaflector on each side of Jana and very close to her. The black surfaces eliminated some of the reflected light striking the sides of the face. Consequently, the face appears narrower, with better shape and contouring.

To add to the slimming effect, I asked Jana to turn her head slightly away from full face. The combination of the lighting modification and the change in pose produced an impressive pictorial difference.

I'm not an advocate of big smiles for portraits. Usually, they tend to distort the face, turning eyes into narrow slits and causing misshapen facial contours. However, every subject is different. Jana's smile in photo 2-5 works very well. It adds character and form to her youthful jawline. But notice that the smile causes the main catchlight in her left eye to diminish. Were I to continue shooting this series with a smile, I would lower the main light about a foot to compensate for the catchlight loss.

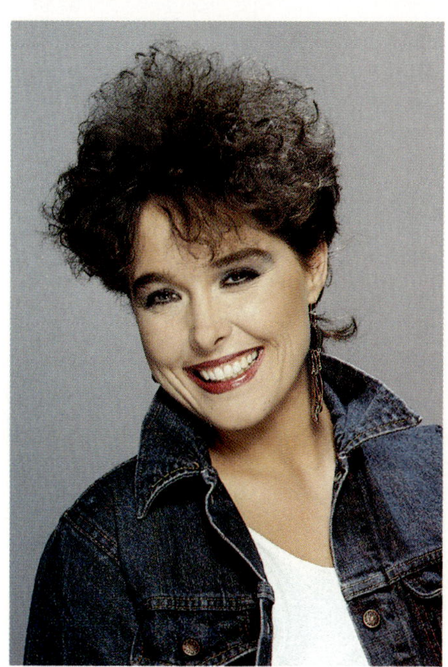

2-5

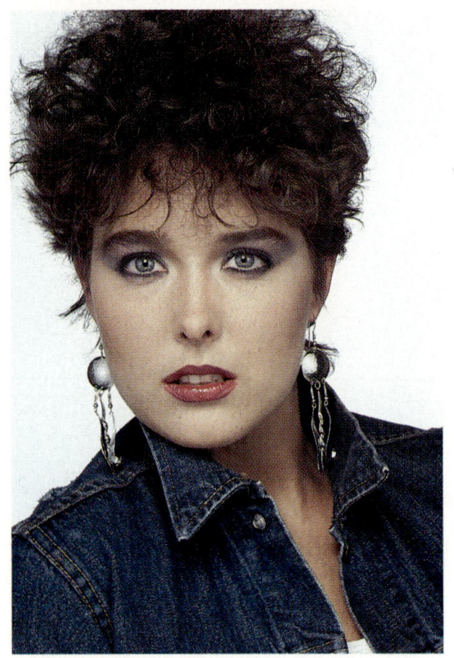

2-6

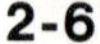

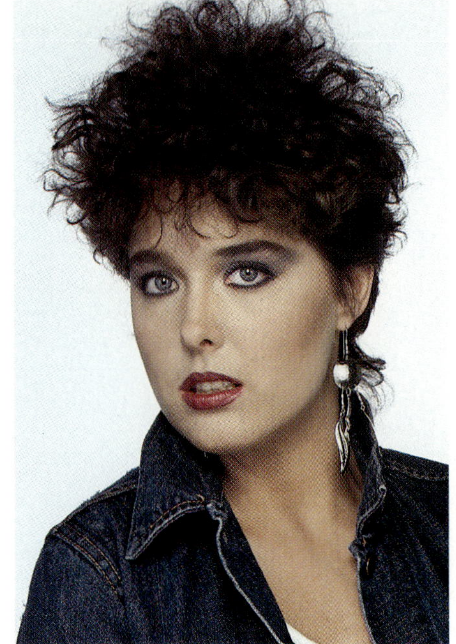

2-7

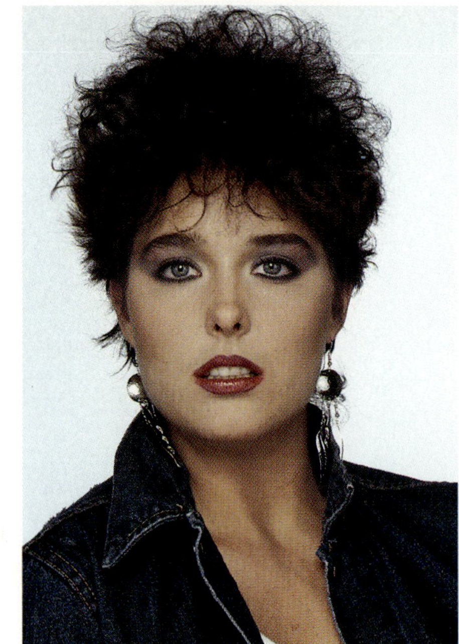

2-8

PHOTOS 2-6, 2-7 & 2-8

The lighting setup for these three pictures is very stylized. It typifies much of the "magazine-cover" lighting used in the late 70s and early 80s. I used two Versatron 800 power packs. The first pack was used with two wide-angle flash heads. They were directed at the white background wall to provide even illumination.

Three flash heads were connected to the second Versatron 800. One was bounced from a 40-inch silvered umbrella and positioned directly above my camera. The other two were in two *softboxes*—large, diffused light sources giving a very soft light. I placed one softbox to either side of the main umbrella. Each softbox gave one exposure step less light on the subject than the main umbrella. The three main units were close enough to touch each other. They were located approximately three feet from Jana's face.

I balanced the exposure of the background wall with the overall meter reading taken from the subject. Consequently, the white background actually recorded as white.

All exposure readings were taken in the incident-light mode. The meter hemisphere was located at the subject's face and pointed toward the center umbrella. To determine background exposure, I took readings from the wall, pointing the hemisphere toward the main light. The reading was made with the subject in position, to allow for falloff.

The illumination for these photos was very soft. Although such lighting can minimize facial flaws and flatter a subject's eyes, the lighting was not right for Jana. Notice how wide her face looks in photo 2-6. I compensated for this in photo 2-7 by asking her to turn slightly. This narrowed her face somewhat. But photo 2-8 provided what I consider the best angle. I has asked Jana to raise her chin. The new angle reveals a more flattering facial shape. Compare photo 2-8 with photo 2-6 and you'll readily see what a difference a slight movement can make in a subject's appearance.

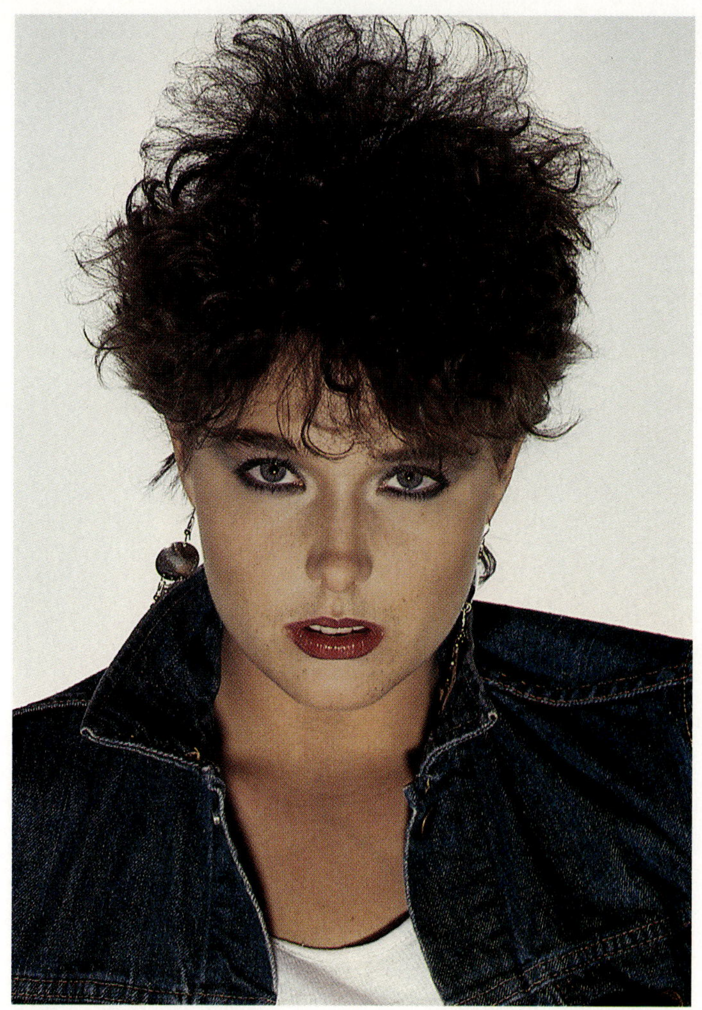

2-9

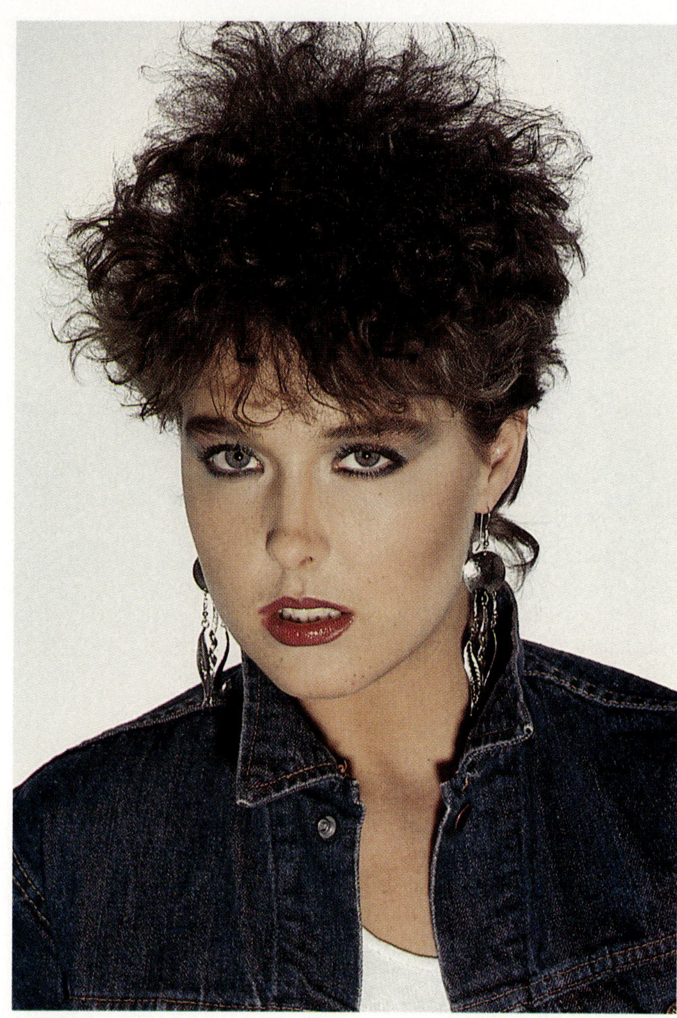

2-10

PHOTOS 2-9 & 2-10

Contrast *increases* as the apparent size of the light source, as seen from the subject, *decreases.* Assuming a constant distance between subject and light, a large light source gives softer illumination and less subject contrast than a small light source.

Photos 2-9 and 2-10 illustrate the point. The main light was a single Versatron 800 flash without umbrella. The resulting light is hard, with significant contrast. The effect is somewhat similar to theatrical spotlighting. Notice that the catchlights in the eyes are now considerably smaller than in the preceding examples.

In most cases, flattering portrait light comes from above. It can vary from an angle slightly above the height of the subject's eyes to an angle approximately 45° above the eyes. In photos 2-9 and 2-10, I departed from this norm and positioned the light below the lens of the camera.

When using a low main light, care must be taken to avoid "monster" lighting. Jana's face has good skin and the roundness of youth. Therefore, I wasn't in danger of getting an unflattering result. In fact the photos are very dramatic. However, to minimize the low angle, I asked Jana to lower her head while lifting her eyes to look at the camera.

For photo 2-10, I asked Jana to turn her head sideways slightly. This enhanced the effect and the mood of the image further. The contrast of spotlighting is apparent in the depth of the shadow along the side of the nose.

Background lighting was produced with a single Versatron wide-angle flash head. It was directed at the wall from the floor, directly behind Jana.

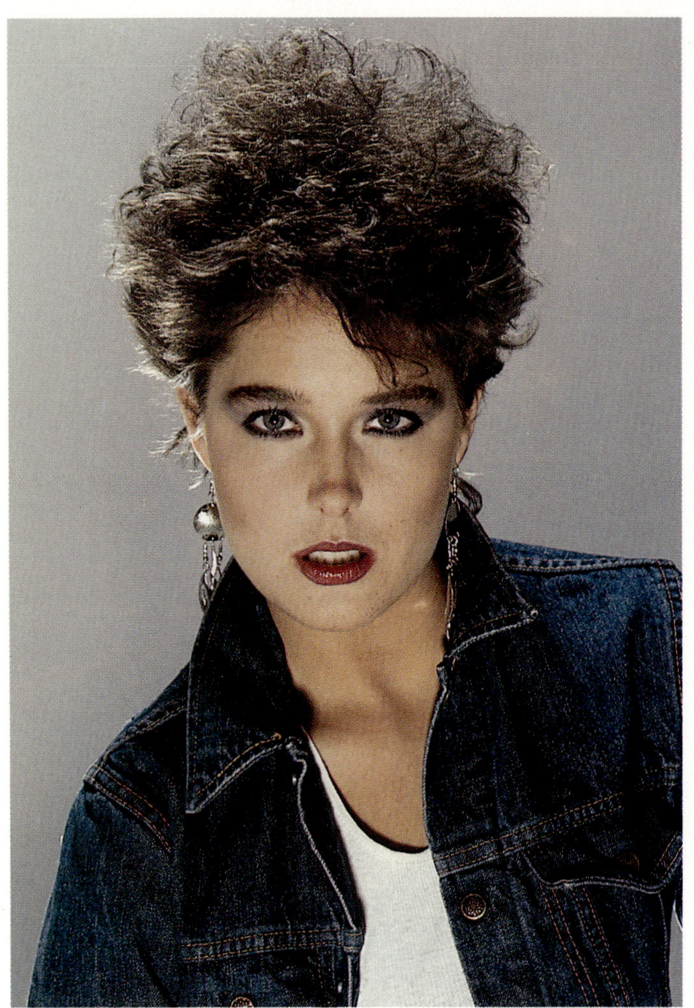

2-11

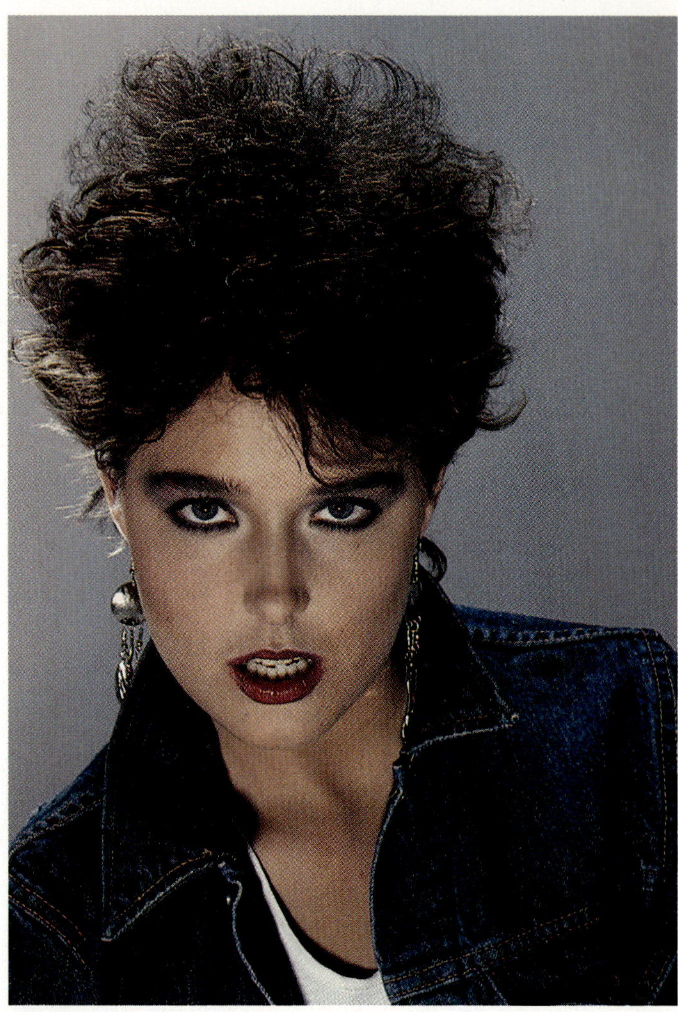

2-12

PHOTOS 2-11 & 2-12

I returned to a gray background—derived from two steps underexposure of a white surface—for these two photos. Notice how the darker background helped to make the face appear narrower. The darkened background also provided the perfect base for the introduction of *edge lighting.*

Two edge lights were used. The first was a hair light, mounted on a boom stand above and slightly behind Jana. On the hair light I used a *grid spot*—a device that concentrates and focuses light to a narrow spot. It enabled me to light the hair without spillage to other areas. The hair light was adjusted to give one exposure step more light to the subject's hair than the main light gave to the face.

The second edge light came from a Versatron flash head, positioned at a 45° angle to the model's back. It provided a rim light to the right side of the model's hair and face, giving the image more impact. Photo 2-12 shows the low-main-light effect I was aiming for.

I raised the background light, causing the area of background directly behind Jana to go even darker. Compare the drama and impact of photo 2-12 with the straightforward softness of photo 2-1. You could be forgiven for thinking they were images of different subjects!

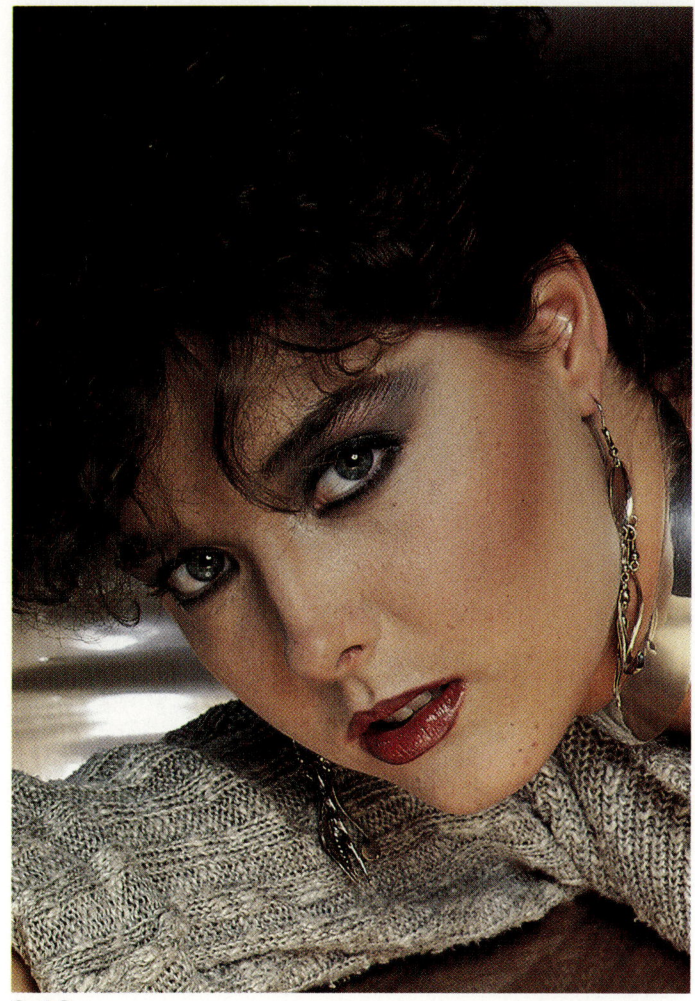

2-13

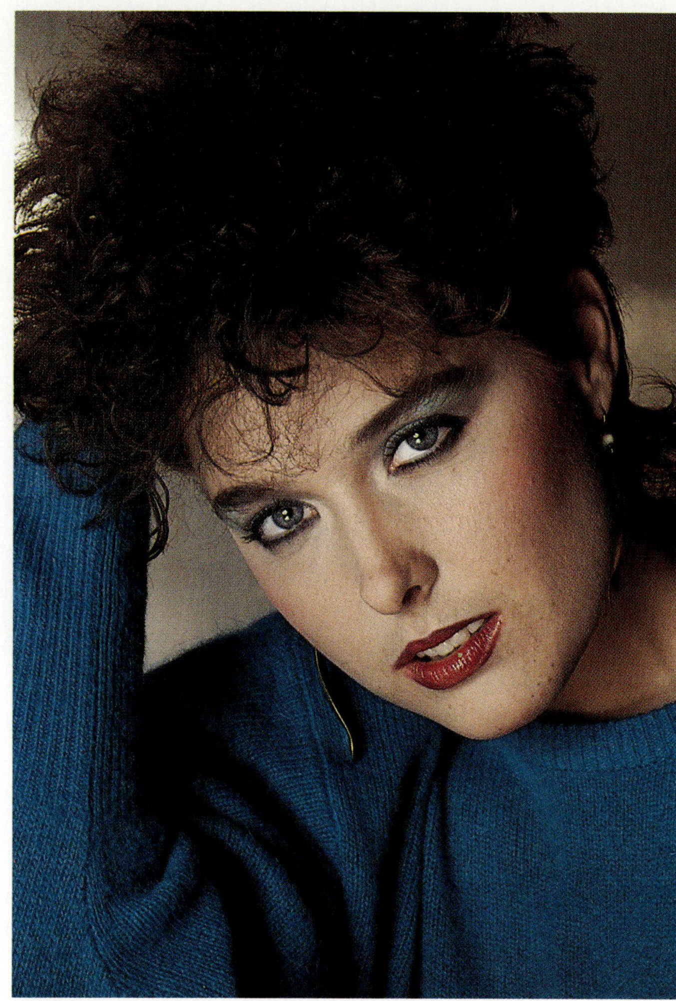

2-14

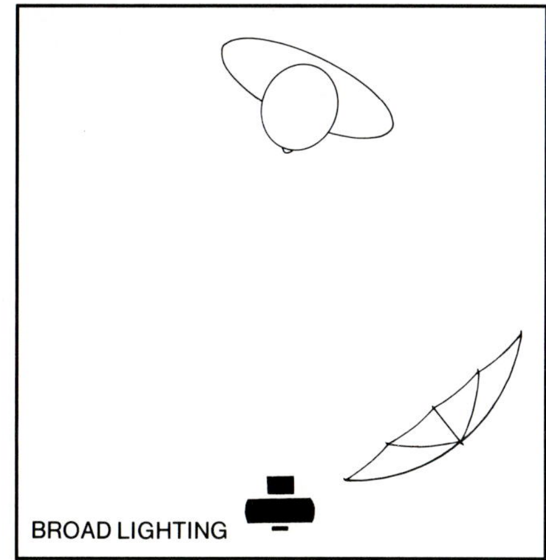

PHOTOS 2-13 & 2-14

For the final series, I replaced the white background with highly reflective gold mylar.

Photos 2-13 and 2-14 both show a three-quarter view of Jana's face. Although she looks pretty in each, subtle lighting variations account for different pictorial results.

Photo 2-13 was taken with *broad* lighting. As indicated in the diagram, I placed the main umbrella light to the right of the camera. Light struck the broadest plane of her face, as viewed from camera position. In photo 2-14, I used *short* lighting—achieved by moving the main light far to the left of the camera. The light struck Jana's face from the narrow, or short, side, as viewed from camera position. It emphasized the frontal plane of the face.

Short lighting gives a wide face a slimmer appearance by creating light falloff on the near side of the subject's face. It allows part of the side of the face closest to the camera to fall into shadow. At the same time, it emphasizes facial structure on the near side of the face. Broad lighting is more appropriate for a subject whose face is naturally narrow.

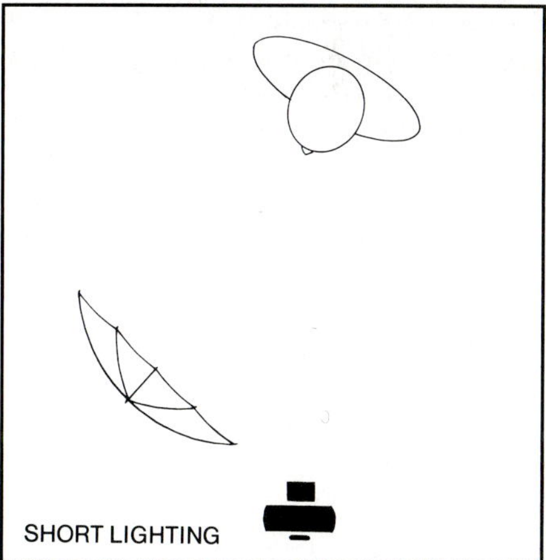

In the examples reproduced here, I prefer the version with the short lighting. You may prefer the broad lighting. But *our* opinions are of little consequence! I'm waiting to hear from Jana!

Character Studies: Photographing the Man

We talk about *glamour* for women and *character* for men! Is this terminology indicative of the classic double standard? Do women really *age* as men *mature*? Let's evaluate this question in terms of photographic application.

Men are as concerned about their looks and appearance as women. They are also just as concerned about the aging process. But society has treated the sexes unequally—which is at once fortunate and unfortunate.

You can get the first indication of unequal treatment by looking at a dictionary. Look up the word *feminine* and you'll see listed such attributes as *gentleness, weakness, delicacy* and *modesty.* Next, check the word *beauty.* What you find will leave little doubt in your mind that, traditionally, typical "feminine" words like *soft, youthful, pretty, lovely* and *flawless* best define the word.

As photographers, we must use our talents and lighting techniques to depict society's view of the fairer sex, as long as those views are desired by our feminine subjects.

Men are judged by an entirely different set of standards. The word *handsome* doesn't only imply pleasing proportions and symmetry. According to Webster's unabridged dictionary, the word carries distinct connotations of *masculinity, strength* and *ruggedness,* rather than *delicacy* and *grace.*

Society's standards allow us far greater flexibility in portraying the man than the woman. Hard, angular lighting—which emphasizes texture—is also far easier to achieve than lighting designed to subdue all flaws and imperfections.

In the photos that follow, I'll evaluate a variety of different lighting techniques on an equally wide range of masculine subjects.

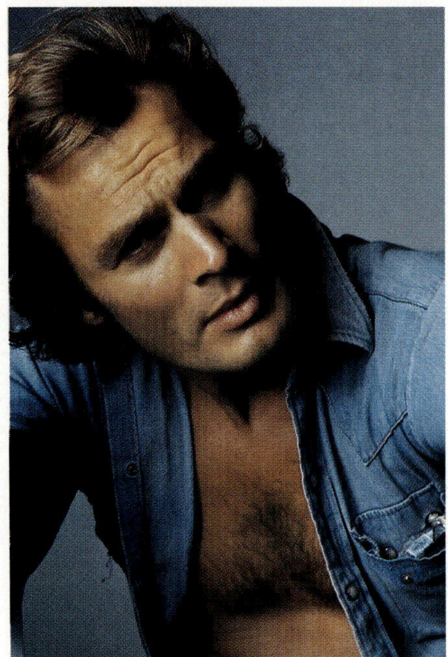

2-15

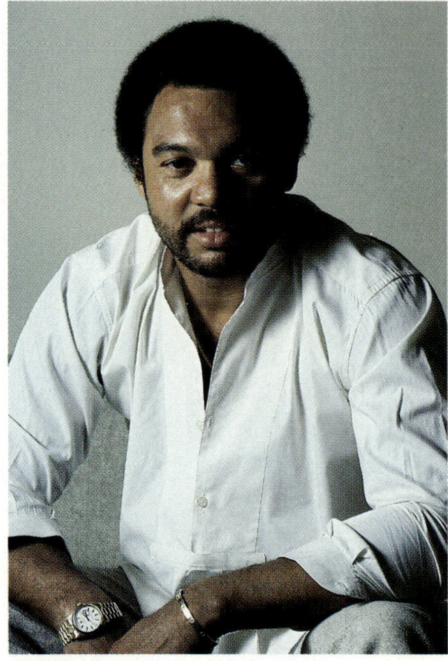

2-16

PHOTO 2-15

Uva Harden is one of the country's most successful male models. His classic good looks are well suited for a variety of lighting applications. In photo 2-15, I used a white umbrella to reflect a single light source. Light placement was considerably higher than normal to emphasize the structure of the subject's face. The high lighting angle caused a shadow to fall on Uva's eyes and no catchlights appeared in his eyes.

The light was metered with a Minolta Flash Meter II, used in the incident-light mode. I positioned the meter's hemisphere at the subject's nose and pointed it up toward the main light.

PHOTO 2-16

So-called *three-quarter* lighting illuminated baseball superstar Reggie Jackson. A single umbrella source emphasized only the right side of Reggie's face. This makes the face appear narrower. I positioned the light close enough to the camera viewpoint to create a small triangle of light on the shadow side of the face. I also lowered the light sufficiently to cause a catchlight in the eye on the shadow side of Reggie's face. This second catchlight gives balance to the image.

Reggie looked relaxed and at ease. This helped to complete a fine portrait.

I metered with a Minolta Auto-Flash III. I placed the incident-light hemisphere at the right side of Reggie's face and pointed it toward the center of the umbrella light.

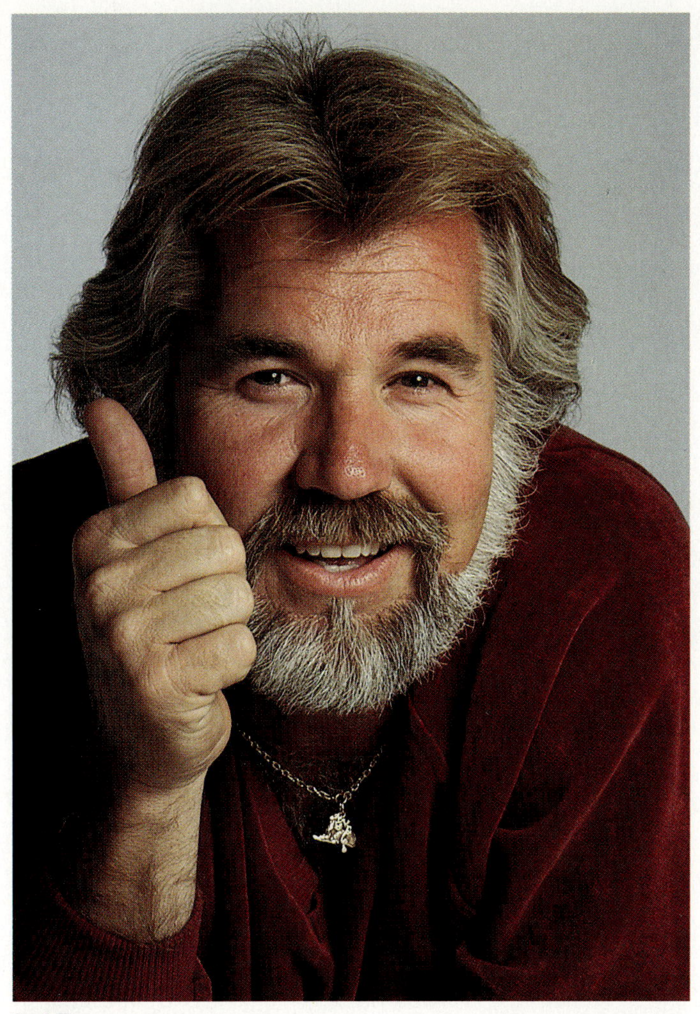

2-17

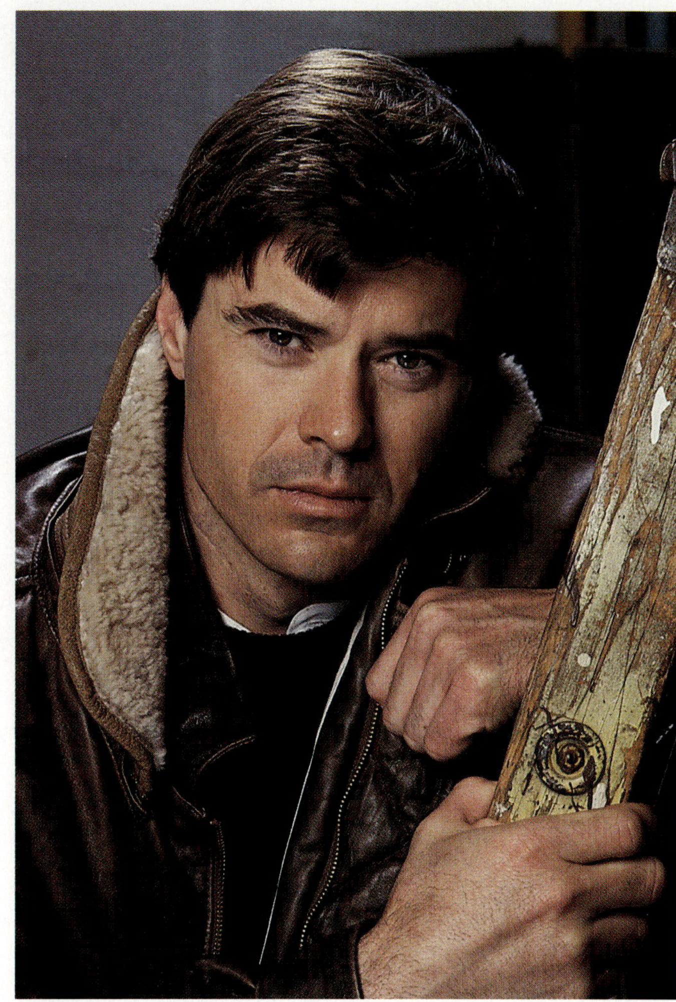

2-18

PHOTO 2-17

The face of Kenny Rogers needs no introduction. It was captured here with classic *glamour* lighting, which is applicable to both female and male subjects. The main light—a 1200-watt-second Rollei pan light—was positioned slightly to the right of the camera. The light placement created shadows on the right side of Kenny's face and nose.

I took the photograph against a white, seamless background. The background recorded as medium gray because it received two steps less exposure than the subject.

I metered the shot by placing the incident-light hemisphere of my Minolta Flash Meter at Kenny's left cheek and pointing it toward the umbrella source.

PHOTO 2-18

To record the strong features of actor Robert Urich, I used two Versatron 800 lighting units and a total of four flash heads.

The main flash head, positioned to the left of the camera, was bounced from a 52-inch umbrella. An incident-light meter reading indicated an aperture between *f*-8 and *f*-11. I placed a small silvered reflector three or four feet in front of Bob. It bounced a little fill light into his face from below and added secondary catchlights to the eyes.

Bob was about 20 feet from the background. At that distance, the background would receive little lighting from the main light. So I added two background umbrellas. They were balanced to produce two steps less exposure than that of the subject by the main light.

To graphically separate Bob's dark hair from the background, I positioned a small hair light on a boom stand above and slightly behind him. The hair-light reading, taken from the top of Bob's head, indicated an exposure of *f*-16. Therefore, it provided 1-1/2 exposure steps more light than the main light. Because the image was actually exposed at a setting between *f*-8 and *f*-11, Bob's hair is overexposed where the hair light struck it. This caused the specular highlights on the hair.

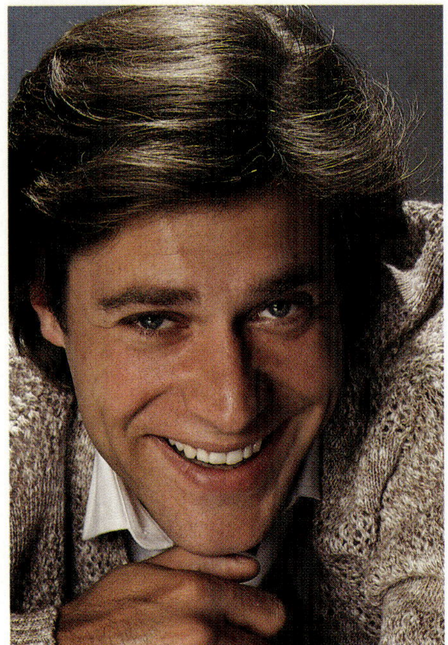

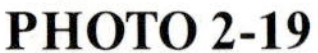

2-19

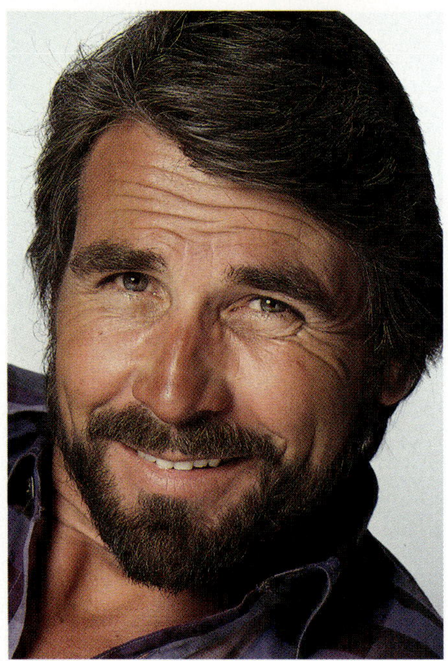

2-20

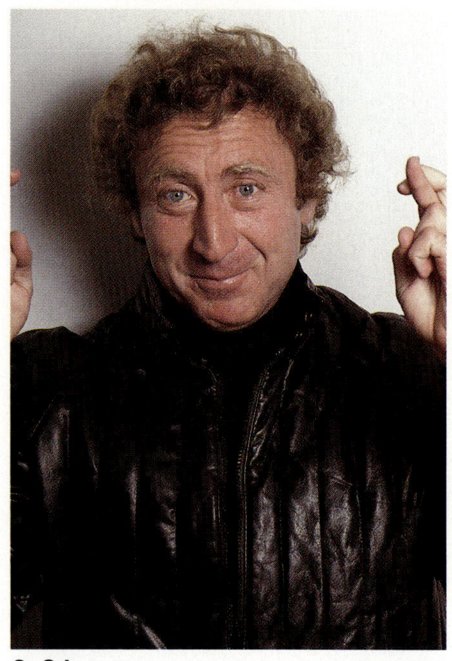

2-21

PHOTO 2-19

Talented John James was the subject for this photo. Main facial lighting was provided by a single flash head, bounced from a 40-inch silvered umbrella. I placed a 27-inch silverer reflector directly below John's face. It brightened shadows and created large catchlights in the eyes.

I metered the main light by placing the incident-light hemisphere of the meter at John's cheek and pointing it between the reflector and main light.

A second flash head was mounted on a boom stand behind John. I attached a grid spot to confine the area of illumination. The light created specular rim lighting on the subject's hair and shoulders. The rim light was set for a 2-step overexposure, relative to the face. I metered the hair light from the top of John's head, pointing the meter's hemisphere directly at the center of the grid spot.

This photo gets much of its impact from the high lighting ratio between the main and hair lights.

John was lying on the floor of the studio and the camera was also at floor level. I placed an electric fan in front of the subject to create slight movement in his hair.

PHOTO 2-20

The main-light configuration used for this portrait of actor James Brolin was similar to that used in photo 2-19. Instead of a silvered reflector, however, I used a seven-foot white Rocaflector below Jim's face. The white surface provided a large, even fill source that lessened contrast and reduced specular reflections from Jim's sun-tanned face. The large, white reflector also lightened the lower halves of the irises in Jim's eyes, adding an extra bit of sparkle.

For additional graphic impact, the background was allowed to record as pure white. I accomplished this by placing two 52-inch umbrellas to either side of the white seamless paper.

The background recorded one exposure step more light than the main-light reading on Jim's face. Exposure, however, was based on the main-light reading.

PHOTO 2-21

Time was at a premium during my session with multi-talented Gene Wilder. This photo was taken in Gene's office at 20th Century Fox.

I set my main light to the right of the camera, about four feet from Gene. It's lower-than-normal height—evident from the two-o'clock catchlights in the eyes—accounted for good facial modeling and a shadow-free area between nose and upper lip. To further lower contrast, I stood a seven-foot white Rocaflector immediately to Gene's right. The unit, just out of camera range, nearly touched his shoulder. The proximity of the reflector helped put some light on the black outfit and accounted for a little edge light on the right side of Gene's face.

This is perhaps an appropriate place to mention the appearance of shadows on the background. I find background shadows perfectly acceptable, as long as they have an intended effect. When used properly, shadows can become an interesting compositional and graphic element. However, few compositional elements are more bothersome than haphazard shadows that appear at random due to sloppy lighting technique.

Who is to say whether the existence of shadows enhances an image? The decision has to be a personal and totally subjective one. As I've said before, the first key to quality photography is the ability to produce on film what you had previsualized.

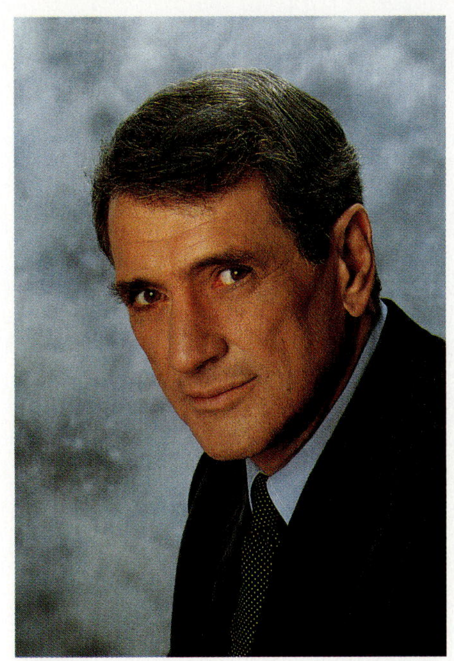

2-22

PHOTO 2-22

The photo of the legendary face of Rock Hudson was produced with two umbrella main lights. Two main-light sources can be versatile. However, when working in this manner, I find it best to use light sources of equal output. By balancing the output of the two lights, I protect myself against unintentional underillumination of the subject with one of the two lights.

The lights can be fired from a single power pack. Alternatively, they can be powered by two separate generators and triggered simultaneously through use of a slave unit.

During photography, I normally have the lower umbrella farther from the subject than the upper light source. In doing so, I preclude the possibility of creating monster lighting. You can, however, position the two lights at the same level, when this achieves the desired effect.

It helps operational ease if each umbrella is mounted on a light stand with wheels. It frees you to work rapidly with a variety of lighting configurations and facilitates some subject movement.

The two-light system allows quick evaluations of light patterns on the subject's face. Lights may be raised or lowered as needed. One light can be positioned close to the subject as the other is moved farther away until it provides the required amount of fill light.

For this shot, the first light—in a 52-inch umbrella—was placed about three feet from Rock's face, slightly above eye level. The second light—in another identical umbrella—was five feet from the subject and at about the height of his chest. I selected the two-light setup because Rock likes freedom of movement while he's in front of the camera. Two light sources not only provide that freedom but also minimize contrast.

I metered the exposure by pointing the incident-light hemisphere between the two light sources.

Three other lights completed the illumination for this photograph. Two background lights, balancing the main-light exposure, evenly illuminated a gray, hand-painted canvas background. The final light source was a hair light mounted on a boom stand. It was placed to register one step more exposure than the total main-light exposure.

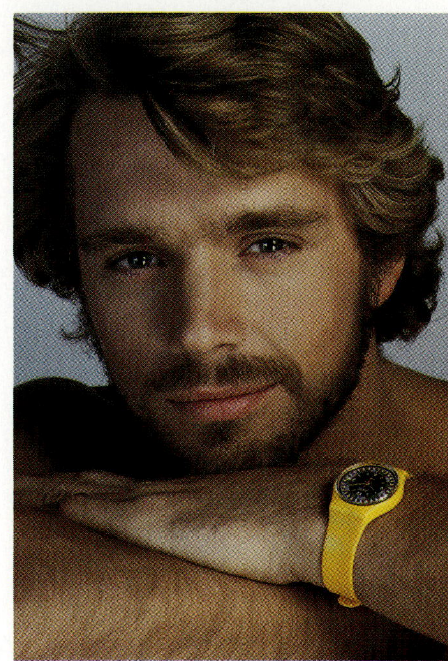

2-23

PHOTO 2-23

Although the organization of this essay may seem to indicate otherwise, photographic lighting techniques are largely interchangeable between the sexes. Certain applications are often more appropriate for one sex than the other, but many are equally suitable for men and women. For example, the technique used for this photo of actor John Schneider is similar to that employed for photos 2-6 to 2-8 of Jana Kay Moore.

The photo of John was produced as a national ad for the *Swatch Watch* campaign. To minimize specular highlights on the watch, I used two softboxes, giving diffused, soft light. One softbox simulates window light; two softboxes used together can give the effect of daylight outdoors on an overcast day.

The main-light configuration consisted of one Rollei pan light, flanked by the two softboxes. The softboxes were positioned to either side of the Rollei light and close enough to touch the edge of the pan. The softboxes were lit by two Versatron flash heads, powered by a Versatron 800 unit. Each of the three lights gave a 400-watt-second output.

The finished image has low contrast and features three exaggerated catchlights in the subject's eyes.

When using multiple light sources, *always* begin by metering the sources separately to determine the intensity of each. In doing so, you eliminate the possibility of one source overpowering the others. Then, turn on all sources and meter them as one unit from subject position. For this photo, I placed the hemisphere of my Minolta Flash Meter at the tip of John's nose and pointed it toward the center of the Rollei pan light.

Two umbrella background lights completed the configuration. They provided a background reading of 1/2 step less exposure than the average of the main lights. Because the actual exposure was based on the main-light reading, the white background recorded as a light gray.

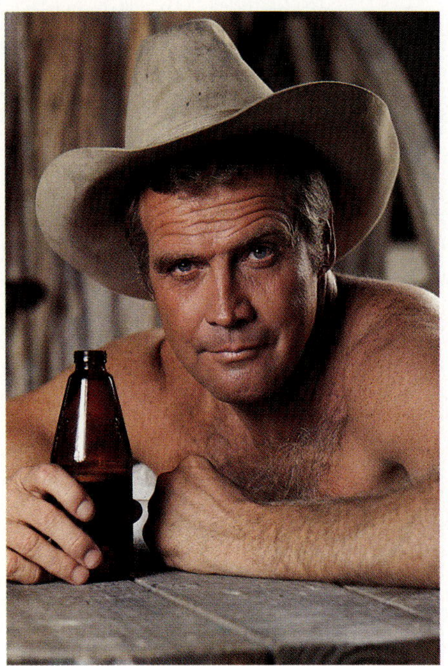

2-24

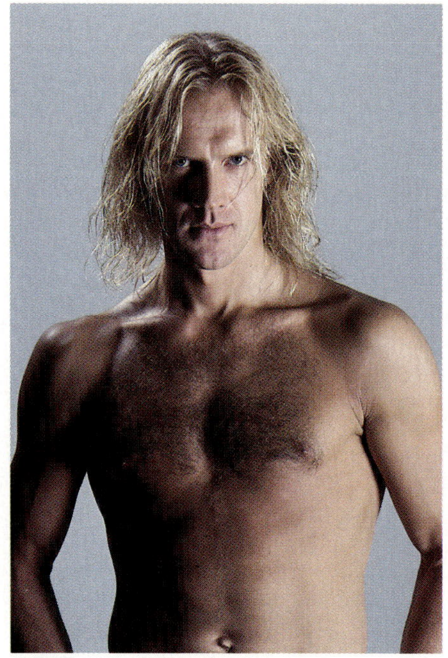

2-25

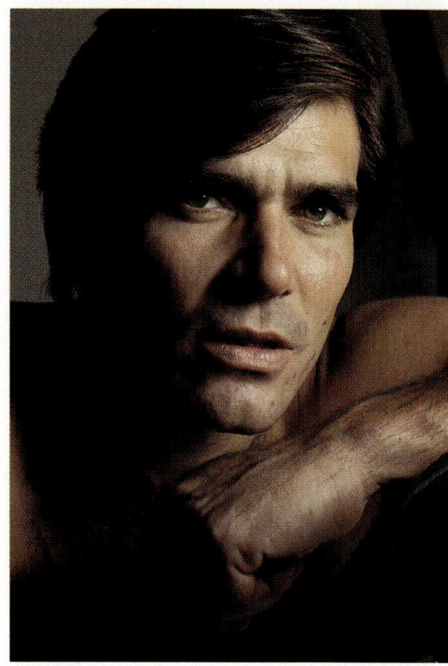

2-26

PHOTO 2-24

This photo of superstar Lee Majors was taken on the set of *The Fall Guy* television show. Although the pose is casual, the lighting consisted of a classic three-light setup. The main light—a 600-watt-second flash, bounced from a 52-inch silvered umbrella—was positioned about four feet from Lee and slightly to his right. It modelled the front of his face.

A second 600-watt-second flash head was used with *barn doors*, which control the spread of light and prevent flare. This light was placed about three feet behind Lee and directed toward his head. It provided rim lighting for the hat and edge lighting to the side of the face.

The main-light exposure reading was *f*-5.6. The rim-light meter reading was between *f*-8 and *f*-11, indicating 1-1/2 steps more exposure than from the main light. Consequently, the rim lighting recorded as overexposure.

The lighting was completed with the addition of a third 600-watt-second flash, bounced from an umbrella. It was used behind the subject to illuminate the background. Its exposure rating was the same as that of the main light. The combination produced a strong graphic image with good tonal balance.

PHOTO 2-25

This photo captures the classic face and form of dancer Alexander Godunov. I bounced a 1200-watt-second flash from a 40-inch silvered umbrella as a main-light source. It was placed a few feet from the subject and aimed up from a low angle.

A second 600-watt-second flash with grid spot was mounted on a small boom stand. I placed it behind Godunov and to his right. The edge light provided 1/2 step overexposure at the subject's right shoulder. However, the amount of light falling on much of Godunov's blond hair provides a little less exposure than the facial light.

The abrupt light falloff of grid spots can be both an advantage and a disadvantage. I advise you to take multiple meter readings around spotlighted areas to ensure accurate exposure.

The relationship of the main-light exposure to the rim-light exposure is often critical. It should first be determined visually and then by metering.

I begin by comparing the tonality of the subject's hair with his skin tone. Next, I compare the tonality of the hair with that of the background. As a rule, the exposure differential between main light and rim light is greater on dark-haired people. Overexposure of blond hair can tend to make it appear too sparse.

Notice that, in spite of the extensive main-light shadow on Godunov's right cheek, the light was sufficiently frontal to create a catchlight in both eyes. This is an important factor in giving the photograph visual balance.

PHOTO 2-26

Top model Chad Deal is the subject of the final image in this section. It represents the simplest and perhaps most dynamic of the lighting techniques—*spotlighting*.

A 600-watt-second flash head with a narrow reflector was directed at Chad from a distance of about eight feet. The subject brightness range produced by the small, specular source was nearly five to one. It minimized middle tones and virtually eliminated shadow detail. However, it produced a graphically dramatic result. The hard, contrasty source emphasized the subject's chiseled, classic features.

Notice that I added light to the background, behind the shadowed side of Chad's face. It gave form and shape to the back part of his head and added balance to the overall composition.

Man and Woman Together

Each person has a unique facial structure and physical appearance. Consequently, it is more difficult to photograph two subjects together. Lighting that flatters a man may be totally inappropriate for his female partner.

Sometimes it is extremely difficult to obtain ideal lighting on two subjects at the same time. But there are ways of avoiding an undesirable compromise. The best way is to position the couple in such a way that the same lighting flatters each individual.

A composition is generally strongest when it has one center of interest. This requirement is easily fulfilled when photographing the individual subject. Confining viewer interest to a single area is more difficult with two subjects.

Metering Two Subjects—The placement of your main lighting depends on the relative emphasis you want to give each of the subjects. To get the effect you want, it's important to meter each subject separately.

For example, if I want to record two faces of similar skin tones equally, I adjust my lighting so my meter indicates the same exposure for each. If I wanted to emphasize one subject and subdue the other, I would adjust my lights to produce an exposure difference of about half a step between the faces.

It's important to also consider tonal differences between subject parts. For example, I might be photographing a man of dark complexion who is wearing a light-colored shirt. I would allow more light to fall on the face than on the shirt. My meter enables me to determine the differential as well as the actual exposure.

Reducing the effective subject brightness range in the above manner is important because film inherently records things with higher contrast than the eye sees them.

In the following examples, the relationship between light, metering and composition is inseparable.

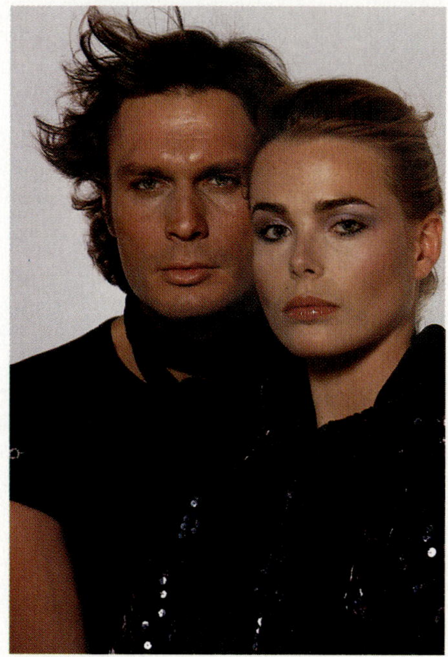

2-27

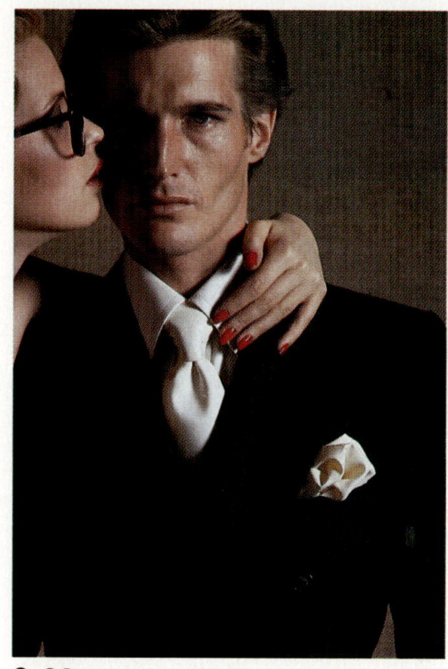

2-28

PHOTO 2-27

For this photograph, a single spotlight illuminated the dynamic faces of Margaux Hemingway and Uva Harden. Because Uva's eyes are set deeper than Margaux's, he required a lower main-light position. The problem was solved by placing Uva higher in the composition than Margaux.

The height relationship between individuals is dictated not only by lighting, but by composition and cropping as well. Subjects should rarely appear to be the same height in a photograph. A height difference creates a composition with movement and greater visual impact.

Although composition is primarily a matter of personal vision, certain guidelines do help. In a detailed portrait from fairly close, such as this one, the top subject's nose should be opposite the lower subject's eyes. In half-length and full-length photographs, you can increase the distance between subject heights. Your aim should be to direct the viewer's attention to a centralized point in the composition. It is confusing to a viewer to have to look back and forth between two distinctly separate centers of interest.

PHOTO 2-28

As I've indicated before, hard, angular light is more appropriate for the man than the woman. In this photograph of Matt Collins and Katthy Cochaux for *Esquire* magazine, I used this to my pictorial advantage.

The photograph was taken with flash bounced from a single 40-inch silvered umbrella placed to the right of the camera. Although Matt was the main subject for this shot, the light was placed with equal concern for Katthy. The angular hard light brushed over Matt's chiseled features, emphasizing them as well as his facial texture. The result is strikingly dramatic. Katthy, by comparison, was lit frontally and her features appear soft and "feminine."

Notice also the relationship between the subjects' heights. I wanted to isolate Katthy's profile against the shadow side of Matt's face. Once again, the nose-to-eye relationship exists. In order for Katthy to attain her required height in the frame, I asked her to stand on a studio cube.

PHOTOS 2-29 & 2-30

The exciting thing about photographing loving couples is that they bring a special energy and emotion to the session. They lend physical and mental support to each other. The couple depicted here—Kristina Kincaid and John Rusnak—are top professional models from Washington, D.C., portraying a romantic role. As is clear from these photos, good models tend also to be talented actors. The feeling conveyed in these images appears as real as if the couple were truly in love.

When you photograph a truly romantic couple, it's often best to let nature take its course—at least for part of the shooting session. To take advantage of a couple's emotional and physical energy, I minimize technical constraints. I did this even with my professional models in photo 2-29, to give them maximum freedom for their acting.

When I lit this couple, I didn't do it with specific facial modeling in mind. Instead, I lit the entire scene in a way that gave the models as much freedom of movement as possible. To achieve this, I placed the main light farther from the subjects than I normally do. The light-to-subject distance was about nine feet.

I raised the main light to a height that would provide *both* subjects with *acceptable* lighting for *most* shots. It's more important to capture genuine but fleeting expressions than to be preoccupied with "ideal" lighting.

For photo 2-30, I placed the main light to the right of the camera, allowing falloff to account for a one-step difference in exposure on the two faces. I took an incident-light reading from Kris' face, pointing the hemisphere toward the main light.

I use four primary ways of directing viewer attention. I can do it with careful composition and the judicious use of accessories in the photo. Or, I can use selective control of depth of field. Thirdly, I can carefully direct eye contact between the subject and viewer. Lastly, I can use my lighting selectively on each subject.

For photo 2-30, I used each of the above, with the exception of depth-of-field control. I positioned Kris so her eyes were about one third of the way into the frame—a location of strong viewer impact. John occupied the remainder of the frame. I directed John away from the viewer as Kris maintained eye contact with the viewer. Finally, I allowed the light to fall off one step on John, reducing his impact in the image.

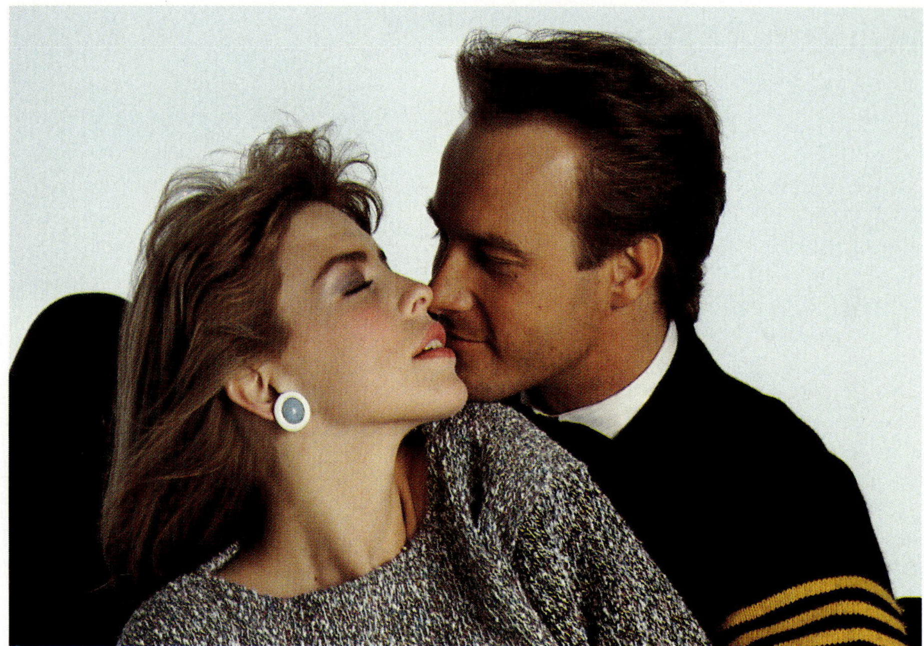

2-29

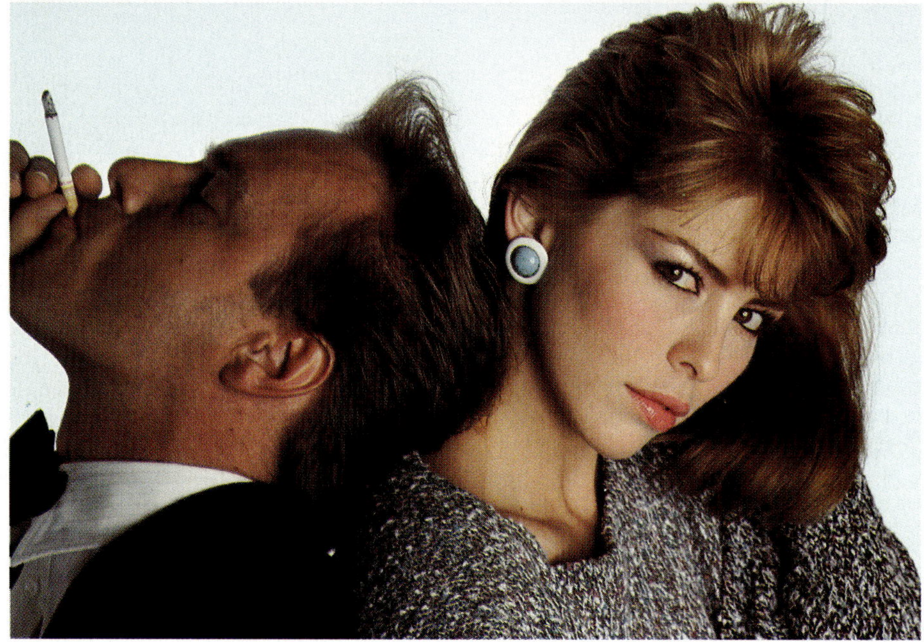

2-30

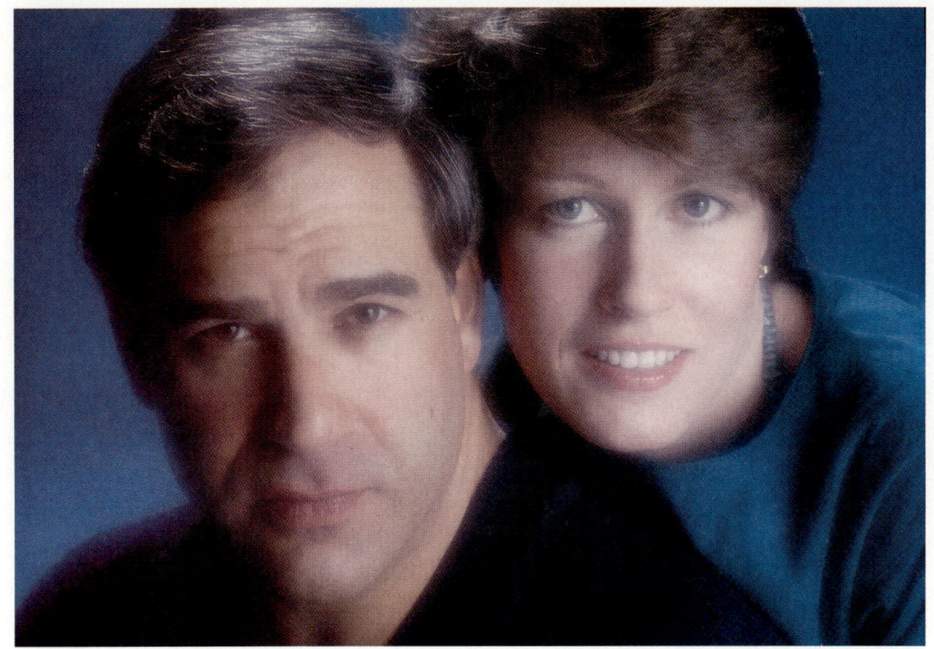

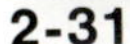
2-31

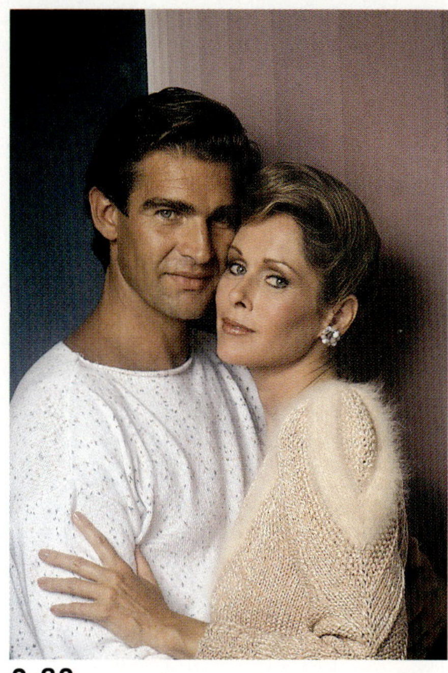

2-32

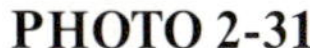
PHOTO 2-31

This handsome couple is Sue and Richard Aronoff of Potomac, Maryland. I made the photograph as part of a private portrait session.

Sue has a thin face with fine features. Richard has a wide face with a rugged, masculine look. I placed my main light to the right of the camera, nearest to Sue. It lit her from the side, emphasizing her delicate features.

Richard was in front of Sue and, therefore, received more angular lighting from the same source. The right side of his face is in shadow. The lighting visually narrowed his face while maintaining the strength of his character.

Because Richard is positioned closer to the camera, his face occupies greater area in the composition. Had this photograph been made with frontal lighting, he would totally overpower Sue in the composition. By using side lighting on his face, his image and Sue's create a perfect balance.

The lighting was completed with the addition of a wide-angle flash head mounted on a boom stand. The light was positioned above the subjects and slightly behind them. The spread of light from the reflector was wide enough to rim light the subjects while at the same time providing background illumination.

PHOTO 2-32

In many creative endeavors, including photography, it can truly be said that "less is more." This photo is a good example of photographic simplicity in both lighting and posing.

Models Zacki Murphy and Giles Kohler were photographed for La Costa Products with one umbrella light to the left of the camera. The cross lighting on Giles brings out his rugged features. The nearly frontal *short light* (see also photo 2-14) on Zacki is ideal for her classic features.

Giles' suntan made him significantly darker than Zacki. By placing him closer to the light source, this tonal difference was reduced.

PHOTO 2-33

Top New York models Lisa Palmer and Greg Bauer are the subjects in this ad produced for Hart, Schaffner and Marx.

Quality lighting is just as important outdoors as in the studio. This photo was taken mid-afternoon on a hazy, bright day in upstate New York. To avoid unflattering overhead light, I asked the models to stand under some overhanging branches. The branches shielded the subjects from the overhead light and allowed the lower, usable light to model their faces.

Notice Lisa's position in relation to the light. The strongest light enters from her left, creating *short lighting* similar to that used on Jana in Photo 2-14. By turning Greg away from the light, he received cross lighting, emphasizing his strong features.

The scene was metered with a Gossen Luna Pro in the incident-light mode. I placed the hemisphere between the subjects and pointed it toward the open sky.

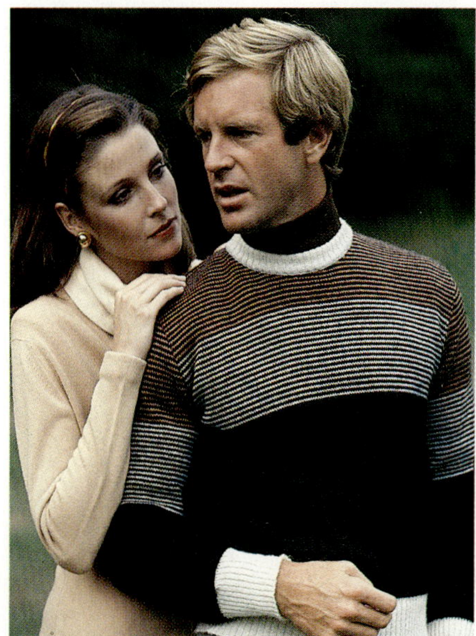

2-33

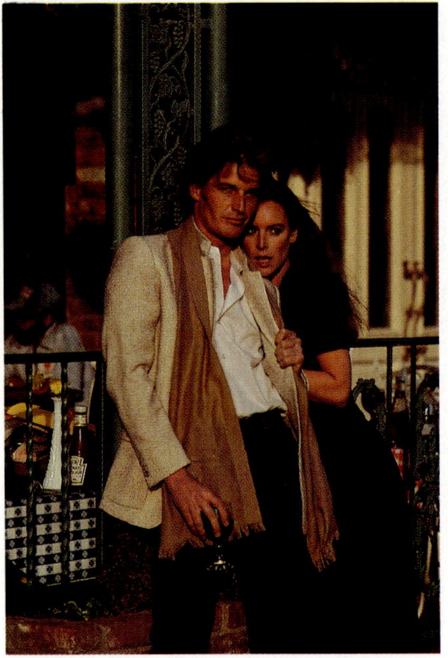
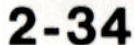
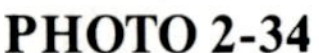

2-34

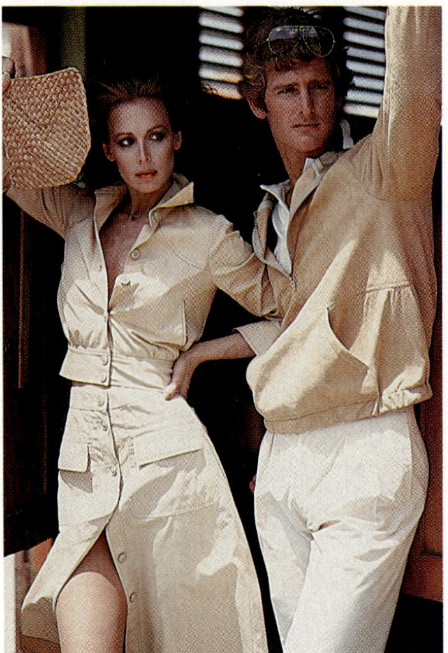

2-35

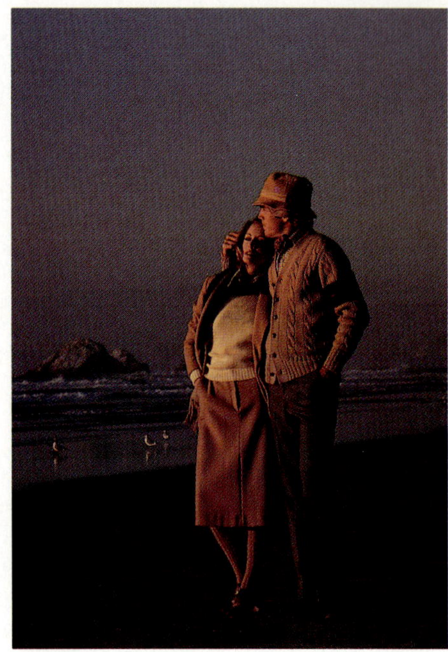

2-36

PHOTO 2-34

In this image I applied basic studio-lighting principles outdoors. Direct sunlight is a prime source of *hard* lighting. Notice the deep shadows and contrast in this ad for *Brittania* jeans, featuring top models Kay Sutton York and Matt Collins.

In the studio, you can position and move lights as needed to produce proper lighting angles and subject modeling. The procedure is a relatively simple one. Outdoors, it's the *subjects* that must be moved so the light strikes them from the best angle.

Unmodified midday sunlight is generally unusable for people photography. The high, harsh light creates pockets of shadow in the subject's eyes. As the sun moves lower toward the horizon, it strikes the subject from a lower, more flattering angle. This photograph was taken just before sunset, displaying two classic faces to their best advantage.

Compare the use of light in this photograph with Photo 54 in the portfolio section of this book. Both images were produced within minutes of each other but with strikingly different results.

PHOTO 2-35

Kay Sutton York and John McMurray are the models in this photograph taken on the Dutch island of Aruba. The shot was part of an eight-page fashion layout produced for *Esquire* magazine.

To block the harsh overhead light, I positioned Kay and John in a doorway with a small awning. This permitted only light from a lower angle to illuminate the faces. Their bodies received the direct overhead sunlight to retain the true feeling of the location.

I took two incident-light meter readings—one at the subjects' faces and one at the highlight part of their clothing. Highly reflective sand on the beach in front of the subjects maintained a lighting ratio of about four to one. Even that was barely within the film's latitude, as evidenced by the nearly burned-out highlights on the clothing.

PHOTO 2-36

Completing this section is a photograph of Lynn Brooks and Scott MacKenzie. I made the image in San Francisco for Gant Shirtmakers. Late-afternoon direct sunlight was used as the sole light source. The effect on the subjects is similar to studio spotlighting—producing high contrast and specularity.

The photo was metered with a Gossen Luna-Pro in the incident-light mode. I placed the hemisphere at subject position and pointed it toward the sun to determine highlight exposure.

Notice the relationship between the heights of the subjects. Because of the relatively distant viewpoint, the height difference can be greater than, for example, in photo 2-27.

CONCLUSION

Photography involves an interplay of many variable elements. The subject influences the camera angle chosen. Camera angle influences lighting. Posing influences both camera angle and lighting. And so it goes on.

As with any art form, photography is dependent upon practice and refinement—technical, visual and esthetic. I encourage you to experiment. Always evaluate your results with care. Record your findings in a book for future reference. Above all else, shoot each image as though you were using your very last frame of film. □

Background Variations

A photographic image is composed of *positive* and *negative* areas. The positive area contains the main subject. Negative area makes up the remainder of the image space and is normally called the *background.* In a balanced image, the two work in harmony. Consequently, negative and positive areas are equally important.

Negative space can enhance or detract from the subject. Therefore, tonality, shape and placement of background elements are critical to the success of a photograph.

The background effects at your command, both in the studio and on location, are limitless. With modern front- and rear-projection systems, we have the pictorial ability to bring the great outdoors inside. In this essay, however, I concentrate on quick and inexpensive backgrounds for a wide variety of photographic applications.

In the Studio

The medium-gray background has dominated editorial beauty and fashion photography for many years—and for many reasons. Gray is a cool, neutral color. By contrast, it emphasizes the warmth of skin tones. Medium gray lends itself readily to a variety of layout and type considerations. For example, type that is either darker or lighter than the background will retain good contrast and legibility. Consequently, the medium-gray background gives the advertising and editorial art director a lot of scope in planning graphics.

SEAMLESS PAPER

My medium-gray backgrounds are actually white seamless paper or a white studio cove. When more light is permitted to fall on the subject than on the background, the white records as gray in the finished photograph.

In photo 3-1, model Cynthia Swearingen is seated approximately six feet from the white seamless background. A single light source, placed approximately four feet from the model, produced a subject exposure of *f*-16. The background exposure recorded as *f*-8. Because the photograph was made at *f*-16, the background was underexposed by 2 exposure steps. This caused the white paper to record as a medium-gray background.

It's a relatively simple matter to produce a background of uniform tone with a seated subject. This is because the subject's shadow falls on the floor behind the subject and is not visible from camera position. A standing subject is a different matter entirely. Because of the subject's height, shadows due to the main light will readily appear on the background. Moving the subject and main light farther from the background doesn't provide a satisfactory solution. It only increases the relative light falloff, causing the background to become darker than you want it, often approaching black.

Photo 3-2 depicts a standing subject against a medium-gray background. The subject was lit with a single main light. In addition, two background light sources were used for an even background tone.

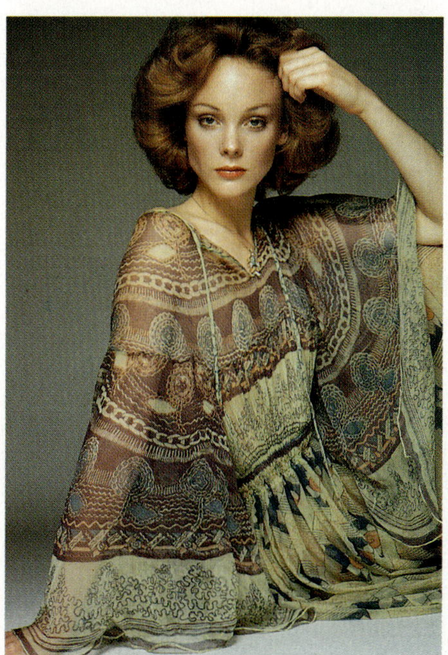

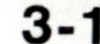

3-1

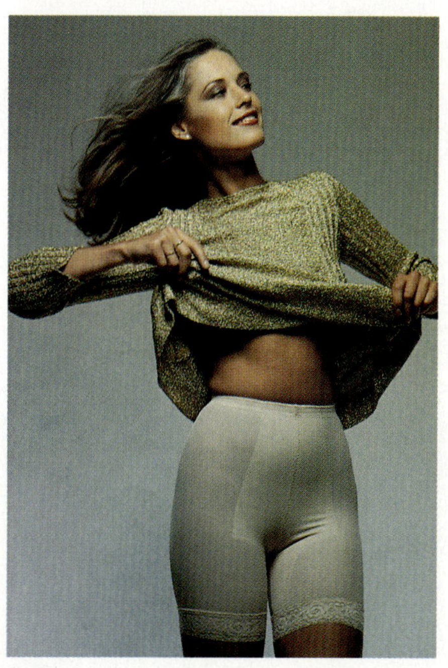

3-2

I generally like to use soft light sources for my background lights —either *softboxes* or large *umbrellas.* They bathe the entire background in even illumination, eliminating shadows.

If you want a medium-gray tone from a white background material, it's important to maintain a 1-1/2 to 2 exposure step differential between the main light exposure and the background exposure.

Variations—The appearance of seamless papers can easily be changed with the introduction of additional light sources. I produced photo 3-3 as a two-page fashion ad for Rich's in Atlanta. I purposely placed the background off-center to depict studio elements on the right side of the photograph. The background behind the models is black seamless paper. It appears to be dark gray, with white highlights.

The effect was produced by placing three electronic-flash heads with narrow-angle reflectors behind the models, close to the background. The background lights were placed to provide three exposure steps more light than was received by the subjects. The patches of white light on the dark background helped outline the models and separate them from the background.

In the previous essay, I mentioned rim lighting. I showed how it can be used to separate a subject from a dark background. The spotlight method, shown here, provides a good alternative.

Spray Paint—Seamless paper backgrounds in a wide variety of colors are available from many photo dealers. To give such backgrounds more "character," you can work wonders with spray paints. With them, you can produce unique background effects with little effort and even less artistic ability.

To make the background for photo 3-4, I applied black spray paint unevenly on white seamless paper. An aperture of *f*-11 with a Nikon 55mm lens produced significant depth of field—and background sharpness. In the image, the clusters of black spray look like blotches of smoke. The visual effect can be controlled in various ways. For example, you can vary the amount of paint used, or change the lens aperture to control depth of field and, therefore, background sharpness.

Before applying paint to a valuable background material, test the spray on scrap paper of the same type. Make sure the paint sprays on evenly, without splattering.

If you should encounter a faulty spray tip, replace it with one from another can of paint. Begin with very light bursts of paint. Return to camera position frequently to check the effect you're creating. Work slowly. If you should apply too much spray in one area, add more elsewhere to maintain a balance.

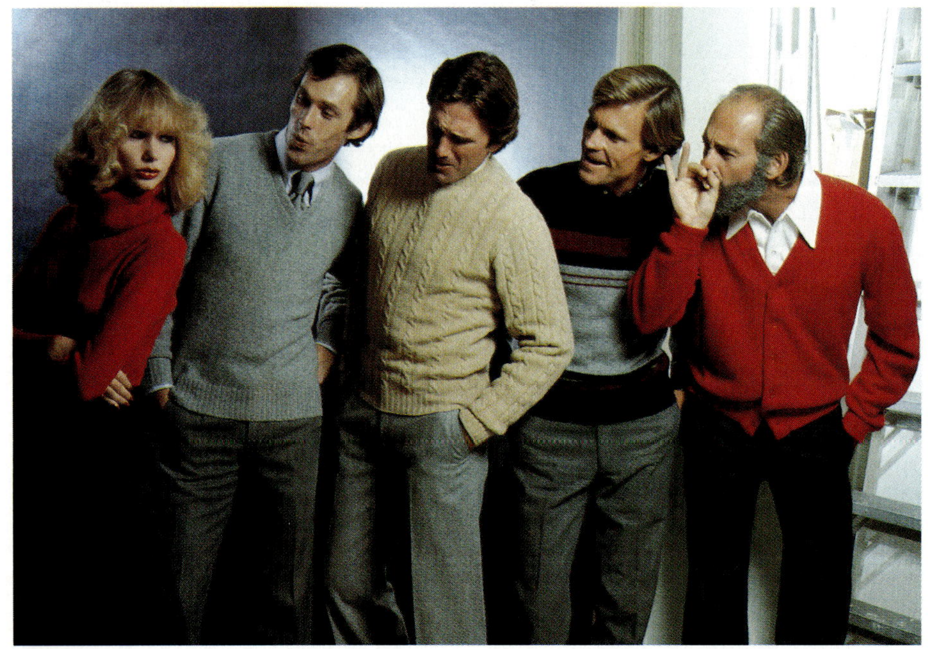

3-3

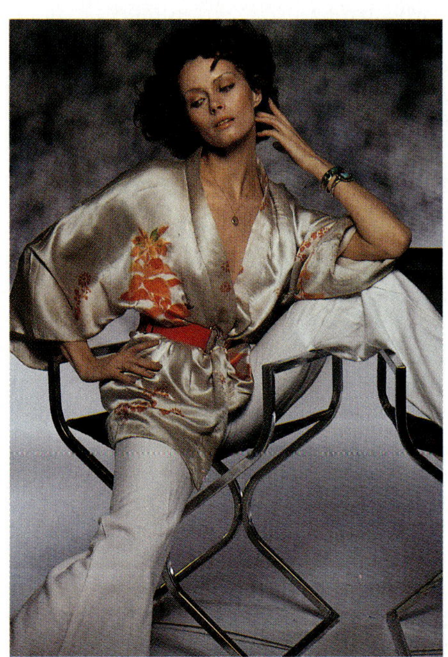

3-4

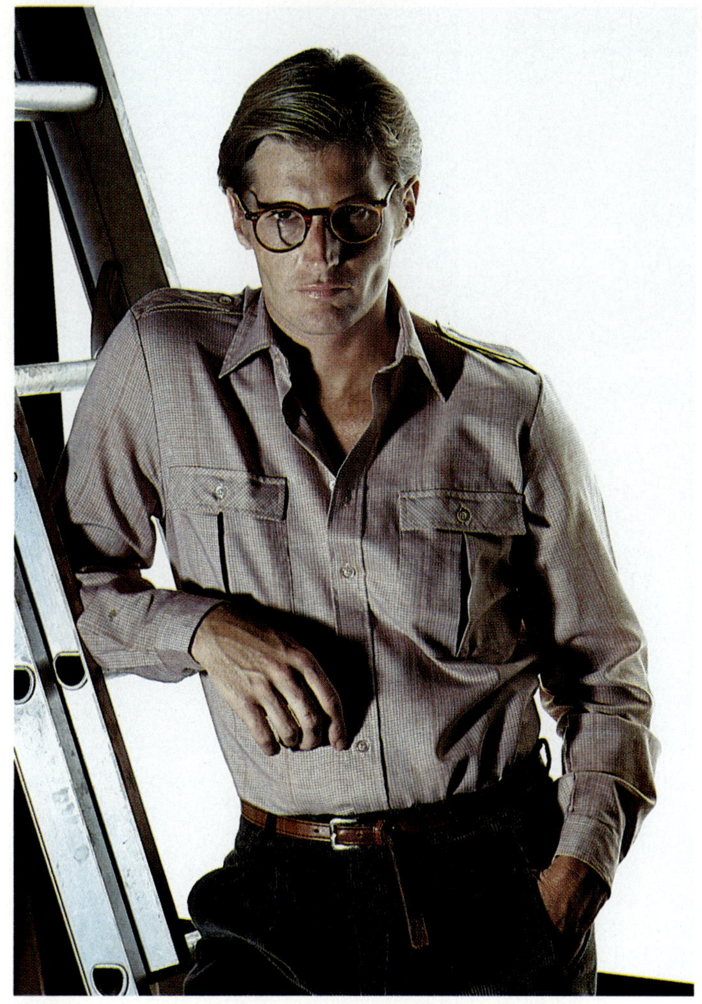

3-5

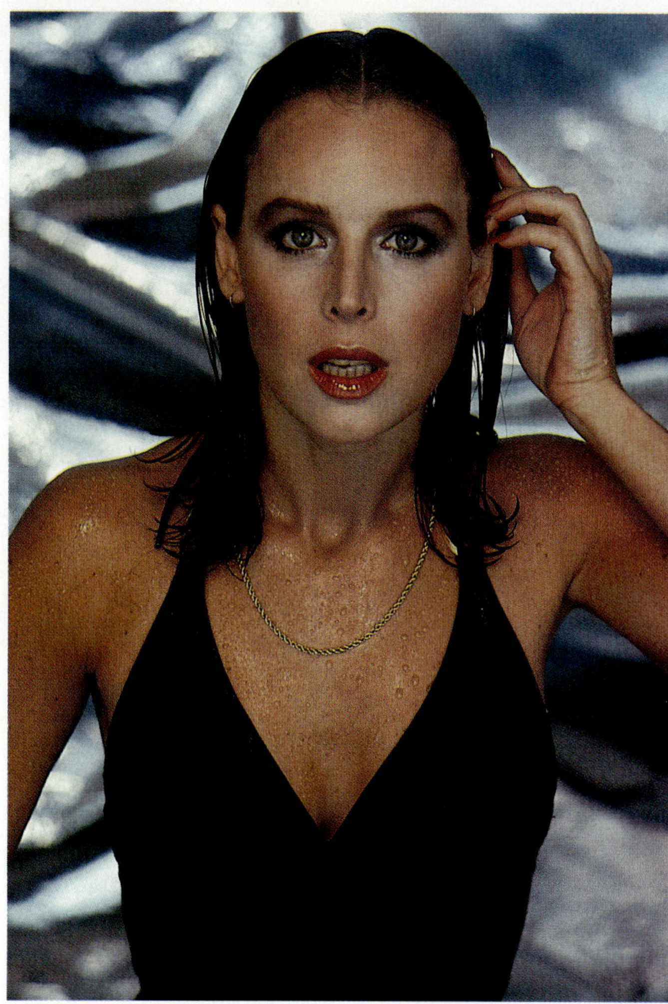

3-6

SIMPLE BACKGROUND PROPS

In recent years, photographic style has become at the same time more dynamic and more relaxed. This is evident in poses as well as in background prop selection. Photo 3-5, for example, gets much of its informality from the ladder.

The background itself for this shirt ad was a large softbox. When this type of light source is directed toward the camera, excessive flare can result. To avoid this, I placed an extra layer of white fabric in front of the softbox. This also ensured more even light distribution, without hot spots.

I adjusted the brightness of the back light to give one exposure step less light at camera position than that recorded from the main illumination on the subject. However, the softbox light striking the subject recorded one exposure step more light than the main light on the subject. This accounts for the edge lighting around the subject.

MYLAR

Reflective mylar is a versatile material for achieving dynamic background effects. It is available in a variety of colors at most large art- or photo-supply stores.

Photo 3-6 was taken for a Revlon ad and also appeared on the cover of *Petersen's PhotoGraphic* magazine. To avoid excessive reflection and the possibility of flare, I angled the silver mylar background away from the camera. I placed blue seamless paper in front of the camera and also below the model. The blue paper was reflected by the silver mylar toward camera position. In the center of the blue seamless I cut a hole just large enough for my 55mm lens to peek through. The blue seamless prevented my own reflection from appearing in the mylar.

I used three lights—a main, balanced with two background lights. I kept the mylar in constant motion by using a small electric fan on the floor next to the model. This automatically gave me a variety of abstract background configurations.

Many interesting visual effects are possible with mylar backgrounds. Results vary with every subtle change in lighting and camera angle. If you keep one of these variables constant, you have much greater control.

A good way to begin a session is by placing the mylar on a background stand. I use either BD aluminum background holders or Mole Richardson C-stands. Each is inexpensive, easy to set up, and lightweight and portable. Position the subject in front of the background and place your camera on a tripod and in place for photography. Set your main light. Then evaluate the pictorial changes that occur as you vary background lighting.

For photo 3-7, a background light with a wide-angle reflector to the subject's left lit the lower part of the composition. I allowed the top portion to record darker. The background was gold mylar. The dark half of the background provided good separation for the subject's blond hair.

Subject lighting was provided by one main umbrella light, flanked by two large softboxes. This illumination gives soft modeling, with minimal contrast, to the model's face and does not affect the background. The background is unaffected because the lack of specularity in the main-light sources minimizes reflection from the mylar.

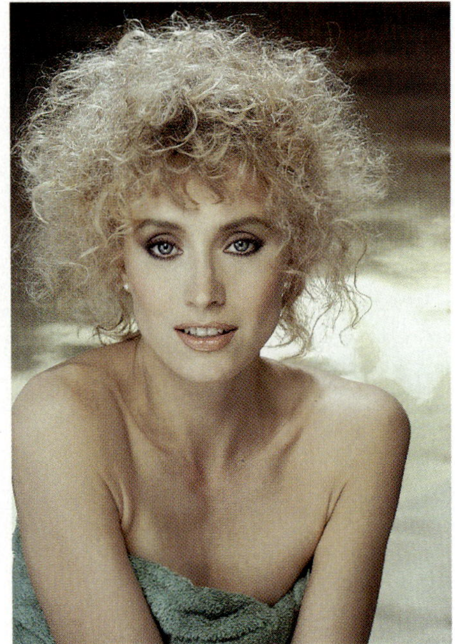

3-7

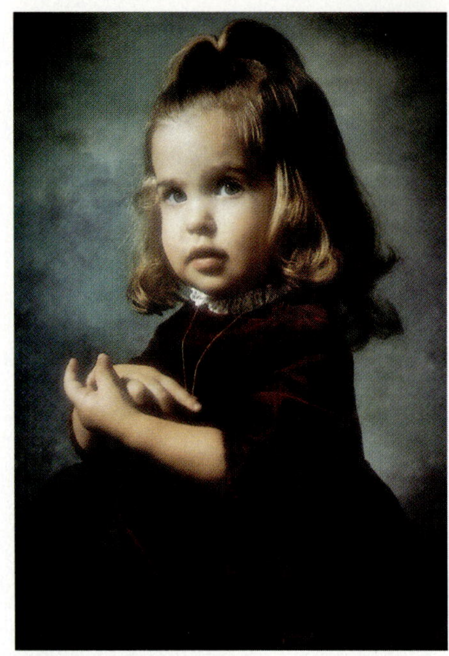

3-8

PAINTED BACKGROUNDS

You needn't be an artist, and you don't need much special equipment, to produce a variety of attractive painted backgrounds. I start with wide rolls of fine canvas or linen, or canvas window shades five or six feet wide.

Stop at your local paint store and purchase a few cans of latex interior house paint. The same store should be able to provide you with an assortment of natural sponges.

A background doesn't take long to paint. In one day, you can easily produce three backgrounds suitable for a wide range of photographic situations. Photo 3-8, a child's portrait made in the Rembrandt style, was taken against a background made with blue, white and black paints. To make the background for Photo 3-9, I used white, yellow, blue and black paints. Both of these backgrounds were easy to make.

Skin tones usually look best against *cool*—or bluish—background colors that tend to emphasize *warm* skin tones. Photo 3-10 of Frank Gifford is a good example. However, as photo 3-11 of Frank shows, *warm* background colors can also enhance rugged, masculine looks and coloring.

Both backgrounds used for the Frank Gifford photos were painted on canvas window shades, using latex house paint. The shades were attached to wooden planks with window-shade mounts. They were supported by lightweight stands. This type of background is easily carried, changed and stored.

How to Paint a Background—Thin the paint with plenty of water. Latex paints dry quickly, but dilution slows the drying process. Try to work all

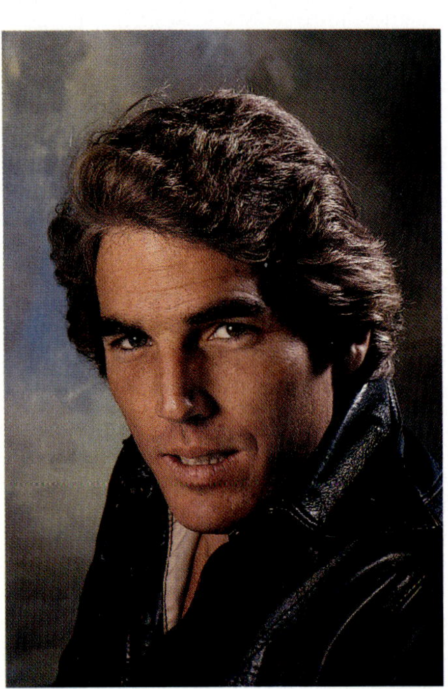

3-9

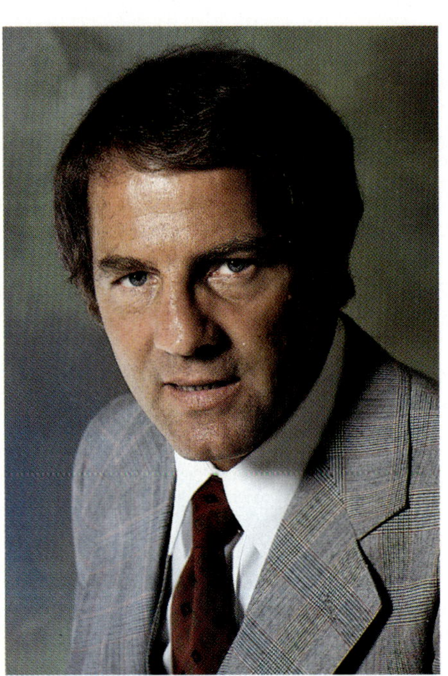

3-10

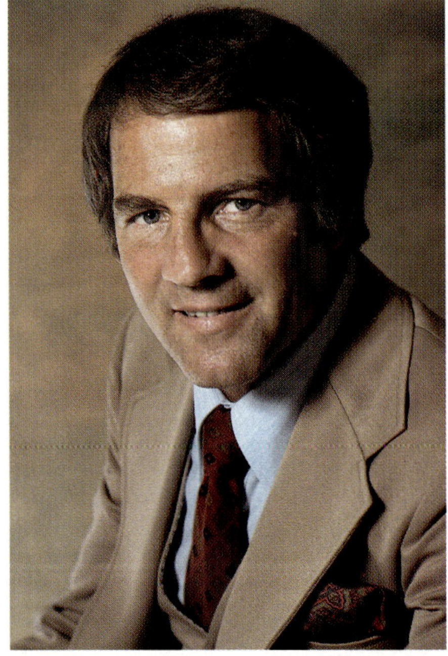

3-11

areas of the background at about the same time, using large sweeping movements with the sponge. Don't be concerned with fine detail that will not be resolved by the camera lens because of limited depth of field.

I start painting at the center of a background and work toward the edges. I paint for a few minutes, then stand back to look at the overall effect from camera position. By squinting my eyes, I can envision the background effect at wide lens apertures. A more direct test is to set up the camera, focus at the subject position and stop the lens down to working aperture. Then, simply look at the background through the viewfinder.

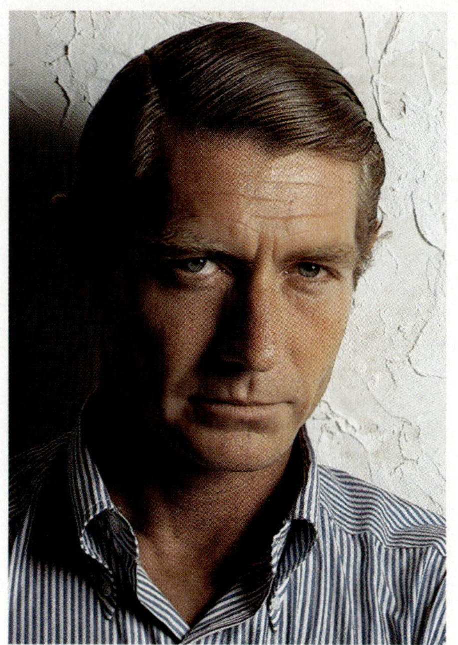

3-12

3-13

TEXTURED BACKGROUNDS—FROM STUCCO TO CARPET

Texture and surface characteristics can play as important a part in your photographic backgrounds as color and tone.

Some of my favorite background textures and surfaces are permanently available on my studio walls. For example, one corner of the studio is stuccoed. In addition I've stuccoed some plywood cubes to match the wall texture. They serve as props and posing supports. Other background surfaces in my studio include high-gloss enamel paint on a cinderblock wall and flat, white latex paint on a metal garage door. I also have a variety of 4x8-foot masonite-backed surfaces featuring such materials as imitation bathroom tile and stained glass.

Most hardware and building-supply stores offer a wide selection of potential background materials. At minimal cost, you can equip your studio with a wide range of backgrounds. They need not be excessively large. A background need be only slightly larger than the total picture area. The viewer won't see what's beyond the borders of the picture.

My stuccoed wall formed the background for photo 3-12. The texture of the stucco effectively complements the model's rugged looks. I placed a small spotlight high, to the right of the camera, to accentuate contrast and texture in both subject and background.

Sometimes it's necessary to construct an entire set for a series of photographs. The corner area of a room was built for photo 3-13. The photograph is part of a fashion layout that appeared in *Esquire* magazine. The set was framed with 1/4-inch plywood on 2x3 studs. A heavy stucco was applied to the plywood.

I used a layer of linoleum to protect the wooden floor in my New York studio during construction. Upon completion of the shooting, I broke the set apart and used the components as wall surfaces in different parts of the studio.

Fabrics provide tremendous background versatility. They can be changed quickly and stored easily. I took photo 3-14 against a background of natural burlap. The burlap was hung from a portable BD background stand and attached with gaffer's tape. Photo 3-15, of top model Pam Southern, was made for The Horchow Collection. It was shot against a background of pleated cotton. I folded the cotton, pressed it with an iron, and mounted it to a sheet of 4x8-foot plywood with a staple gun.

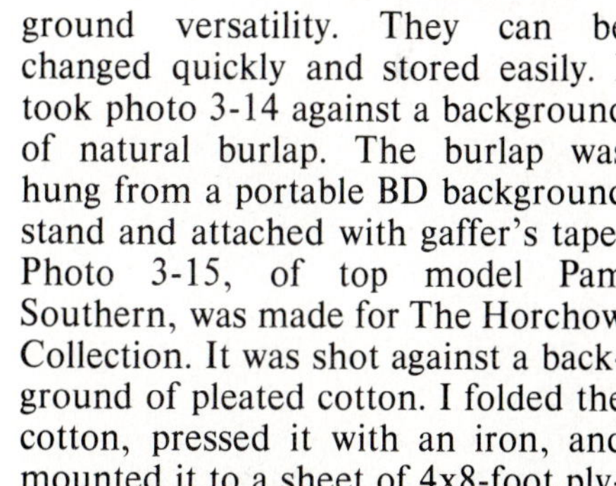

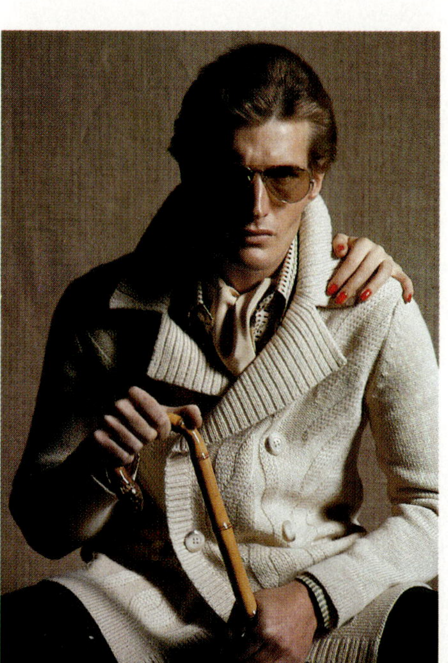

3-14

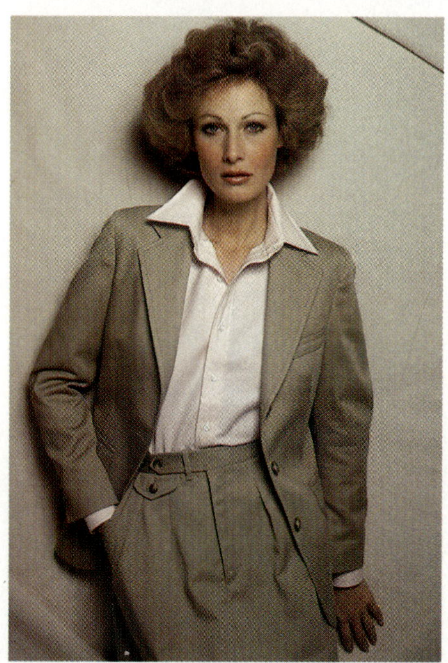

3-15

3-16

THE VERSATILITY OF WHITE

Photo 3-16 was taken against a metal garage door in my Los Angeles studio. I had painted the door white because a white surface provides greater background flexibility than any other color. It reflects colors accurately and can be manipulated by exposure to yield gray and black, as well as white.

White backgrounds also allow for rapid background color changes in a variety of ways. For example, you can use colored gels on the background lights. For photo 3-16, I placed a 3200K photoflood behind my car and pointed it at the right side of the background. The warm light became a beautiful amber against the white wall when photographed on daylight-balanced film.

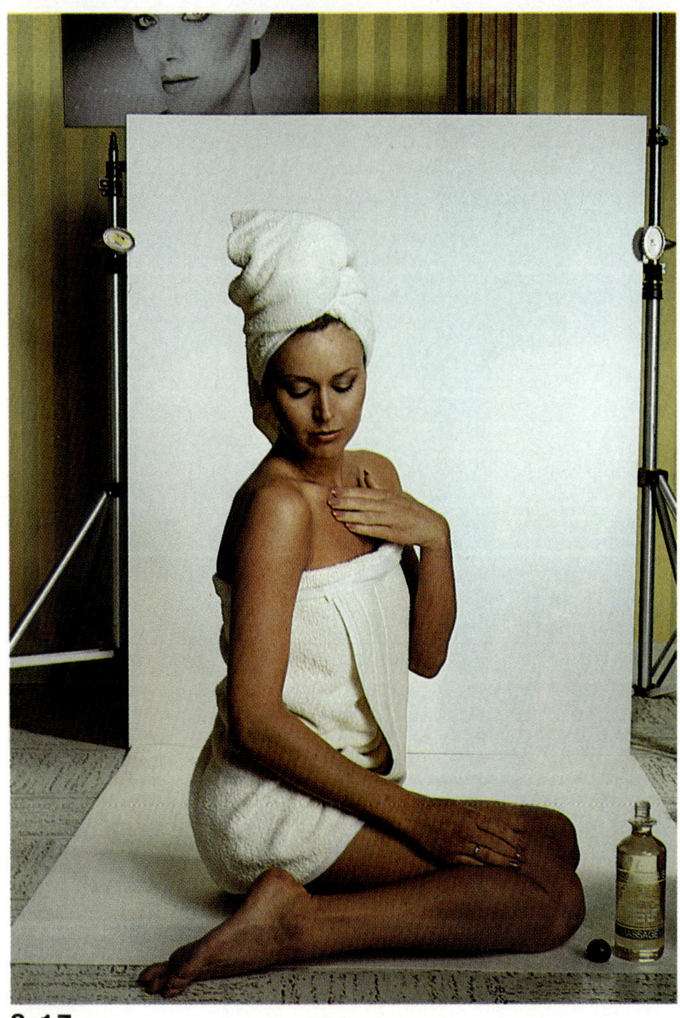

3-17

On Location

When you're shooting away from the studio, you must find suitable backgrounds at the shooting location or bring them with you. Generally, the purpose of shooting on location is to show some of the character of the place. Sometimes, however, you'll need a neutral, plain background.

MINI-STUDIO FOR LOCATION WORK

Photo 3-17 shows a portable background setup consisting of two large pieces of white cardboard. One piece is placed on the floor and the other is used as a vertical background.The latter can be secured to two light stands or other suitable supports. A couple of stand clamps will hold the cardboard in place.

I like to take credit for devising this remarkably portable background. It was born from a spur-of-the-moment need. It provides great versatility with relatively few, inexpensive elements. I've used this setup on several location sessions, sometimes interchanging the white cardboard with cards of different pastel shades. Photo 3-18 was made in this "mini-studio."

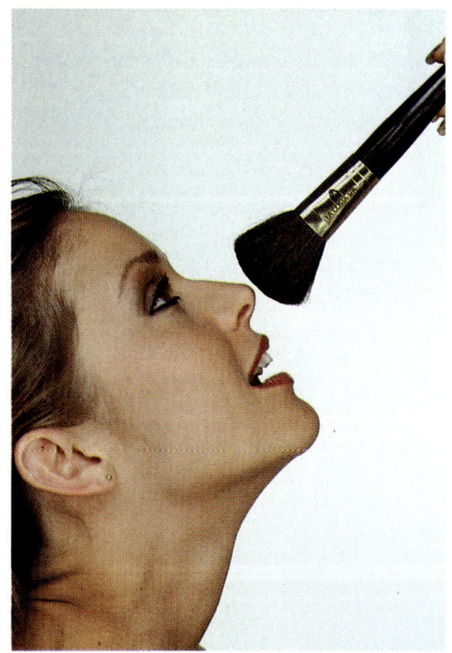

3-18

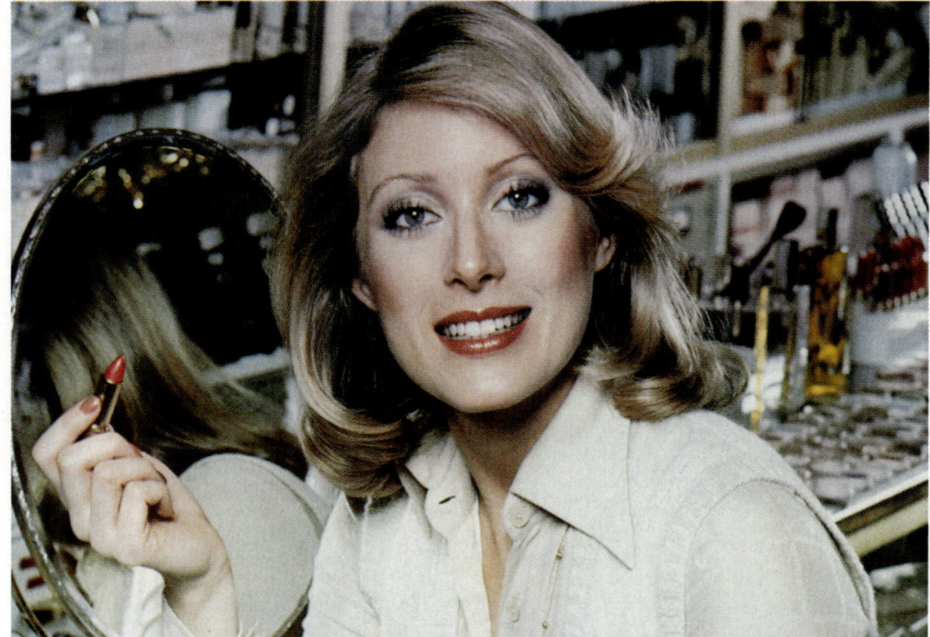

3-19

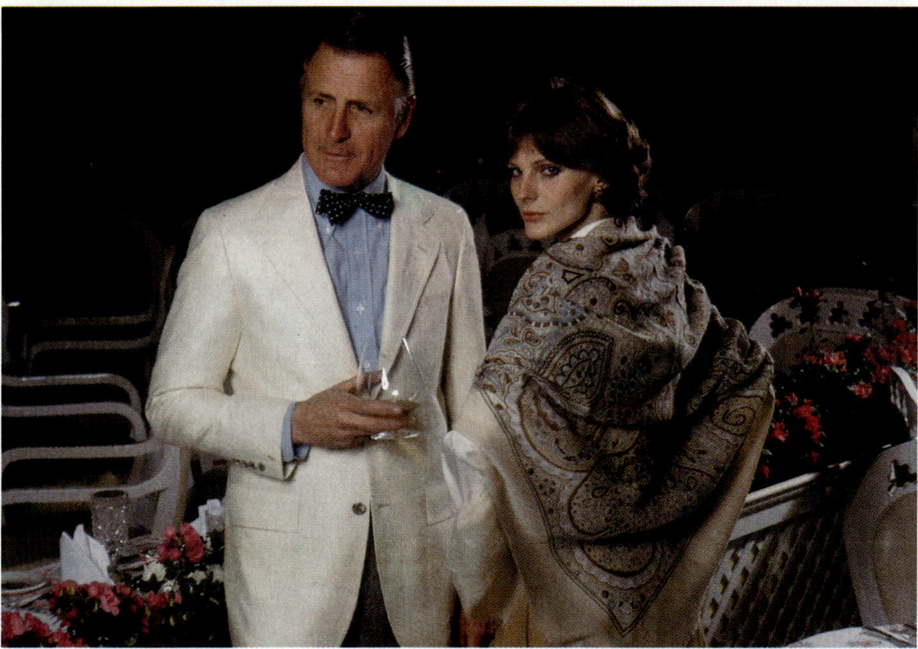

3-20

LOCATION BACKGROUND CONTROL

In much photography, the location forms an essential part of the images. Location backgrounds can lend mood and reality to photographs. Such "real-life" backgrounds can be controlled and varied in several ways. You can select the viewpoint, choose the camera angle, vary the lighting and control depth of field.

Pretty Laura White is the subject of photo 3-19, taken for *Family Circle* magazine. Few backgrounds are "busier" than a department-store cosmetic counter—but that was the required scene for this assignment.

I used three basic techniques to prevent the background from compositionally overpowering the subject. First, the model was placed at an oblique angle to the counter. The receding counter concentrated viewer attention on the foreground and Laura. Next, I selected a large enough lens aperture to render background elements recognizably but not with great detail. Finally, I gave the model half an exposure step more light than the background. The viewer is subtly attracted to the brightest part of the photograph—the subject.

Photo 3-20 was made at New York's elegant Tavern On The Green restaurant. The restaurant was closed for the photography session and I had the freedom to do what I wanted. However, the background was empty and did not lend itself to making exciting photographs. I minimized the view of the background by shooting from a high angle. In addition, I gave the background three exposure steps less light than the subjects. To add a little extra emphasis to the subjects and eliminate the visual blending of their heads with the background, I added a rim light. It gave 1-1/2 exposure steps more light than the main light.

Telephoto lenses and large lens apertures can work wonders on location. With them, you can depict your main subject with sharp detail but, thanks to limited depth of field, be assured of a soft, diffused, nondistracting background.

OUTDOOR BACKGROUND SELECTION

Location background evaluation and selection is a major undertaking. It's little wonder that it also is a lucrative business. In every large advertising city, such as New York, Los Angeles or Chicago, professional *location finders* operate extremely successful businesses. They serve the needs of photographers and motion-picture makers. It's easy to appreciate their services. I've personally spent as long as a week seeking ideal backgrounds for a simple one-day photography session.

To avoid last-minute problems or the need for costly location-search services, I make a point of recording interesting backgrounds as I drive around doing normal daily chores. I maintain a location directory on computer and also keep notebooks and Polaroid photographs. I list general location details, background colors and textures, how much space is available for photography, the dis-

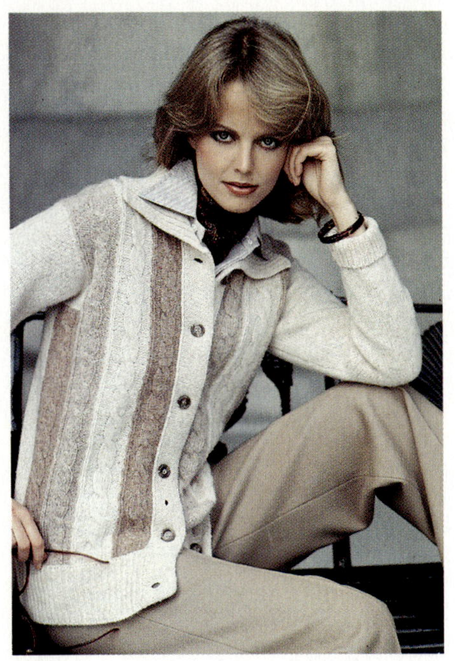
3-21

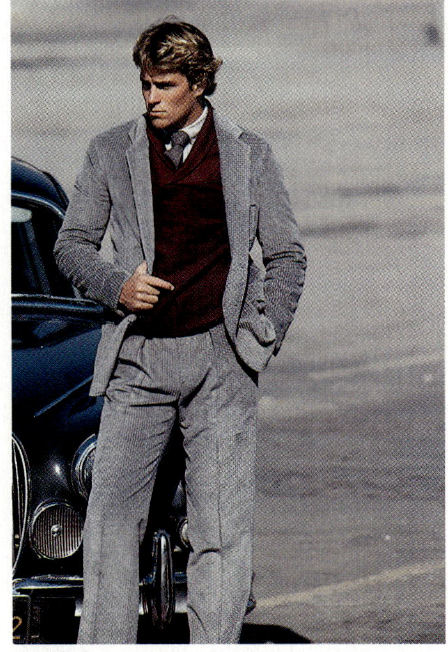
3-22

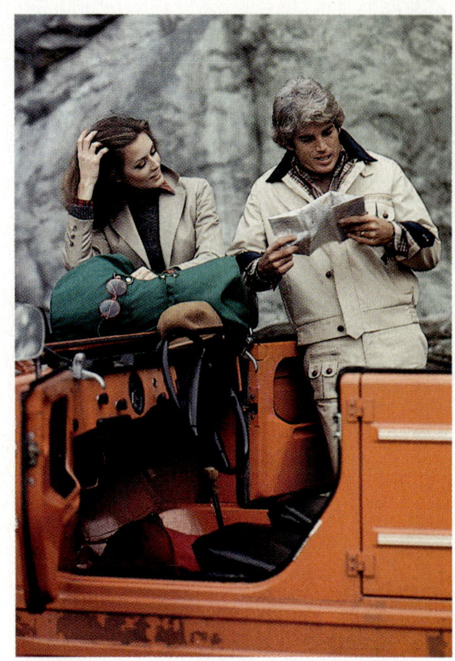
3-23

tance and traveling time from my studio, cost of use of the location, if any, and the position of the sun at different times and seasons.

The four backgrounds shown next were all selected to simulate the neutral tonality of a medium-gray studio background.

In urban areas, buildings are the greatest source of background diversity. Photo 3-21, which was taken for Hart, Schaffner and Marx, was shot with an 85mm *f*-1.8 Auto-Nikkor lens at *f*-4. Limited depth of field softened the gray background masonry to almost a continuous tone.

Actor Ted McGinley is the subject of photo 3-22. It was taken with one of my favorite Nikon lenses, the 300mm *f*-2.8 telephoto. At *f*-4, the 300mm lens softens the background of even a full-length shot. For this photo, the background was an empty parking lot beside a highway in Malibu, California.

In rural areas, space is often virtually unlimited. When you can place subject and background farther apart, you can often use shorter lenses and still get the limited depth of field you need. Because of the considerable distance between my subjects and the background in photo 3-23, I was able to shoot with a 55mm Nikkor. At *f*-5.6, the background is rendered as an undistracting, gray blur.

I used a different technique for photo 3-24, taken for *Virgin Island Rum* on an overcast day. By using a portable 100-watt-second flash and underexposing the daylight by half an exposure step, I made the background record as a uniform, medium gray.

BOLD COLORS AND DYNAMIC GRAPHICS

You can always find a possibility for creating strong graphic images. Photo 3-25 is a good example. I took it in Queens, New York, in an area that was less than appealing in terms of background esthetics. To achieve an effective, dramatic background for actor-model Steve Shortridge, I raised my camera by standing on two metal camera cases. As a result, I got a clean, uncluttered background. The subject, in his white outfit, stands out

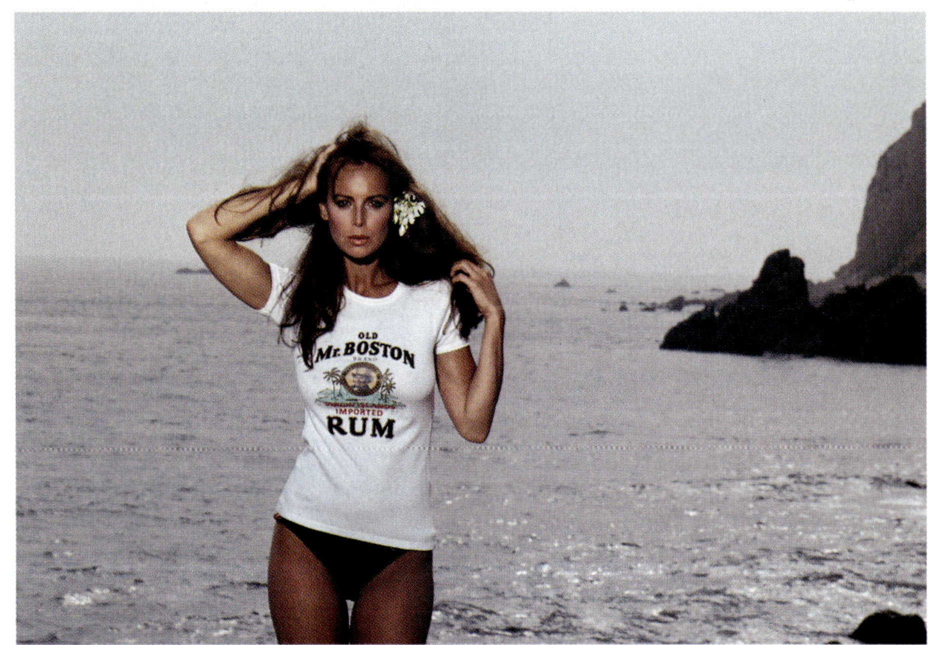

3-24

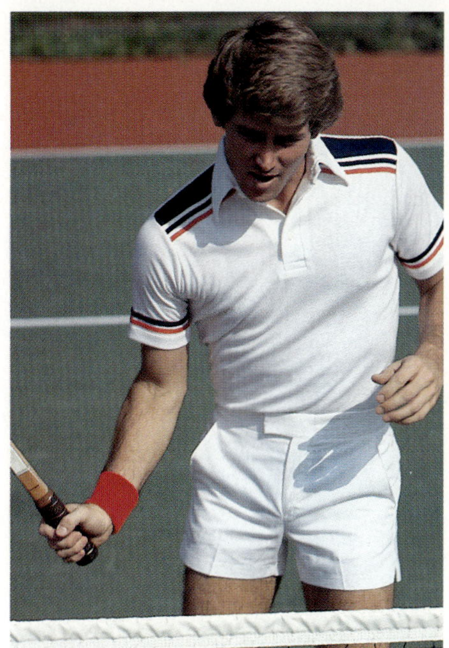

3-25

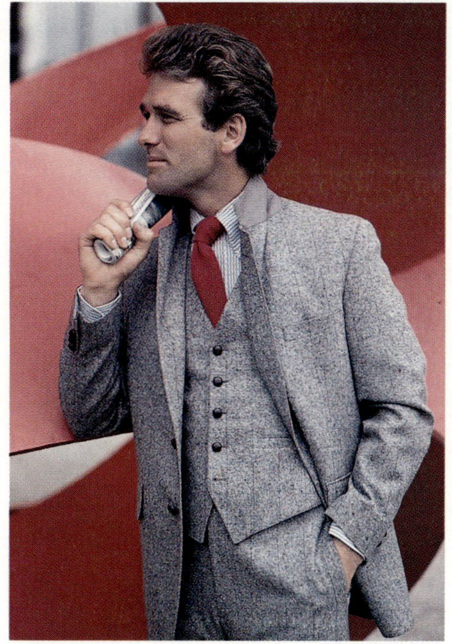

3-26

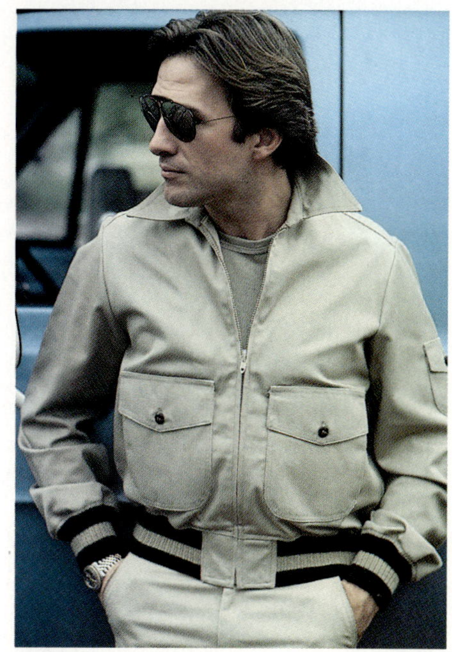

3-27

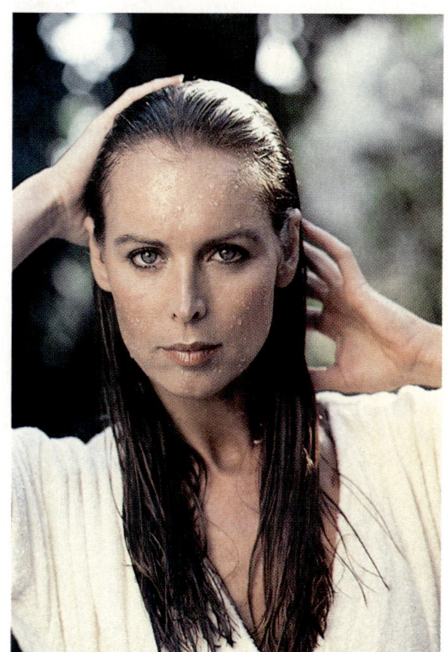

3-28

clearly against the dark court surface.

Art objects can provide colorful background variety for many photographic situations. Photo 3-26, for textile manufacturer J. P. Stevens, was taken with an 85mm Nikkor at *f*-1.8. The wide aperture gave minimal depth of field, causing the red sculpture behind the model to appear even more abstract than the sculptor had intended. Incidentally, it's no coincidence that the red background and the model's tie are a perfect color match.

Colorful backgrounds need not be sophisticated to be effective. A blue panel truck by the side of a road in Miami, Florida, made an ideal background for photo 3-27. I used a 105mm *f*-2.5 Auto-Nikkor at wide open aperture. The limited depth of field allowed me to render the subject in sharp focus and the truck with less detail.

BACKGROUND FOLIAGE

Foliage can be a source of background problems. As light filters through leaves, a background can become excessively distractive, making viewer concentration on the subject difficult.

To eliminate the distraction caused by backlit foliage, I need to use a relatively long lens to limit depth of field. Photo 3-28 is a good example. I took it for Max Factor. It was midday. The sun was above and just behind the subject. The direct sunlight produced distracting spots of light behind the subject. To soften these spots, I had to put them out of focus. I did this by using a 200mm *f*-4 Nikon telephoto lens at its widest aperture.

For final printing, the image was cropped at the top to eliminate the two large spots of light. The result was a pleasing image without any background distractions.

CONCLUSION

The ultimate aim and purpose of beauty and glamour photography is subject enhancement. It is possible for a background to be magnificent, yet unflattering to the subject. Therefore, you must be selective. Study the images appearing in contemporary fashion magazines and evaluate the reasons for pairing specific subject types with certain backgrounds. Learn, but remain open to change and experimentation. During a photography session, try some background changes without altering lighting or subject pose and attitude. Evaluate the results carefully. □

4

Effective Posing

In many ways, this was for me the most difficult essay of the book to prepare. I know that many photographers would like a comprehensive listing of poses from which to select. However, effective posing depends on many factors and truly doesn't lend itself to a structured, tabulated approach. I'll try to give you some useful guidelines, based on my own practical experience.

CLASSIC PORTRAIT POSING

In my book *Pro Techniques of People Photography,* also published by HPBooks, I discussed the basics of classic posing for men, women, and couples. The classic rules provide important guidelines. When all else fails, return to the basics—at least at the start of a session.

In private portraiture and photography of well-known personalities, the subject is the most important factor. Therefore, the purpose of a pose is to show the subject to the viewer to best advantage. The subject's body position should be comfortable and easy to assume as well as appropriate to the character study desired by both subject and photographer.

In commercial beauty and fashion photography, where the main aim is to attract attention to a product, the subject is often of secondary importance. Because of these different priorities, the rules of classic posing are often more important in private portraiture.

In spite of the above, more and more of today's portrait clients, both private and public, find classic posing constrictive and undesirable. I consider them correct in their belief that classic posing—as practiced by the majority of the nation's portrait studios—is a relic of the past. It originates from the time when slow films and long exposures were the order of the day.

CONTEMPORARY PORTRAIT POSING

Today's lighting technology, camera equipment and films give you almost unrestricted control. In a fraction of a second you can easily capture the fleeting subtleties in a subject's character. With a motor drive or auto winder and fast flash recycling, you can shoot lively picture sequences within seconds.

The Natural Pose—In contemporary portraiture, the best poses are usually those assumed naturally by the subject or created spontaneously by you, the photographer, for a specific situation. In effect, successful posing is usually the result of a combined effort by subject and photographer. Each must contribute to the creative process. When the subject's body is in an appealing and appropriate position, you can capture a variety of subtle attitude changes before asking the subject to change the basic position.

When a subject has difficulty following my verbal directions, I assume the pose myself and ask the subject to take my position behind the camera. This lets the subject see what I wish to achieve compositionally. As I demonstrate the pose I also explain the visual effect I'm aiming for. For example, I may tell a mature woman why I'm forcing my head toward the camera: Because it elongates the neck and gives a better line to the jaw. When people know the reason for a requested pose, they find it far easier to assume the position.

I find that most subjects become more relaxed as a session progresses. Often, posing attempts that don't work early in a photo session work beautifully toward the end, when you've built increased subject confidence.

STUDY CURRENT MAGAZINES

As you look through a magazine, the sheer impact of a dynamic photograph may arrest your attention. It may be difficult to define precisely which creative element moved you. It was probably an interplay of many. Posing is just one of the many important aspects of photography that can "make or break" an image.

Don't hesitate to copy magazine images that you find appealing. Even if your particular subject is unable to assume the exact pose shown, this provides a fine starting point from which to experiment with variations.

MALE AND FEMALE POSING

Excluding posing, you generally have considerably more creative pictorial freedom with men than women. With men you can use extreme camera angles and harsh, contrasty lighting. You can see some of this variety in photos in this book as well as my other book, *Pro Techniques of People Photography,* also published by HP Books.

Where posing is concerned, however, women offer greater flexibility. For that reason, I've chosen to illustrate posing a woman in this essay.

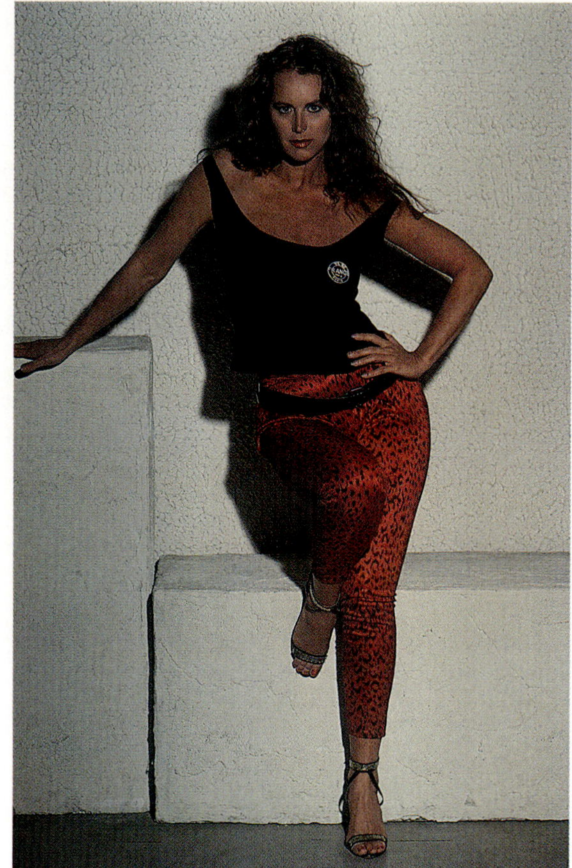

4-1

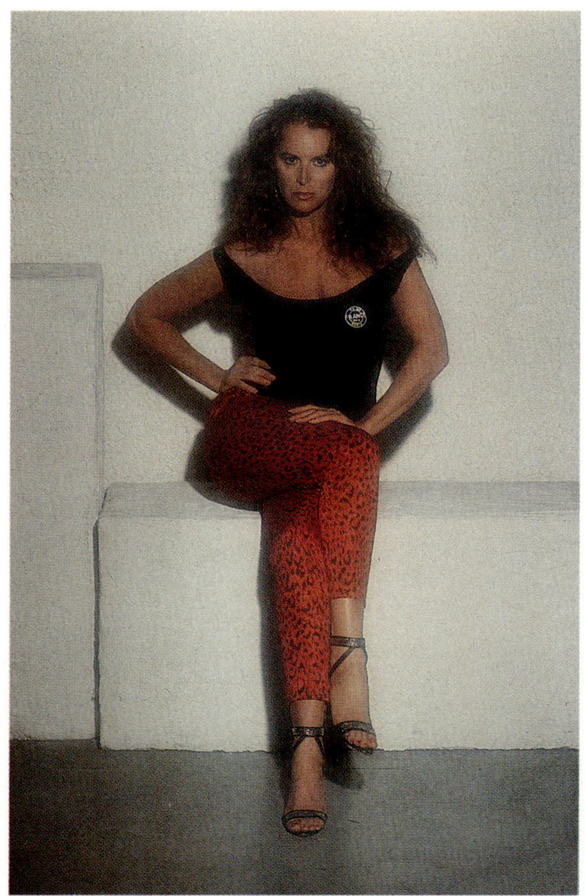

4-2

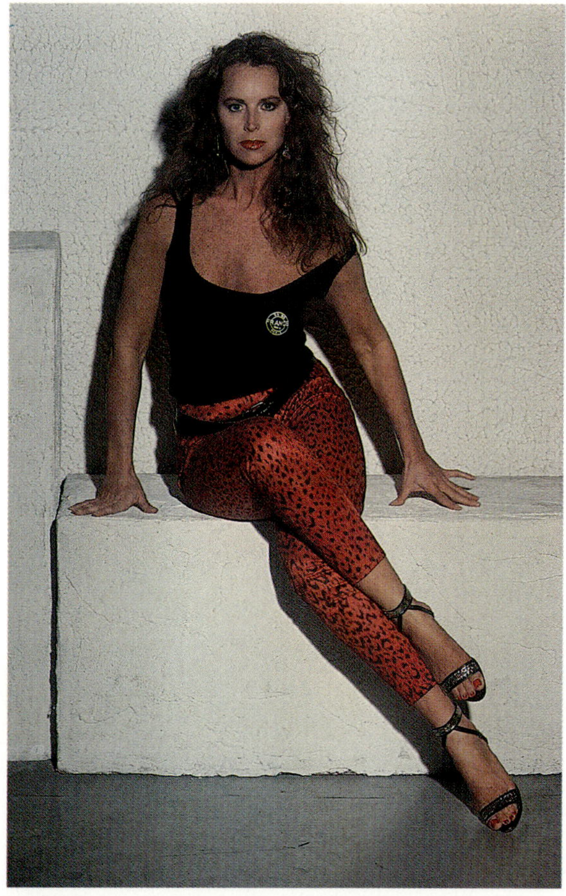

4-3

POSING A WOMAN

Many elements affect the selection of poses. They include the subject's age, appearance and physical condition, and the clothing selected for the session.

For the examples illustrating this essay, I selected a casual outfit consisting of a tank top and slacks. The outfit provided maximum posing versatility and allowed the model's leg positions to be seen clearly.

As you look through the images, you'll become aware of a distinct photographic *flow*. One image seems to lead quite naturally to the next. Be warned, however, that variations that work well with one subject may be much less successful with another. It depends on the characteristics and abilities of the subject. Evaluate each subject carefully as your shooting session progresses.

Although the changes from one pose to another are often slight, they are significant. The subject—especially a female subject—is astutely aware of subtle changes in body and attitude. Minimal changes—such as the shifting of body weight, the position of a hand, the tip of the head or turn of the torso—may be barely noticed by the casual observer. However, they are vitally important to the subject and the ultimate effectiveness of the photographic image.

The session, shot specifically for this essay, was based on a hypothetical assumption: I had been assigned to shoot an ad for a European fashion or cigarette account. Why European? Because European accounts tend to give model and photographer greater flexibility than their domestic advertising and editorial counterparts.

The photographs in this essay depict some basic body positions and subtle variations of each basic pose:

While standing, the model slid her right foot along her left leg (photo 4-1). In doing so, her weight was shifted toward her left side. Her hip was thrust out, adding sensuality to the image. She looks more elongated and feminine than if she were standing squarely on both feet.

Notice, incidentally, the posing cubes I used throughout this series. It's important to maintain a variety of such props in a range of sizes and shapes to satisfy different subject shapes and sizes.

From her standing position the model sat down, crossing one leg over the other (photo 4-2). Because the model was wearing slacks, the entire shape of her legs is evident in the photographs. For that reason, she did not apply the full weight of her upper leg to the lower leg. This prevented unflattering distortion of either leg.

As a variation, the model shifted her weight to her right side (photo 4-3). Because her body was no longer balanced, she supported her weight

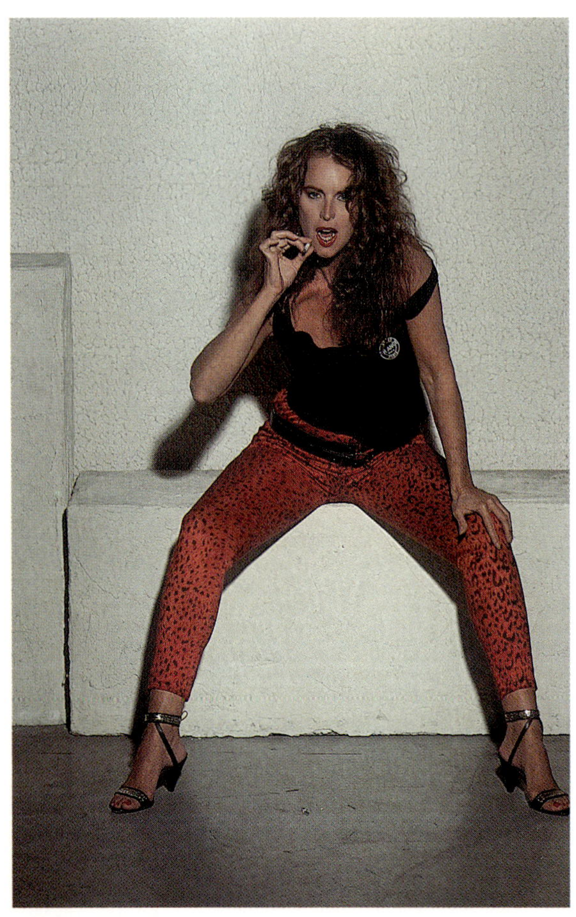

4-4

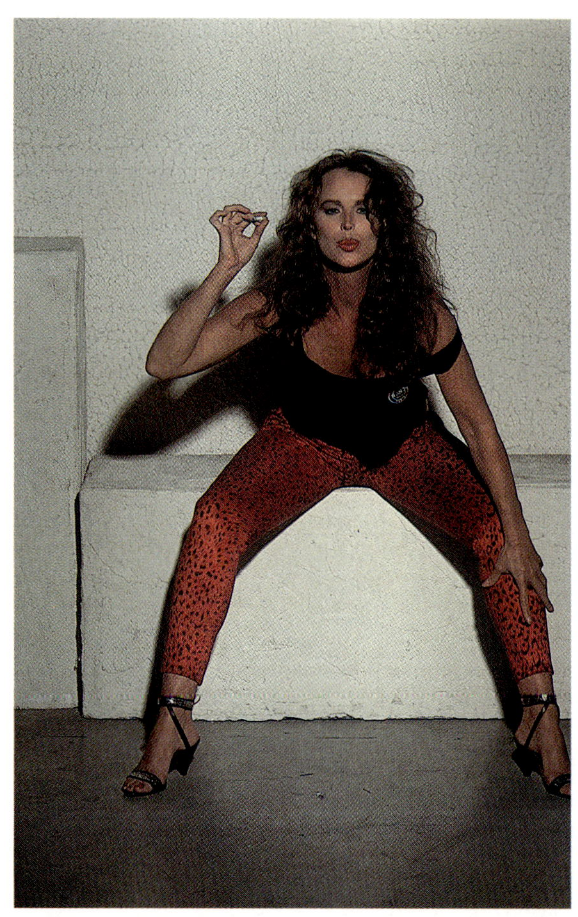

4-5

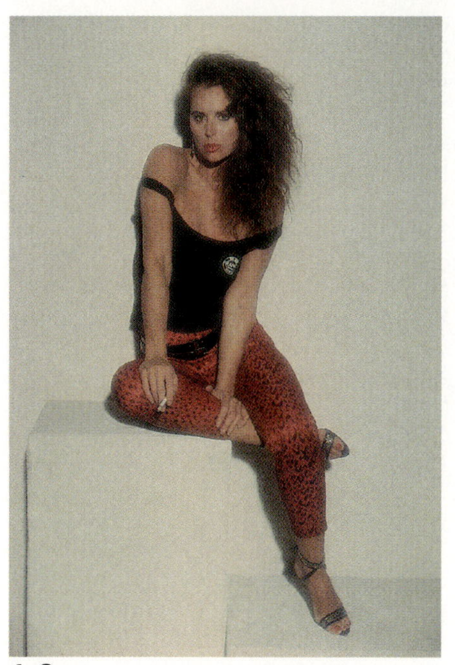
4-6

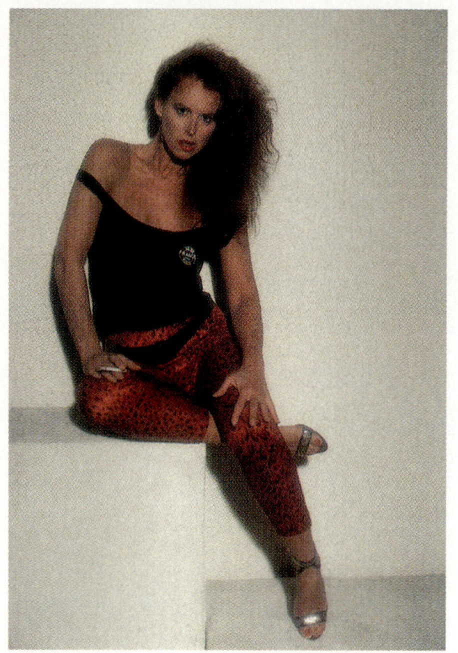
4-7

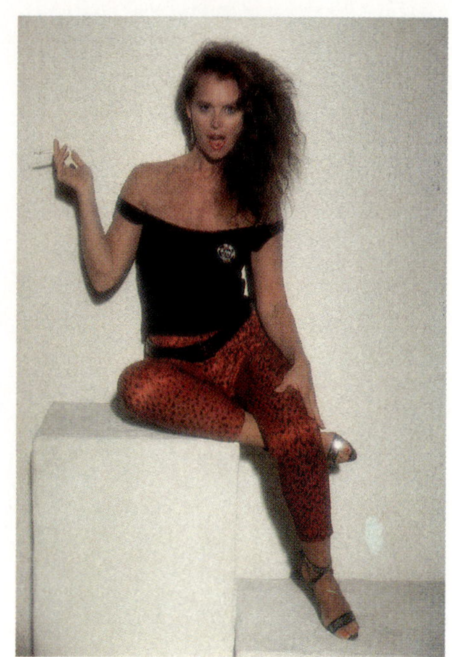
4-8

with her right hand on the cube.

The model remained seated, this time with her legs parted (photos 4-4 and 4-5). She used a cigarette as a prop. The only change in her pose occurred from the waist up. Notice that in photo 4-5, where the model's torso is thrust forward toward the camera, her left arm extends down her left leg. At the same time she moved her right elbow out to maintain both a comfortable physical and pleasing compositional balance.

Notice the subtle change in the position and height of the model's right shoulder in the next sequence (photos 4-6 to 4-9). Each slight alteration created a totally new look.

I take care to avoid photographing the backs of a subject's hands. Hands, like elbows, can easily become very unflattering. Showing the sides of a hand and the full length of fingers produces soft, graceful lines in an image.

In photo 4-9, I had the model seated in profile position but asked her to look directly at the camera.

In this book, you'll see several examples of basic poses on the studio floor. Photos 4-10 and 4-11 show how posing cubes of various heights offer additional scope for pose changes. The model positioned her legs so both were visible and created slender, graceful outlines. It's usually most flattering if the leg closest to the camera is bent. Notice how the entire

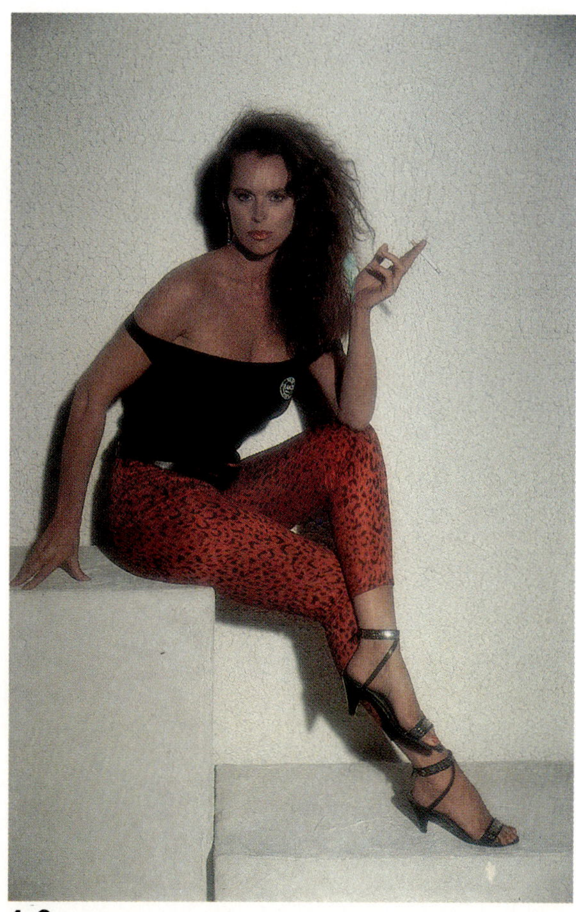
4-9

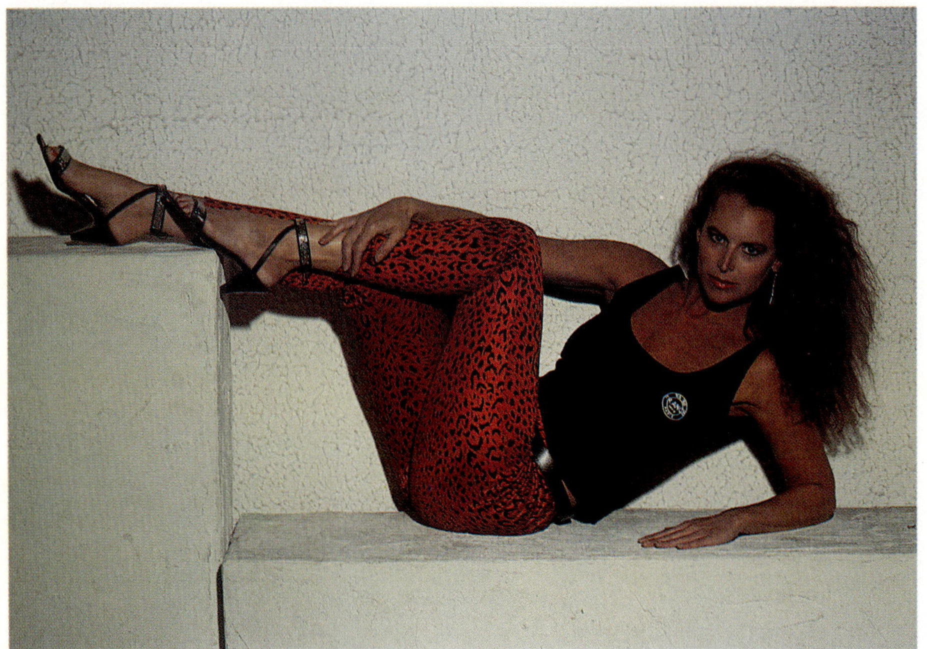

4-10

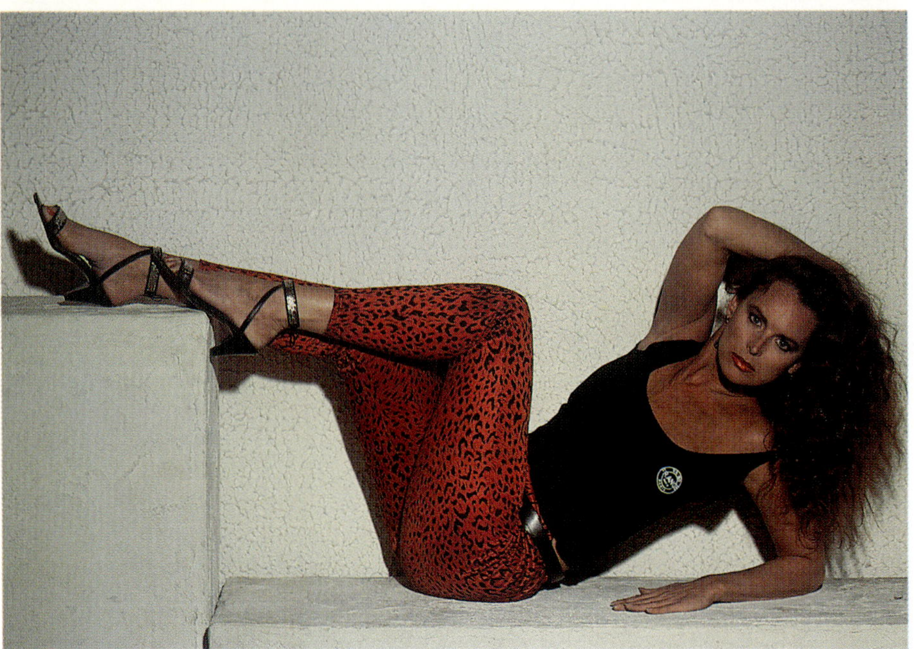

4-11

effect of the photograph changes when the model moves her hand from her leg to her head.

The final image (photo 4-12) shows how facial attitude and expression are integral parts of the total pose.

CONCLUSION

In beauty and glamour photography, a pose need not always be comfortable to be successful. What is imperative is that the subject *appears* to be comfortable in every pose. That's where your judgment as photographer and director comes in. Make sure that the poses you select are appropriate for the garment, be it an evening gown, a swimsuit or a pair of slacks.

As I've said before, I don't maintain an inventory of *standard* poses. I treat every situation individually—analyzing the subject's needs and the requirements of the styling and overall composition. With a little practice you, too, can produce striking poses that are not from the "rule book" but enhance each subject's body, attitude and wardrobe uniquely. □

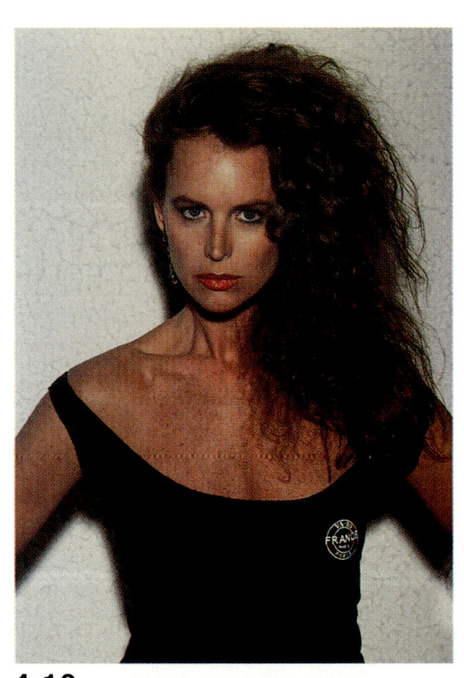

4-12

Makeup and Hairstyling

In Essay 6, I discuss the use of models and stylists. To obtain the model, as well as the makeup artist and hairstylist, for the specially made images appearing in this essay, I used agencies such as I describe.

In Los Angeles, some of the finest hair, makeup, and fashion stylists are represented by HMS Bookings, Inc. The principals of this agency, Margaret L'Hommedieu and Catherine Brickley, and agency publicist John McMurray, helped me select the styling talent for this beauty session. Makeup was by Jeff Jones and hairstyling by Steve Reiley. I was most fortunate in securing the services of these two fine artists on the same job. Their talent and creativity is astounding, and their collective client list reads like an international *Who's Who*.

Our pretty subject for the session was Tracy Bayne, a 22-year-old professional model and actress. She's represented by Mary Webb Davis Models, Inc. of Los Angeles. Margo Law, representing this agency, helped me select Tracy from many models' portfolios and composites.

The accompanying photograph shows the team that made this essay possible. I'm standing behind the camera in silhouette. In front of Tracy Bayne, our model, is makeup artist Jeff Jones. Hairstylist Steve Reiley is behind Tracy. I thank them all for doing an excellent job!

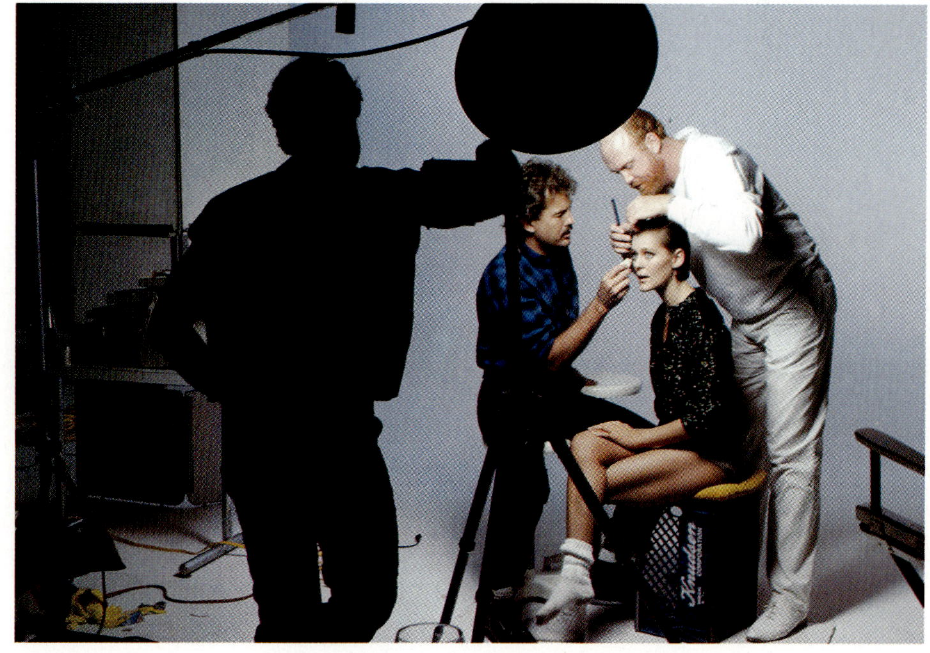

Photos 5-1 through 5-19 were lit by the 800-watt-second Versatron main light in pan reflector visible in this photo. Back lighting—one light to either side of the model, each bounced from a 52-inch umbrella—was provided by two Versatron 800s at full power.

Makeup

Here's a step-by-step demonstration of makeup suitable for beauty and glamour photography:

PHOTO 5-1
The session began with our model freshly scrubbed, free from all makeup. Her hair was unstyled.

PHOTO 5-2
Jeff applies a non-greasy moisturizer, creating a moist, smooth surface for application of the makeup.

PHOTO 5-3
Jeff applies a cream concealer around Tracy's eyes and along the smile lines, using a medium Windsor-and-Newton #6 brush. Then, using a small wedge sponge, Jeff blends the edges of the concealer with Tracy's skin.

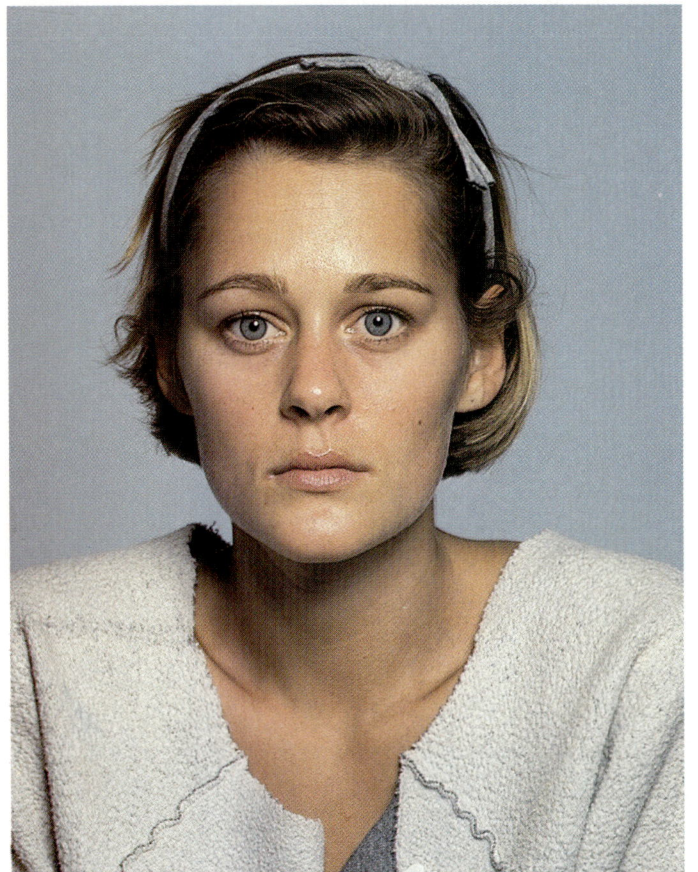

5-1

5-2

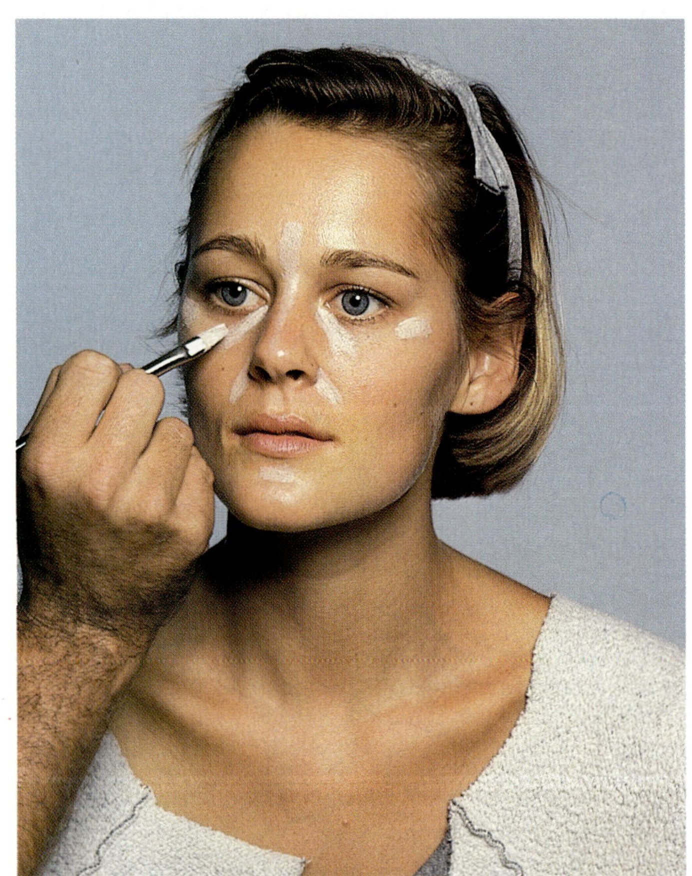

5-3

PHOTO 5-4

With a clean wedge sponge, Jeff applies a liquid foundation to further smooth the complexion and even out the skin tonality. Next, a light application of translucent face powder over the entire face and eye area is added to dull excessive gloss and also give the makeup a lasting quality. Jeff then uses a damp sponge to *set* the foundation.

PHOTO 5-5

This is how our model looked after application of a peach eye shadow over the eye area from the base of the lashes to the tip of the eyebrow. Notice the warmth and allure of the eyes.

PHOTO 5-6

A soft-brown eye shadow is applied to the outer half of each eye to apparently raise the ends of the eyes and visually increase their separation. This application also adds depth and drama to the eyes. The eye shadow is applied with a small brush.

Jeff also applies the same brown shadow along the eyelids and blends it

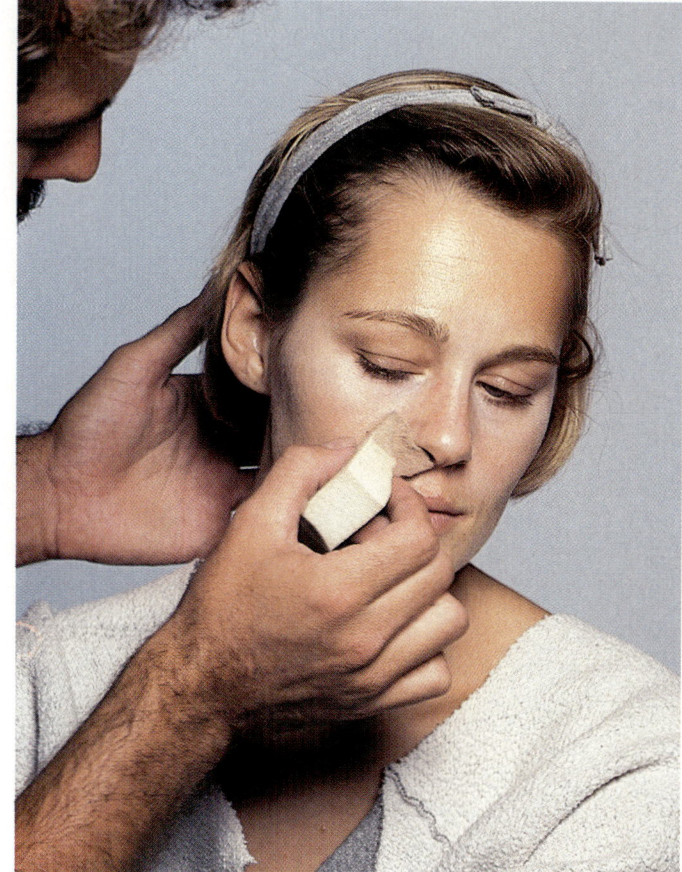

5-4

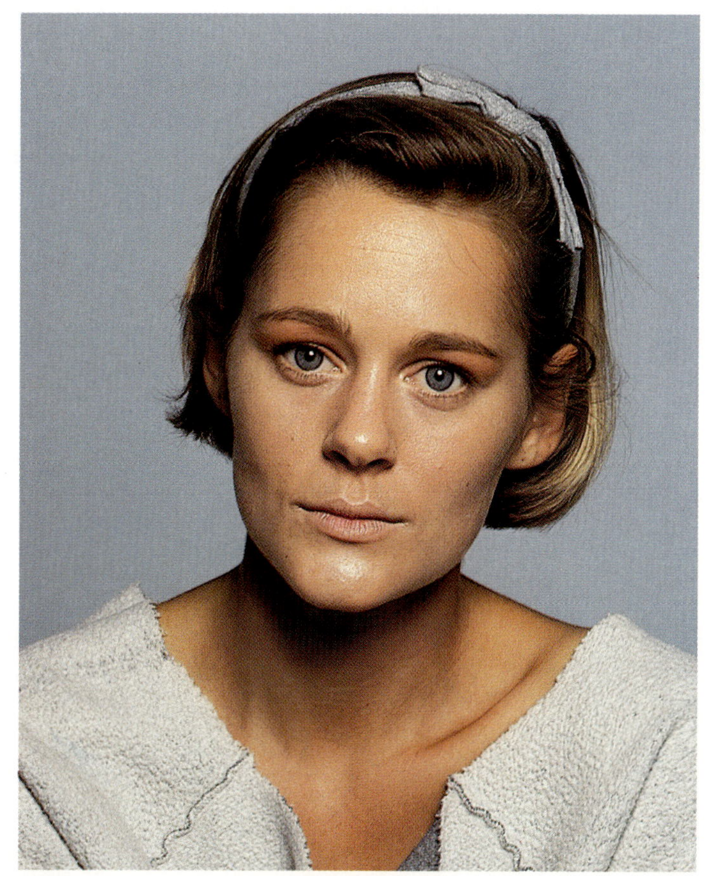

5-5

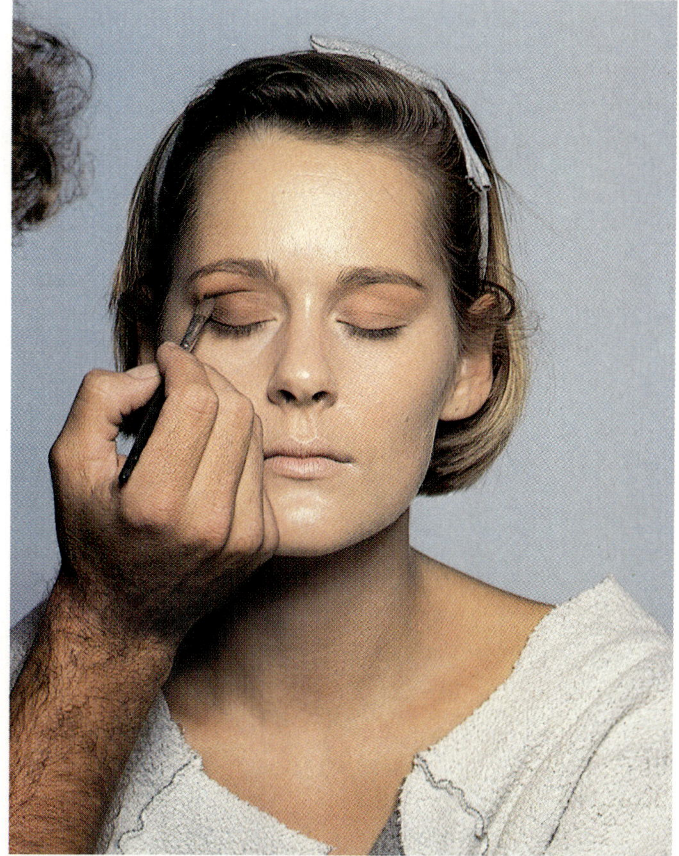

5-6

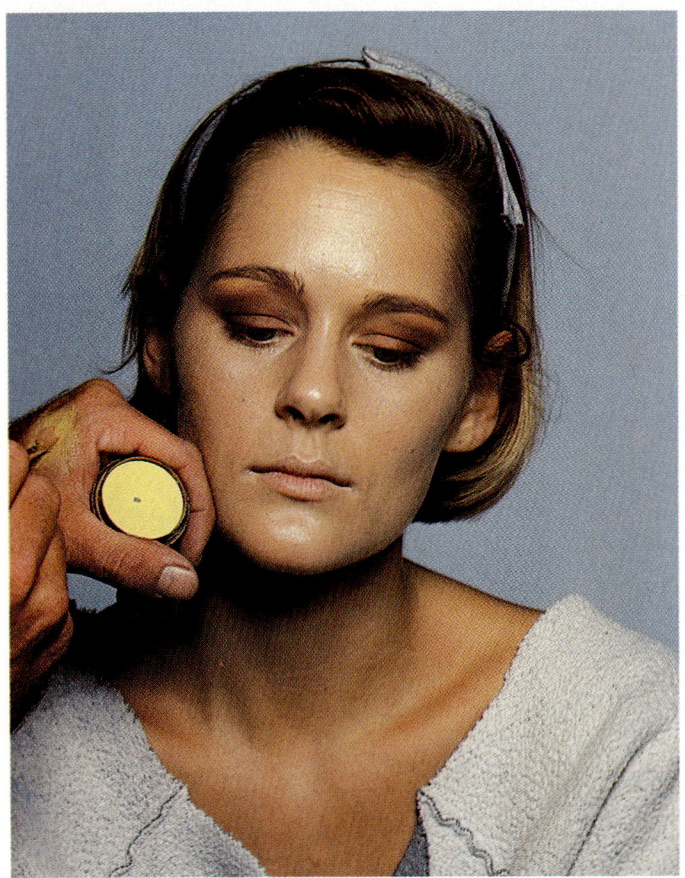

5-7

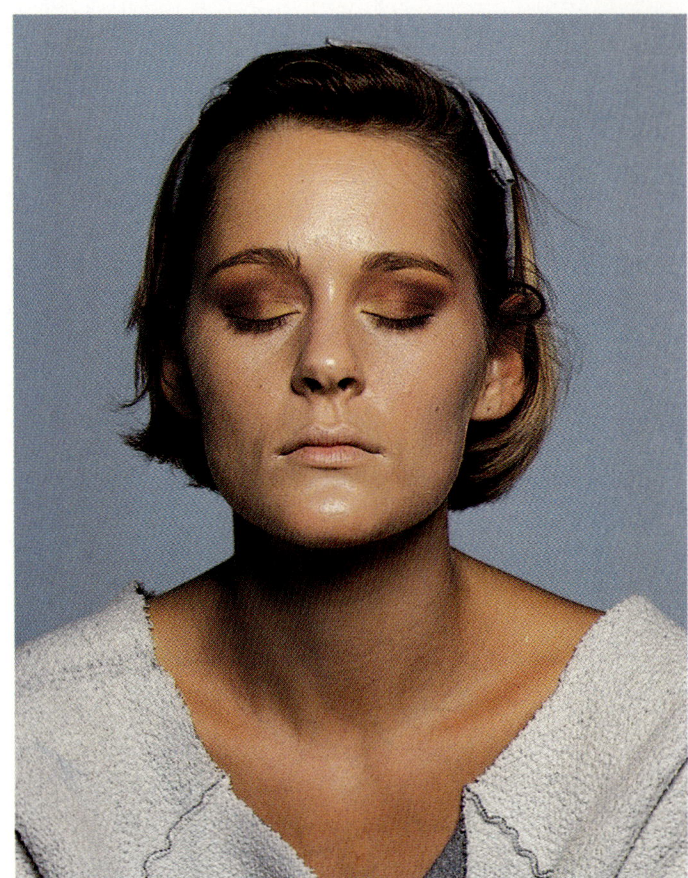

5-8

to the top of the eye socket, below the eyebrow. To locate the area to be shadowed, ask the model to "look" straight ahead while her eyes are closed. Then apply the shadow at the start of the fold in the fatty tissue of the eyelid. Begin by applying the shadow at the fold and then soften the edges.

Jeff suggests testing the shadow on your hand before applying it to the subject's face. The hand serves as a useful artist's palette, indicating the depth and amount of color you are using.

PHOTO 5-7

Jeff adds a soft, gold highlighter on the brow bone below the eyebrow. Using a damp, soft brush, he blends additional color under the eye to emphasize the lower lashes and the lower eye area.

After this step, Jeff adds a thin line of charcoal black above the eyelash hairs to accentuate the lash line and add depth to the upper lid. The line is made thicker toward the outer ends of the eyes. This gives the ends of the eyes an apparent *lift.*

PHOTO 5-8

Jeff also uses the charcoal black under each eye, toward the outer corner, to add thickness and depth. With a very thin eye-liner brush, he softens and blends the edge of the eye liner on the upper lid and outer edge of the lower lid. A small sponge applicator may also be used to soften the liner line. This photo shows in detail the eye makeup Tracy has received so far.

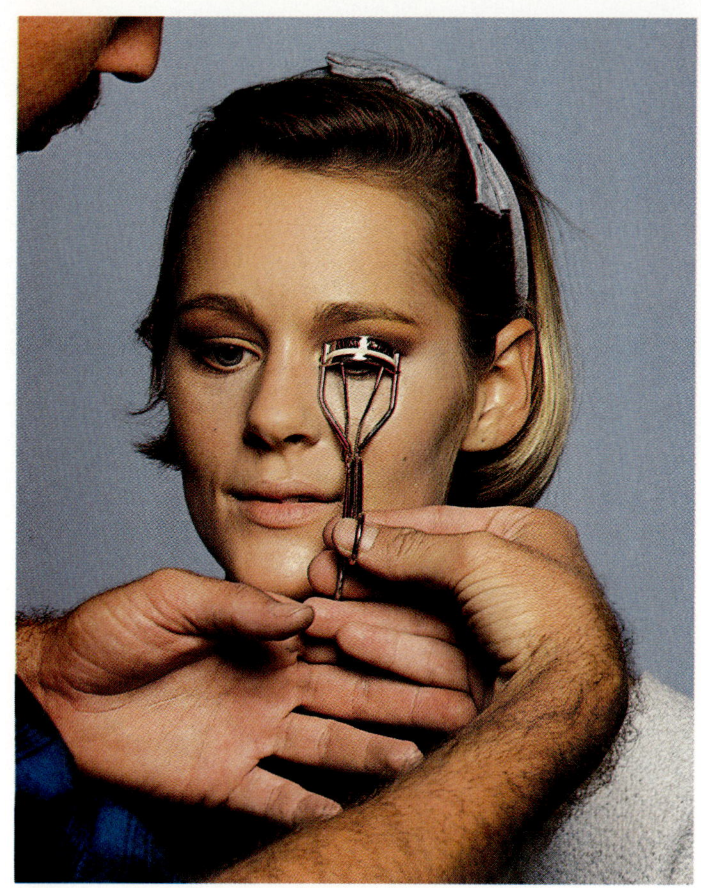

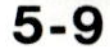
5-9

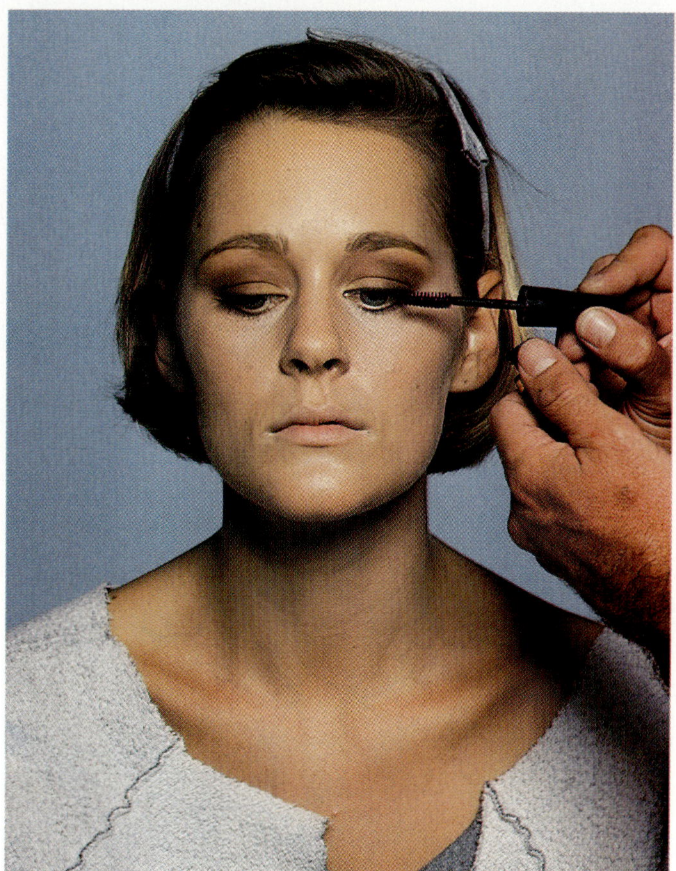

5-10

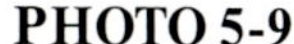
PHOTO 5-9

Jeff uses an eyelash curler on Tracy's lashes. Curled lashes sparkle and also increase the apparent size of the eyes.

PHOTO 5-10

Black mascara is applied to the upper and lower lashes. Jeff prefers black mascara to brown or brown-black. It allows less mascara to be applied and so avoids caking on the lashes.

PHOTO 5-11

A lash brush separates the eyelashes and distributes the mascara evenly between the lashes from root to end.

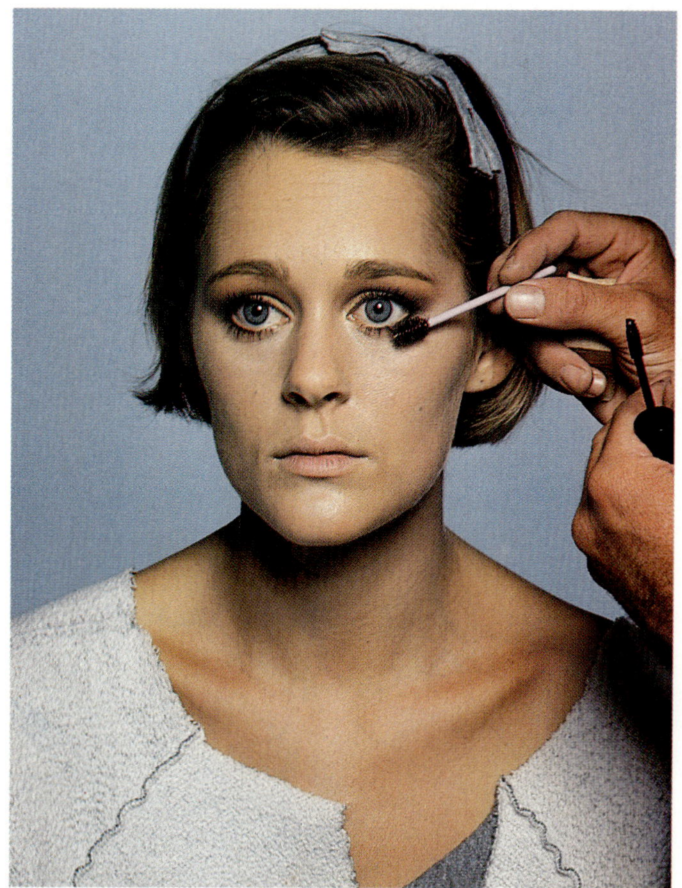

5-11

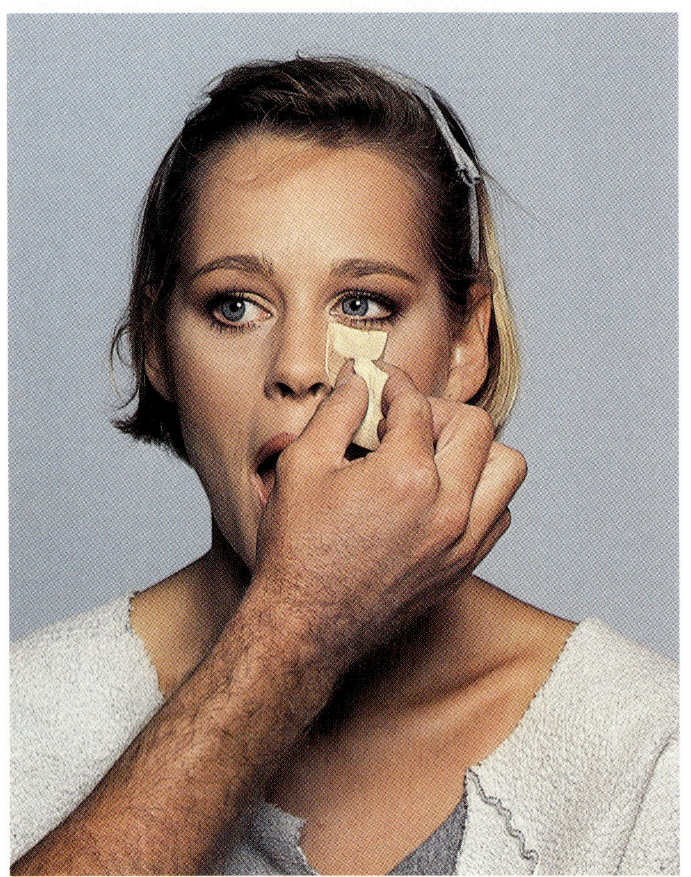

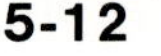
5-12

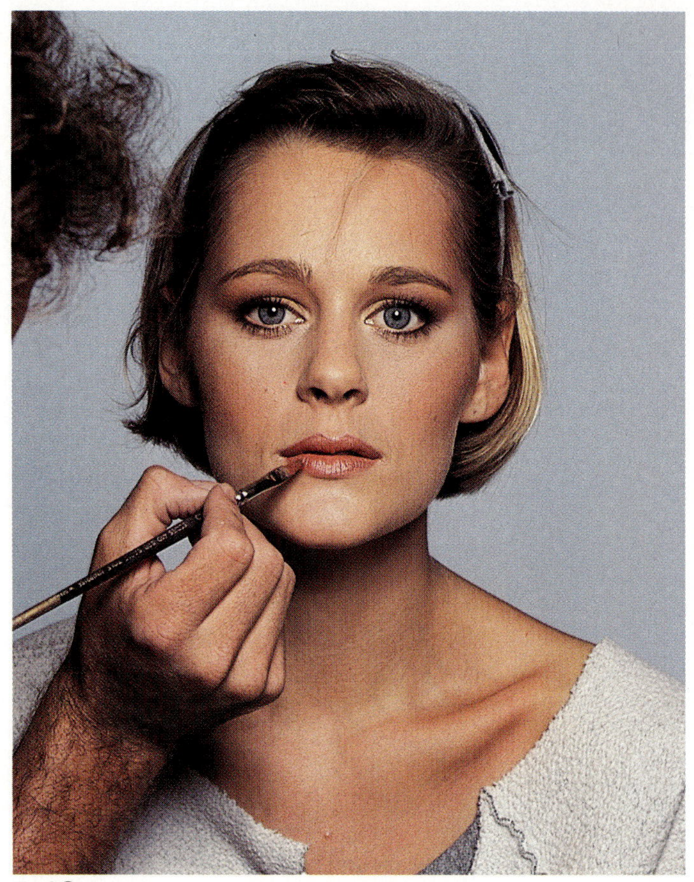

5-13

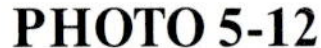
PHOTO 5-12

Jeff applies a peach shade of blusher to the high points of the cheek area. To determine the area of the cheek to receive the blusher, ask the model to smile. Apply the blusher to the *apple* of the cheek—the front part—and blend toward the tip of the ear.

Apply the excess blusher remaining on the brush to each side of the forehead at the temples. This helps maintain better unity between the facial features. Jeff also applied a small amount of peach blush to the tip of Tracy's chin.

PHOTO 5-13

Before this photo was made, a soft, mauve, lip pencil had been used to shape and define the lip area. The lip pencil prevents consequent application of lipstick from *bleeding.* In this photo, Jeff applies a soft peach lip color on top of the lip pencil. Strange as it may sound, mauve is the closest color to actual lip tissue.

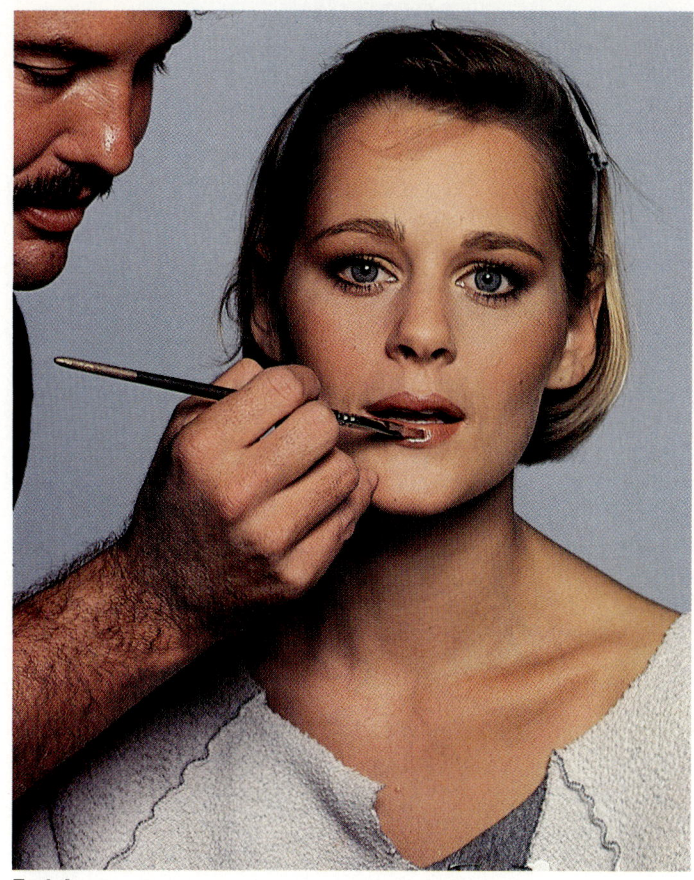
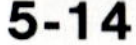

5-14

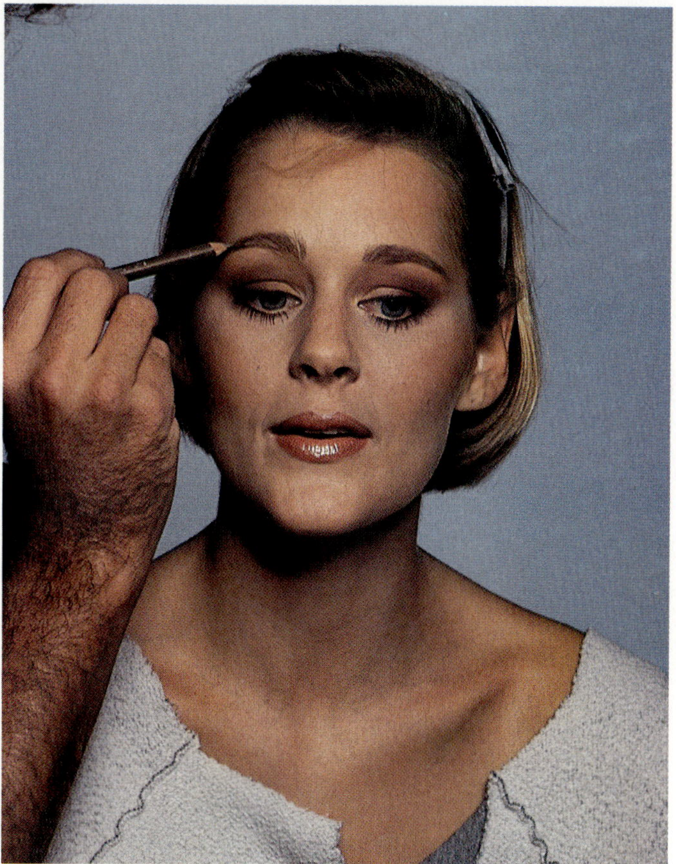

5-15

PHOTO 5-14
Jeff adds a small amount of gold, frosted lip gloss to the center of the lower lip to give fullness to the mouth and create a subtle pouting effect.

PHOTO 5-15
With a medium ash-blond pencil, Jeff fills in small separations in the eyebrow hairs. The pencil is lightly stroked in short movements in the direction the hair grows.

PHOTO 5-16
Having had a final brush of the eyebrows, Tracy's makeup is completed.

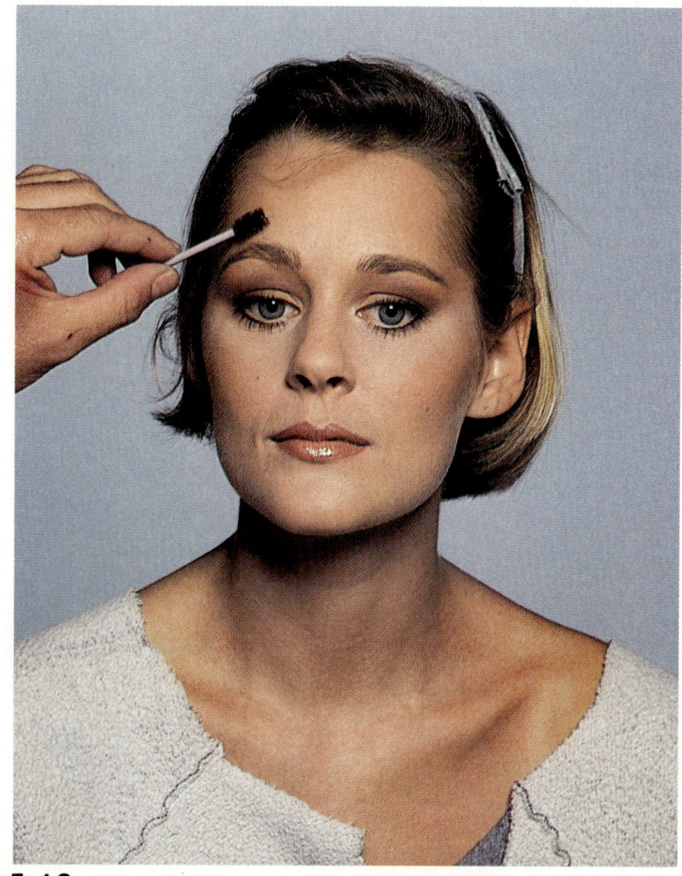

5-16

Hairstyling

There's an important difference between makeup and hairstyling. Makeup involves *basic* techniques concerning facial contouring, tonal enhancement and the emphasis or suppression of specific features. In many ways, it is similar to photographic lighting techniques. Hairstyling, however, is greatly affected by trends in *fashion*. This means that the art of corrective makeup for photography changes little, while hairstyles can change as rapidly as clothing styles. Furthermore, hairstyle choice is a very personal matter, often based on subjective considerations rather than on fashion. For the above reasons, I've avoided *specific* guidance on hairstyling.

After shampooing and before using a hair blower, dryers, curlers or crimping irons, Steve recommends using a setting lotion designed for blow-drying. This prevents tangles. Steve recommends Tenex, or Pantene's Hot Set. The setting lotion adds body to fine hair but does not weigh the hair down.

PHOTO 5-17

Steve used a waving iron on Tracy's straight hair. The waving iron—which is actually two curling irons put together—produces a soft, wide-wave effect. A crimping iron, by contrast, would produce a harsh, zig-zag effect. The flexible curl produced by the waving iron lends itself to a wide variety of styling treatments.

Always start curling from the scalp, working outward toward the hair ends.

PHOTO 5-18

To get a fluffier, bouncy look, Steve tousled Tracy's hair. After Jeff added some blue eye shadow to Tracy's eyes, Steve added a scarf of the same color to her hair. Tracy wears earrings to match the eye shadow and scarf.

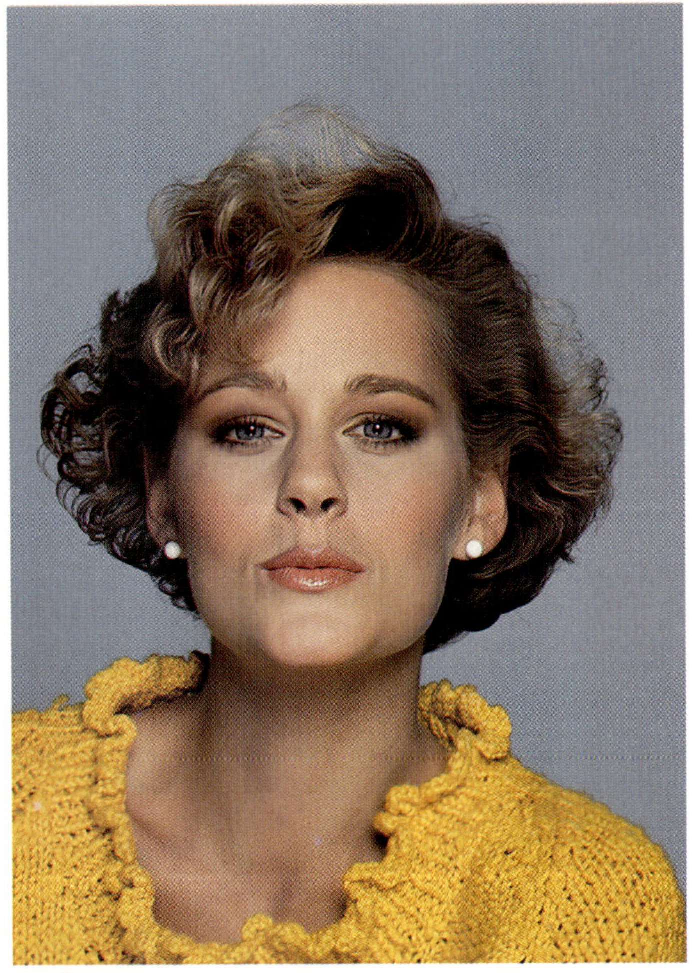

5-17

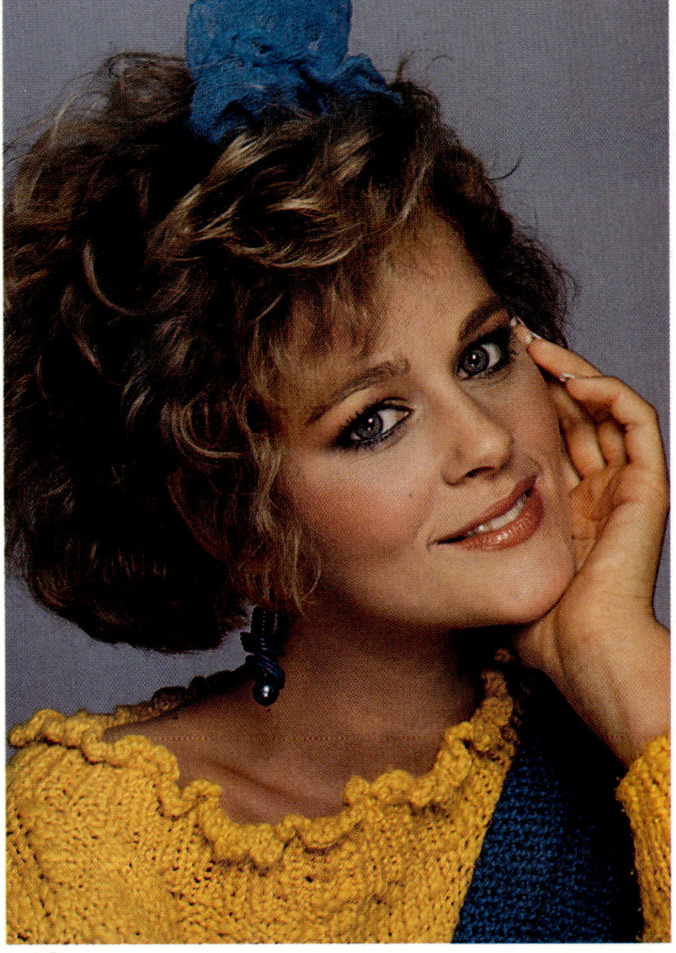

5-18

PHOTO 5-19

To transform Tracy's daytime hair-style into a sophisticated evening coiffure, Steve wets her hair with water and then applies a sculpting lotion, available at any beauty shop. The sculpting lotion allows the hair to be shaped and formed.

Using his fingers and a comb, Steve sculpts the hair into finger waves reminiscent of the 30s. For a little extra drama, he adds a few spit curls over the forehead.

To transform the makeup, Jeff begins with black powdered eye shadow, applying a little to the outside corner of each eye and blending it into the eyefold and fatty tissue. An extra accent of black is added beneath each eye, at the corner.

For the best effect, evening makeup should be applied to a light base, providing more contrast for shadows, cheek colors, highlighting and lip colors. Jeff lightened Tracy's skin tone by mixing a light water-based foundation and applying it over her existing makeup with a wedge sponge. The result is a striking china-like look.

Rather than the earthy peach tones used for the daytime makeup, Jeff adds some light and medium pink tones for the blush and a deeper pink on the eyelids to soften the black eye shadow.

PHOTO 5-20

This photo shows clearly the result of the eye and face makeup. Earrings complete the sophisticated evening effect.

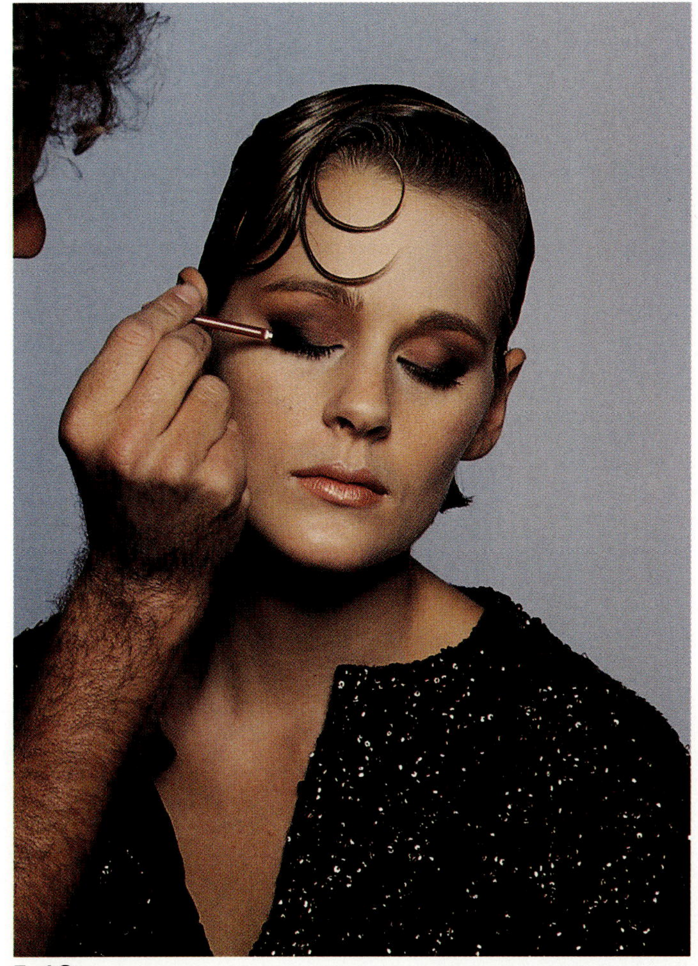

5-19

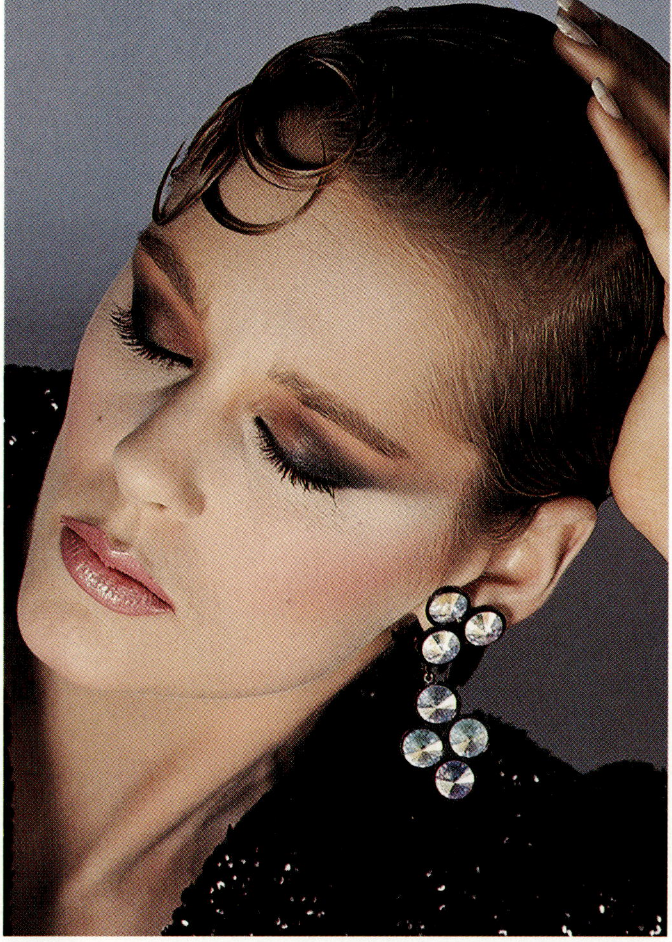

5-20

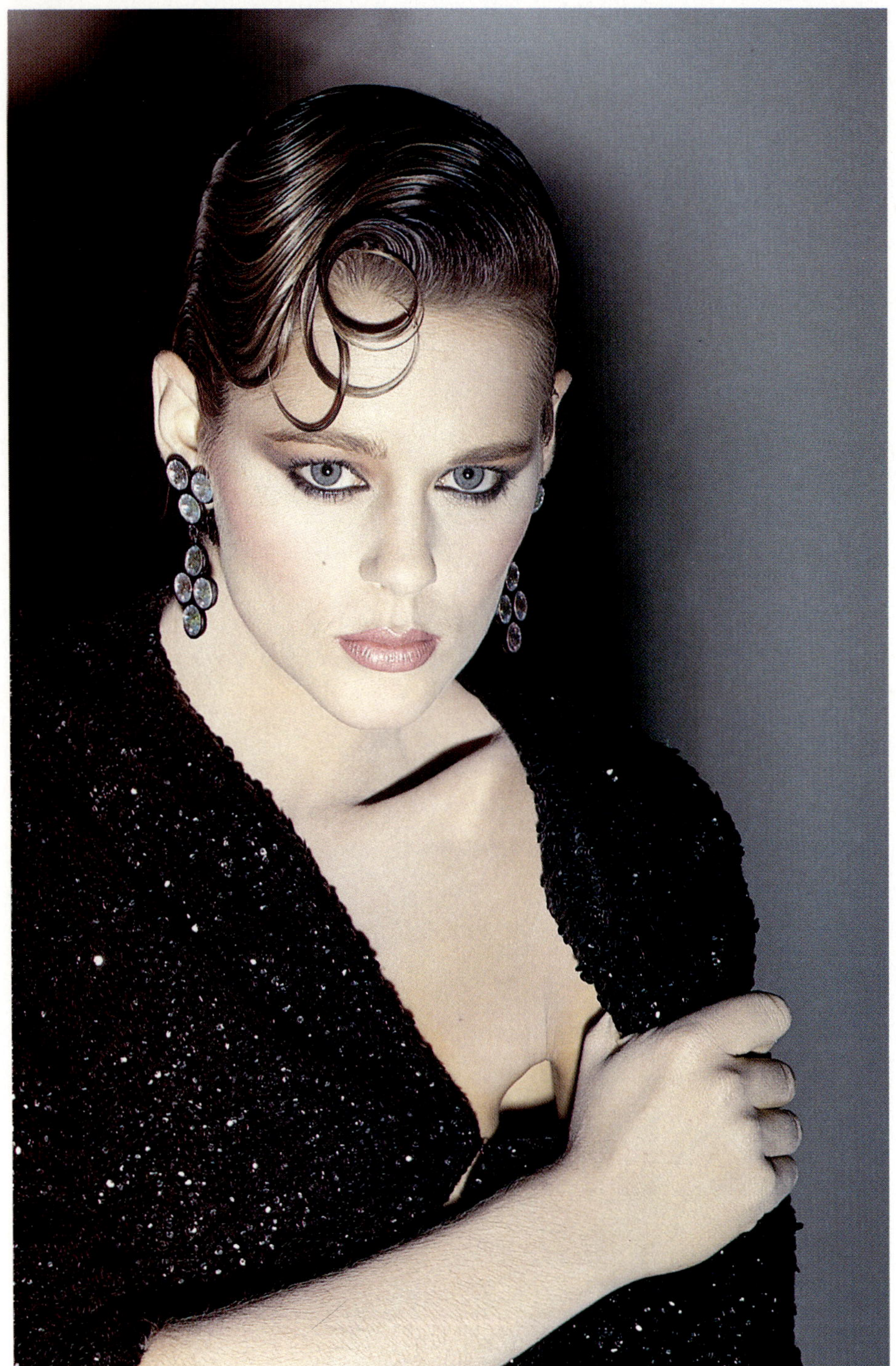

5-21

PHOTO 5-21

For this photo, it was necessary to add body makeup to the exposed skin areas beyond the face. The body makeup provides smoothness and color continuity between face and body.

Makeup, hairstyle, dress and earrings all contribute to produce a sophisticated evening look. Photographically, the pose and lighting add to the effect. □

Turning Pro— Commercial Photography

We all need rewards for our efforts. People involved in creative activities, such as photography, need the fulfillment brought by producing something beautiful or meaningful. However, the most obvious and basic reward is the paycheck. Many talented and ambitious amateur photographers eventually want to make their living by doing what they love most. This essay is intended for them.

DEFINITIONS

Basically, this book is about *people* photography. This essay and the next are about how to become a professional. In this essay, I'll discuss *commercial people photography.* Essay 7 is about *portraiture.* What's the difference?

Commercial photography is produced for sales and promotional purposes. Commercial photos of people are most often used in advertisements. The primary purpose of such photography is not to show the face or character of a *specific* person, but to use the most *suitable* face, character or body that can be found to sell or promote a product or idea.

The suitable faces and bodies are provided by professional models. This essay is about dealing with models, model agencies and art directors. It also deals with the preparation of a portfolio of your work—your main tool in selling yourself. I'll also discuss the nature of the photographic market in different types of communities.

Portrait photography, the subject of the next essay, refers to photographs taken of people for the main purpose of depicting their specific appearance and character. Portraiture is generally done for the person photographed, or for relatives and friends. Most of the time, it has no other commercial value.

I photograph well-known persons in the entertainment and business worlds for both personal and "commercial" purposes. Sometimes the photos are made for use in ads, sometimes for the promotion of the client's career, and at other times simply for personal use.

The Market

Basic photographic technology is the same for all photographers. However, the professional application of photography can differ greatly. It depends not only on what you shoot, but on where you're located.

Major advertising cities, such as New York, Los Angeles and Chicago, demand photographic specialization. For example, a New York art director in need of glamour photographs would call on someone who has made a name for himself in that specific field of photography. He wouldn't ask a general, all-round photographer or a food or architectural photographer to submit his portfolio and bid for the assignment.

In the major advertising markets, there's a wealth of beauty- and glamour specialists from which to select. Outside those areas, there's more reliance on general commercial photographers who are capable of handling many types of assignments. They may be specialists in some limited areas, but depend for their living on their all-around capabilities.

I've had the opportunity of working in both environments. I started in Washington, D.C. and its surrounding suburbs. I now have studios in New York City and Los Angeles. Each kind of location has its advantages and limitations.

IT'S COMPETITIVE

When you're an amateur, your efforts are rewarded with simple accolades such as a kind word from a friend you had photographed, or a blue ribbon at a local print competition. As a professional, it's more difficult to earn your reward. In effect, you have to earn it twice. First, you must get the assignment, sometimes against heavy competition. Then, you must fully satisfy the client, to ensure that he'll call on you again.

Buyers of photography can afford to be highly critical. They know that there are many talented photographers to choose from. Only the best photographers remain at the top of this competitive ladder. The worst soon fall by the wayside altogether.

If your passion for photography is so great that it is as much a part of your life as breathing, you have no choice but to enter the ranks of the professional. I'll try and help you make it—so read on!

Professional photography has a painful *Catch-22*—you can't get hired without experience, and you can't get experience without being hired. In spite of this, many photographers have made it—and so may you! There are guidelines that can help. What follows is my personal advice. Much of it is based on my experiences as a beginner, my development, and my eventual success. To address the majority of readers first, I'll begin with the secondary advertising-photography market.

SECONDARY ADVERTISING CITIES

It is far easier to enter the world of professional advertising photography in the secondary photographic markets than in such cities as New York, Los Angeles or Chicago.

Definition—The secondary advertising markets in the United States include most areas outside New York, Los Angeles and Chicago. The areas involved may be large cities, small towns or rural areas. For simplicity, I'll call them all *secondary markets* in the text that follows.

Bear in mind, however, that the advertising business is in a constant state of flux. Some of the major national advertisers are beginning to select advertising agencies in the so-called secondary markets. Because of this, cities such as San Francisco, Boston, Dallas, Houston and Atlanta have an ever-increasing demand for creative photographers who specialize.

Advantages—In the secondary market, the progression from amateur to professional usually takes less money, time and effort. There's generally less competition, so there is a greater opportunity to secure photographic assignments.

The level of technical and creative proficiency required to generate an income from photography is often less in a relatively small community than in the big city. This doesn't imply that the small-town photographer has less talent or need try less hard than his big-city counterpart. It does mean, however, that a photographer whose limited talent and creativity is capable of sustaining a business in a small town might never make it in the major photography markets.

In the secondary photo market, you enjoy the benefits of variety. The nature of your photographic assignments changes on a regular basis. Some like this while others would prefer to specialize in the one area in which they know they are best.

Many secondary-market photographers can operate successful businesses from their homes, without the need for a separate studio. Consequently, their financial needs for getting started are less.

Keeping in Touch—In smaller communities, you have the advantage of being able to get to know your market more intimately. There are fewer clients and advertising agencies. Those having responsibility for hiring photographers are often answerable to fewer people higher up in the corporate structure.

In a small community, it's easier to analyze and maintain an up-to-date record of the current status of industry in the area. Local newspapers indicate major changes in local businesses or the development of new ones. Consequently, your advertising and promotion efforts are easier to control.

Versatility is Important—The commercial photographer establishing a business in a secondary market must be capable of taking on many varied assignments. Generally, such an area simply can't support specialists. There isn't enough work. The photographer may be called upon to shoot fashion and beauty one day, products the next, and portraiture the next. His assignments may include real-estate, school-yearbook and newspaper photography. He *must* be a jack-of-all-trades. He should *try* to be somewhat of a master at all! It's a challenging, stimulating life!

MAJOR U.S. MARKETS

It is estimated that there are three or four thousand commercial photographers in the 22 square miles of Manhattan. The numbers in Los Angeles and Chicago are just as staggering. Obviously, competition is the key word. Each year a crop of new photographers, many from the major schools, storm the major markets, hoping for a small slice of the photographic pie. There are far more photographers than the market can sustain. The prospects of a change to a "seller's market" are slim.

How to Show Your Work—In the major photo markets, it's rare for a beginning commercial photographer to personally encounter an ad agency's art director. If an art director were to schedule appointments with every new photographer that called, he'd have little time for anything else.

Most major advertising agencies ask photographers to drop off their work samples, or *portfolios,* on a specific day—sometimes as long as three months from the time they're asked to call. They are told to pick up their portfolios a day or two after the call.

While a portfolio is at an agency, it's seen by most of the art directors at special viewing sessions. If they are impressed by your portfolio, you may expect your phone to ring at some time in the near future, with the offer of an assignment. If they are not impressed, your phone will remain silent—and you had better try elsewhere.

Quality and Dependability—The major commercial market is not a place for experimentation during an assignment. It is a place for professionalism, quality and dependability. A good photographer can quickly earn the respect of his clients. However, one bad shooting session can just as quickly lose you a valuable client.

If you are to survive, you must be familiar with every technical aspect of your craft. You must also understand precisely what the client wants, and be sensitive to the customs and procedures prevalent in the business world you're dealing with.

Pressures are High—An agency's account executives and art directors are under great pressure to produce advertising photography quickly and economically but with consistently good quality. Top models and stylists can cost thousands of dollars per day. Locations can rent at thousands of dollars per day. The magazine space devoted to an ad can cost as much as $100,000 for a single page of space for one month. Consequently, the photographers selected are specialists who've proven they are capable of producing on demand.

Art directors maintain a stable of photographers with whom they've worked previously. The strength of the existing relationships is based on past performance and past successes. Therefore, it's difficult for the newcomer to establish himself in the major photography markets.

Success Breeds Success—I'm often approached by beginning photographers seeking a solution to a predicament. They've talked with advertising agencies, shown their portfolios to art directors, and have had favorable verbal responses. However, they have yet to get an assignment. The young photographers are frustrated and confused.

Viewed from the client's viewpoint, the situation is easily understood. Art directors have confidence only in those photographers who have successfully serviced their needs or the needs of other clients. A portfolio alone isn't enough.

I've looked at beginners' portfolios with absolutely magnificent photographs. But they were *nothing more* than photographic prints. They had not been published. Furthermore, each photo may have taken half a day to make—or several shooting sessions. You can't tell by looking at the images.

A published magazine tearsheet indicates a professional success. It indicates that—when the money was on the line, the models were on set, the location was reserved, and the pressure was on—the photographer produced a successful photograph! That's the experienced professional's edge over the beginner.

People You'll Work With

The work of a professional involves more than a simple photographer-client relationship. You must get accustomed to working with advertising agencies, art directors, model agencies, models and stylists.

ADVERTISING AGENCY

An advertising agency is an organization specializing in communications. Its functions may include market research, sales planning and effective marketing through advertising. Creative photography plays a major part in these endeavors.

Creating and maintaining a desirable corporate image involves many considerations, ranging from logo and stationery design to advertising on television, billboard, and in print.

To manage its various accounts, an advertising agency employs *account executives.* A typical account executive may handle one large account or two smaller, non-competitive accounts. He works with a staff of *copywriters* and *art directors* to develop a creative concept for the client and see it through to completion.

To satisfy a client's needs, an advertising agency uses the talents of many people not directly employed by the agency. The creative photographer is an important part of this team.

To more easily serve the needs of their major clients on a national scale, several national advertising agencies have branch offices in secondary-market cities. Generally, these branch offices also handle smaller, local accounts.

ART DIRECTOR

The advertising agency is the intermediary between the advertiser and the buying public. The agency's art director determines the creative course of the advertising. For example, he decides whether his client's needs are best served with a freehand illustration or a photograph. The art director is also responsible for hiring the talent for ad production. To be hired for an assignment, you must impress the art director.

Make a list of the major advertising agencies in your area. Note the clients each serves and the names of art directors responsible to each client.

I try to familiarize myself with the advertising campaign I'm soliciting prior to making an appointment at the agency. In doing so, I can arrange and design my portfolio with photographs selected specifically for the target client. If, for example, I'm approaching the art director handling *Arm & Hammer* baking soda, I'll check magazines such as *Family Circle, Woman's Day,* and *Good Housekeeping,* to view their current advertising.

If the ads contain a typical "housewife" in a kitchen, holding the product box, I'll load my portfolio with pictures that reflect that concept. It would be to my disadvantage to include photographs of teenage girls in studded leather outfits!

MODEL AGENCY

A model agency is more than an assembly of pretty people. It provides comprehensive representation for professional models. In addition to selling the services of its models, many agencies provide legal, accounting and contract-negotiating services for the models.

The successful model has abilities similar to those of the professional actor or actress. It's not surprising that many successful actors began their careers as models. The model that can, on command, present a variety of emotions, attitudes and poses can earn high fees.

Headsheet—A photo of each model represented by an agency appears on the agency's *headsheet.* The headsheet—which is generally in the form of a booklet—contains important data with each model's photo. This data may include height, color of hair and eyes, special features, such as especially attractive hands, feet or legs, and the model's hourly and daily fee.

Comp—As a sales tool, each model carries a *comp,* or composite—a card containing photos of the model in a variety of situations and poses. The comp contains similar data to those printed on the headsheet. The agency generally helps models select the best pictures for the comp. Photo 6-1, on the next page, shows one side of professional model Kay Sutton York's comp.

Both the agency's headsheet and each model's comp are used to mail or carry to prospective clients to enable them to select the most suitable model for a specific requirement.

STYLIST

I remember the day I took the train from my home in Washington, D.C. to New York City for my first appointment with a major magazine. My portfolio shots were primarily attempts at fashion and beauty photography, with a smattering of product photos, and a few character studies thrown in for good measure.

The art director flipped through my book without uttering a word. Coming to my favorite photograph, she stopped and asked, "Who styled this picture?" I wasn't sure what she meant. I had never heard reference to *styling* before. "Who decided to put that particular scarf with that blouse, and who put that leather bag on the male model's shoulder?" she asked. "I guess I did," I replied sheepishly. She indicated that the clothes and accessories just didn't go together.

I felt insulted and frustrated. I told her I had come to show my photographs, not the clothes the models were wearing. She corrected me, pointing out that what was *in* my photos was *part of* my photos.

I had learned a valuable lesson that day: The photographer alone is responsible for every aspect of the finished photograph. Consequently, you owe it to yourself to either learn what style is about or work with a professional stylist whenever an assign-

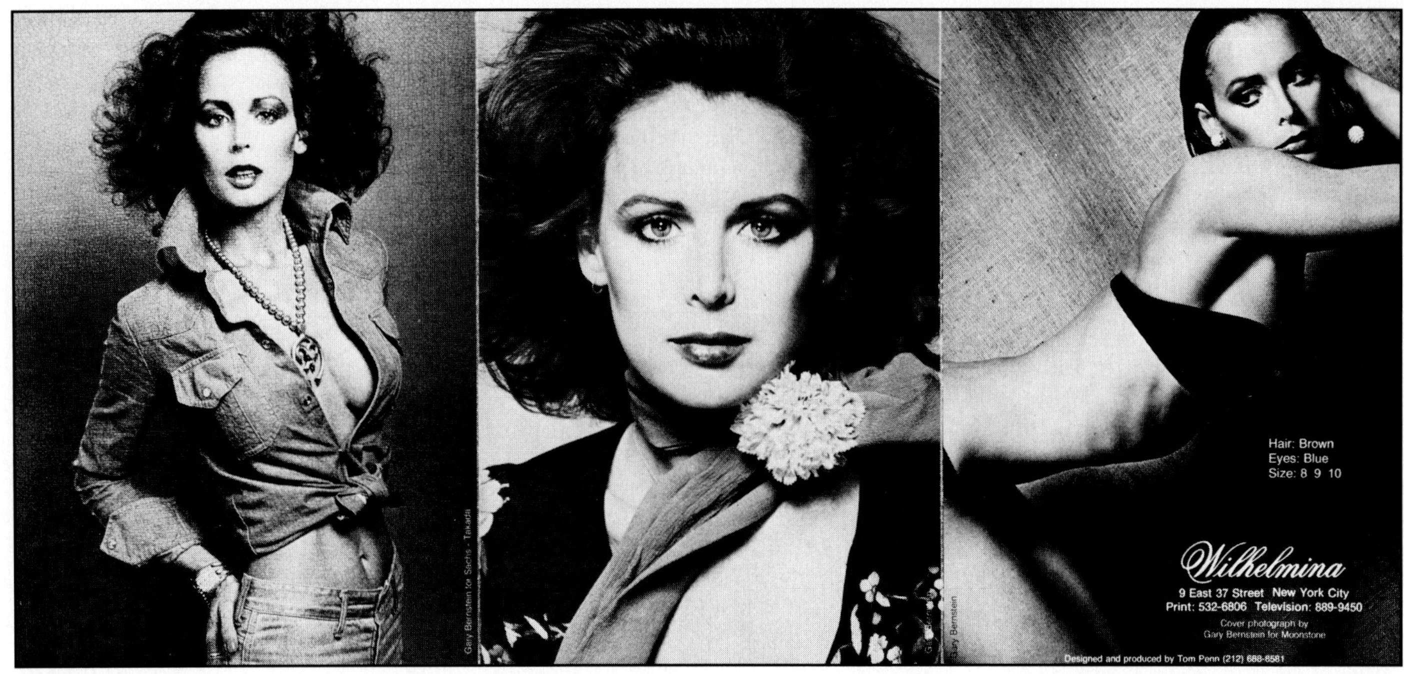

6-1

ment warrants it. Much of the credit for the clean, finished and contemporary look of fashion and beauty images must go to stylists.

Later in this essay, I'll show how models and photographers work together to produce their mutual work samples, or portfolios. Beginning stylists of make-up, hair and fashion are usually equally willing to provide their services for your test session in return for portfolio photographs.

Where to Look—In a large city, you should have little difficulty finding stylists willing to test with you. Established stylists are often represented by agents or agencies that represent only stylists for photography and film. In a smaller city, finding styling services may be more difficult.

For hair styling, I suggest you contact local hair salons. Usually, a salon has not only qualified hair stylists, but also makeup artists. It's generally not difficult to persuade them to have their creations recorded on film, even if they're not interested in pursuing a career in photographic styling.

REPRESENTATION

At the start of your photographic career, I believe it's important to represent yourself. Especially in the secondary advertising markets, it's to your advantage to meet with clients and ad agency executives in person. It establishes the personal rapport so important to lasting business relationships. Your understanding of the photography and advertising businesses will be that much more complete through your agency and editorial associations. Even in the major ad markets, there's no substitute for self-representation.

Agents and Representatives—When a photographer's workload becomes so great that he can't afford to "make the rounds" to clients and agencies any more, he should consider hiring an agent or representative.

Choose Carefully—The agent or rep must be your alter ego. He must truly represent your personality and attitude as well as your photographic abilities. Many a job has been lost because of a strained agent-client relationship. Consequently, good agents are in great demand.

I produced a considerable amount of photography in Washington, D.C. without ever using an agent's services. I always found the time to meet with my clients personally. In doing so, lasting friendships, which exist to this day, were established. After a couple years, however, I wanted a bigger slice of the commercial pie and moved my studio to New York City. Soon after setting up there, I was shooting a lot of magazine and catalog assignments. Getting around in New York took more time than in Washington. And there were so many clients to see!

Soon after my first few editorial magazine layouts appeared, I was approached by a top photographers' agent. I was very flattered because the agent also represented four photographers of international fame whose work I had admired for years. Naturally, I accepted her offer of representation.

In New York, editorial magazine layouts establish a photographer's reputation more rapidly than any form of *public relations.* Because a printed photo credit appears on each magazine feature, prospective advertising clients can associate a photographer's name with his abilities.

Soon after my pictures began appearing in magazines regularly, I was called by an ad-agency art director representing one of the largest shirt manufacturers in the country. "We want you to shoot our new fall campaign," he said. "Would you send over your portfolio so we can prepare some layouts based on your magazine tearsheets?" he asked. I asked my new agent to deliver my portfolio to the art director.

A Useful Lesson—I was with the art director a few weeks later, when he related the following story: "Gary, I think you should be aware of something," he began. "When your agent came to the agency, she brought another photographer's portfolio with her. She tried to talk me into using her other photographer rather than you!"

Later that day, I questioned my agent about her actions. She confessed that her other photographer hadn't been working of late. Because I had been working, she thought I wouldn't mind if she secured the assignment for him. I severed my relationship with my agent that same day—a little shocked but a lot wiser. It was the first and last time I used an agent who represented more than one fashion and glamour illustrator at the same time. Since then, I've enjoyed harmonious relationships with several agents.

I've related this story to make an important point: Although advertising photography involves artistry, it's also big business. Never allow your concern with esthetics to overshadow your concerns with the business end. You should retain the ultimate control of all activities relating to your photographic operation.

Career Development

To begin a successful career, you must have *direction.* You must determine the type of photography you feel most suited and inclined to produce. If it's beauty, glamour and fashion, make a habit of studying the major fashion magazines each month. Publications such as *Vogue, Esquire, G.Q.* and *Harper's Bazaar* are useful guides to contemporary styling and photographic technique.

Analyze the differences between *advertising* illustration (photo 6-2) and *editorial* photographs (photo 6-3) in each magazine you see. Advertising photography is hired and directed by the advertiser—sometimes directly and sometimes through an advertising agency. The purpose of the photography is to sell the product. An advertising photograph is usually designed to leave room for the advertising company's logo and name and some text.

An editorial photograph is designed and produced by or for the magazine itself. Although a product or fashion may appear in the photograph, the manufacturer has little, if any, say about the production and appearance of the photograph or the design of the page. Consequently, the style of photography is often looser and freer than it would be for a commercial ad.

If you love glamour and fashion photography, you should be aware that assignments in those fields are likely to be few and far between, especially in the secondary photo market.

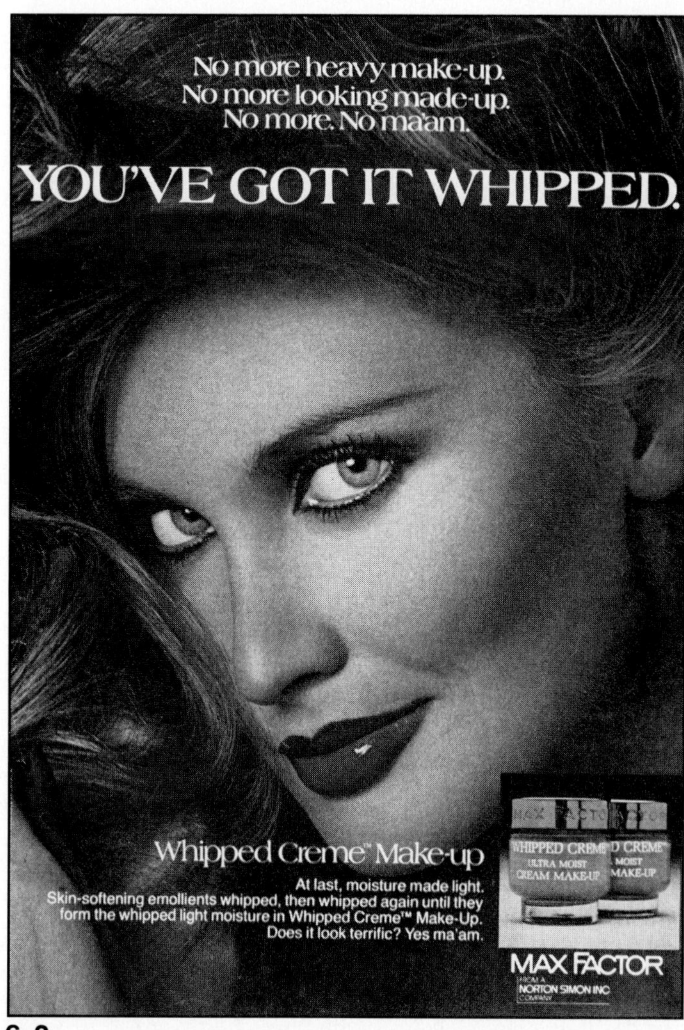

6-2

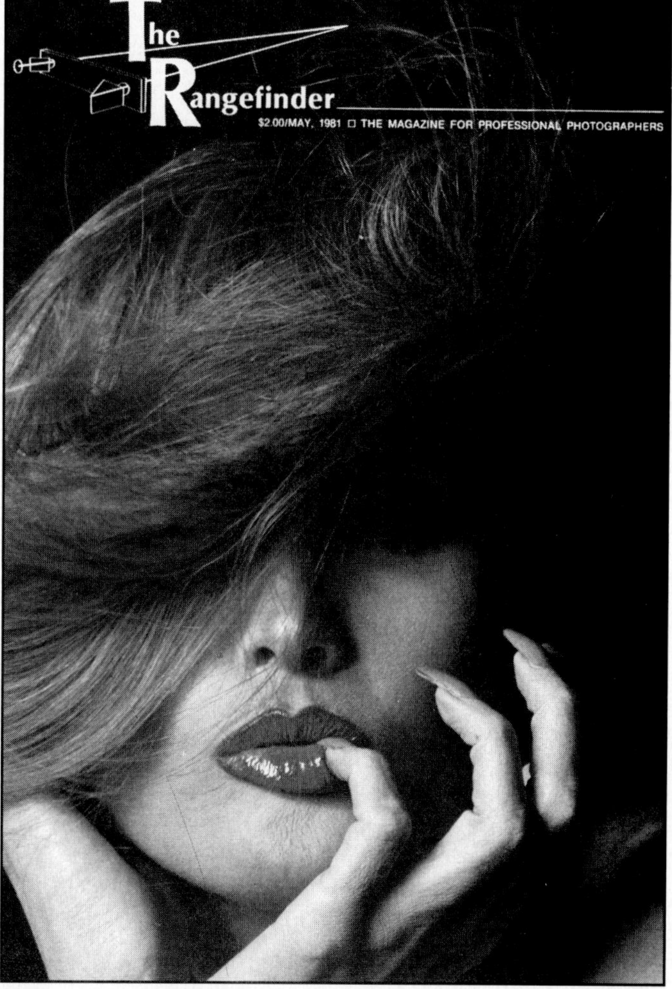

6-3

ASSISTING

An assistant is a photographer's helper. He is responsible for a wide range of tasks. He may be cleaning a darkroom one minute and handing a celebrity a product to be advertised the next.

Many of the world's most successful photographers began as assistants in established studios. An equally large number, including myself, have become successful without ever serving as assistants.

The assistant helps the photographer prepare for his photo sessions. However, the assistant performs his most important function during a session. He loads cameras, moves equipment and props, positions lights, holds reflectors and takes meter readings. He should always be ready when the photographer needs something, such as another camera body or a different lens.

A Good Start—Although I wasn't an assistant myself, I believe it can be a great advantage to start a photographic career that way. This is especially true if you can work for a successful, well established photographer. You can learn a lot by observing a photographer's lighting techniques and operational procedures. The knowledge you derive depends largely on your rapport with the photographer. You'll benefit the most if he entrusts you with many varied tasks and is prepared to patiently answer all your questions.

To become an assistant, contact studios in your locality. If you can select a studio that does the kind of photography that interests you most, all the better. If you can't, start anywhere. Once you have "your foot in the door," you have half the battle won.

IMPORTANCE OF THE PORTFOLIO

A photographer's most effective sales tool is his *portfolio*—a compilation of photographs, transparencies and tearsheets, carried in a suitable case. This is your calling card. You show it at interviews with potential clients. It should represent your full range of photographic abilities.

Your portfolio must speak for you. It's not unusual for a busy art director to request portfolios, not photographers, when hiring for an upcoming assignment. Consequently, your portfolio may be the only opportunity you have to secure a job.

Your portfolio grows with the growth of your career. As you work on more exciting assignments and experiment with different techniques, update your portfolio. Let your prospective clients know what you can do *now*—not what your capabilities were six months or a year ago.

Your First Portfolio—To prepare your first portfolio—before you've had any assignments—you must rely on test shooting sessions. Create situations that might call for ads, then shoot the ads. Of course, you won't be able to include tearsheets until some of your work has been published.

Give your test sessions the same concern you would give a major assignment. It represents your "practice" before the "big game." Make tests in many varied areas of photography, especially if you're in a secondary advertising area. Remember, in such an area you may be asked to shoot a fur ad on Monday, a salad-dressing ad on Tuesday, sports photographs on Wednesday, architectural shots on Thursday, and so on. Be prepared!

Analyze which model type is best suited for a specific job. Should she be a teenager or older, blond or brunette, an athletic type or an elegant fashion model? Professional models are selected with the same care used in casting actors and actresses. Use the same selectivity in planning your test sessions.

Pay careful attention to fashion, hair styling and makeup. Use contemporary magazines as a guide to your styling. Determine the best locations and the most appropriate lighting for your photography.

Don't make an appointment with a single ad agency until your portfolio is in top form. If you have 15 images that are great and three that are mediocre, eliminate the mediocre ones or shoot them again. Art directors look for consistency in quality. Their jobs depend on it. Show them only the best you're capable of.

SETTING UP A PORTFOLIO TEST SESSION

Many large towns have at least one model agency or school. Make an appointment to see those in your area. Show the interviewer your beginner's portfolio. You can show b&w or color prints, or slides. Indicate that you would like to shoot some test photos, using agency models. The agency will probably show you a collection of composites and glossies depicting the models available for testing.

The best way to select models is by personal interview. Pictures can be misleading and don't tell the whole story. Rapport is one of the keys to strong photography. A personal interview enables you to discuss with a model the best clothes, hair-styling and location for the test session. An agent may arrange a specific day and time when you can personally interview prospective models, either at the agency or at your studio.

When you first begin testing, you'll probably be offered the agency's least experienced models. They, too, must develop a good portfolio before they are capable of promoting their talents professionally. You won't be offered the current agency stars. They are likely to be in constant demand and to have little time for testing. Top models rarely lend their time or talent to beginning photographers—with or without payment. However, today's beginner may be tomorrow's superstar, and you may be working with better material than you realize.

Talent and Attractiveness Count—Physical attractiveness should be only one of the criteria you use in selecting your test models. It's important for a model to convey believable emotions and attitudes. It's not surprising that many models become successful actors and actresses.

How to Pay a Model—Barter is an ideal way of paying for testing services. The model provides her services in return for your photography. You provide her with free prints or transparencies.

When I began shooting, it was customary for the photographer to pay for all expenses, including film, processing, prints, and even wardrobe and location costs, when applicable. Now, it's not unusual for photographer and model to share expenses. Regardless of the method you use, remember that few successful businesses have been established without some initial financial investment.

SELF-PROMOTION

When you've had some work published, capitalize on your success with self-promotion. There are many ways of making clients aware of your photography. For example, you can buy additional copies of magazines containing recently published ads and mail tearsheets to target clients with a cover letter. Or, you can have separate promotional sheets or posters, depicting your best work, printed and circulated.

Purchasing advertising space in some of the many creative directories on the market is another effective way of self-promotion. Such directories include *The ASMP Book, The Creative Black Book, American Showcase* and *The Art Director's Guide.* However, probably the most effective way to promote yourself is to continuously make appointments with agencies and art directors. Show them your newest tearsheets and make them aware of your progress.

THE STUDIO

My first studio was in a suburban Maryland high-rise apartment building. The one room was on the 16th floor and had a large north-light window. When I didn't want the daylight, I placed blackout curtains on the window. I generated a lot of photography from within the walls of that 9x18-foot room.

My seamless background was at one end of the room and a small client area was at the other end. Where possible, features of the studio served multiple purposes. For example, my end tables doubled as posing cubes.

The ceiling was less than eight feet high. I taped seamless paper to the ceiling and the wall, simulating a continuous cove. This enabled me to use a low camera angle without having the wall-ceiling line show in my photos.

Camera and lighting equipment was stored in closets and the models changed in the bathroom. This creative heaven was mine for a scant $200 per month. Of course, the price of commercial and residential rentals has gone up since then.

Although it may not be a necessity in secondary advertising markets, I recommend that you have a studio right from the start—even if it's a modest place. Agents feel more comfortable sending their models to a business address than a home. A studio also indicates a commitment to the profession of photography, even if only a financial one.

A strange double standard exists in the major advertising areas. There's little question that a studio is needed when you start out in your career. "Where's your studio?" was the first question asked of me at every one of my early client interviews in New York City. However, once you've established a reputation for quality photography, that question is rarely asked. In fact, a studio is then the least of a client's concerns. Unfortunately, you need a studio most when you are least likely to be able to afford it.

Many of the world's top fashion and beauty photographers rent studios as and when they need them. These photographers travel widely. Maintaining a studio in each of their regular working locations would be unnecessary and prohibitively costly.

THE ASSIGNMENT

After visiting all the agencies—maybe more than once—and showing your photographs to all of the art directors, you wait and hope for the phone to ring. If an art director requests your services for an advertising assignment, what do you do? There are very few hard and fast rules in the creative advertising business. My career has been one of daily variety. Therefore, the following scenario does no more than capsulize a probable course of events.

Getting Briefed—When you meet the art director at the agency, he will already have met with his client, the advertiser. They will have agreed on a firm direction for the advertising. You'll be presented with one or more *layouts*—drawings produced by the art director, indicating the proposed ad design, with locations for body copy and headlines.

Your goal is to satisfy the requirements of the layout exactly. Remember, the client has already approved the layout and the agency must produce what the client wants.

Be Inventive—When you have satisfied the needs of the layout, you're sometimes free to shoot variations on the basic theme. However, remember that modeling fees are very high, so don't waste time. If there's additional time for variations, the art director will give you the go-ahead.

During the course of the shooting, try subtle visual alternatives. Change the composition and the model's position. However, always satisfy the basic needs of the layout.

Booking Models—Models are usually selected by the art director and photographer together. However, it's the photographer's responsibility to book the models. This is done by calling the appropriate agency and talking to the booking agent. If your first choice is unavailable, alternative models of similar type and character will be suggested.

Some art directors like the photographer to make the initial model selection and leave the final decision to the client. In such a case, I'll tentatively book a few different models I feel would satisfy the needs of the assignment. A *tentative* booking reserves a model's time without requiring a firm booking commitment with payment.

I ask the model agency to send the art director two sets of comps of the models I had reserved. The art director gives the second set to the client. The final booking is made when the client has made his selection.

Another photographer or client may call the agency, requesting a model you've tentatively reserved. He'll be told that the model is reserved for that particular day, but he can have a *secondary.* This means he'll be first in line for the model's services, if you release her.

You should become familiar with all model-agency policies. Usually, tentative bookings must be canceled within 48 hours to avoid a charge for the models that had been reserved. Be careful with your clients' money. In the long run, it will be to your advantage, too.

Your Other Responsibilities—As photographer, you are responsible for setting up the entire photo session. You must book locations, stylists and assistants as needed. It's not unusual for job expenses to exceed the fee for photography. Before taking action on behalf of a client, secure an agency purchase order, spelling out responsibilities and obligations.

Fees—Commercial photography is highly competitive and jobs are at a premium. At the beginning of a career, you're subjected to many pressures, both esthetic and financial. You alone can determine the value of your services. Charge appropriately, using the ASMP or APA Guide to Photography for guidance. Once you've established your rates, it's difficult to change them. □

7

Turning Pro—Portrait Photography

More professional photographers practice portraiture than any other photographic specialty, making the field highly competitive. Each city, big or small, has a selection of photographers who call themselves *portraitists.*

Added to that competition are the mass-production portrait studios in many department stores. These operations offer fixed-light, fixed-background, fixed-exposure portraiture that does not call for skilled, creative photographers. Such studios make low-cost portraiture available to virtually everyone.

QUALITY IS IMPORTANT

As is the case with many products, the quality of the photos received from the mass-production operations is often commensurate with the price paid. Unfortunately, many private portrait studios offer a product that's not much better. For this reason, I believe that portrait photography offers good, creative photographers exceptional potential for business success.

My earliest professional photography was portraiture. I began shooting portraits as a college undergraduate at Penn State. I used my hobby to earn money. At that time, it was customary for the many fraternal organizations on campus to be photographed by one of the local studios each year.

Except for the faces, the images were all identical. Expression, background, lighting, camera angle and clothing style varied little from photo to photo. In many respects this school portraiture constituted the forerunner of today's mass-production portrait studios.

Individual Treatment—I tried a different approach by photographing each student in the natural environment of the fraternity or sorority. I used available light. The photographs were candid and casual, allowing the subject to express his or her individuality. The Bernstein portrait program became a grand success.

After being in commercial photography for about 15 years, I have recently returned to portraiture. It happened by accident and with some initial reluctance on my part.

At a party, a businessman asked if I would photograph his wife. I declined the offer, indicating that I shot commercial assignments only. He was very persuasive and I yielded. Since that time, display of the portrait I made has led to many other private portrait sessions. I now shoot a few private portraits each month. It has become a permanent, self-generating part of my photographic business.

I don't believe my success in portraiture is due to luck. I have given a lot of thought to the philosophy and technique that have led me to a profitable portrait business. Perhaps the most important key to success is being totally interested in, and sympathetic toward, each subject you photograph.

Be Familiar With Fashion and Makeup—It's not easy to style a glamour or beauty photograph if you aren't knowledgeable about fashion and makeup. Up-to-date instructional guides exist at reasonable cost in the form of modern fashion magazines. Simply pick up copies of *Vogue, Harper's Bazaar, Gentlemen's Quarterly, Esquire, Glamour* or any of the other fashion and beauty publications on the market and start reading—and looking.

BUSINESS CONSIDERATIONS

In the previous essay I defined the basic differences between portrait and commercial photography. Let me make some further comparisons.

Consumer Product—The commercial photo is a *business* product, paid for by business. The personal portrait is a *consumer* product and is paid for by individuals—in all income brackets. As such, personal portraiture is more subject to fluctuations in the national economy. When times are good, the portrait market thrives; during economic recession, it suffers.

As a safeguard against economic fluctuation, many portrait studios couple the portrait business with wedding photography. The wedding market is relatively constant. Photographs of the memorable event are as standard and essential as the wedding cake.

Self-Sufficiency—All participants in a commercial photo session are paid for their efforts. This includes the photographer and the subject— usually a professional model or celebrity. In private portraiture, only the photographer is paid. The client relies totally on the photographer's skills. Consequently, the man or woman behind the camera must accept full responsibility for the subject's motivation and for the technical and creative quality of the result.

Payment—The commercial photographer bills for services after completion of the job. If he's fortunate, he'll receive payment within 90 to 120 days of his billing. When I shoot a private portrait session, I require a 50% deposit prior to the date of the session and the balance of my fee upon completion of the shooting. Any additional photographs desired by the client after viewing the proofs must be paid for when the print order is placed.

There are two reasons for advance payment. First, quality photographic prints, retouching and finishing services are expensive. I learned the hard way that portrait clients have a difficult time making final print selections—particularly when confronted with a variety of good images. They may have a change of heart *after* placing the order for finished prints. By the time the lab is informed of such a change, it's often too late, the order having already been completed. If so, the photographer bears the cost of unused prints and services.

The second reason for advance payment is more psychological. For the photographer, the check will clear the bank prior to delivery of the finished product, so payment is assured. For the customer, the prints are fully his and he'll take them home and enjoy them. Were the photos not fully paid for, the customer would be much more likely to scrutinize them—and perhaps request a change in his print order.

ESTABLISH YOUR TARGET MARKET

As I indicated in the previous essay, a commercial photographer's potential clientele and portfolio requirements differ with location. The same is true for a portrait photographer. Selecting the studio location is a vital part of business strategy.

Every city possesses potential clients in each income bracket. Only the larger metropolitan cities, however, offer enough potential clients in each of the income brackets to allow just one to be selected as a target market. In areas of lesser population, the portraitist must find clients in all walks of life.

The nature and income of the clientele determines precisely what you should offer, how much you should charge, and what your advertising and publicity strategy should be.

THE STUDIO

The average portrait studio is smaller than its commercial counterpart. The commercial photographer is often confronted with assignments that require large sets and backgrounds, extensive lighting, and several professional models. He often needs assistants and stylists. He must also be prepared to accommodate art directors and account executives who must attend the photography session.

Most portrait studios use relatively small backgrounds. There are rarely more than five or six individuals at one sitting. Consequently, the portrait photographer's rental, utility and other expenditures are relatively low.

Studio Not a Necessity—Just as in the commercial field, the successful portrait photographer with an established reputation may not require a studio at all. Many leading portraitists work without extensive studio facilities. They do most of their photography in the clients' homes. Other photographers operate successful portrait businesses from their own homes.

However, the majority of photographers prefer the convenience and standard lighting provided by the familiarity of their own studios. The studio is also a logical center for meeting with clients, storing and organizing equipment, backgrounds and props, and displaying past efforts in a gallery setting.

SAMPLES AND DISPLAYS

As you saw in the previous essay, the commercial photographer needs a portfolio of samples before he can approach potential clients. The portrait photographer must also shoot test sessions and accumulate a variety of portrait samples. Shoot your test sessions the same way you plan to photograph paying clients.

Begin with your friends and relatives. Ask them to pose for you. Select the most attractive, photogenic individuals you can find. No one can resist pure, natural beauty. All your subjects will aspire to look like the attractive samples you show.

After shooting, you must make the important decision of how to finish your display prints. Of course, each additional lab application adds to your expenditure. However, the money is well spent if your samples stimulate large print orders and healthy profit.

My own portrait displays consist of canvas-bonded prints finished with a high-gloss spray. The canvas is laminated to masonite or stretched on a canvas frame like a painting.

EQUIPMENT

The community of portrait photographers seems to love tradition, sometimes to the point of regarding outdated equipment and techniques as a virtue rather than a limitation. The equipment needs of the commercial photographer are often assumed to be quite different from those of the portraitist.

These generally accepted fallacies include the belief that the commercial photographer who portrays people requires greater lighting power and faster flash-recycling times than the portrait photographer. This shortsightedness is a joy to equipment manufacturers because it provides them with a secondary equipment market and added income.

Such attitudes not only contribute to the propagation of second-rate equipment, but are a direct cause of the low standing of the portraitist on the professional photographers' economic ladder.

If you plan to be a portrait photographer, get the finest, most up-to-date equipment you can afford.

Each of my cameras is equipped with a motor drive or auto winder. They enable me to shoot fast and capture many subtleties of expression, a critical factor for the success of a portrait session.

I use Nikon cameras and accessories and so, naturally, recommend this equipment to the newcomer to 35mm portraiture. Buy the top model, if you can afford it. Or, buy whatever else suits both your pocketbook and taste.

I use 35mm Kodachrome 25 color-slide film for nearly all my color portraits. Slide film enables you to shoot large quantities of images at minimal cost per image. Kodachrome 25 gives results of exceptional quality.

Many long-established portrait photographers still feel the need for a film format larger than 35mm. Some use 2-1/4-inch-square or other medium-format cameras. Many others shoot on 4x5 sheet film. They have yet to experience the image quality possible with 35mm cameras and films.

More importantly, they fail to realize the most essential factor about portrait photography: A subject is only impressed with photographs in which he or she looks good. It's that simple!

Most photographers are impressed with an image in which every strand of hair is rendered sharply, but it won't sell portraits. A subject won't look for a 3:1 lighting ratio, either. Nor will he measure shadow densities with a densitometer. However, he will admire and appreciate an image that has captured the essence of his character and personality. And that, in my opinion, is best captured with a 35mm camera because of ease and speed of handling.

KNOW YOUR CLIENT

The modern woman who visits a portrait studio is astute. She is a magazine reader and knows about current trends in fashion and design. Some American publications now rival their European counterparts in size and by the amount of advertising featured.

I believe that many a woman's secret dream is, or was, to be a professional model. Only relatively few meet the stringent requirements. There is no reason, however, why the remainder can't be photographed like professional models.

With this thought in mind, I developed what I call *fashion portraiture.* I provide the subject with a series of images similar to those I produce for fashion magazines and celebrities. For many of my subjects, it is the fulfillment of a fantasy.

Men, too, are aware of current trends in fashion—and in photographic style. In general, they find the style of editorial and advertising photography they see appealing and appreciate being photographed in a similar way.

PREPARING FOR A SESSION

I discuss a session with each client before I begin photographing. This general discussion covers moods and attitudes, poses, props and clothing. I also use the conversation to eliminate any pre-photography jitters the subject may have and build up her confidence. In most probability, the subject has never experienced a *glamour* or *beauty* portrait session of this kind before. I want her to have the pleasure of discovering that the experience is every bit as exciting as it appears on television or in the movies!

Clothing and Props—If a woman wants to be photographed in formal attire, I suggest she bring three different formal outfits with complete accessories—fur, jewelry, bags, gloves, and so on. Most subjects like a diversified session in which I photograph them in both formal attire and casual clothing. In such cases, I may shoot them in as many as four different outfits.

Hair and Makeup—Most of my female subjects visit their hairdresser prior to the photography session. Some will also have their makeup done at a beauty salon. Others feel capable, and more comfortable, doing their own hair and makeup. In any event, I always ask the subject to bring her personal makeup with her to the session. This way, touchups and corrections are possible.

Final Touches—On arrival at my studio, the subject is shown to the dressing room. I'm shown the wardrobe and accessories brought for photography. I make the clothing selections and pick the accessories for each series of photographs. If hair or makeup corrections are needed prior to photography, to complement an outfit, they are suggested and directed by me.

Background—While my subject is dressing, my assistant and I select backgrounds that complement the outfit. Sometimes we'll prepare as many as three backgrounds, so a transition can be made rapidly and the photography can proceed without undue delay.

LIGHTING

In most portrait situations, I use four lights or less during an entire session. Sometimes a single umbrella light is enough. At other times, I may use a main light, two background lights, a hair light, and a reflector. Only when photographing a group of several people would I sometimes need more than the basic four lights.

My assistant and I plug in all lights and place them at their approximate positions at the start of the session. Everything is organized for ease and rapidity of operation. I may begin with a single light and, as I see the need, add others.

Buying Lights—As I mentioned earlier, the *types* of lights suitable for commercial photography of people are also suitable for private portraiture. The only difference is that the commercial photographer often requires to illuminate a larger area and, therefore, needs *more* light.

Purchase lights that accept a variety of head configurations, including wide- and narrow-angle reflectors, focusing spots, softboxes and umbrellas. Versatility is the most important consideration. Recycling capability is also important. I need lights that recycle to 200 to 400 watt-seconds in no more than 1.25 seconds. This enables me to use my camera's auto winder or motor drive to full advantage, so that I can capture fleeting changes in a subject's expression.

Another essential factor—so obvious it shouldn't require mention—is dependability. If your lights fail to function, their versatility and recycling abilities mean nothing.

There are several manufacturers of good, reliable electronic flash equipment. I use the Versatron and Porta-Master lines produced by Photogenic Machine Co. of Youngstown, Ohio. I have four Porta-Master 400 units. These are small, portable and self-contained. They have a capacity of 400 watt-seconds.

Each Porta-Master 400 is shipped with a flash head and standard reflector, a light stand and a sync cord. This constitutes a great setup for the beginning photographer and is ideal for location assignments. Each Porta-Master 400 unit is capable of firing three additional flash heads.

When I need more light than the Porta-Master 400 can provide, I use the Versatron 800. It provides 800 watt-seconds of power, features fast recycling and has a full line of accessories.

For more information about equipment, see the list on page 160.

SHOOTING THE PORTRAITS

I ask the subject to assume a relaxed pose on the set. I begin by posing myself in the way I want the subject to pose. I start most sessions by evaluating the subject's appearance under a single light source. If all looks well, I check the lighting balances with my flash meter, taking incident-light readings from various parts of the subject. I also check the lighting relationship between subject and background. Then I begin shooting.

When the subject makes a change in clothing, I often change background and lighting, to provide a wide variety of images to select from.

In one session, I usually expose 10 to 15 rolls of 36-exposure 35mm slide film. This means I make an average total of more than 400 exposures.

PROOFS

I receive my processed film uncut and unmounted. I cut each film into six strips of six frames each. My lab places these strips in an 8x10 negative carrier and enlarges the 36 shots on a 16x20-inch piece of Type-R paper. The result is a 16x20 proof sheet, showing each of the 36 images at almost wallet size.

When viewing the 16x20 proofs, the subjects see every exposure made—including the shots in which they blinked. Occasionally, they'll see a light meter next to the face, when my assistant moved in for a reading. In short, they see the good and the bad of the session. From this proof sheet, the subject selects and orders enlargements. I include a copy of my price list with the 16x20 proofs.

PRICING PORTRAITS

The commercial photographer enjoys the benefits of numerous pricing guides in determining approximate charges. There are no similar guides for the beginning portraitist. Your best avenue is to find out from other portrait photographers in your area what current prices are. This gives you some ideas as to where to start. As your abilities, clientele and reputation increase, so will the fees you can demand.

My sitting fee includes photography, proof sheets, two 8x10 enlargements and one 5x7 enlargement. The enlargements may all be of the same image or of different images.

The images selected by the client are converted from 35mm slides to 4x5-inch *internegatives.* Any desirable retouching is done on these negatives before they are enlarged onto an untextured paper. Final retouching can be done on the print. The print is sprayed for a lustre finish.

Most of my clients want more than the relatively small prints included with my fee. They order large canvas-mounted prints, beginning with the 11x14 size. I offer prints in sizes up to 60 inches long. My pricing for prints is the same for original orders and reorders at a later date.

ADVERTISING AND PROMOTION

The most obvious way you can advertise your work is through displays in your studio and its window. Another effective method is by word-of-mouth. People will hear from satisfied customers or from those who have seen and admired your work.

Other avenues for promotion include local portrait exhibits at banks and public buildings, as well as direct mail advertising with color mailers. Whatever approach you select, remember that your best publicity will be your known quality and dependability. Be sure your photography is consistently good. Be sure that you conduct both the business and photographic side of your operation in a manner that makes customers feel at ease and enjoy the session.

Success comes only with experience and dedication. If your main ambition is to be a beauty and glamour photographer, make everyone look beautiful! □

8 Portfolio

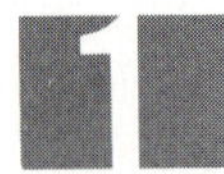

Subject: Margaux Hemingway
Client: Fabergé Cosmetics
Art Director: Richard Barrie
Location: Gary Bernstein Studio, New York City
Camera: Nikon F2
Lens: 105mm *f*-2.5 Auto-Nikkor
Lighting: Three 1200-watt-second Thomastrobe electronic flash units
Film: Kodachrome 25
Exposure Metering: Minolta Auto-Flash II, incident-light mode
Exposure: *f*-8 (shutter at 1/60 second)

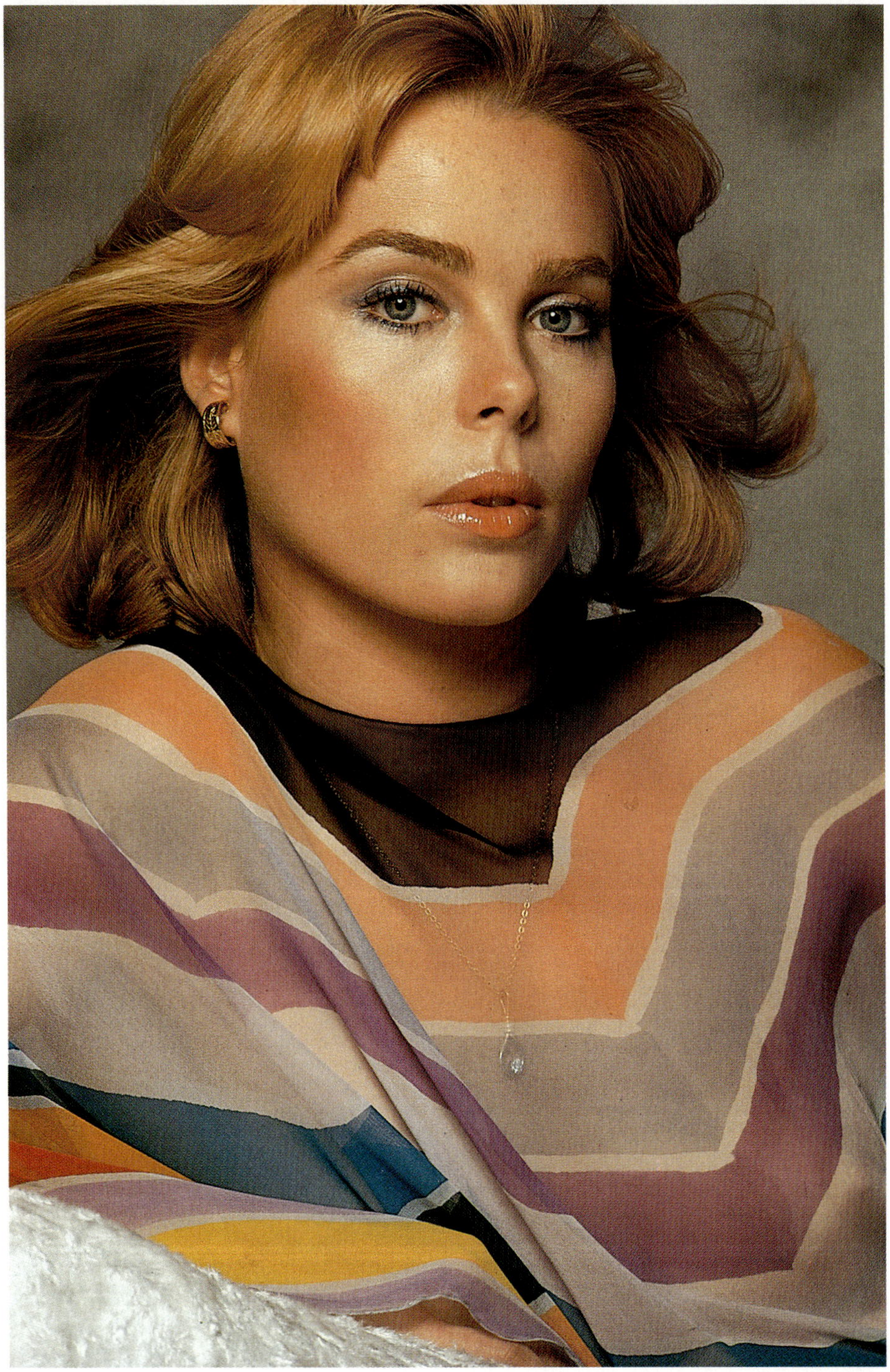

For this photo of beautiful Margaux Hemingway, I used a white, seamless background that had been spray-painted to create the illusion of smoke.

I needed enough depth of field to allow Margaux freedom of movement but also wanted to record the background out of focus. I achieved this by placing the subject approximately 10 feet from the background, using a short telephoto lens, and setting my subject and background lighting for an *f*-8 exposure.

Notice the white fabric in the lower-left corner of the frame. What you see is just a corner of a large piece that I had draped over half a dozen pillows. I keep a variety of random fabrics in the studio—everything from silk to burlap—to harmonize or contrast with any outfit. The pillows can be raised or lowered at will to give me complete posing and composition flexibility. They also tend to provide a subject with comfort and a feeling of security. □

Television commercials photographed with 35mm still cameras, rather than movie or TV cameras, are called *photomatic* commercials. They are an inexpensive way of shooting test commercials. Because the images form an animated sequence, viewfinder accuracy is imperative. The image must be cropped to conform with the proportions of a TV screen. I use a Nikon focusing screen marked specifically for television-screen cropping. A tripod-mounted camera is also essential.

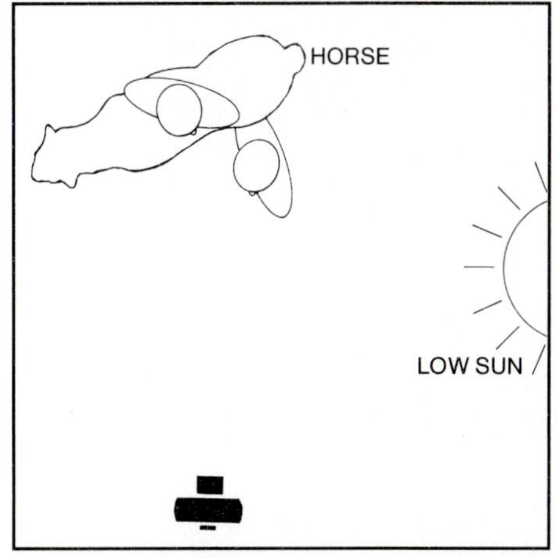

Photos making up a sequence of this kind are sorted—or *edited*—and music and a voice track are added. If the photomatic commercial is a success, the client has one of two choices: He can air the photomatic commercial as it is or convert it into a movie version.

The photo shown here is part of a sequence in which the male model approached the woman and helped her off the horse. I positioned the woman for best modeling from the sunlight because we were "selling" the beauty of her hair. The harsh late-afternoon sun created excessive contrast on the male model, causing his face to fall into deep shadow. To avoid this, I asked the man to glance over his shoulder as he approached the horse, as shown. Eventually, he had to turn back toward the female model. To brighten the shadow on his face, I used a silvered reflector.

Subject: Professional models
Client: Alberto-Culver, Inc.
Ad Agency: Lee King and Partners, Inc., Chicago
Producer: Sharon Sturgis
Art Director: Deborah Pavitt
Location: Zuma, California
Camera: Nikon F3
Lens: 180mm *f*-2.8 Auto-Nikkor
Lighting: Late-afternoon sunlight
Film: Kodachrome 25
Exposure Metering: Gossen Luna Pro, incident-light mode
Exposure: 1/250 second at *f*-5.6

To determine exposure, I pointed the hemisphere of my incident-light meter directly at the sun from subject position. □

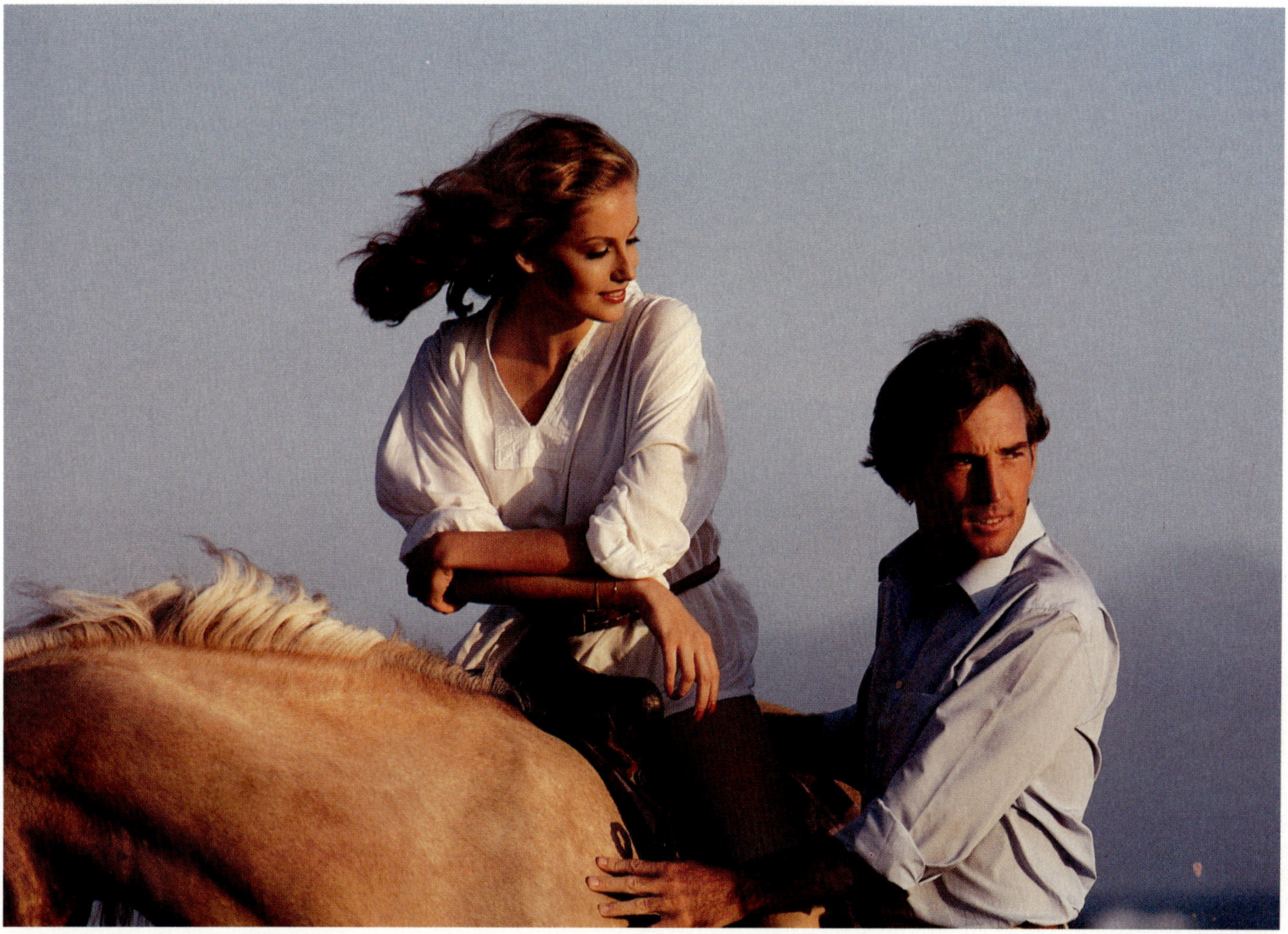

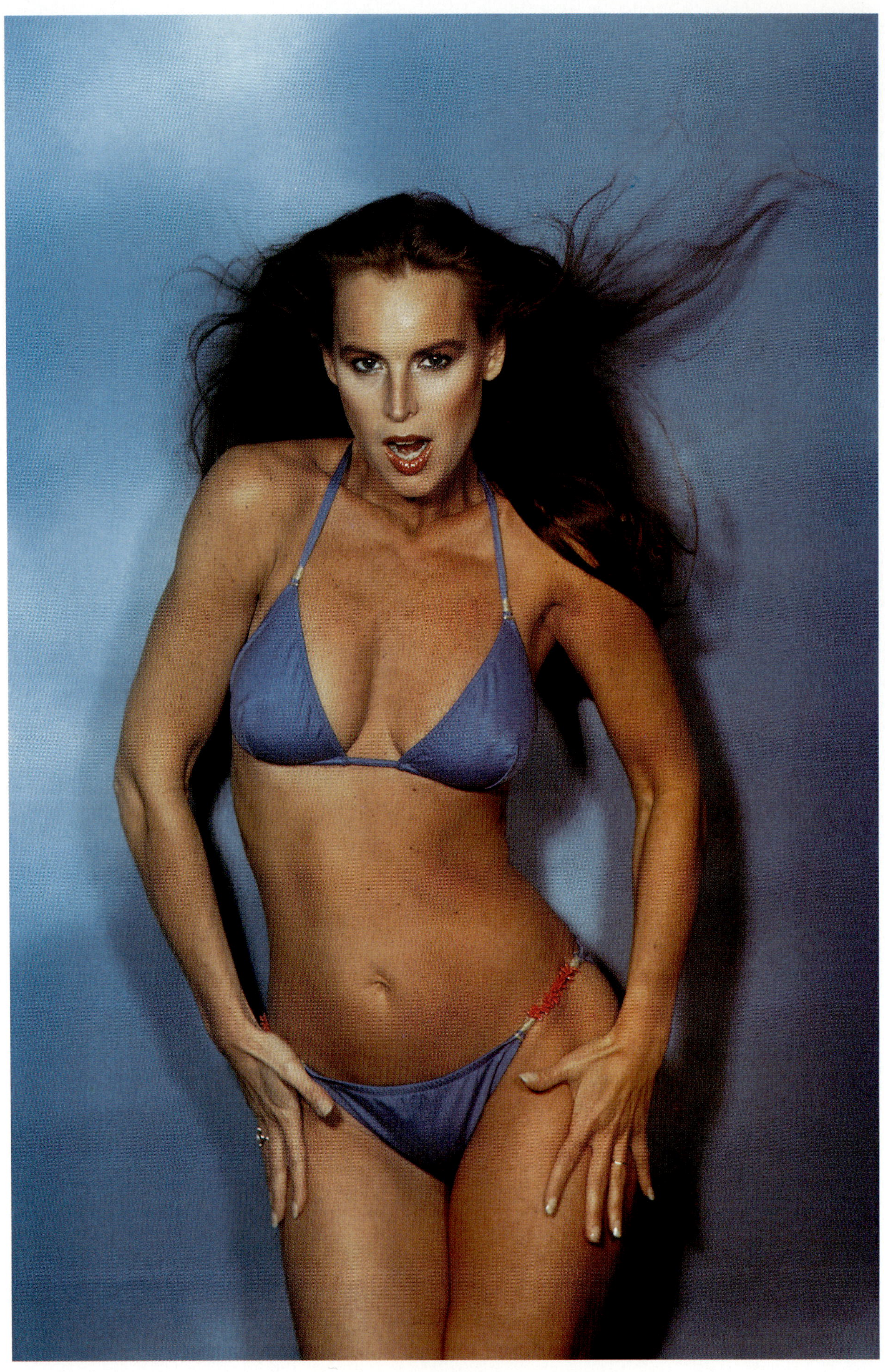

Using the spray-paint technique described in the essay on backgrounds (page 25), I prepared a seamless background of blue sky and white clouds. The background was placed in my living room, supported by a portable BD background holder.

I connected two flash heads to a 1200-watt-second power pack. Each 600-watt-second head had a wide-angle reflector. The lights were positioned at a height of about six feet.

I used two white, V-shaped reflector panels—one on each side of my camera—and aimed each flash head at the center of the "V" in the standing reflectors.

Placing the incident-light hemisphere on my Minolta flash meter at subject position, I metered each light source separately, carefully shielding the meter's hemisphere from the other light. In this way I established that the subject received equal illumination from each head. I then metered the total illumination on the subject by placing the hemisphere at the center of the subject's face and pointing it toward the camera. It recorded *f*-8—the exposure I used to make the picture.

Notice the directional, yet soft, quality of the lighting and its evenness throughout the composition. The setup is ideal for use with a couple of small, portable flash units, too. You can control the lighting effect by simply increasing or decreasing the angle of the "V" in the reflectors.

Two large sheets of white foamcore board make excellent reflectors. Score the vertical center line of each board with a razor blade and bend the board into a V-shape. Or, cut each board along its vertical center line and then tape the two halves together. □

Subject: Professional model
Client: Pro Arts, Inc.
Art Directors: Gary Bernstein and Kay Sutton York
Location: Gary Bernstein home, Beverly Hills, California
Camera: Nikon F3
Lens: 85mm *f*-1.8 Auto-Nikkor
Lighting: Two 600-watt-second electronic flash units
Light Control: Two white reflector panels
Film: Kodachrome 25
Exposure Metering: Minolta Auto-Flash II, incident-light mode
Exposure: *f*-8 (shutter at 1/60 second)

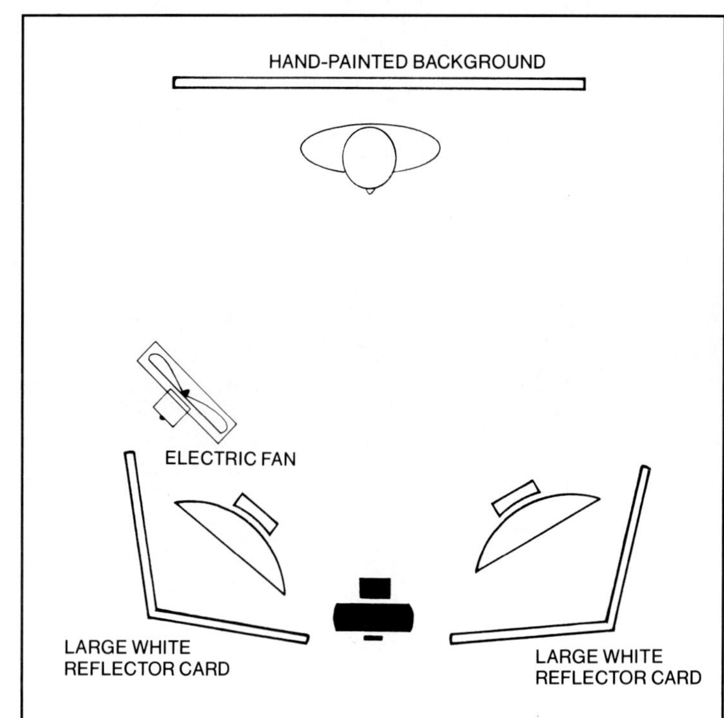

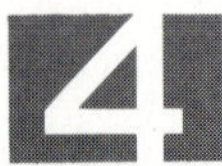

Subject: William Shatner
Client: Jean-Paul Germain, Ltd.
Art Director: Gary Bernstein
Location: Gary Bernstein Studio, Los Angeles, California
Camera: Nikon F3
Lens: 85mm *f*-1.8 Auto-Nikkor
Lighting: One 800-watt-second Photogenic Versatron electronic flash unit
Light Control: One 40-inch silvered umbrella; one small Photogenic Silfoil silvered reflector
Film: Kodachrome 25
Exposure Metering: Gossen Ultra-Pro, incident-light mode
Exposure: *f*-11 (shutter at 1/60 second)

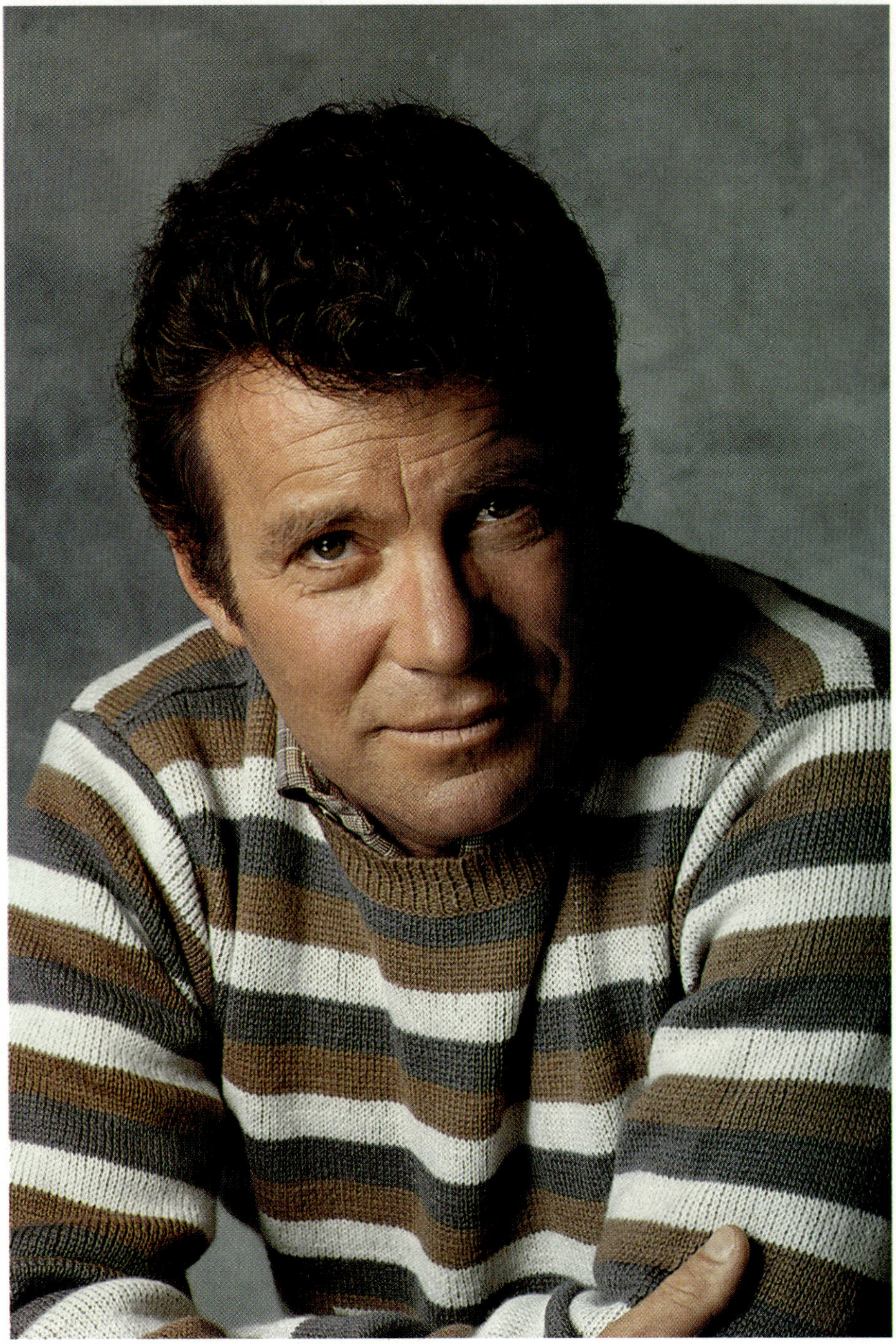

I would call this photo of talented actor William Shatner a casual, yet elegant, portrait. It was taken against a canvas background which I had painted with black, white and gray latex house paints. Using large natural sponges and lots of water, I painted the entire 10x30-foot backdrop in about four hours. That was a few years ago and the background has provided me with a wide variety of uses since then.

You need not be an artist to produce a variety of attractive painted backgrounds, but you do need the right tools. I began my background painting by using 5x6-foot canvas window shades. The shades were large enough for most portrait situations, yet compact enough to be easily portable.

Using latex paints mixed with water, I work all areas of the background at the same time. I take regular breaks to view my efforts from a typical camera distance. You can mount a camera on a tripod, focus on a fixed object at subject position, and evaluate your efforts with a variety of lenses and apertures. Just keep on painting until the background looks the way you want it.

The greatest advantage of an unevenly painted background is that it can be lit unevenly or exposed incorrectly and still look spectacular in a photograph. □

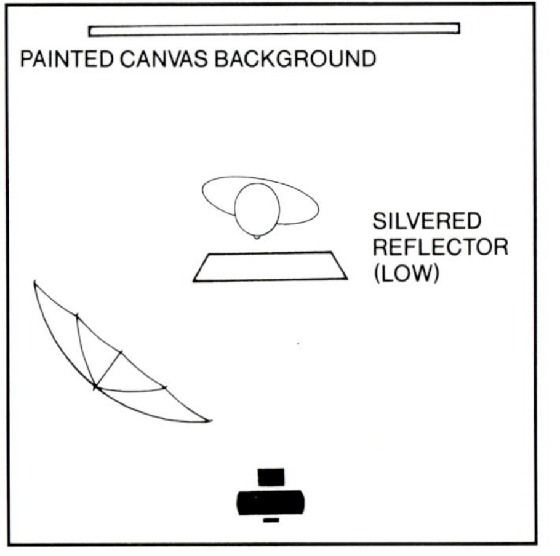

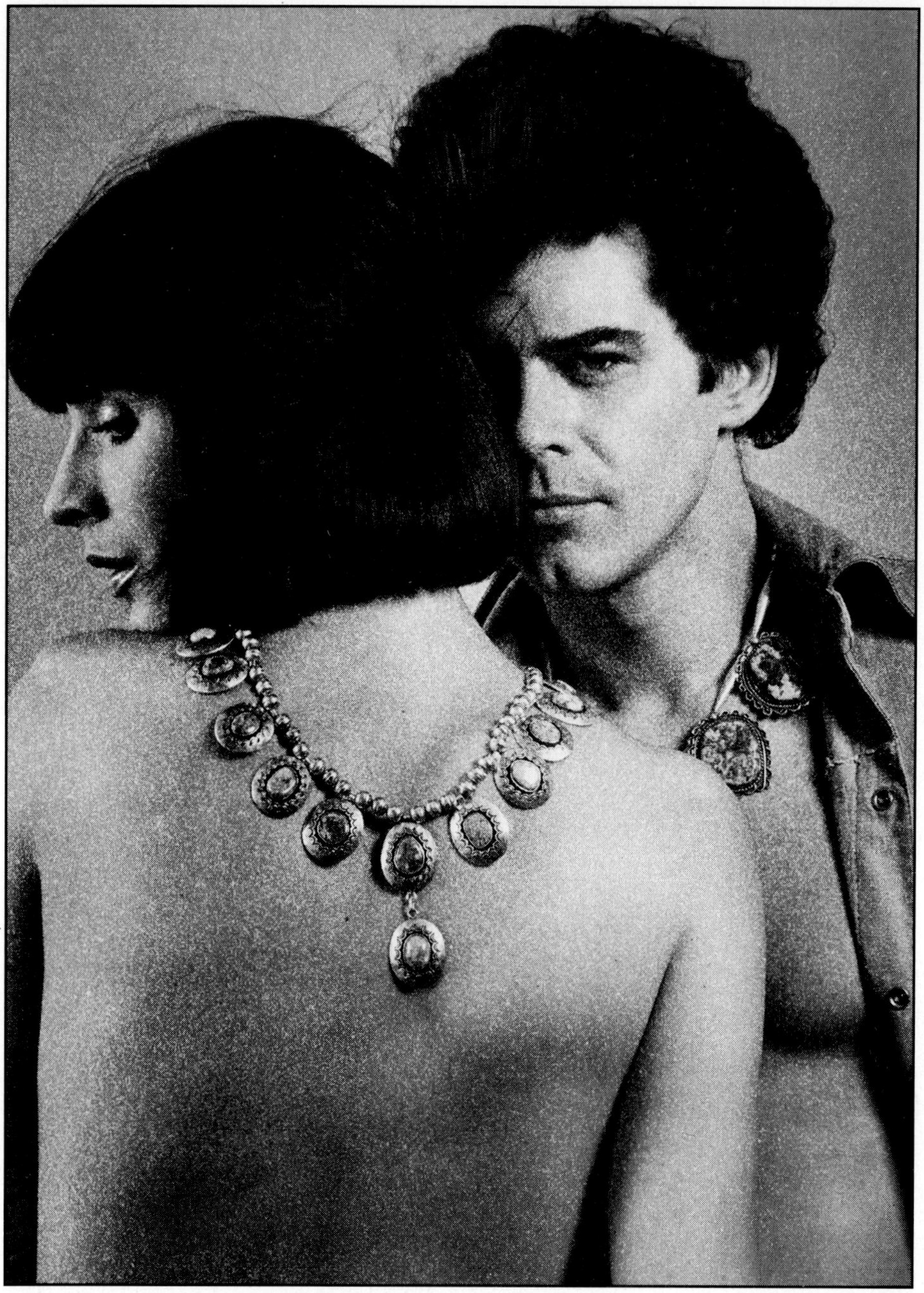

Subject: Professional models
Client: Saks-Takada Salon, New York City
Location: Saks-Takada Salon, New York City
Camera: Hasselblad 500EL/M
Lens: 150mm *f*-4 Zeiss Sonnar
Lighting: Two 1200-watt-second Thomastrobe electronic flash units
Light Control: Two 40-inch silvered umbrellas
Film: Kodak Plus-X Pan
Exposure Metering: Wein Electronic-Flash Meter, incident-light mode
Exposure: *f*-22 (shutter at 1/250 second)

Saks-Takada is a specialty salon in New York City. This photo was produced to depict not only the talent of the salon's hairstylists, but also some of the jewelry available at the gift department. I took the shot at the salon, against four-foot-wide white, seamless background paper supported by a portable BD background holder.

Notice the position of the male model. He is behind the woman and partly hidden by her. To maintain his impact in the composition, I asked him to bring his head well forward. His importance is further emphasized by his eye contact with the viewer.

I used a separate main light for each of the subjects. A small umbrella light to the left of the camera provided the beautiful profile lighting on the woman. A second source, placed to the right of the camera, illuminated the male model from the side. Each source recorded *f*-22 with my incident-light meter placed at the subject positions.

There are no catchlights in the models' eyes. This departure from the norm was intentional. I wanted the bodies to appear sculptural and impersonal, acting merely as supports for the intricate jewelry. By avoiding catchlights, I toned down the vibrancy of the models, allowing the jewelry to be dominant in the composition.

I printed the final image through a coarse-grain texture screen to further enhance the abstract effect of the two bodies. □

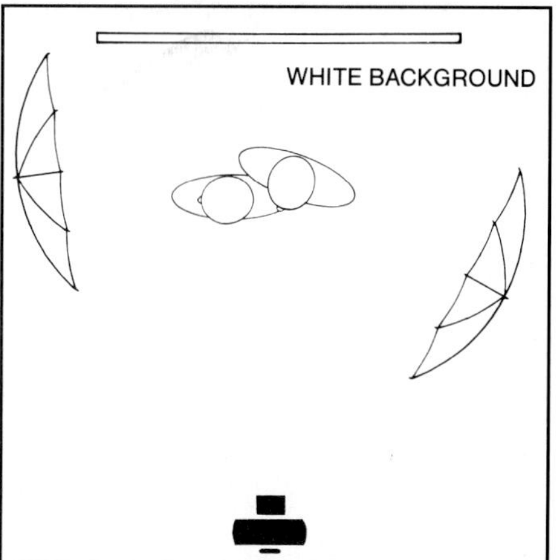

Subject: Two body builders
Client: Paramount Fitness Equipment Corporation
Art Director: John Nicholson
Location: Gary Bernstein Studio, Los Angeles, California
Camera: Nikon F3
Lens: 85mm *f*-1.4 Auto-Nikkor
Lighting: One 800-watt-second electronic flash unit; Two 1200-watt-second electronic flash units
Film: Kodachrome 25
Filtration: Blue gelatin filters on background lights
Exposure Metering: Minolta Auto-Flash III, incident-light mode
Exposure: *f*-5.6 (shutter at 1/60 second)

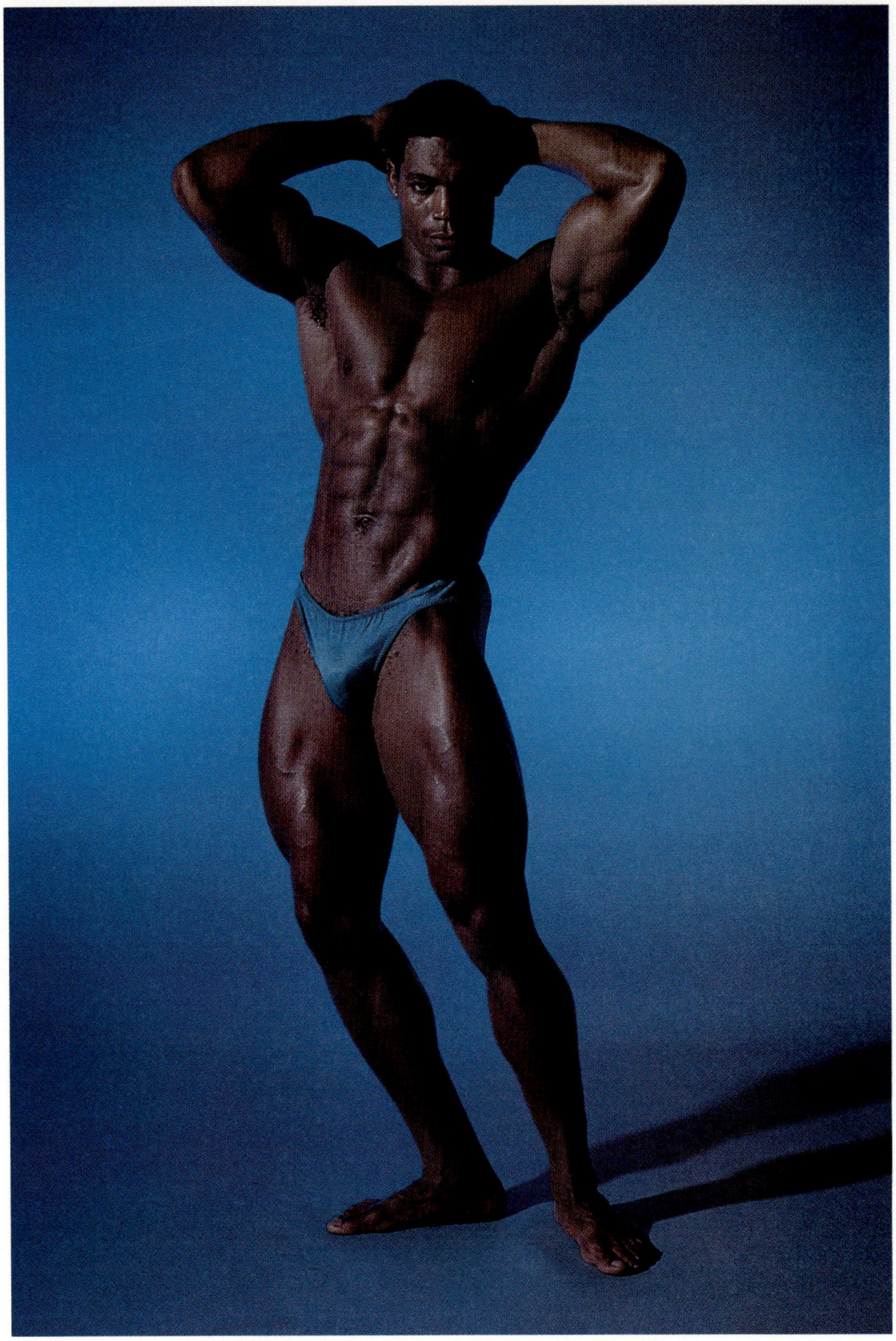

These two shots for Paramount Fitness Equipment illustrate that pictorial continuity can be maintained in spite of considerable lighting changes. The photos are part of a continuing national advertising series.

The layout called for a series of active figures against a vibrant blue, seamless background.

Nine-foot-wide blue seamless paper was supported by two stands at a height of about 12 feet. I used two 1200-watt-second flash units with wide-angle reflectors as background lights. Over each reflector I taped a blue gelatin filter. The blue filtration caused the normally bland paper to glow like blue neon light.

To emphasize the chiseled contours of the male subject, I placed the 800-watt-second main light—with wide grid spot—on a boom stand to the subject's right. This point-source light created high contrast and gave the muscled torso dramatic specularity. I metered the highlighted side of the body by placing the incident-light hemisphere at the subject's right side and pointing it toward the main light. The meter recorded *f*-5.6—the same as the light falling on the background.

Without changing the background lighting, I replaced the spot main light with a flash in pan reflector for the photo of the female subject. This light was in a frontal position. The relatively soft illumination emphasized the feminine charm of both face and body. Again, the light was set to balance with the *f*-5.6 recorded from the background. □

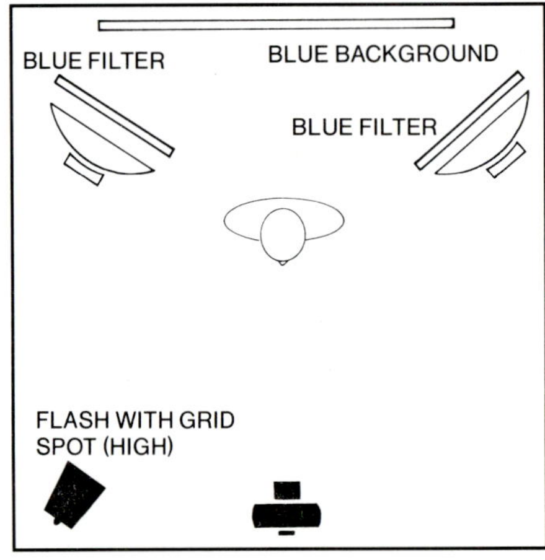

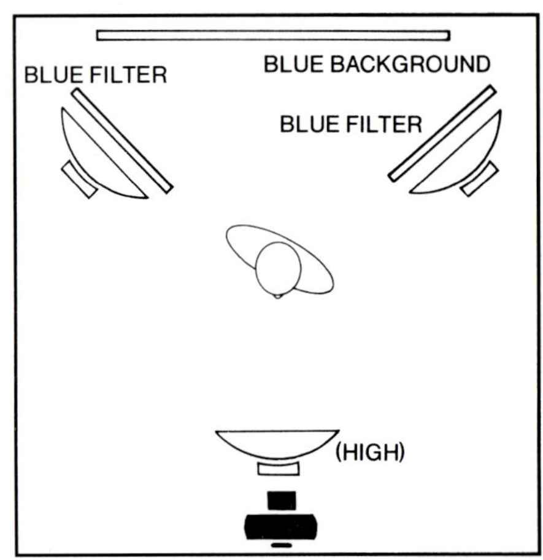

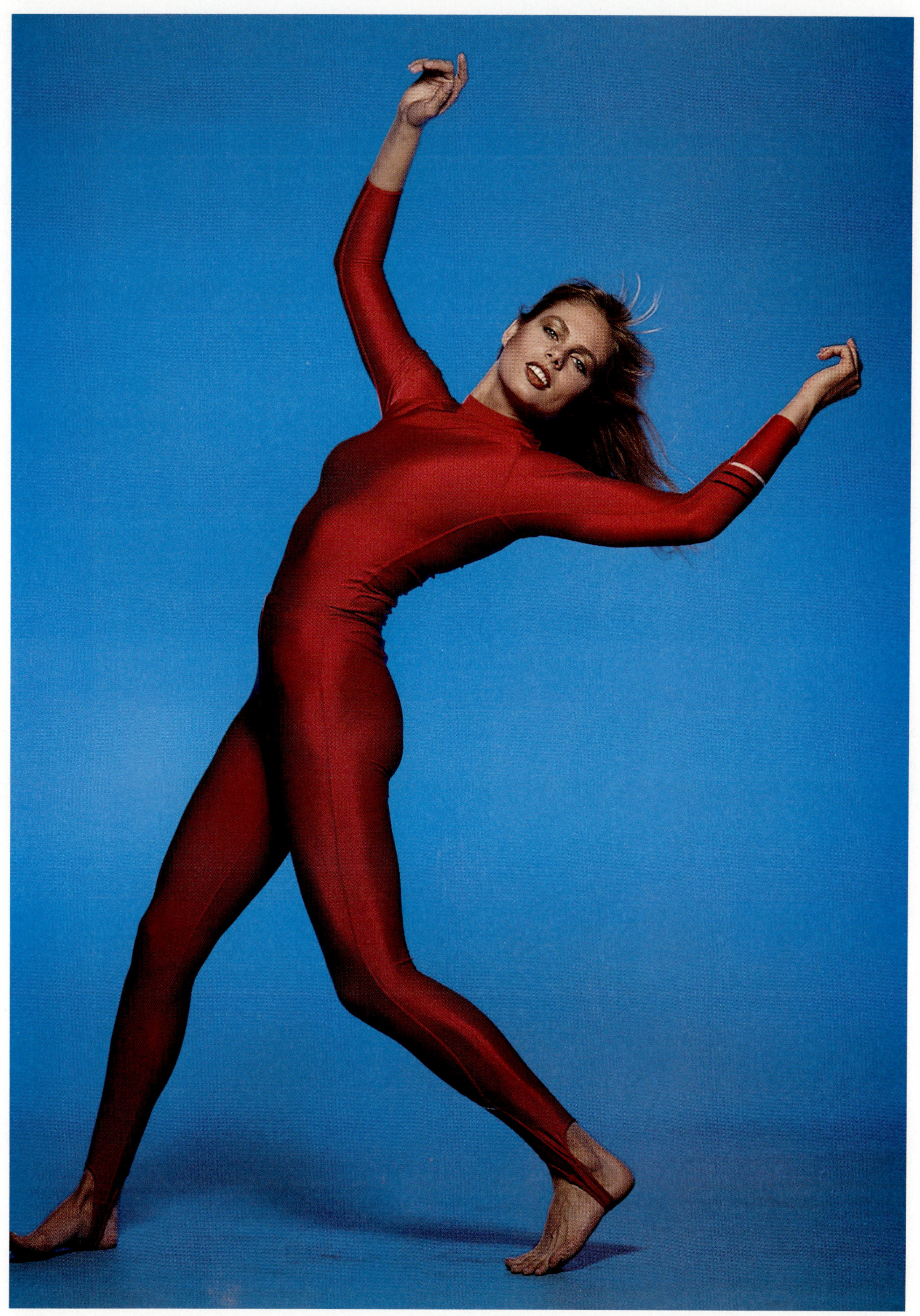

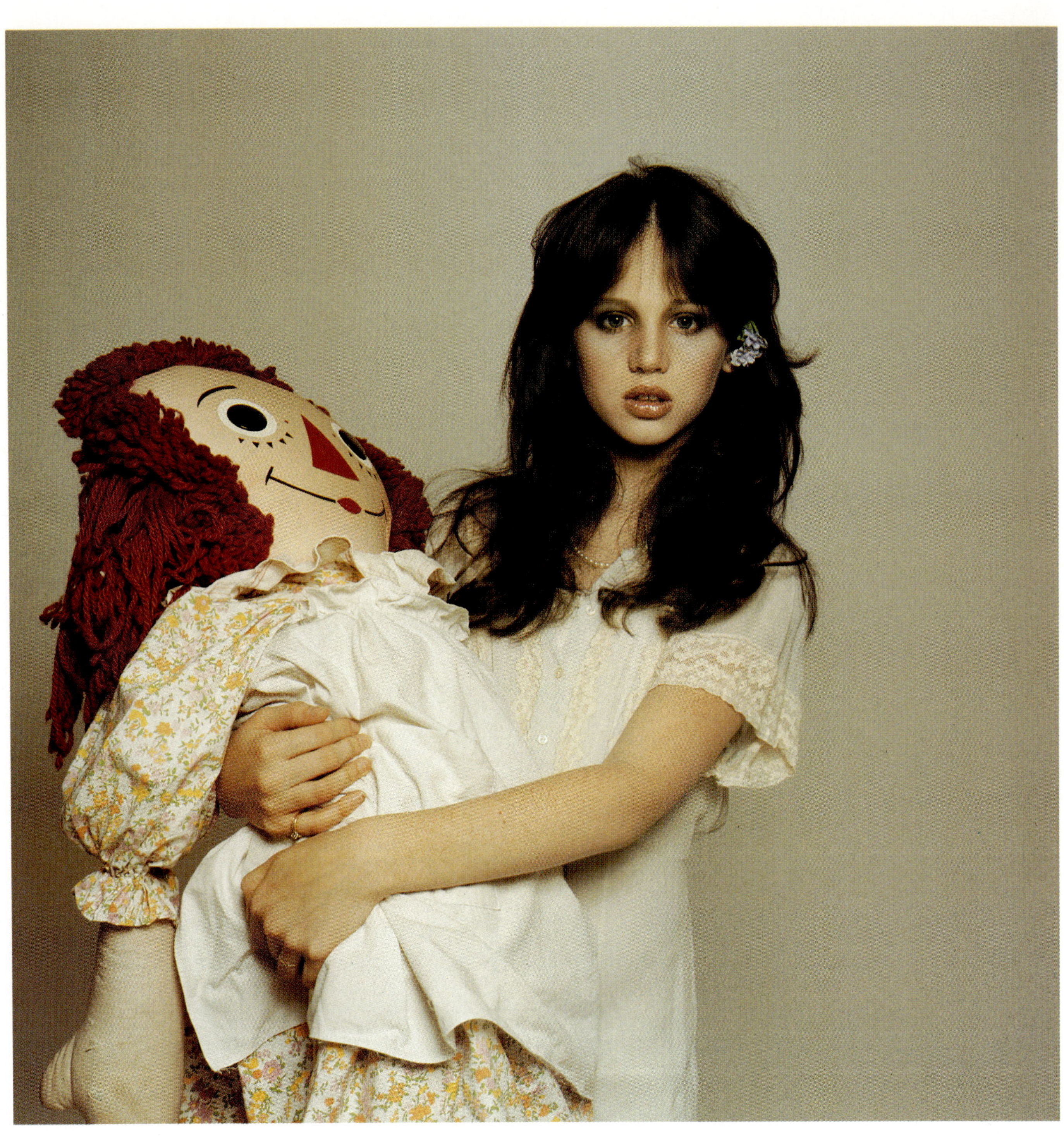

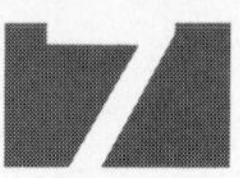

Subject: Eleven-year-old girl
Location: Gary Bernstein Studio, New York City
Camera: Hasselblad 500EL/M
Lens: 80mm *f*-2.8 Zeiss Planar
Lighting: One 1250-watt-second Rollei flash in pan reflector
Film: Ektachrome 64
Exposure Metering: Minolta Auto-Flash II, incident-light mode
Exposure: *f*-16 (shutter at 1/250 second)

The best portraits of adults usually project some emotion, such as joy, humor, affection, and even anger. Sometimes the emotion is spontaneous and sometimes it has to be elicited through the photographer's skillful direction.

Photographs of children are a different matter. The charm of a child's portrait often lies in the innocence and spontaneous sense of wonder displayed by the child. This portrait of my oldest daughter at the age of 11 is a charming example. To enhance the drama of her unreserved stare, she received eye makeup and a bit of rouge, courtesy of my wife. The subject's direct confrontation with the camera, and the huge rag doll, further help to attract viewer attention.

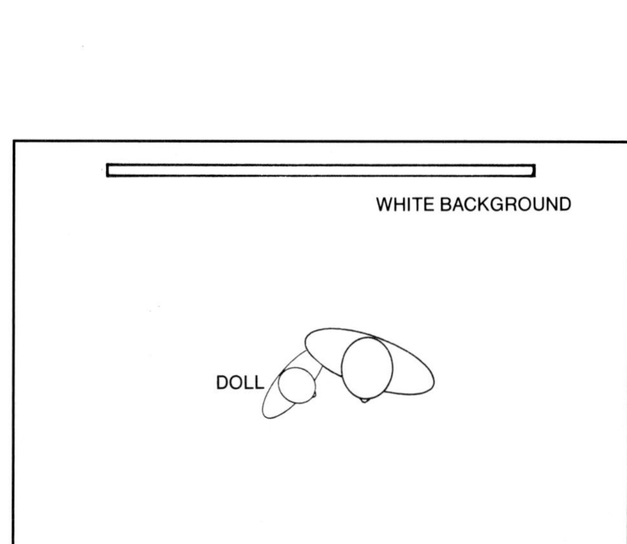

I used a standard lens and shot from a low angle. This helped to further exaggerate the size of the large doll because it was closest to the camera. For the same reason, the child's hands also appear disproportionately large.

A pan reflector provides very uniform light distribution. In spite of this, I metered the scene at two locations—the subject's face and the doll's head—to be sure that each received equal lighting and, therefore, equal emphasis in the composition. □

Subject: Professional model
Location: Aruba, Netherland Antilles
Camera: Nikon F2
Lens: 55mm *f*-3.5 Micro-Nikkor
Lighting: Late-afternoon sunlight
Film: Kodachrome 25
Filtration: Homemade diffuser
Exposure Metering: Nikon through-the-lens, center-weighted
Exposure: 1/125 second at *f*-4

Many factors play a part in the creation of photographic impact. They include lighting, lens selection, shutter speed, lens aperture, camera angle and the film type used. An important non-technical factor is *styling.* This involves the selection and proper use of clothing, accessory items and props appearing in a picture. Even in the apparently simple case of a nude on a beach, styling is a major consideration.

This is one of the photographs I made for my first book, *Burning Cold.* I wanted all the images to remain "contemporary" for many years. To achieve this, the model and I made certain styling decisions. First, the model's hair was to be either wet or dried naturally throughout the series. Not a trace of hairstyling would be evident. Second, makeup would be minimal, with no trendy or fashionable colors or designs. Last, jewelry would be elegant and of high quality—the kind that remains forever "classic."

Prior to leaving for location, we purchased a variety of towels and natural fabrics in a wide range of colors and textures. For this photo in late-afternoon sunlight, we selected a melon-colored towel and draped it across the model. Its tone is slightly lighter than the model's skin. It acted almost like a vignette, directing viewer attention back toward the center of the image. □

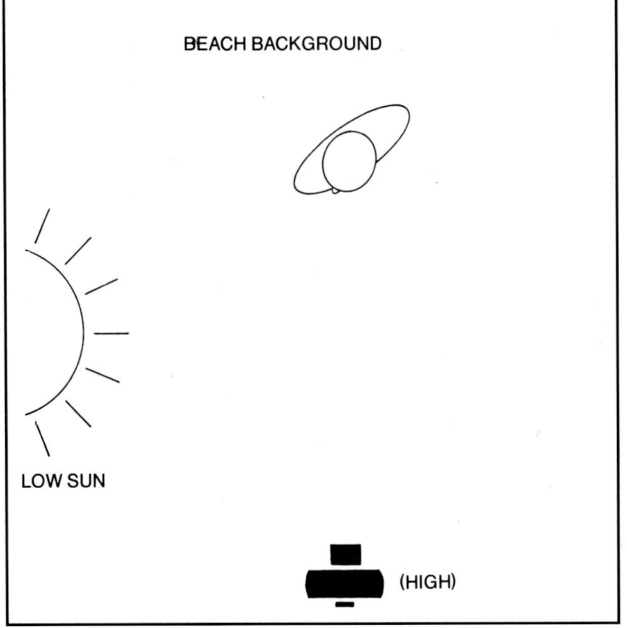

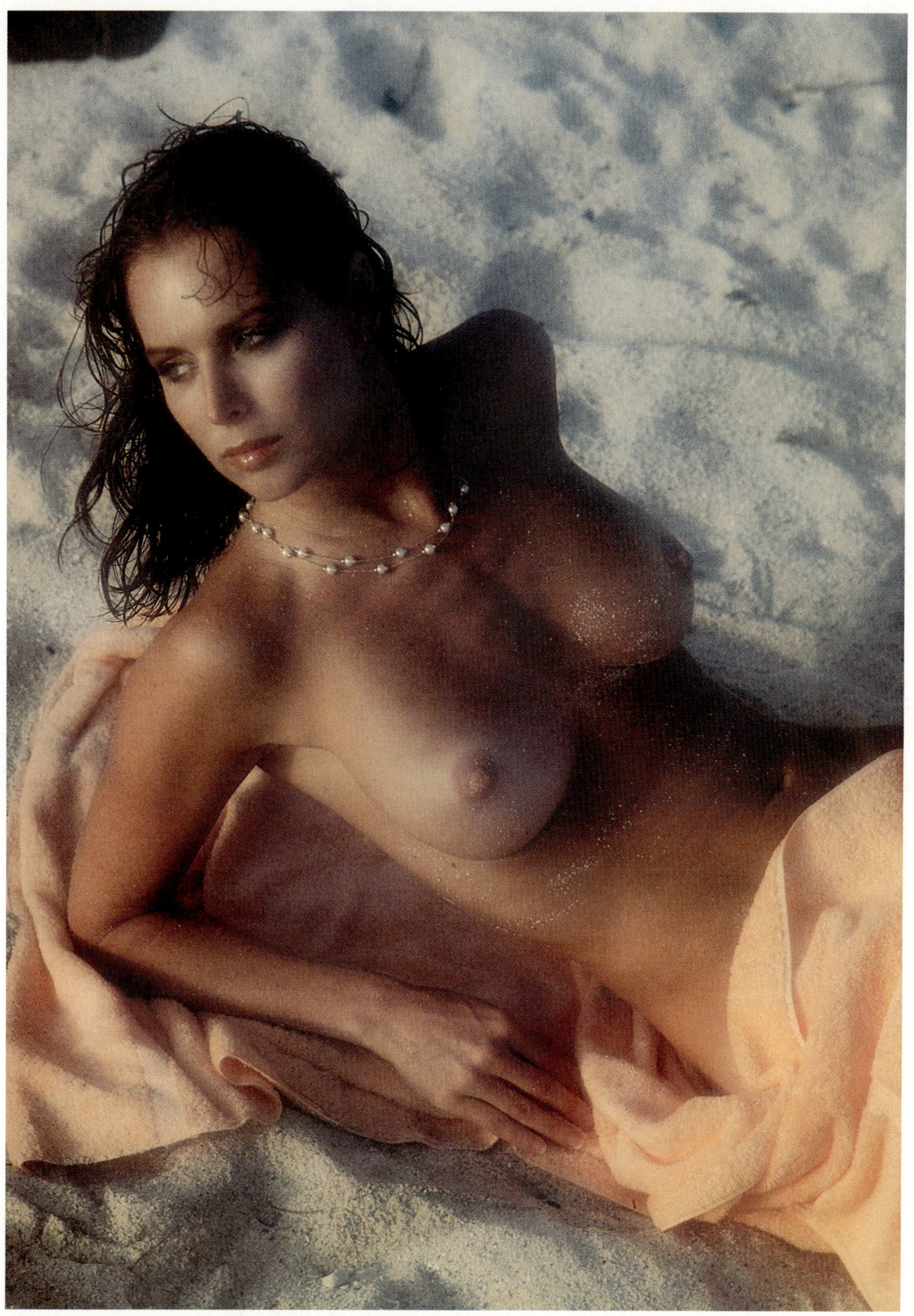

Subject: Paul Anka
Location: New York City
Camera: Nikon F2AS
Lens: 105mm *f*-4 Micro-Nikkor
Lighting: One Balcar 600-watt-second electronic flash unit
Film: Kodachrome 25
Exposure Metering: Minolta Auto-Flash II, incident-light mode
Exposure: *f*-8 (shutter at 1/60 second)

It was wonderful working with musical genius Paul Anka. I was anxious to capture his extraordinary energy on film. Paul has a full face with wonderful skin tone—a combination that's perfect for *spotlighting*. I used a single light in a 14-inch silvered umbrella. Because the source was a long way from the subject—about 10 feet—it acted like a spotlight.

Spotlighting creates specular highlights and high contrast. Placing the light at an extreme angle to Paul's right caused a deep shadow on the left side of his face. This visually narrowed his face while emphasizing his strong facial features. Notice that the light was sufficiently frontal to record a catchlight in both eyes. The second catchlight is important because it gives balance to the image.

The background was gray industrial carpeting. Its vertical striation provided a visual balance with the horizontal stripes in Paul's sweater. An *f*-8 aperture on my short telephoto lens provided sufficient depth of field, with the background softening slightly.

I placed the hemisphere of my incident-light flash meter at the highlight side of Paul's face and pointed it at the single light source. The famous Anka smile recorded as "pure music." □

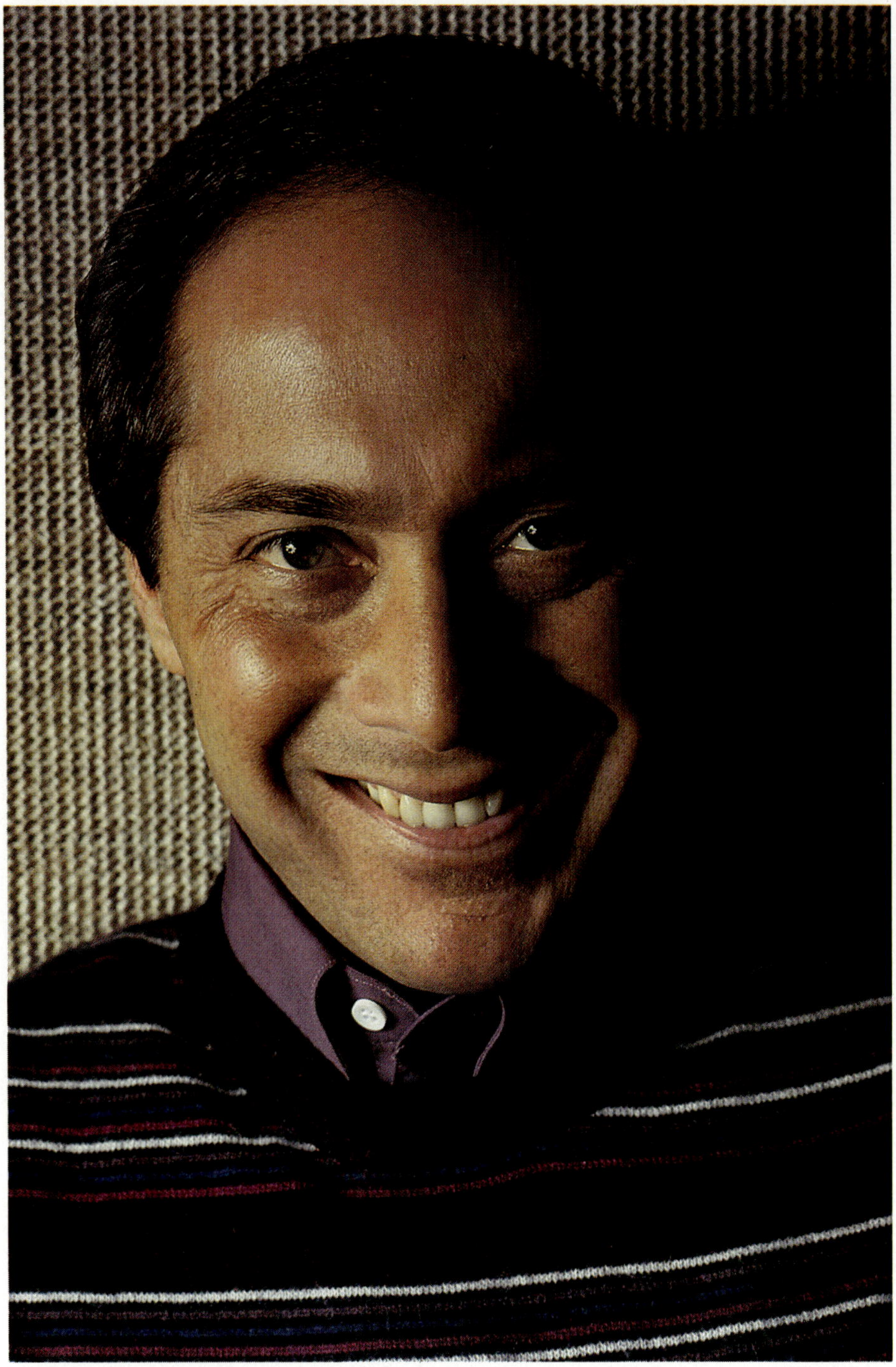

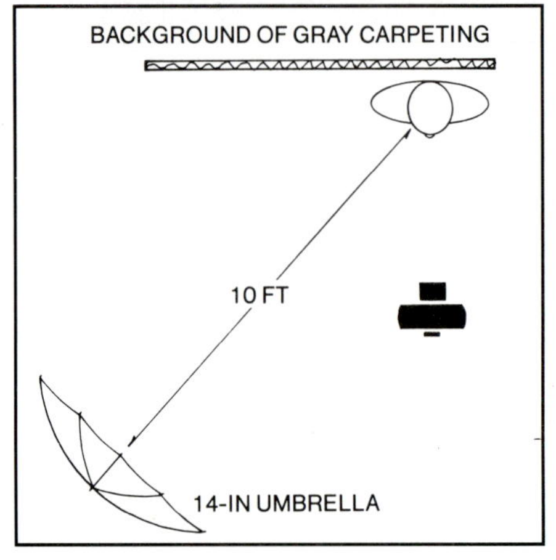

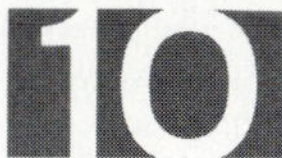

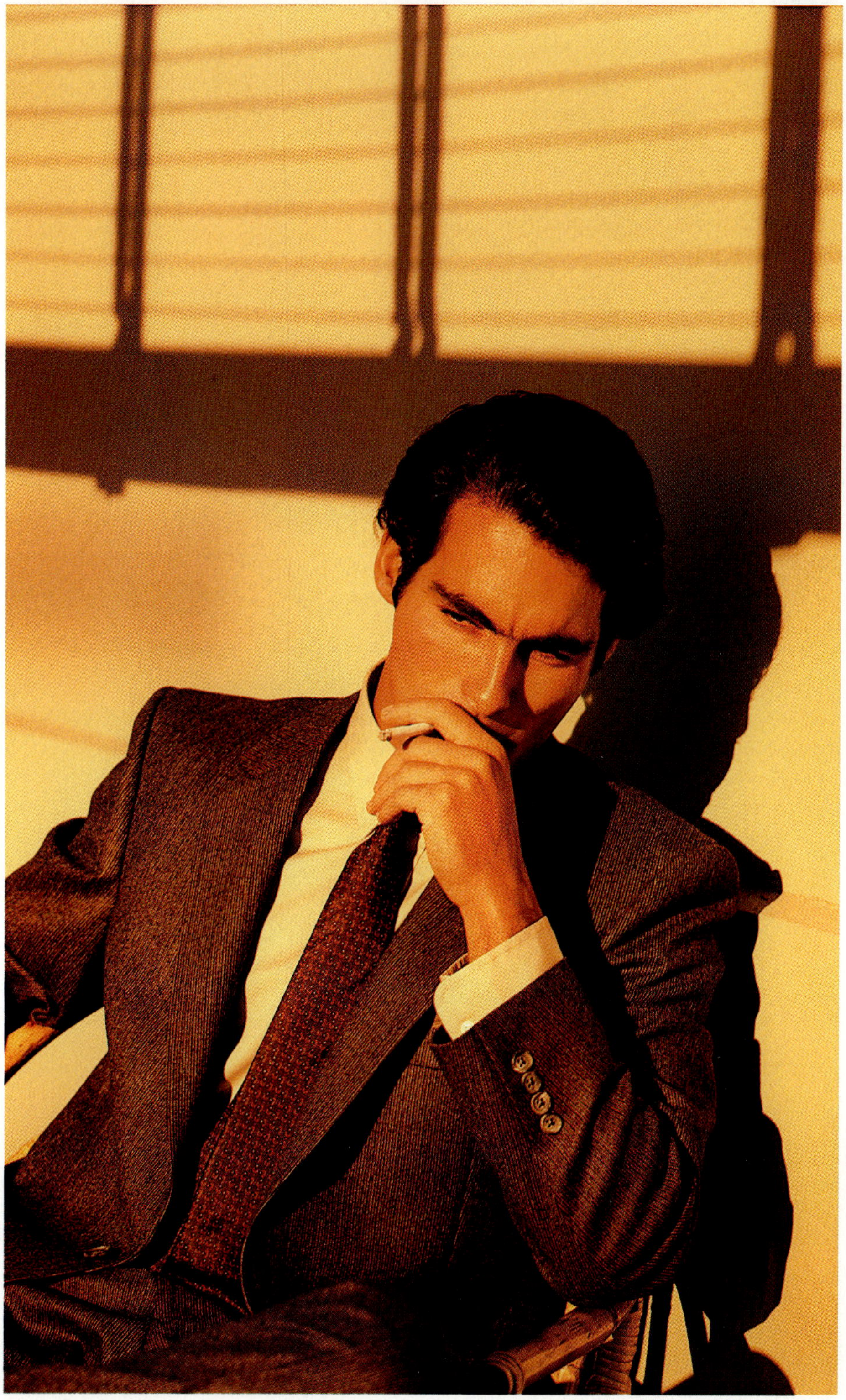

Subject: Professional model
Client: Fire Magazine
Location: Gary Bernstein Studio, Los Angeles, California
Camera: Nikon F2AS
Lens: 85mm *f*-1.4 Auto-Nikkor
Lighting: Midday sunlight
Film: Kodachrome 25
Filtration: Orange filter
Exposure Metering: Nikon TTL, center-weighted
Exposure: 1/250 second at *f*-8

I took this image in the early afternoon on the street outside my Los Angeles studio. It was produced for the cover of a trade fashion magazine. The model's low placement in the frame allows for the addition of the magazine's logo and a cover blurb.

Perhaps the most difficult form of light to use for people photographs is a high, overhead sun. The light angle and contrast render eye sockets as deep pockets of shadow. I asked the model to turn his head away from the sun and tip his head slightly, allowing the sun to fully illuminate one side of the face while producing a triangle of light on the far cheek.

I mounted a venetian blind between the sun and the background to get some interesting shadows on the wall. By using an orange filter on the camera lens, I was able to simulate the "warmth" of late-afternoon sunlight much earlier in the day. I metered through my Nikon's center-weighted meter, thereby avoiding any filter-factor calculations. □

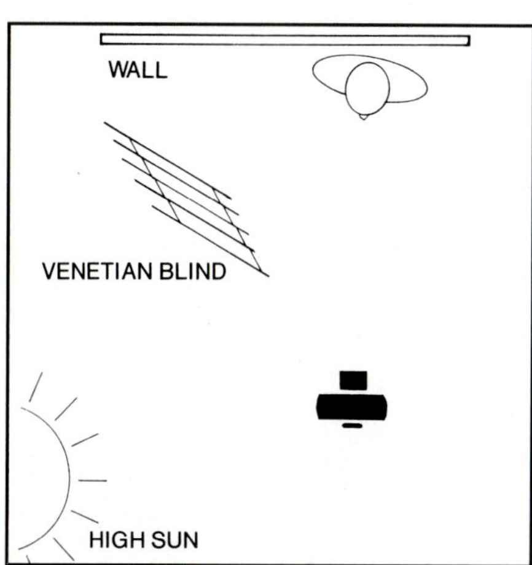

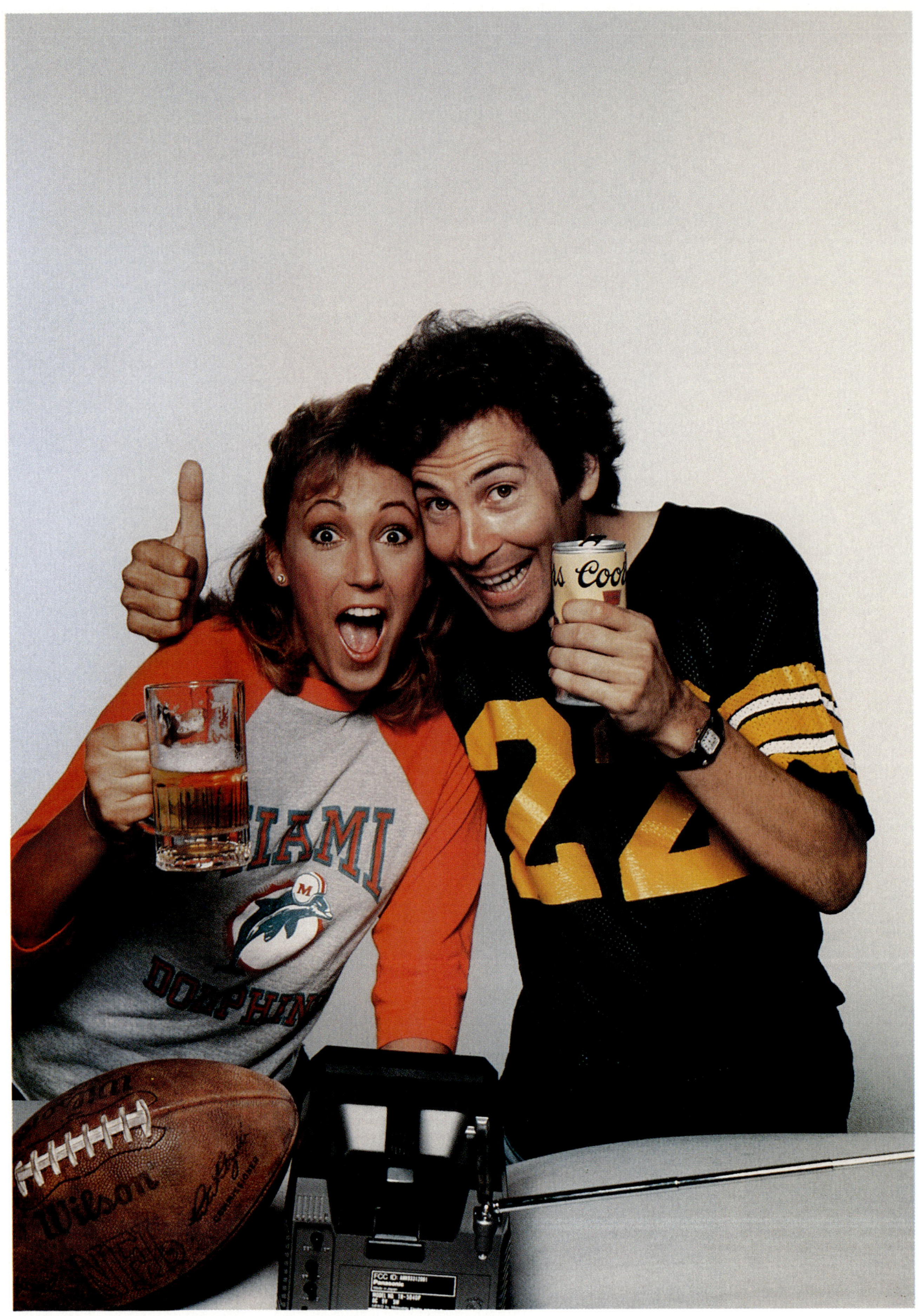
22
Wilson

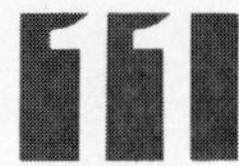

Subject: Professional models
Client: Intro Magazine
Art Director: Linda Homler
Location: Gary Bernstein Studio, Los Angeles, California
Camera: Nikon F3
Lens: 85mm *f*-1.8 Auto-Nikkor
Lighting: Three 800-watt-second Photogenic Versatron electronic flash units
Film: Kodachrome 25
Exposure Metering: Minolta Auto-Flash III, incident-light mode
Exposure: *f*-22 (shutter at 1/60 second)

This photo was taken for the cover of *Intro* magazine's fall football issue. Using readily available props and basic lighting, I created an image that depicts great energy and excitement. The models were wonderful. They responded beautifully to my yelling, cheering and screaming from behind the camera. Excitement isn't as easy to generate in a single frame as in a picture sequence or movie. You have just one split-second chance to express the mood.

Because I expected the models to be relatively active during the shooting, I used enough main lighting to provide an *f*-22 aperture. The extensive depth of field this provided enabled me to shoot without constantly worrying about critical focus. Extended depth of field also ensured sharpness of all the props.

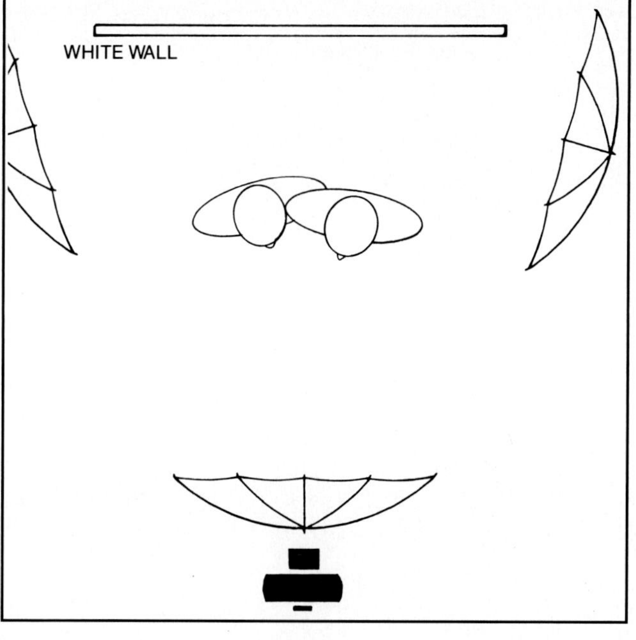

Notice the low position of the subject elements in the composition. This gave the art director flexibility in the placement of the magazine logo and cover headlines and text.

I used two umbrella lights to illuminate the background evenly. The background lights were set for 1/2 exposure step less light than that received by the subjects. Consequently, the white wall recorded as a light gray.

I asked the models to tip their heads toward each other. In doing so, they formed a single entity in the composition. In spite of the activity of the photograph and the abundance of props, the viewer's attention is directed toward the models' faces. □

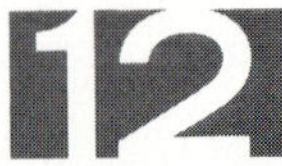

Subject: Private portrait session
Location: Beverly Hills, California
Camera: Nikon FM2
Lens: 85mm *f*-1.4 Auto-Nikkor
Lighting: Indirect sunlight
Light Control: White walls
Film: Kodachrome 25
Exposure Metering: Nikon TTL, center-weighted
Exposure: 1/125 second at *f*-5.6

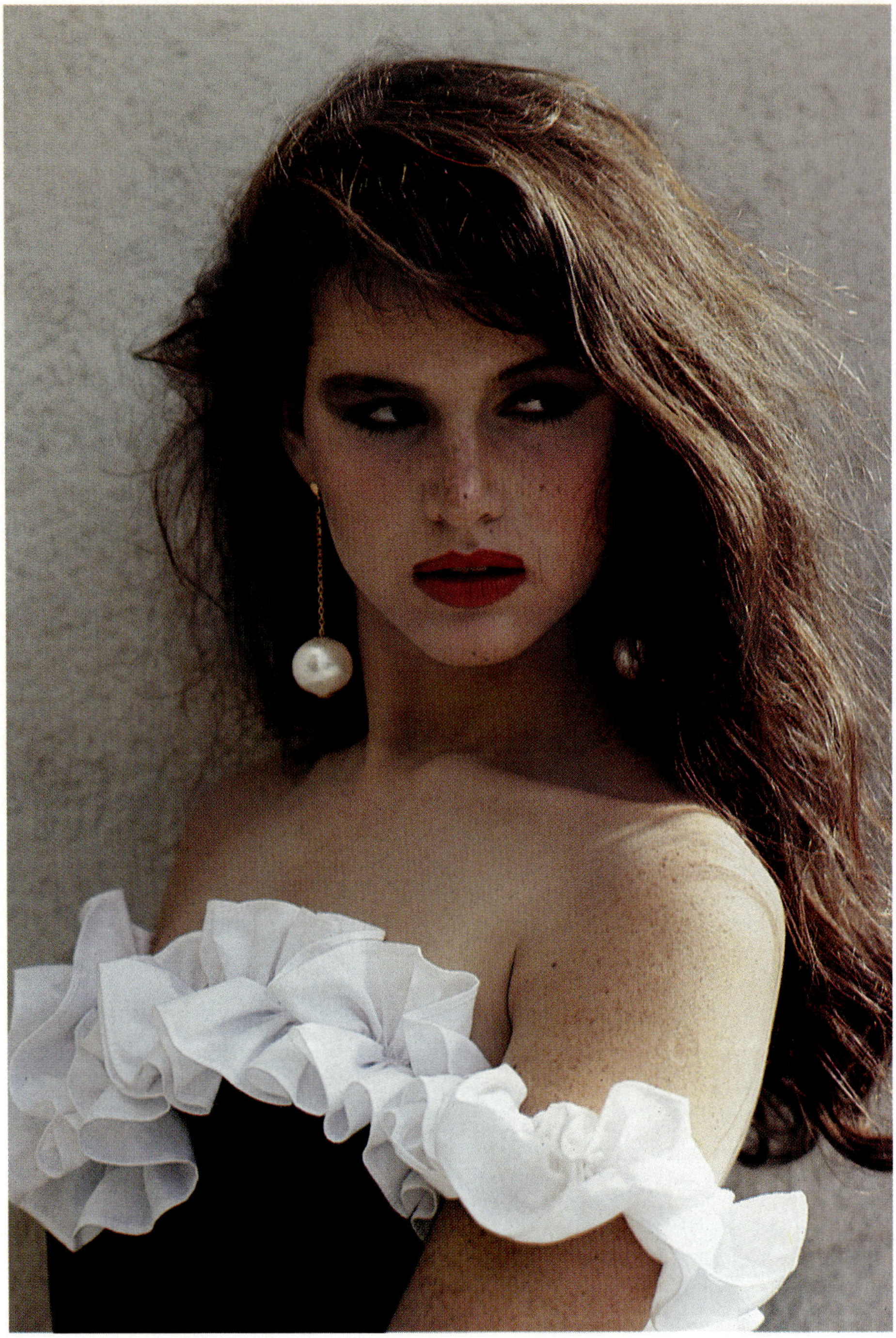

On sunny days in large cities like New York, I like to shoot on streets adjacent to tall, light-colored buildings. The sunlight reflected from the expansive building surfaces yields a beautifully soft, yet directional, light that's ideal for beauty and glamour photography.

I used the same principle to make this indirect-sunlight image on a street in Beverly Hills, California. The direct sunlight was too harsh and struck the subject from too high an angle to be useful as main-light source. I found an ideal location for bouncing the light from three adjacent walls. I positioned my model with her back to a wall uniformly illuminated by skylight and reflected sunlight. Two frontal walls reflected the sunlight onto the model, providing soft and uniform illumination.

I brought the subject forward from the background wall sufficiently to allow the direct overhead sunlight to reach her hair and arm.

A word of warning: When you're making color photos, the reflective walls you use should be white or light gray. If the walls were colored, they would reflect that color onto the subject, causing an unwanted color imbalance in the image. □

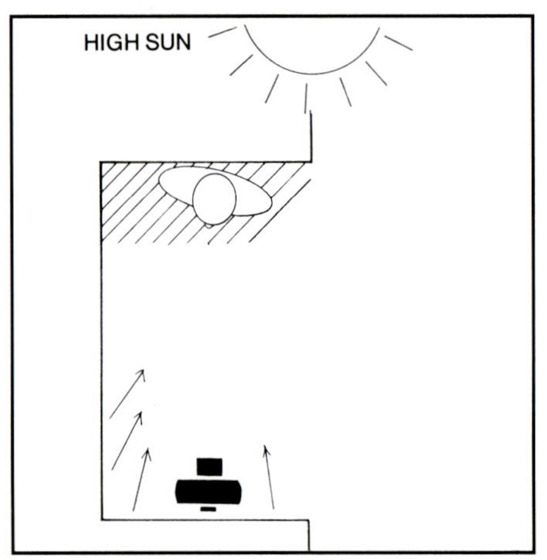

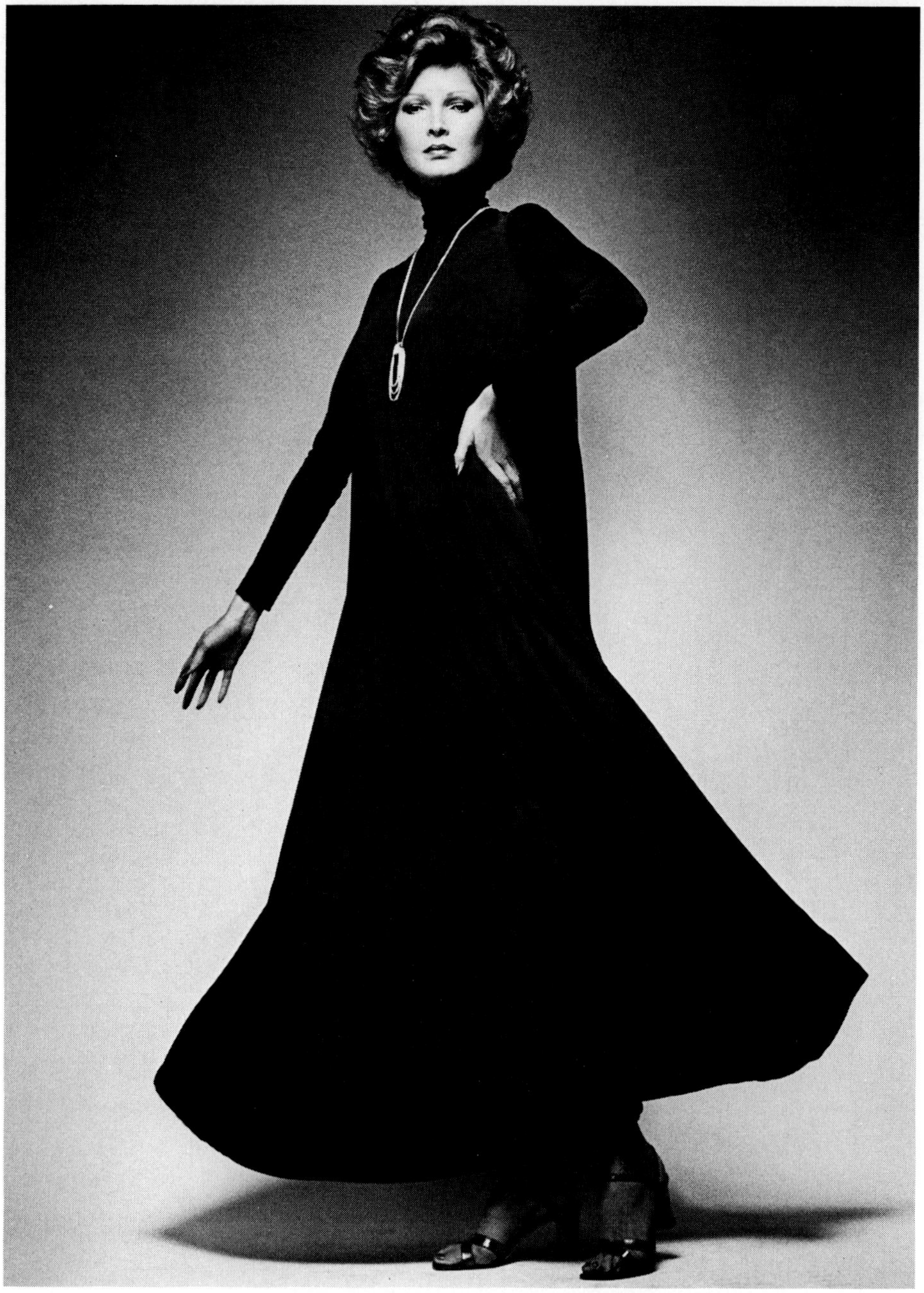

13

Subject: Professional model
Client: Garfinckles, Inc.
Ad Agency: Barra Graphics, New York City
Art Director: Bob Barra
Location: Gary Bernstein Studio, New York City
Camera: Hasselblad 500EL/M
Lens: 80mm *f*-2.8 Zeiss Planar
Lighting: One 1200-watt-second Thomastrobe electronic flash unit
Light Control: One 40-inch silvered umbrella
Film: Kodak Tri-X Pan Professional
Exposure Metering: Wein Electronic-Flash Meter, incident-light mode
Exposure: *f*-16 (shutter at 1/250 second)

This classic fashion image was produced as an ad for a Washington, D.C. department store. It shows the elegance you can convey with single-source lighting. To make the image, I selected the 2-1/4-inch-square format instead of 35mm. The larger negative ensures the best possible enlarged image. Clients also prefer to select from the larger contact prints produced from these negatives.

I used a standard-focal-length lens for two reasons: The lens elongated the model's form without the perspective distortion caused by a wide-angle lens. The lens also provided extensive depth of field, allowing the subject freedom of movement during the session. My camera position was at floor level.

Notice the movement in the model's gown. I asked her to stand with her back to the camera and then spin toward me. At the end of her 180° spin, she stopped but the dress continued to swirl. I exposed the film at the precise moment the gown had opened to its fullest spread.

The main light—a 1200-watt-second flash, bounced from a 40-inch silver umbrella—was placed on a boom stand about eight feet in front of the model. The apparent vertical cone of light was caused by the very high placement of the main light.

Few faces—especially those with deep-set eyes—can accept such a high lighting angle. In this case, I had the perfect face to work with. □

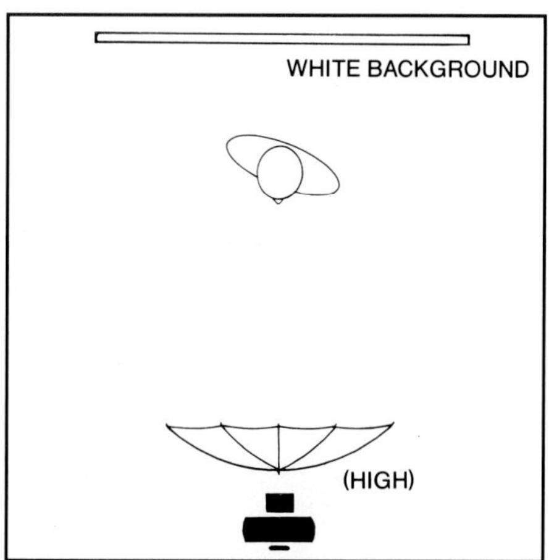

14

Subject: Professional model
Client: Winona School of Professional Photography
Location: Winona School of Professional Photography, Mt. Prospect, Illinois
Camera: Nikon F3
Lens: 55mm *f*-3.5 Micro-Nikkor
Lighting: Three 400-watt-second Photogenic Porta-Master electronic flash units
Light Control: One 32-inch Halo on main light; two 45-inch Halos on background lights
Film: Kodachrome 25
Exposure Metering: Minolta Auto-Flash III, incident-light mode
Exposure: *f*-5.6 (shutter at 1/60 second)

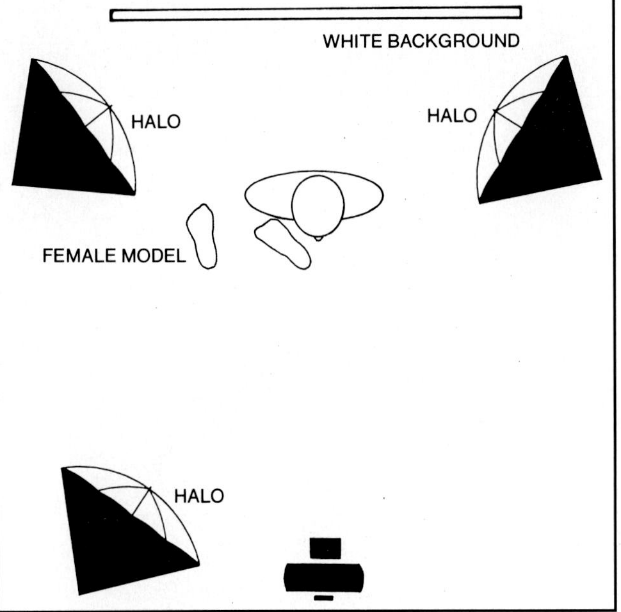

I made this shot while teaching a class at the Winona School of Professional Photography. I love teaching. The contact it provides with other photographers, both young and old, is stimulating. Teaching also affords me an opportunity to add special new photographs to my own portfolio. And, as this example shows, I also have a lot of fun at these sessions!

I decided to exploit photographically the decidedly adolescent manner conveyed by my young male model. I thought the sophomoric "leg-grabbing" antics would complement perfectly his dressy, "preppy" attire.

The main light was a single Halo, placed to the left of the camera. Two background lights in 45-inch Halo umbrellas were positioned to overexpose the main light by about 1 exposure step to provide a pure white background. □

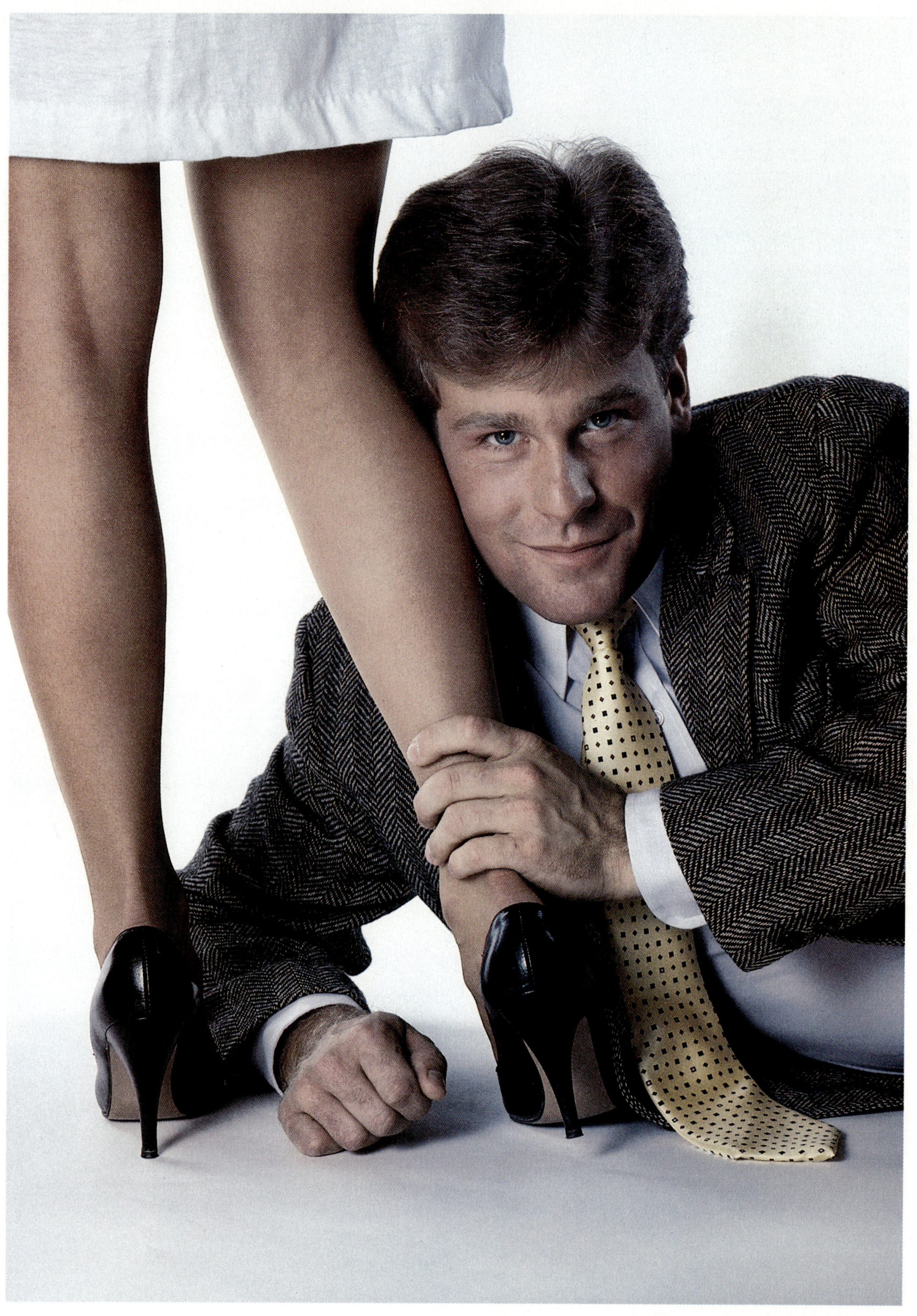

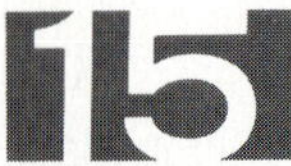

Subject: Professional model
Client: Hart, Schaffner and Marx, Inc.
Art Director: Scott Davis
Location: Gary Bernstein Studio, Los Angeles, California
Camera: Nikon F2AS
Lens: 85mm *f*-1.8 Auto-Nikkor
Lighting: One 600-watt-second electronic flash in umbrella
Film: Kodachrome 25
Exposure Metering: Minolta Auto-Flash II, incident-light mode
Exposure: *f*-8 (shutter at 1/60 second)

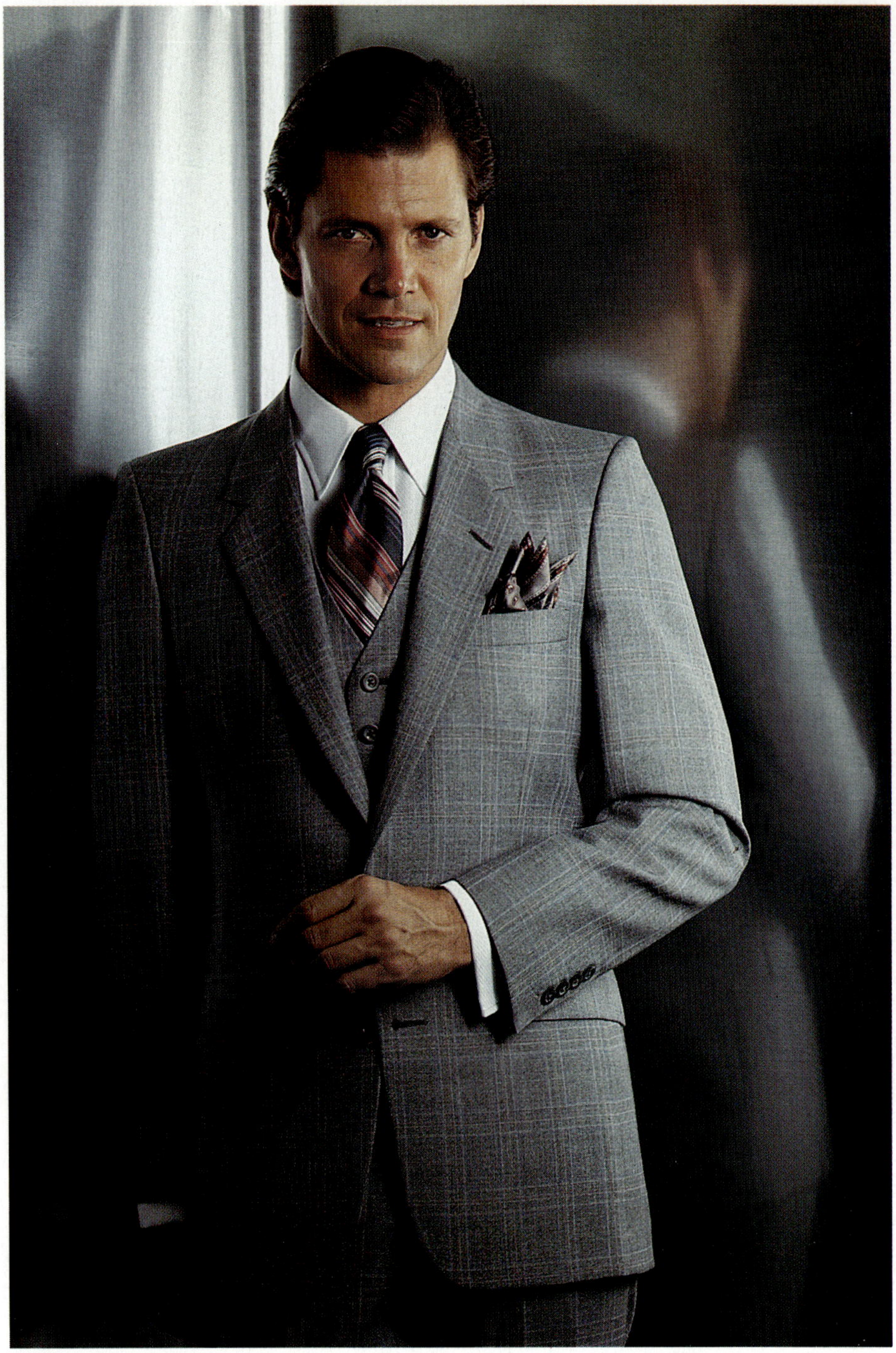

Reflective mylar is perhaps the most versatile of all background materials. It's unfortunate that, so far, I've been unable to find rolls wider than four feet. For this photo, I used a long piece of silver mylar horizontally in a corner of my studio. The mylar extended from just above the model's head to a couple of inches below the bottom of the frame. To maintain the composition accurately, I placed my camera on a sturdy Gitzo tripod.

Reflective surfaces are beautiful. However, they can cause unwanted reflections in the form of flare. To avoid this, I placed the main light well to the right of the camera. When using highly reflective surfaces, I consider modeling lights essential. They enable you to view the lighting effect before exposure. Also, remember the basic law of physics: The angle of reflection equals the angle of light incidence.

The main light bounced off the background to the model's right, producing beautiful edge lighting along the side of the face. Notice, incidentally, that the highlight side of the model's face and the highlight on the background are almost equally bright—an indication of the reflective efficiency of silver mylar. □

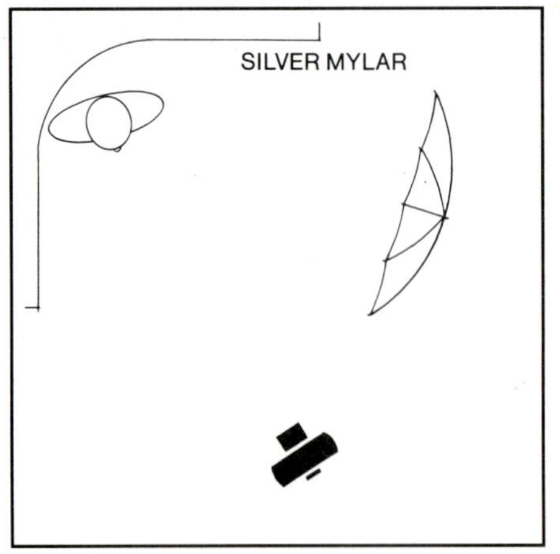

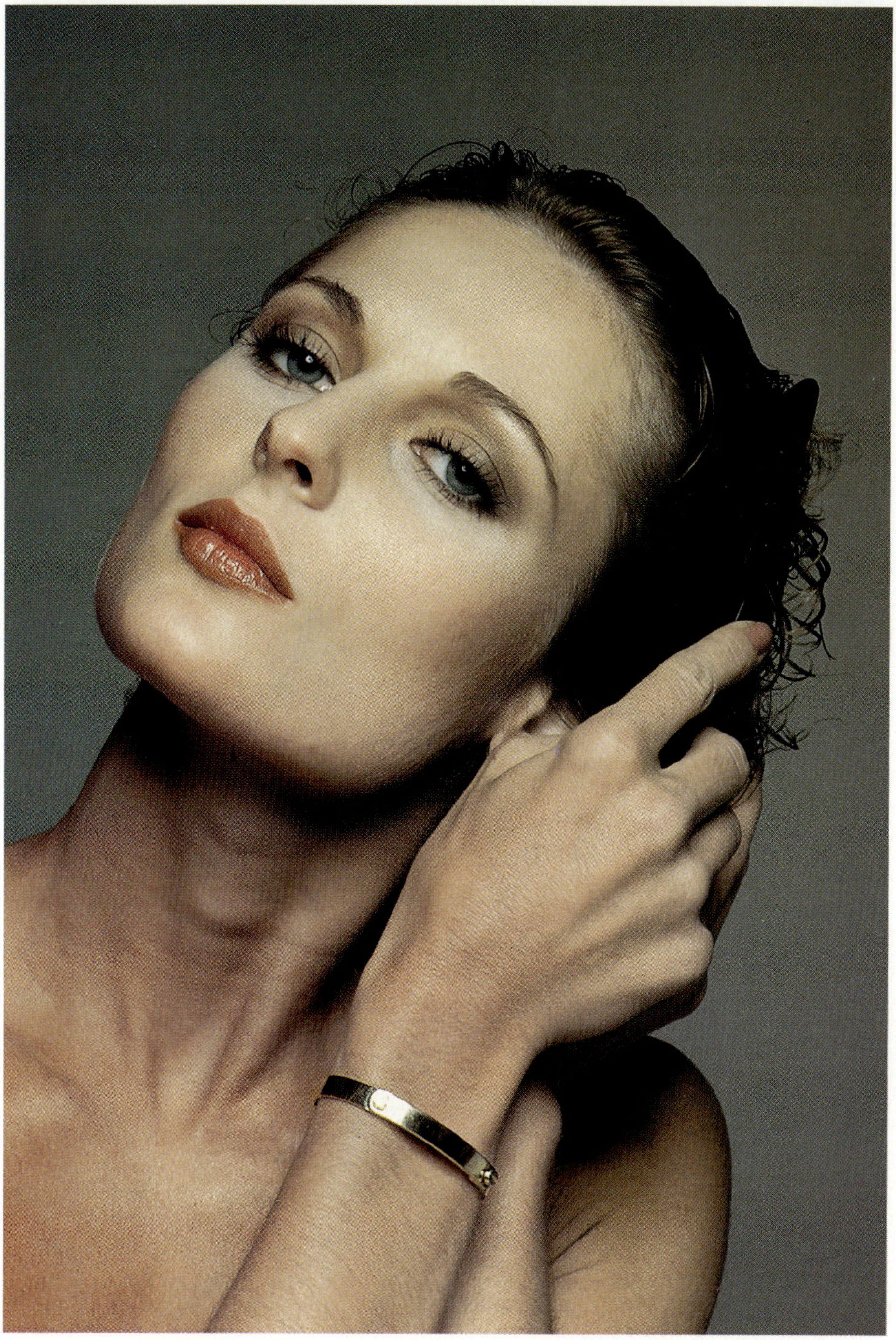

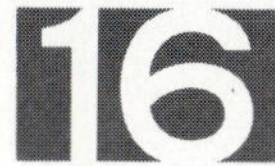

Subject: Professional model
Client: Revlon, Inc.
Ad Agency: 50th Floor Workshop
Art Directors: Mirella Forlani Buchanon and John Revson
Location: Gary Bernstein Studio, New York City
Camera: Nikon F2
Lens: 85mm *f*-1.8 Auto-Nikkor
Lighting: One 1250-watt-second Rollei electronic flash unit in pan reflector
Film: Kodachrome 25
Exposure Metering: Minolta Auto-Flash II, incident-light mode
Exposure: *f*-16 (shutter at 1/60 second)

Beauty photographs are used to advertise a wide variety of products—not only those associated directly with cosmetics and hair products. This is because of the universal appeal of a beautiful face.

This photo was shot for Revlon to promote a special offer on Aldo Cipullo's *Friendship Bracelet.*

To avoid perspective distortion in the head-and-shoulders shot, I used a short telephoto lens. I used a small lens aperture to get sufficient depth of field to allow the model some freedom of movement without giving me excessive focusing concerns.

I wanted the clean, crisp quality of Kodachrome 25 to record the model's flawless complexion. To be able to shoot at *f*-22 with this slow film, I needed a lot of light. I used a 1250-watt-second Rollei flash in pan reflector at a distance of about four feet from the subject.

The model was approximately four feet from the white, seamless background. The main light fell off by 2 exposure steps, accounting for the medium-gray background requested by the client.

Normally, I avoid photographing the back of a woman's hand. It tends to look broad and unfeminine. In this case, I had to shoot the back of the hand to display the bracelet clearly. By placing the main light to the left of the camera, I achieved a 1/2-step light falloff on the hand, giving it less emphasis than the face.

Before photographing, I sprayed the bracelet with a dulling spray to tone down specular reflections. □

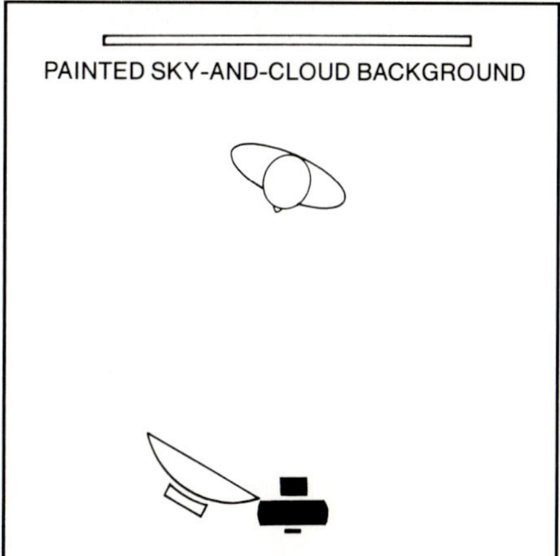

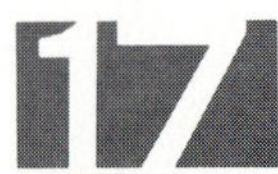

Subject: Professional model
Client: Winona School of Professional Photography
Location: Winona School of Professional Photography, Mt. Prospect, Illinois
Camera: Nikon F3
Lens: 180mm *f*-2.8
Lighting: Three 400-watt-second Photogenic Porta-Master electronic flash units
Light Control: One 32-inch Halo for main light; two 45-inch Halos for background lights
Film: Kodachrome 25
Exposure Metering: Minolta Auto-Flash III, incident-light mode
Exposure: *f*-5.6 (shutter at 1/60 second)

I used three Halo lights—one as main light and the other two on the background. The background Halos were set for about 1 step more exposure than the main light, giving a pure white background. This was essential for the graphic effect I wanted to achieve with the hat, face, earrings and checkered outfit.

The camera angle was low. I directed the model to look at the main light above the camera rather than at the camera lens. On viewing her eyes through the camera, however, I saw too much white below the irises. I then asked her to look about six inches below the main light. This slight change centered the irises in the eyes beautifully. Because the model doesn't make eye contact with the camera lens, the viewer of the photograph is able to study the subject without inhibition. □

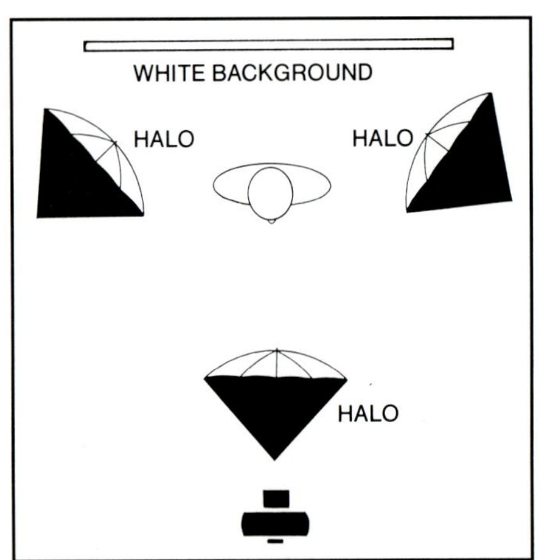

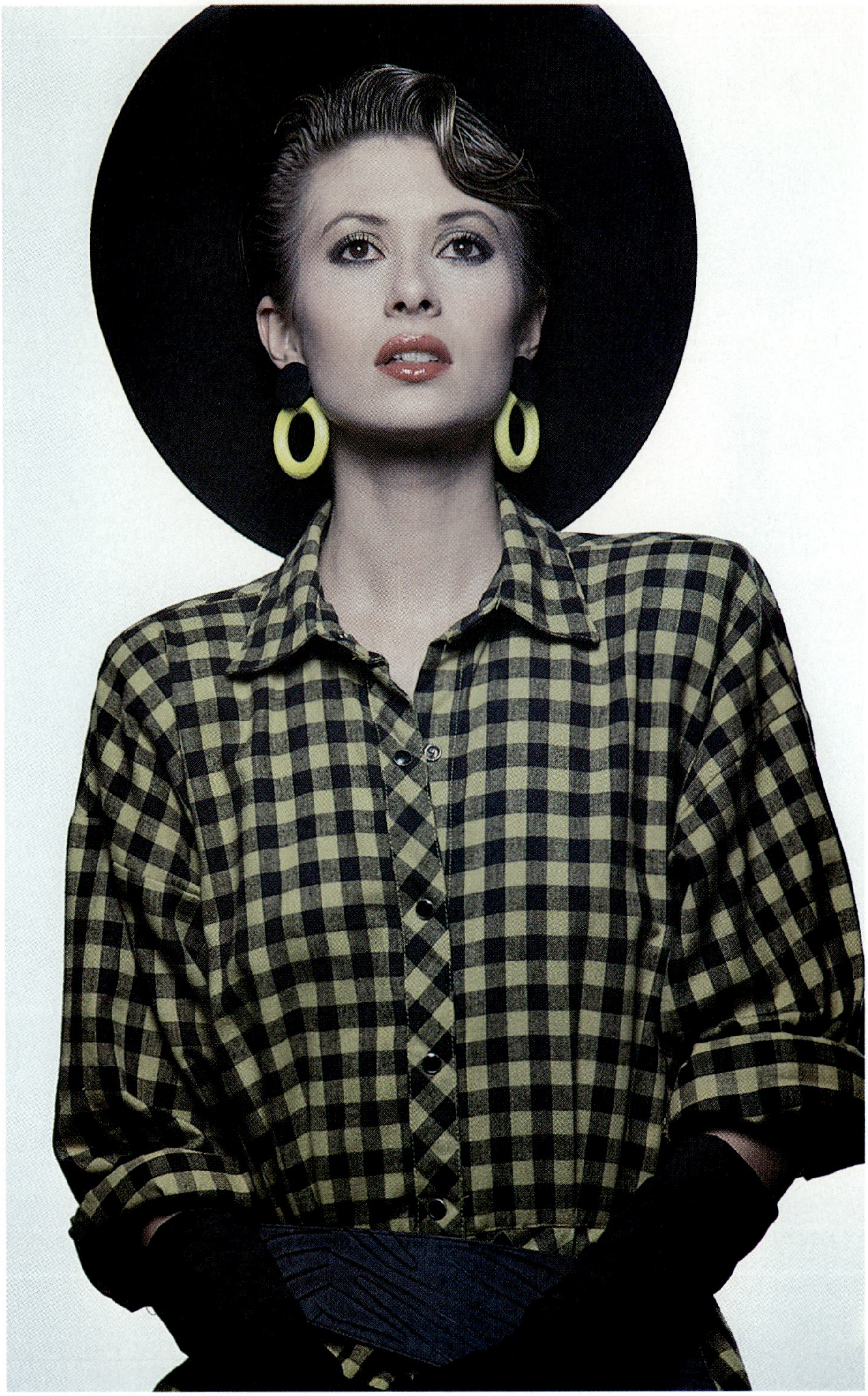

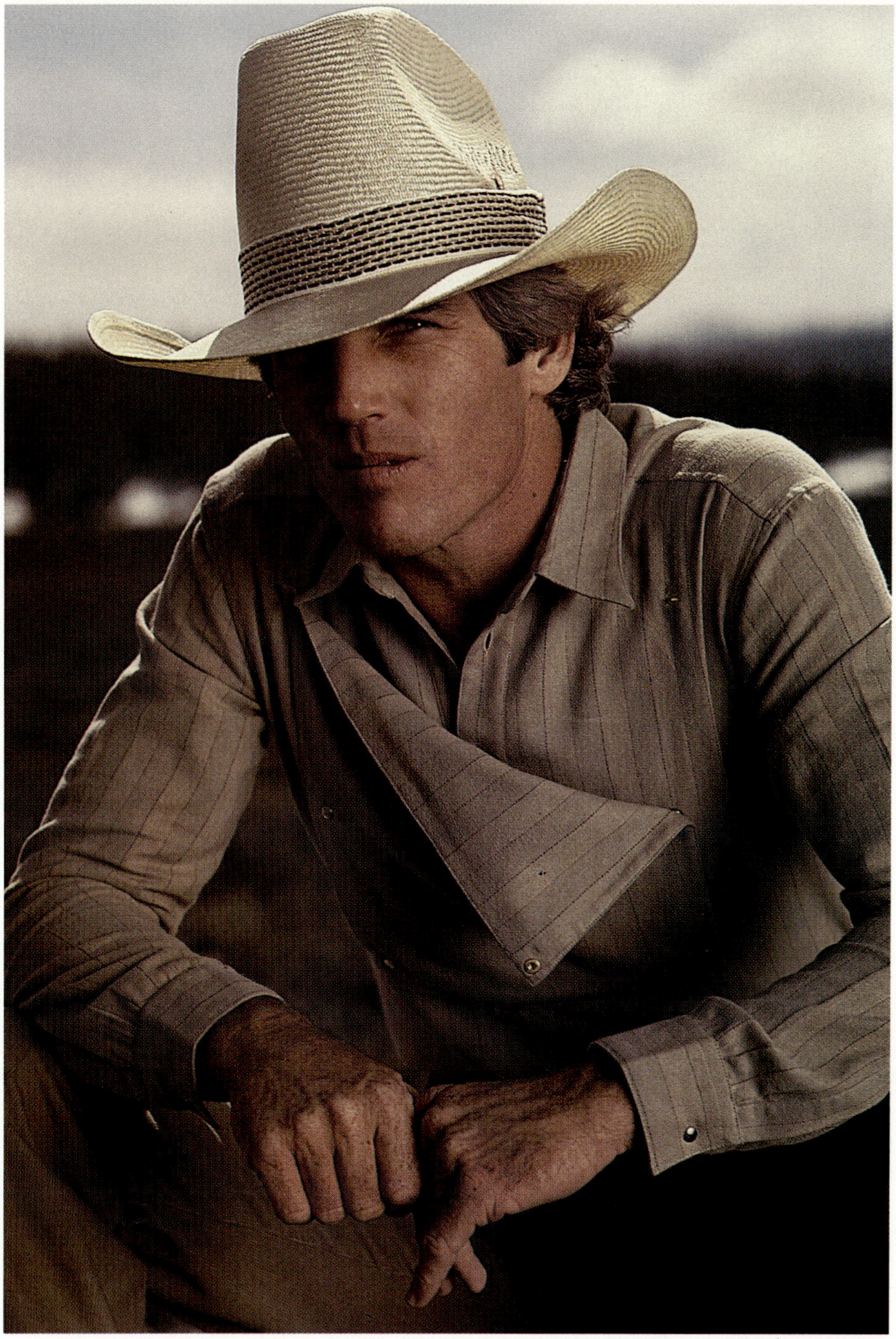

18

Subject: Professional model
Client: Cone Mills, Inc.
Ad Agency: The Marschalk Company, Inc.
Art Directors: Noel Rosenbower and Barry Pohorence
Location: Reno, Nevada
Camera: Nikon F2AS
Lens: 50mm *f*-1.4 Auto-Nikkor
Lighting: Mid-afternoon hazy sun
Light Control: Gold Rocaflector
Film: Kodachrome 25
Exposure Metering: Minolta Auto-Flash II, incident-light mode
Exposure: 1/250 second at *f*-5.6

There was a glorious time when client budgets seemed limitless. If something was needed, the money was available to do it—and do it in the best possible way. Before making this shot, for example, I had photographed a series of eight fashion ads for Cone Mills in sunny and warm Los Angeles. We had two outfits left to shoot—a ski outfit and the Marlboro cowboy shirt shown here. Someone suggested that we "sure could use some snow" for the ski-outfit shot. So we dashed to the airport and hopped on a plane for Lake Tahoe. After completing the ski shot, we drove to Reno, where we produced this final photograph.

It was cold and overcast in Reno. From time to time, hazy afternoon sunlight peeking through the clouds. The natural light was wintery and blue—similar to open shade. I placed a large, highly reflective gold reflector on the ground in front of the model. As the sun appeared—rimming the top of the hat—the gold tonality was reflected into the subject's face, giving warmth to the resulting image. The reflector also bounced a specular catchlight into the model's left eye. This little sparkle is critical to the photograph's success. □

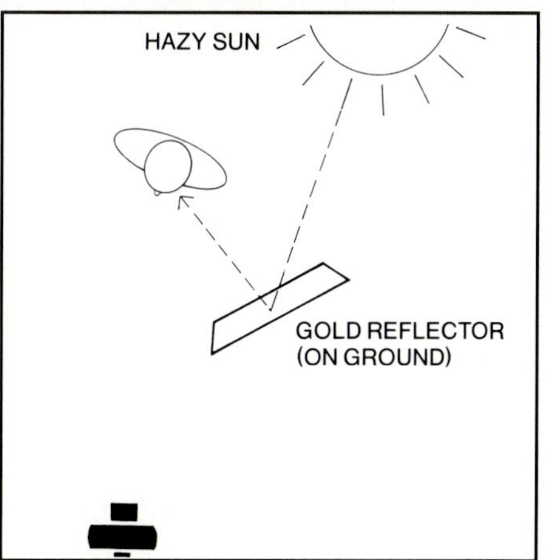

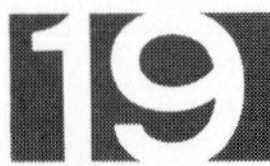

Subject: Six professional models
Client: Winona School of Professional Photography
Location: Winona School of Professional Photography, Mt. Prospect, Illinois
Camera: Nikon F3
Lens: 55mm *f*-2.8 Micro-Nikkor
Lighting: Two 2400-watt-second Speedotron flash units with four 1200-watt-second flash heads
Light Control: 32-inch Halo on main light; barn doors on back and side lights; Photogenic Silfoil silver reflector
Film: Kodachrome 25
Exposure Metering: Minolta Auto-Flash III, incident-light mode
Exposure: *f*-16 (shutter at 1/60 second)

I made this photo while I was teaching at The Winona School of Professional Photography. The models, provided by The Arlene Wilson-Casablancas Agency in Milwaukee, Wisconsin, couldn't have been better to work with. They were wonderful! It's not easy holding a precise pose for an extended period of time— especially when there are to be six models in the same image.

I wanted the entire image to be in sharp focus. To get the needed depth of field, I used 4800 watt-seconds of lighting power, allowing exposure at *f*-16. I connected two flash heads to each of two 2400-watt-second generators. Each head was used at its full 1200 watt-seconds of power. One flash head, placed in a 32-inch Halo umbrella, was the main light. Another provided the rim lighting from the rear.

I connected two flash heads with narrow-angle reflectors and barn doors to the second 2400-watt-second power pack. These lights were positioned to either side of the set to give additional edge lighting to the three models at the rear. This helped to graphically separate their forms from the black background. The barn doors confined the rim lighting to the edges of the models, preventing the light from striking my lens and thus avoiding flare. The edge lights provided 1-1/2 exposure steps more light than the main-light Halo gave to the subjects.

When I'm working with a large group—especially if the posing is going to be difficult—I try to have the basic lighting set up before placing the models on the set. The placement of the lighting for this shot took about an hour. The photography took about 10 minutes. □

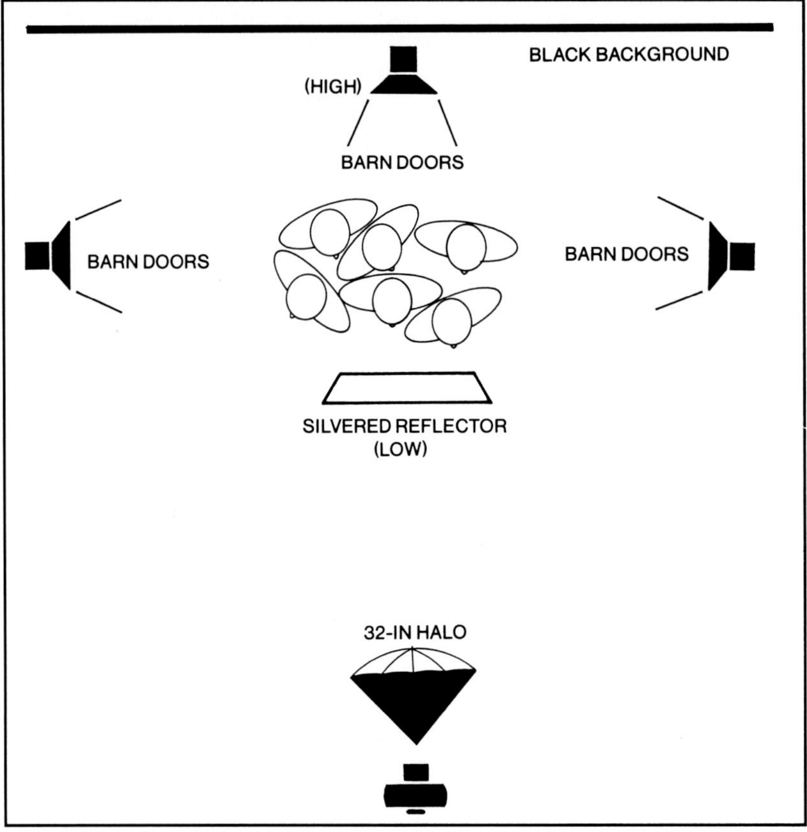

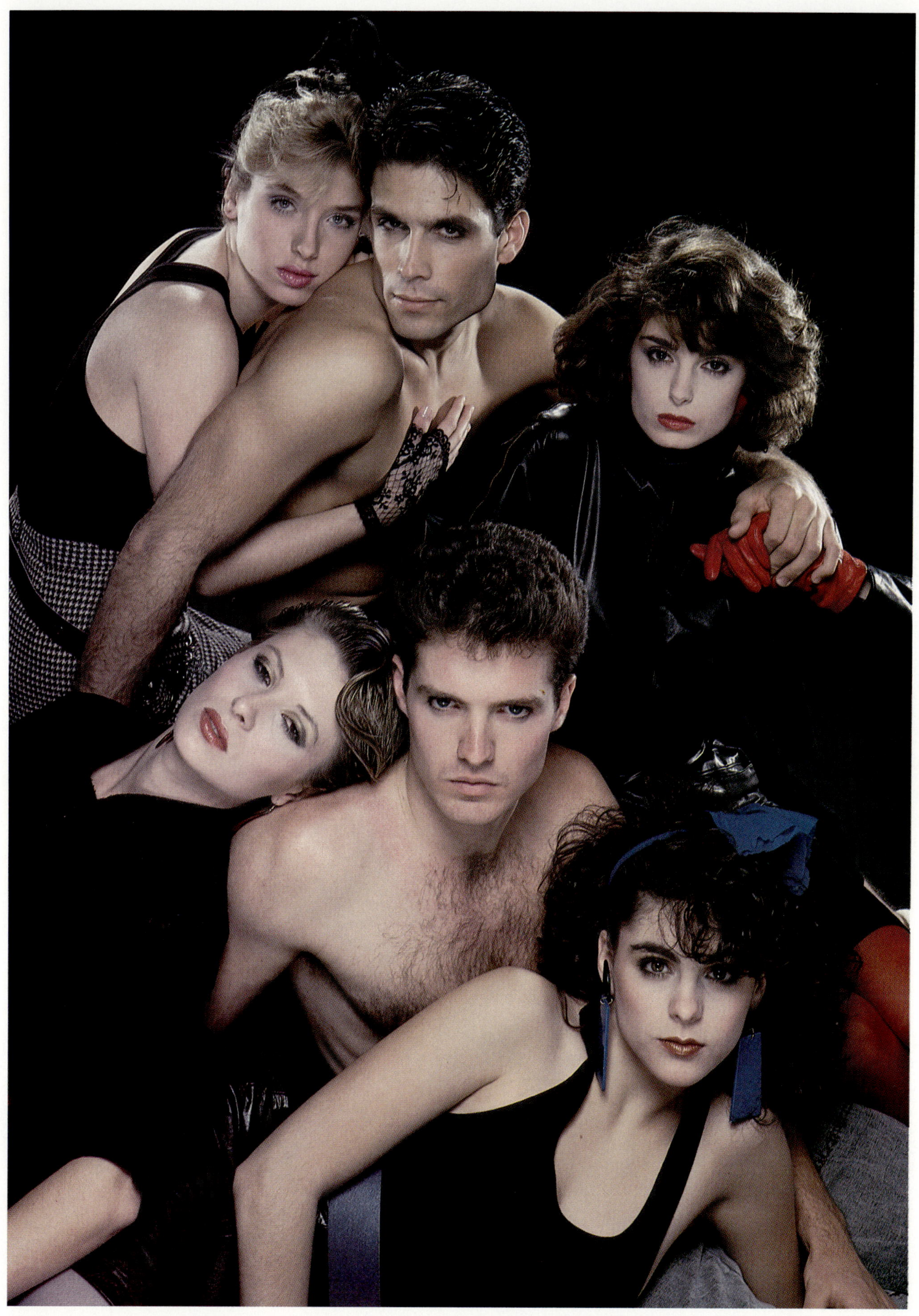

Subject: Professional model
Location: Central Park, New York City
Camera: Nikon F
Lens: 105mm *f*-2.5 Auto-Nikkor
Lighting: Open shade
Light Control: Small silver reflector on stand
Film: Kodak Tri-X Pan
Exposure Metering: Gossen Luna Pro, incident light mode
Exposure: 1/250 second at *f*-8

This shot is part of a test session I conducted in my early years in New York City. It was raining at the time the photo was taken, so I placed my subject under the thick, protective overhang of trees in front of the Plaza Hotel. By asking my subject to lift her head, I was able to achieve beautiful facial modeling from the open sky area.

Unfortunately, the top of the dark hair was lost against the dark background. I placed a portable 27-inch silvered reflector on a light stand to the right of the camera. The reflector bounced a bit of edge light along the left side of the model's hair, but the top of the head still lacked a clear outline. My subject mentioned that she had sunglasses with her. Holding them on top of her head provided the needed graphic separation. □

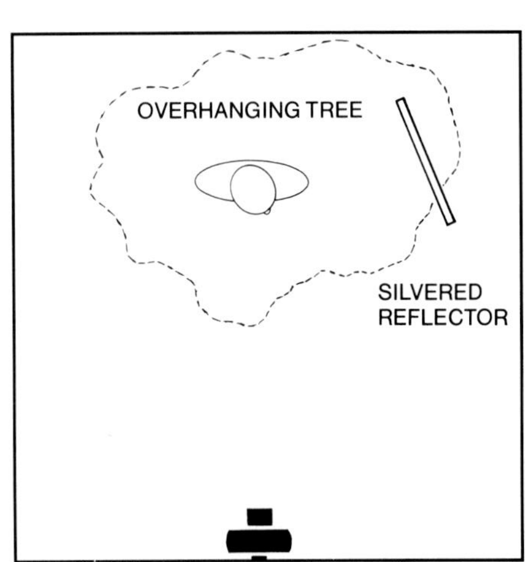

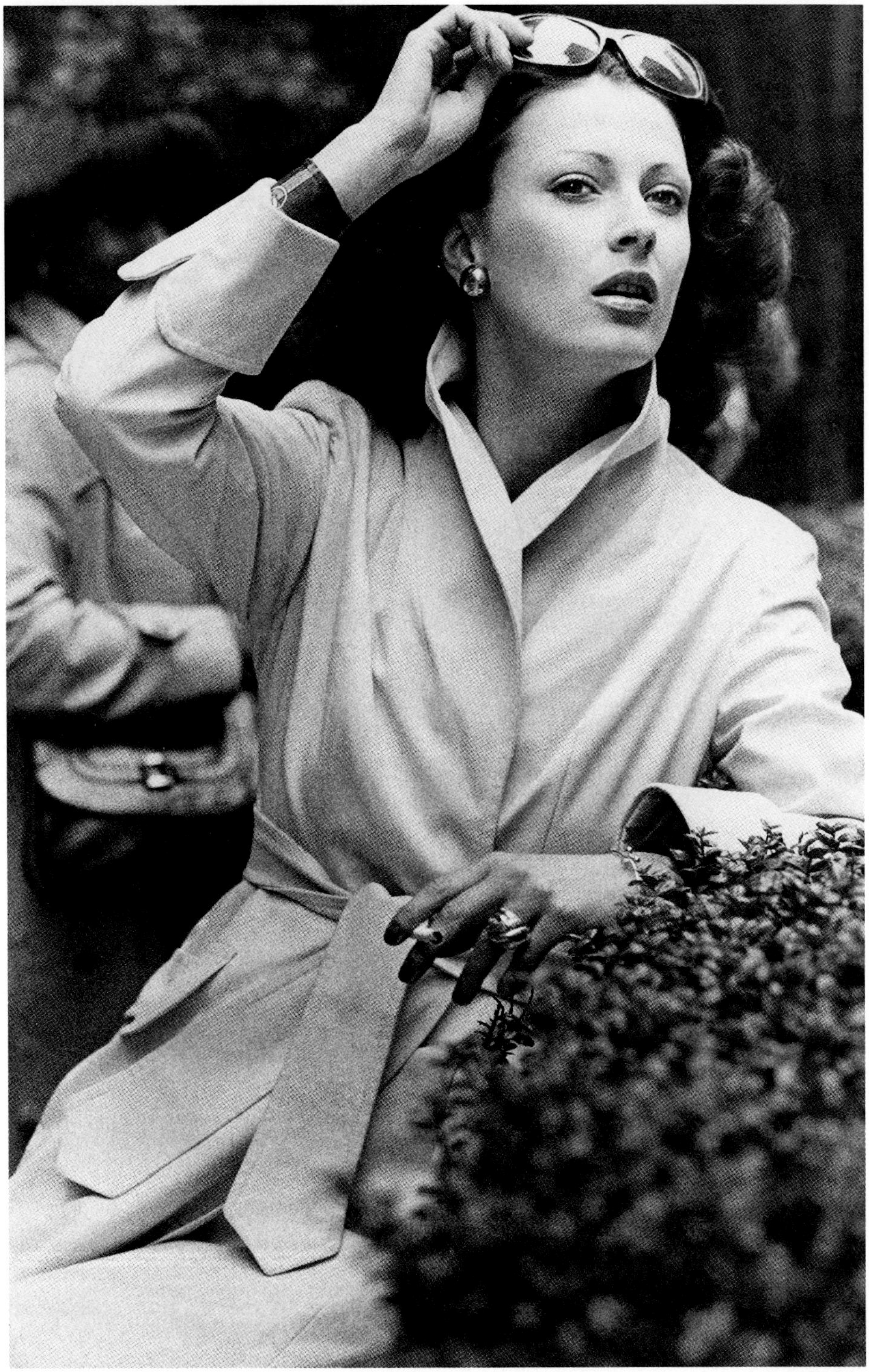

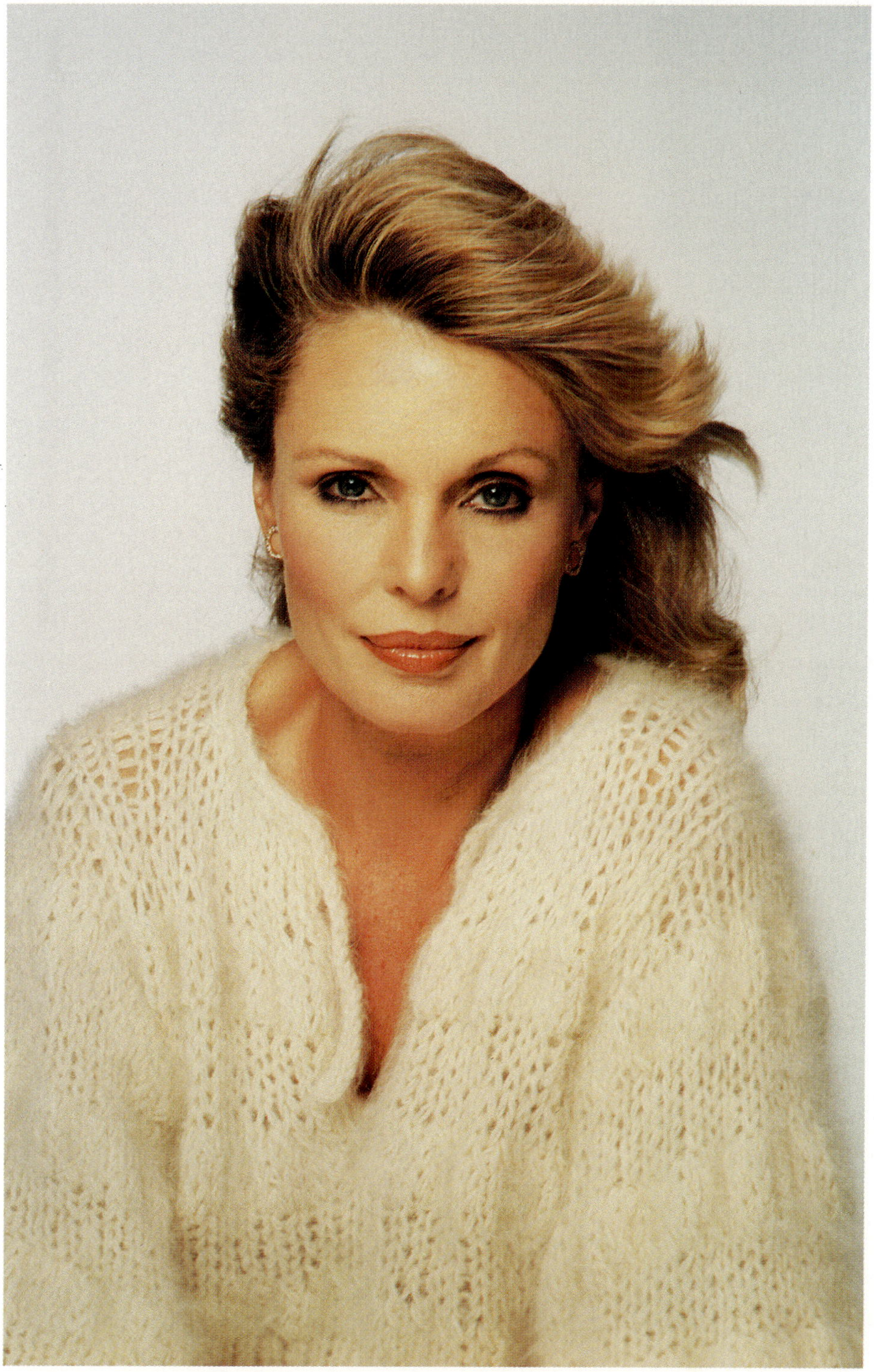

Subject: Rosemarie Stack
Location: Gary Bernstein Studio, Los Angeles, California
Camera: Nikon F3
Lens: 85mm *f*-1.8 Auto-Nikkor
Lighting: Three 800-watt-second Photogenic Versatron electronic flash units
Light Control: Pan reflector on main light; 40-inch white umbrellas on two background lights; one small Photogenic Silfoil silvered reflector
Film: Kodachrome 25
Exposure Metering: Minolta Auto-Flash III, incident-light mode
Exposure: *f*-8 to *f*-11 (shutter at 1/60 second)

This portrait of beautiful Rosemarie Stack, perfume entrepreneur and wife of Robert Stack, adorns the living room of Bob and Rosemarie's Bel Air home. The photo was taken in my Los Angeles studio against a continuous, white background illuminated by two 800-watt-second flash heads in umbrellas.

The background lights were set to deliver 1/2 exposure step more light than the main light in pan reflector. Below Rosemarie's face, I placed a small Photogenic Silfoil reflector to soften shadows slightly.

Rosemarie was posed on the studio floor for the shot, leaning toward the camera. I, too, was on the floor, assuming a low camera angle. Rosemarie's white sweater and golden tresses frame her fine features. The gentle breeze of an electric fan helped to complete a vision of loveliness. □

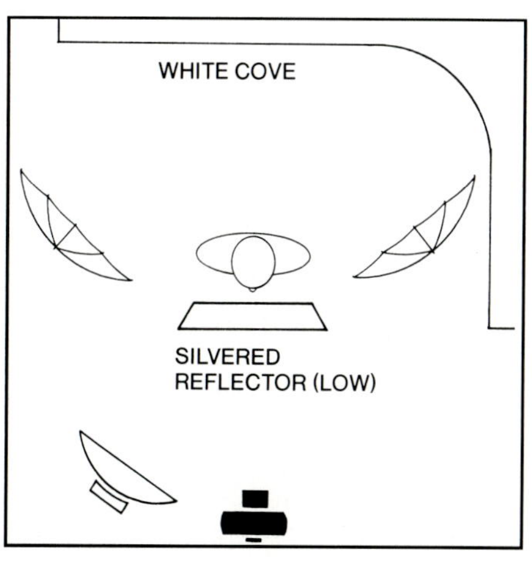

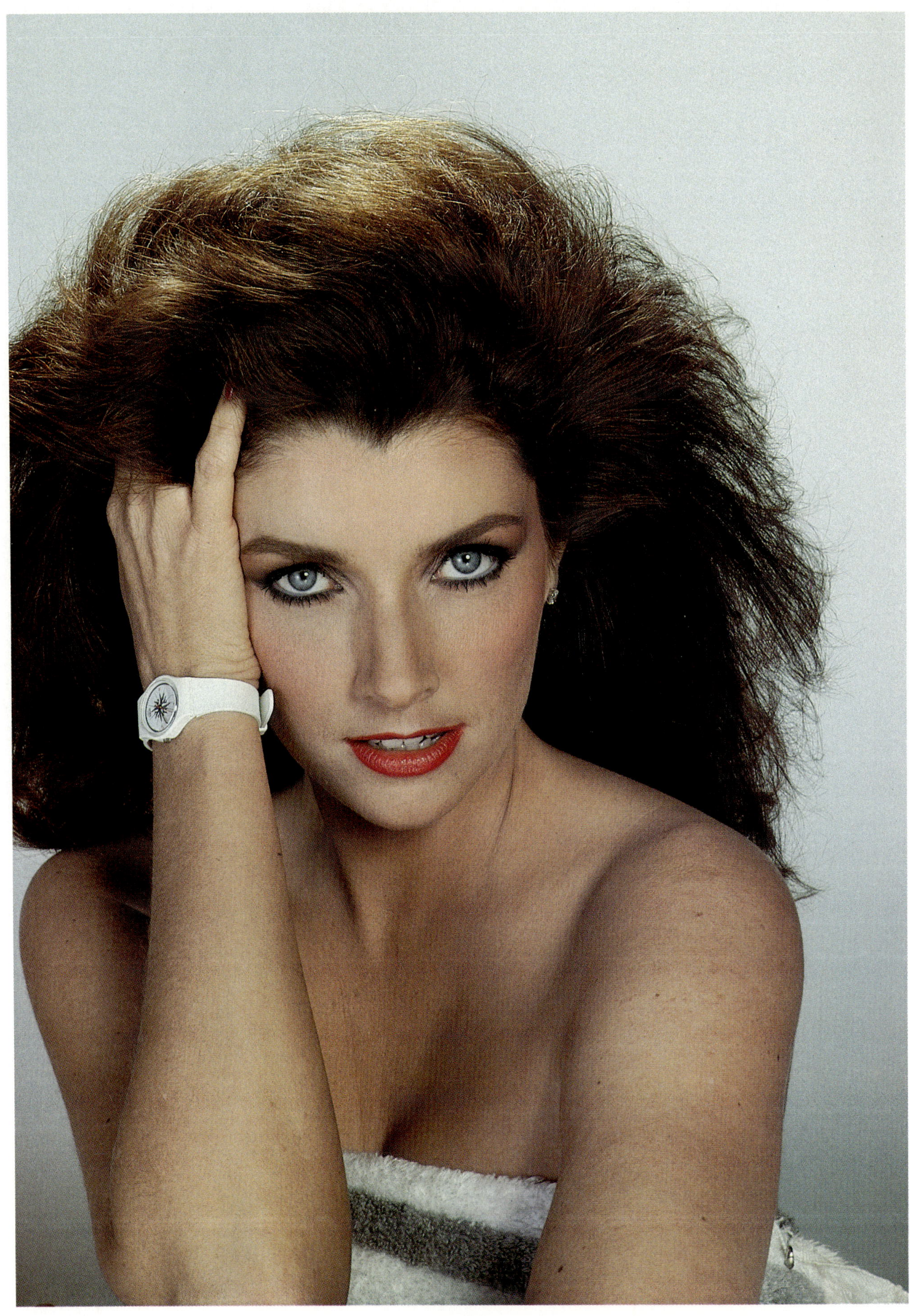

Subject: Morgan Brittany
Client: Swatch Watch USA, Inc.
Location: Gary Bernstein Studio, Los Angeles, California
Camera: Nikon F3
Lens: 85mm *f*-1.4 Auto-Nikkor
Lighting: Six flash heads, powered by three 800-watt-second Photogenic Versatron electronic flash units
Light Control: One pan reflector and two softboxes for main lighting; two wide-angle reflectors for background lights; one grid spot for hair light
Film: Kodachrome 25
Exposure Metering: Minolta Auto-Flash III, incident-light mode
Exposure: *f*-11 to *f*-16 (shutter at 1/60 second)

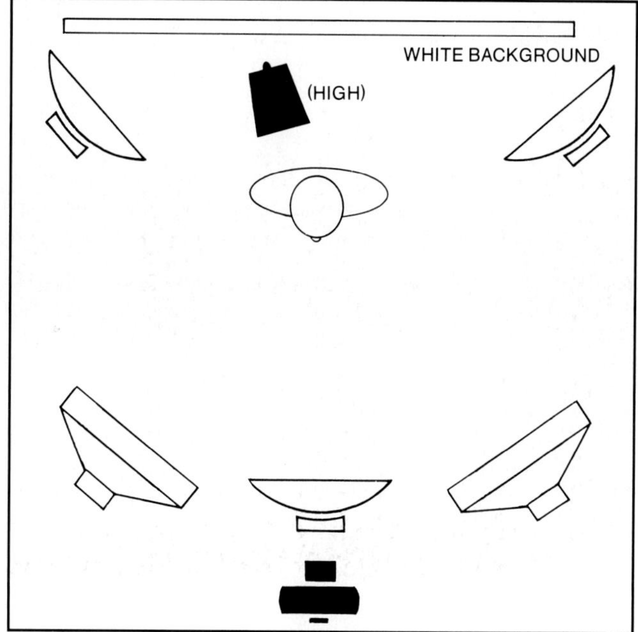

I used six lights to make this photograph of lovely Morgan Brittany. To produce soft, frontal lighting, I used one flash in an 18-inch pan reflector at camera position, flanked by two medium-sized softboxes. This arrangement provided relatively soft lighting on the watch surface, while adding sparkle and large catchlights to Morgan's blue eyes.

Notice that Morgan's face received more exposure than her body. This was done to direct viewer attention to the face and the watch. To get abrupt light falloff like this, place the main light very close to the subject.

The uniform, light-gray background tone was created by lighting white, seamless paper with two flash heads in wide-angle reflectors and underexposing by 1/2 exposure step. The hair light delivered 1 exposure step more light than the main light. The final touch of glitter, however, was provided by Morgan herself. □

Subject: Actress/model (Private portrait session)
Location: Gary Bernstein Studio, Los Angeles, California
Camera: Nikon F3
Lens: 105mm *f*-1.8 Auto-Nikkor
Lighting: One 800-watt-second electronic flash in pan reflector; one 400-watt-second umbrella fill light
Film: Kodachrome 25
Exposure Metering: Minolta Auto-Flash III, incident-light mode
Exposure: *f*-8 (shutter at 1/60 second)

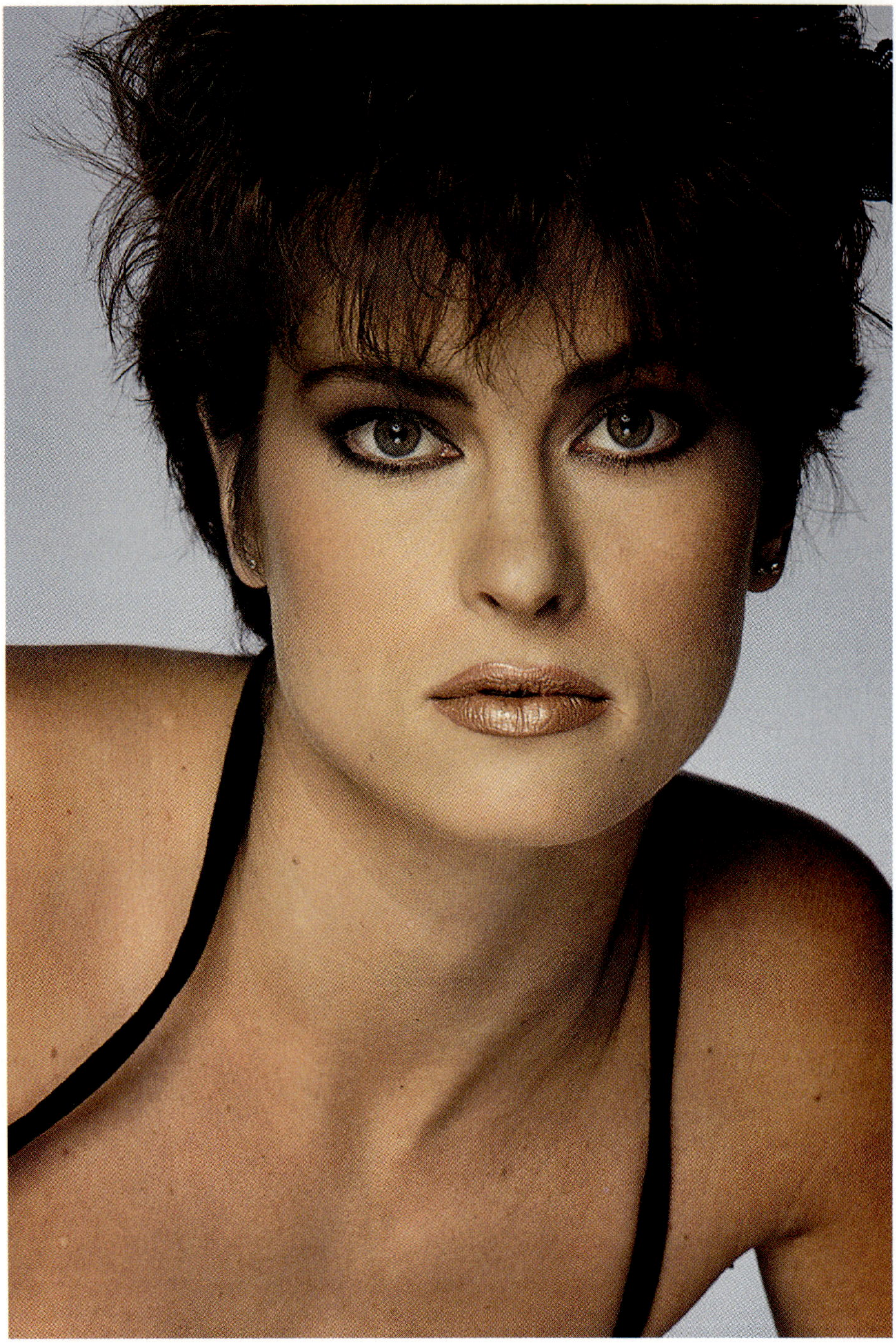

I took this photo as part of a portfolio series commissioned by the subject. I used a basic two-light setup. The main Versatron 800 was bounced from a pan reflector. I also used a Porta-Master 400, bounced from a small umbrella, as fill light.

I positioned the main light on a boom stand in front of the subject. The light was set to deliver an *f*-5.6 to *f*-8 exposure on Kodachrome 25 film. To brighten the subject's pretty eyes and lighten the eyelid area, I placed the fill light slightly below camera position. The two lights together gave an *f*-8 meter reading.

Every lighting change, addition or subtraction alters the resulting image. Consequently, an infinite variety of lighting effects is at your disposal. Lighting decisions are personal and the only way to plan lighting is by evaluating its effect on each specific subject.

There are times when a separate fill source is more valuable than a silver reflector. The difference is primarily in the direction of the light. Reflectors are frequently placed to provide fill light from below. Light from a secondary source, such as the umbrella source used here, is usually more directional and from a higher angle.

Notice that the model is leaning forward. She was lying on the floor with her weight on one forearm. The resultant weight shift gives the image a sense of motion.

The gray background is a result of 1-1/2 exposure steps less light on white, seamless background paper than on the subject. □

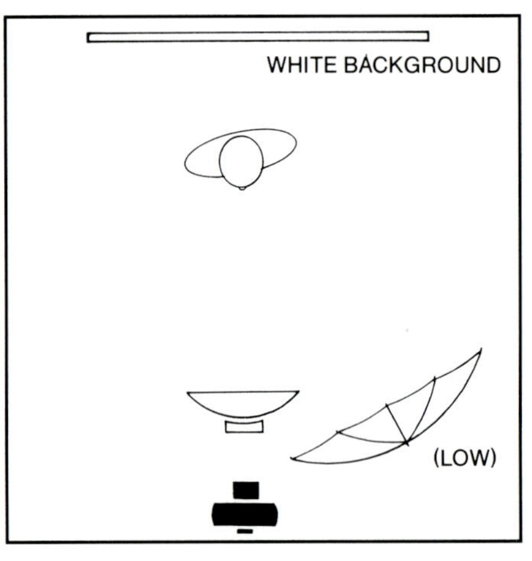

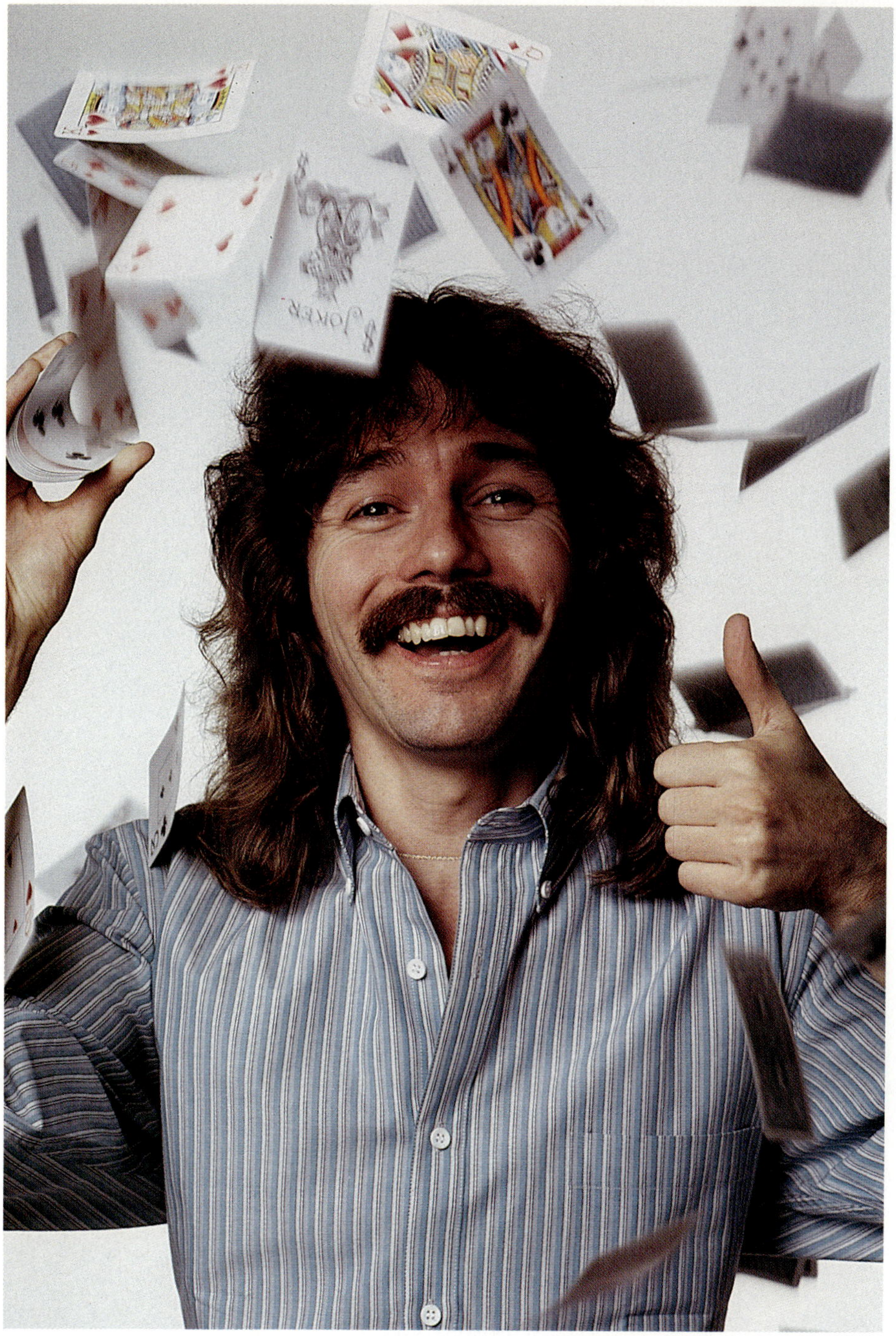

Subject: Doug Henning
Client: Jean-Paul Germain, Ltd.
Location: Gary Bernstein Studio, Los Angeles, California
Camera: Nikon F3
Lens: 105mm *f*-2.5 Auto-Nikkor
Lighting: Three Balcar 600-watt-second electronic flash units
Light Control: Three 40-inch white umbrellas
Film: Kodachrome 64
Exposure Metering: Minolta Auto-Flash II, incident-light mode
Exposure: *f*-11 (shutter at 1/60 second)

There are relatively few situations in which precise electronic-flash duration is critical. However, it was an important consideration for this shot of Doug Henning, that genius of magic. I wanted a flash duration short enough to freeze Doug's image, yet long enough to allow the moving cards to blur. A Balcar Monobloc, used at full-power, has a duration of about 1/800 second. The speed was perfect for the desired effect with the fast-flying cards.

I used a 600-watt-second main light in umbrella, mounted on a boom stand in front of Doug. The light was positioned close enough to Doug to give an *f*-11 exposure. This aperture provided sufficient depth of field to record at least some detail in nearly all the cards.

Behind Doug, I placed two additional 600-watt-second flash units, also with umbrellas. The background lights overpowered the main light by about 1 exposure step, ensuring a pure white background that would allow the cards to record clearly.

Doug's wonderful sense of humor shows in the photograph. I remember having jokingly suggested that we should use a deck of cards containing only jokers. The fact that one appeared so prominently in front of Doug's face, however, was pure coincidence! At least, I think it was! □

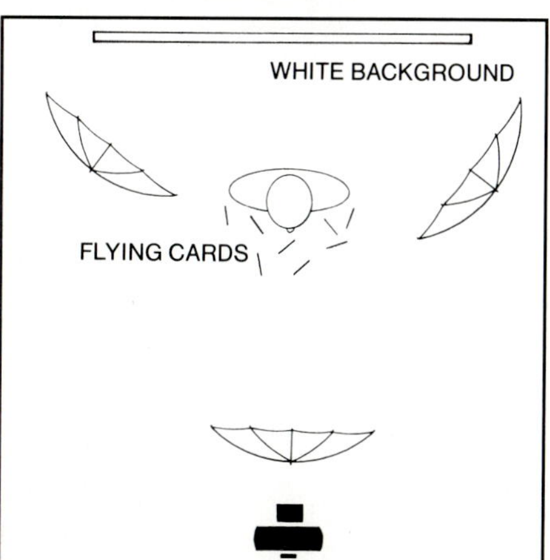

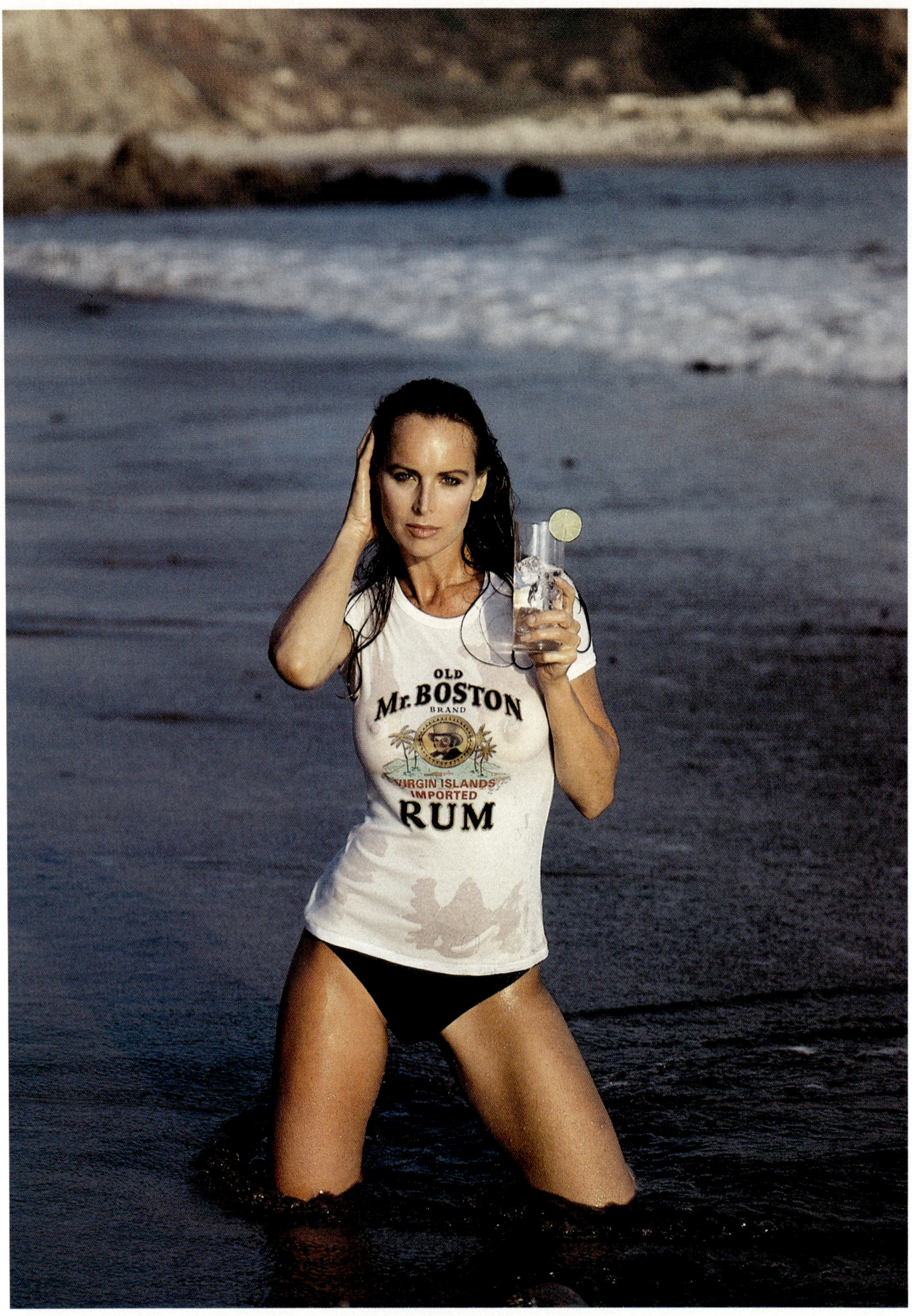
OLD
Mr. BOSTON
BRAND
VIRGIN ISLANDS
IMPORTED
RUM

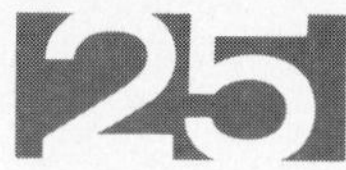

Subject: Professional model
Client: Virgin Islands Rum
Ad Agency: Mathieu, Gerfen and Bresner, Inc.
Art Director: Bill Berenter
Location: Pacific Palisades, California
Camera: Nikon F2AS
Lens: 105mm *f*-2.5 Auto-Nikkor
Lighting: Direct sunlight
Light Control: Black card
Film: Kodachrome 25
Exposure Metering: Nikon through-the-lens, center-weighted
Exposure: 1/125 second at *f*-5.6

Photography involves a careful balance of lighting. In a studio, you have total control. You can add light where you need it and remove it where you don't want it.

Outdoors, you sometimes have too much light coming from too many directions. As this example shows, it isn't difficult to remove light that you don't want to affect the image—even on a bright, sunlit beach.

The reflective sand caused the subject to be illuminated uniformly from too many directions. To remedy this, I placed a large, black card to the right side of the subject. This eliminated reflected light from a sand bank next to her. It improved the modeling and contrast in the face.

The scene was photographed for Virgin Islands Rum to advertise Old Mr. Boston Rum. □

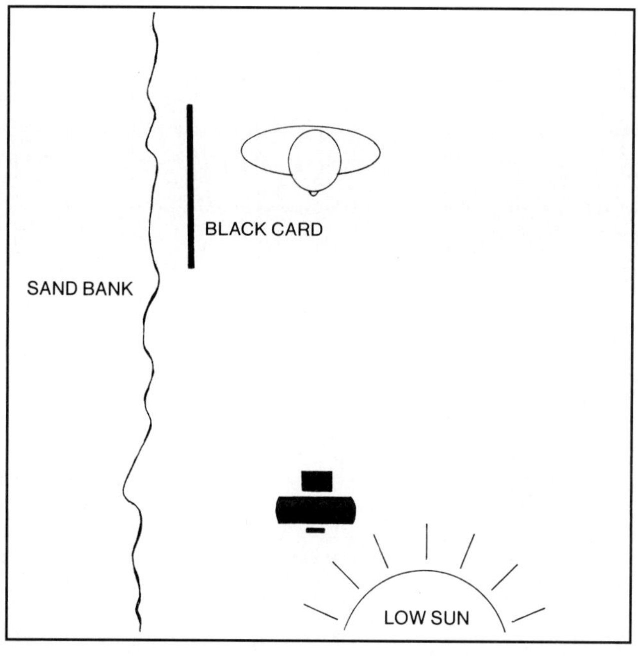

Subject: Gabrielle, German countess
Location: Gary Bernstein Studio, New York City
Camera: Nikon F2
Lens: 105mm *f*-2.5 Auto-Nikkor
Lighting: One 1250-watt-second Rollei flash in pan reflector
Film: Kodachrome 25
Exposure Metering: Minolta Auto-Flash II, incident-light mode
Exposure: *f*-16 (shutter at 1/60 second)

Gabrielle, German countess and professional model in New York City, was the subject for this picture series. I shot the sequence to illustrate the variety of usable portrait images that can be made with a fixed main-light position.

The best location for the main light varies not only from individual to individual, but also with the movement of the subject.

Light usually looks best when it strikes the subject from above eye level. The eye sockets should be illuminated equally unless one side of the face is deliberately placed in shadow. Generally, each eye should contain a catchlight. If you view the eye as a clock, the most flattering lighting for most subjects tends to produce a catchlight located between 10 and 12 o'clock or 12 and 2 o'clock.

The shadow of the subject's nose should point downward or sideways and not touch the upper lip. If the shadow touches the upper lip, the light is too high.

This series of photos shows how the basic lighting requirements can be retained without movement of the main light, even when the subject moves. Sometimes, for optimum results, a *slight* adjustment of the light position may be called for as the subject changes position. □

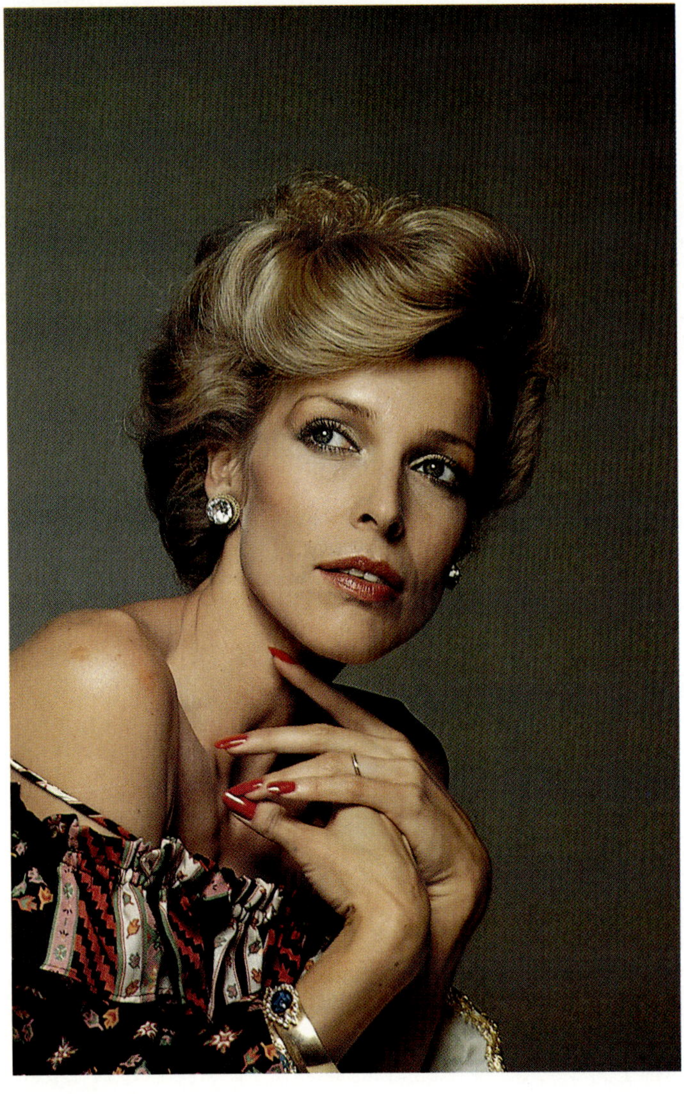

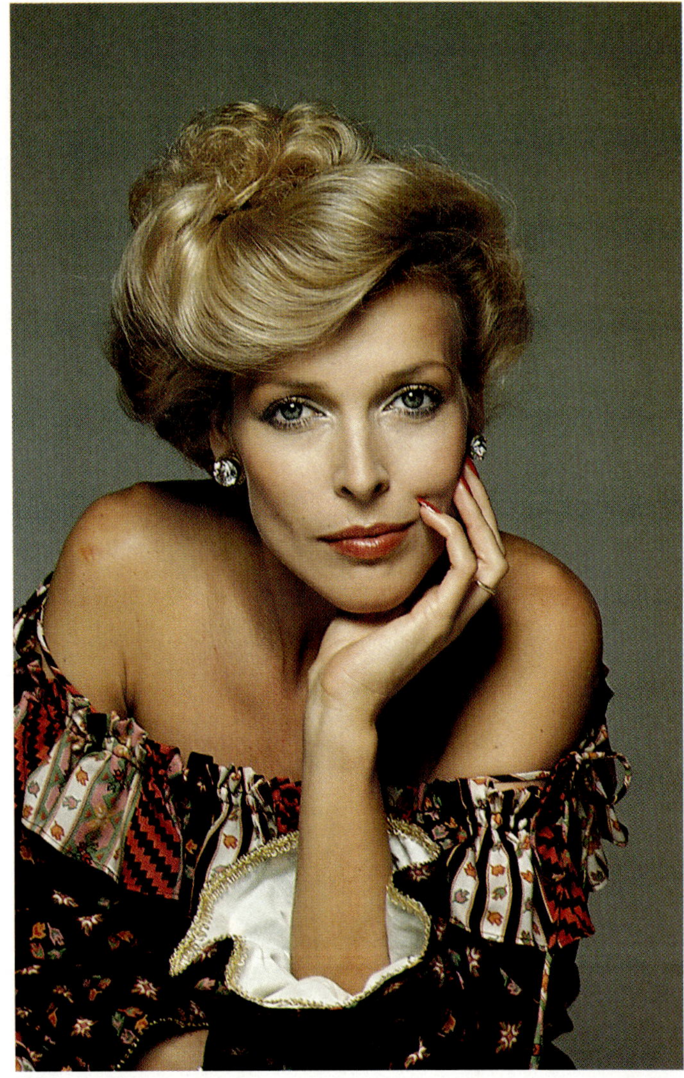

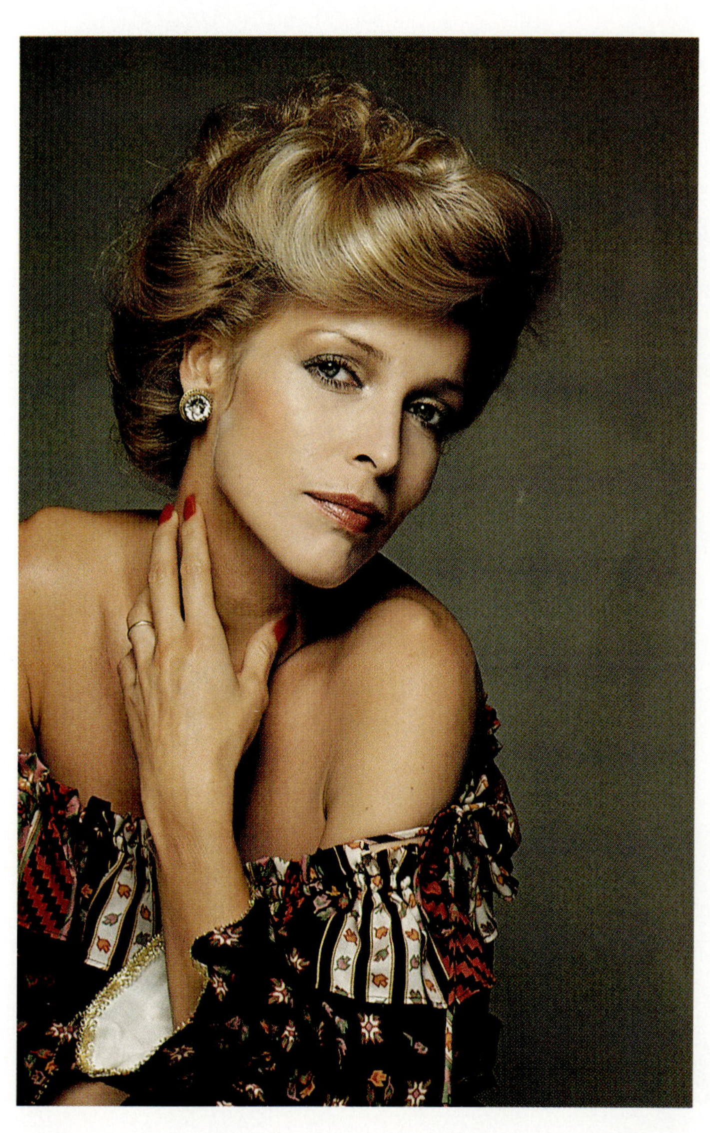

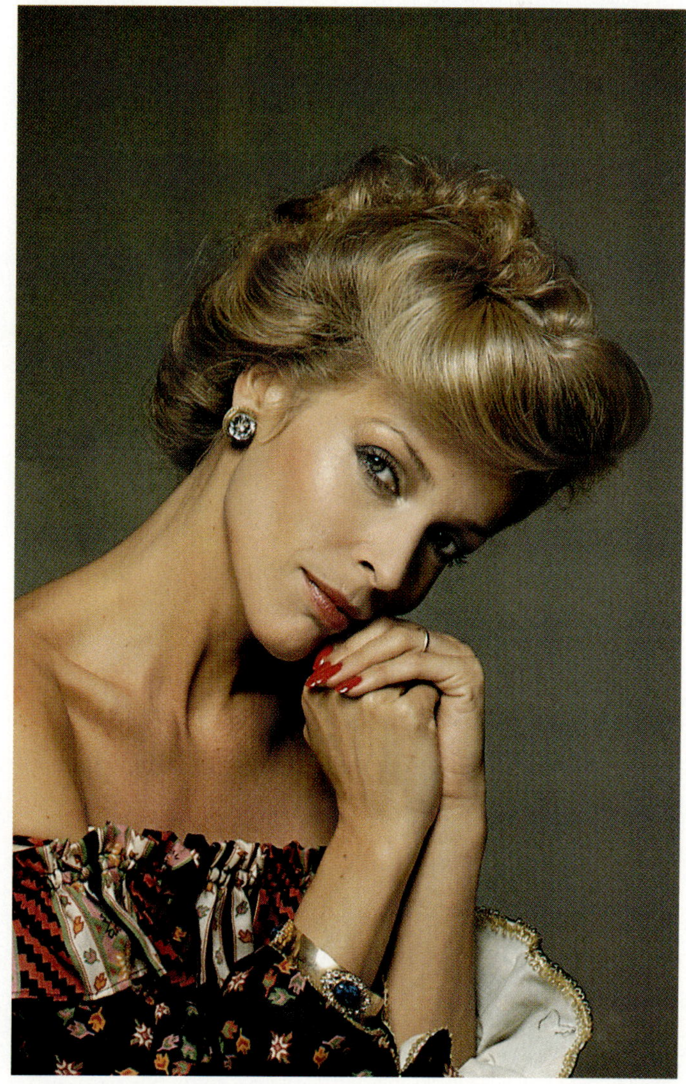

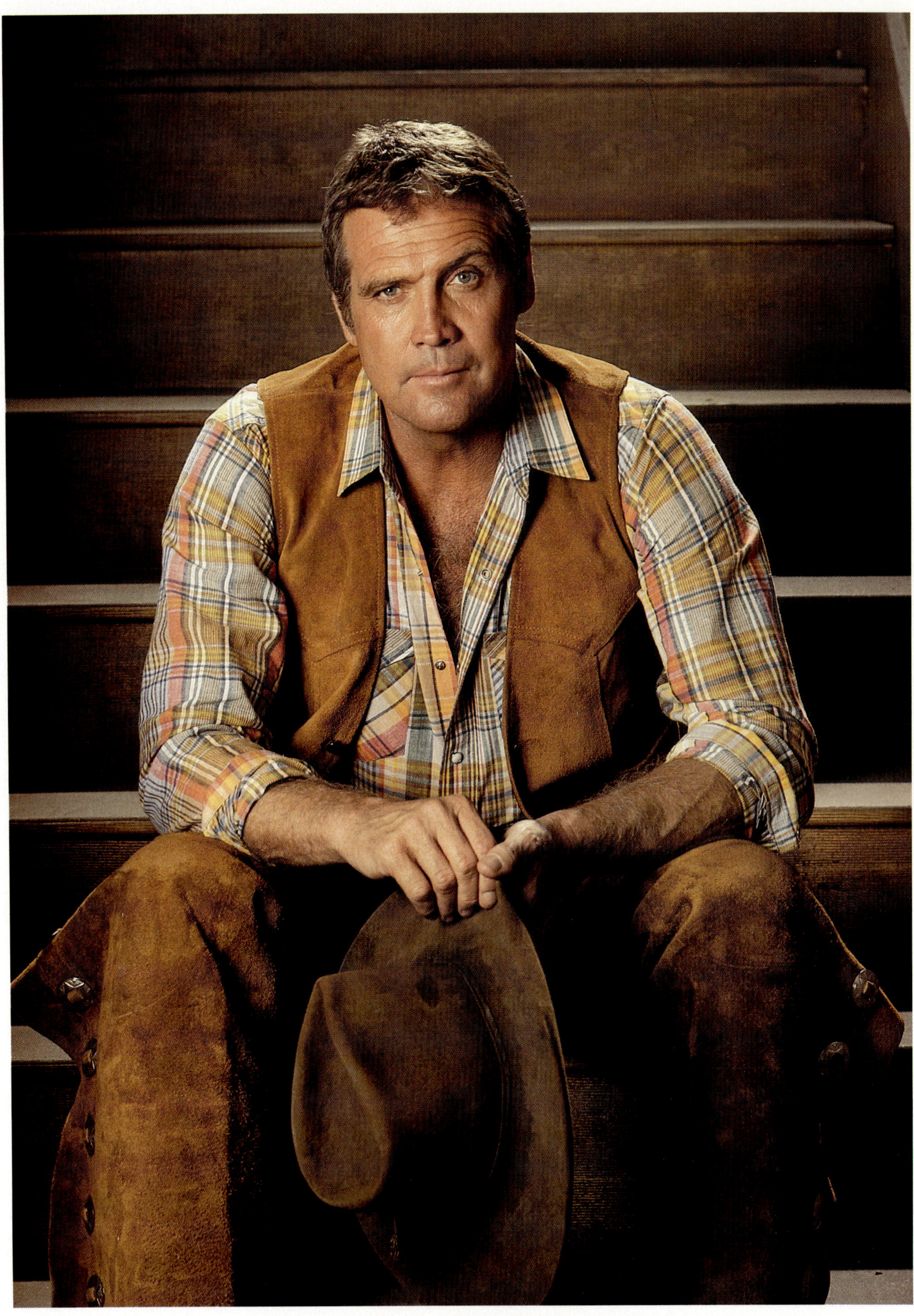

Subject: Lee Majors
Client: 20th Century Fox
Ad Agency: PMC, Inc.
Art Director: Denny Bond
Location: 20th Century Fox Studios, Los Angeles, California
Camera: Nikon F3
Lens: 55mm *f*-3.5 Micro-Nikkor
Lighting: One bare 600-watt-second electronic flash unit; one 600-watt-second electronic flash unit in white 32-inch umbrella
Film: Kodachrome 25
Exposure Metering: Minolta Auto-Flash III, incident-light mode
Exposure: *f*-8 (shutter at 1/60 second)

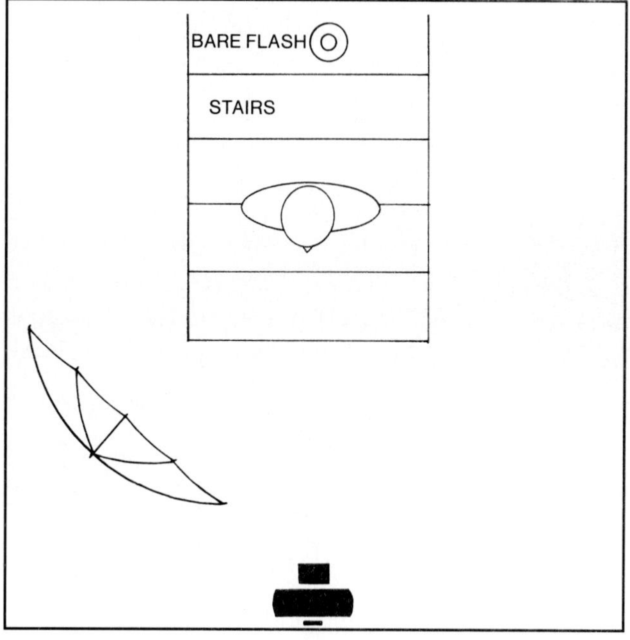

I made this photograph of Lee Majors on a Western set at 20th Century Fox Studios. I wanted the lighting to create the impression of a bare bulb hanging from the ceiling at the top of the stairs. I placed a single, bare, electronic flash in the appropriate position, just behind Lee. To simulate frontal room lighting, I added a second flash, low to Lee's right. The light was bounced from a white 32-inch umbrella.

Each light was metered separately. In metering the bare flash behind Lee from subject position, I had to shield the meter's hemisphere from the main light to get an accurate reading.

The bare flash recorded *f*-11 to *f*-16. To create a rim of highlight around Lee, the main light was set for an exposure of *f*-8 on Lee's face. Exposing at *f*-8 created 1-1/2 steps overexposure on Lee's hair and shoulders. The result is a detailed image with believable location lighting. □

Subject: Professional model
Location: Beverly Hills, California
Camera: Nikon FM
Lens: 105mm *f*-2.5 Auto-Nikkor
Lighting: One 40-watt tungsten desk lamp; one 100-watt tungsten table lamp
Film: 3M 640T color-slide film
Exposure Metering: Nikon through-the-lens, center-weighted
Exposure: 1/125 second at *f*-4

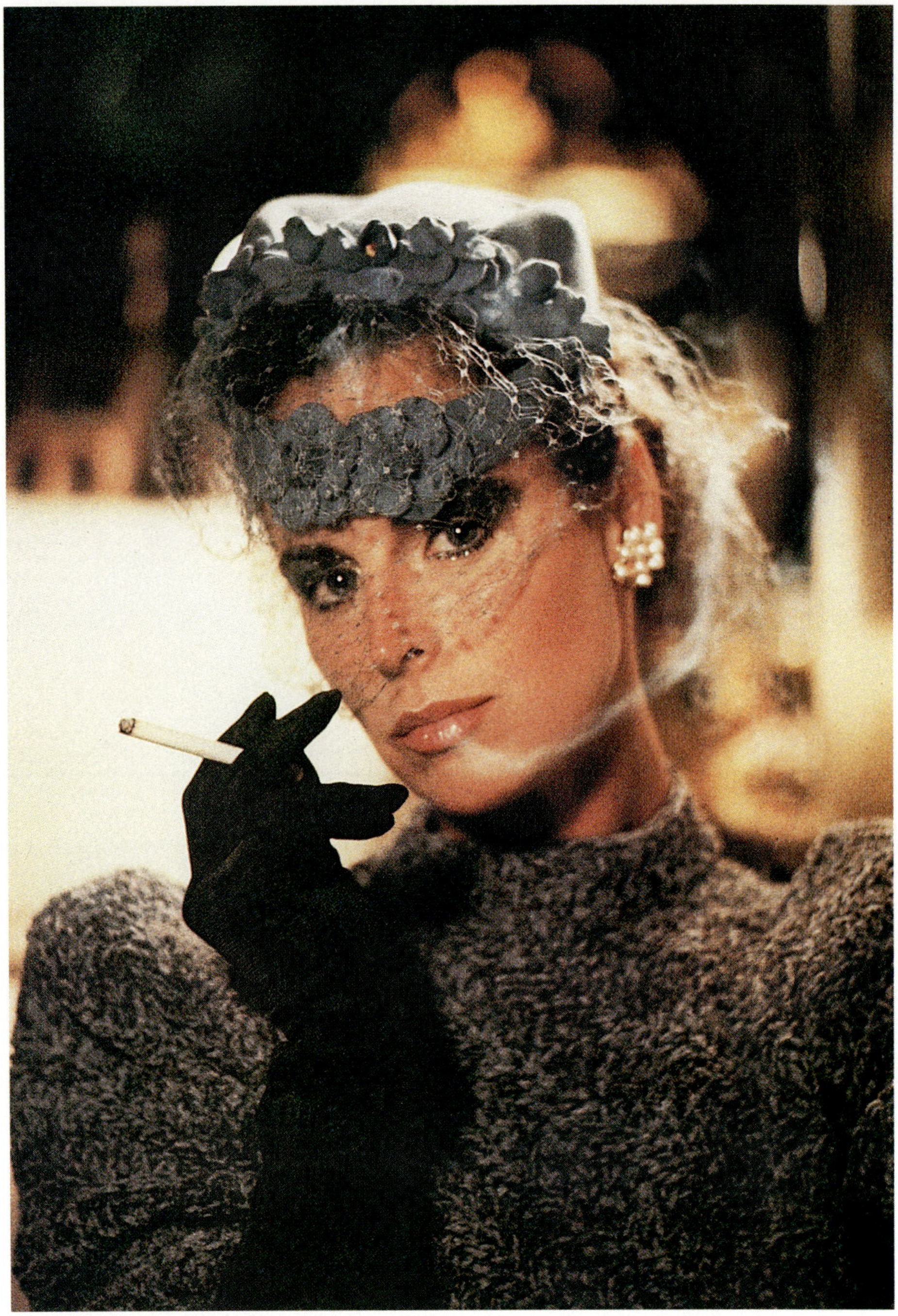

Successful images are a consequence of mastering technique and learning to see the effect light has on film. The amount or cost of equipment has little to do with creative photography. This photograph, taken as a personal test for my portfolio, is a perfect example. I shot it at my house late one evening, using an inexpensive 35mm camera and two domestic tungsten lamps.

I envisioned a photograph of an elegant woman smoking a cigarette in a chic restaurant. I seated the subject on the floor, with her back toward a wall mirror. The main light—a small desk lamp with a 40-watt bulb—was placed on a coffee table in front of the subject. I located the light and adjusted my camera position so the light was reflected in the mirror. A table lamp, with 100-watt bulb, was behind the subject. I determined the lighting balance visually, without a meter.

Shallow depth of field played a critical part in creating an abstract, dynamic background for this photograph. At an aperture of *f*-4, the lens recorded an indistinct reflected background. The visual effect suggests distance, size and grandeur.

For adequate exposure, I rated the ISO/ASA 640 film at EI 1500 and had it push-processed. This also gave the image its characteristic grainy appearance. □

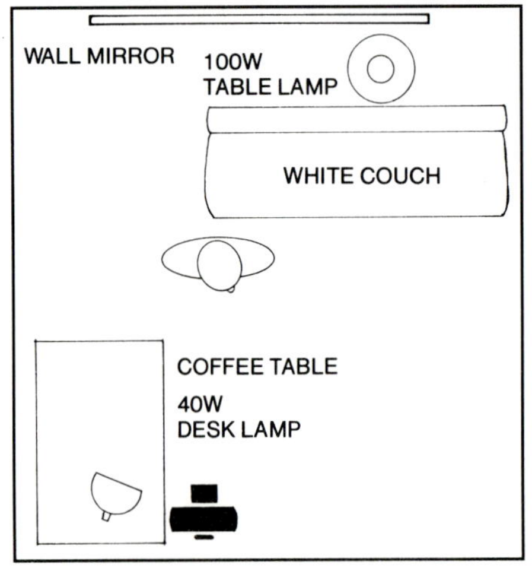

Subject: Susan Lucci
Client: Swatch Watch USA, Inc.
Location: New York City
Camera: Hasselblad 500EL/M
Lens: 150mm *f*-4 Zeiss Sonnar
Lighting: Three Photogenic Versatron 800-watt-second electronic flash units
Light Control: One pan reflector; two white 40-inch umbrellas; one Photogenic Silfoil reflector
Film: Ektachrome 64
Exposure Metering: Minolta Auto-Flash III, incident-light mode
Exposure: *f*-11 (shutter at 1/250 second)

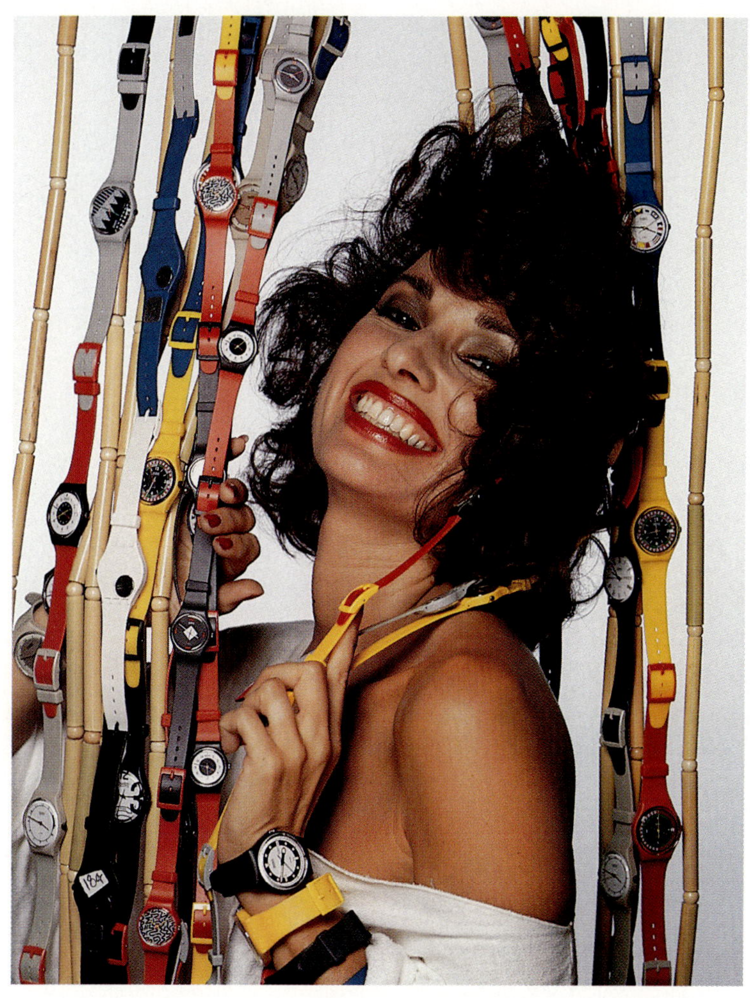

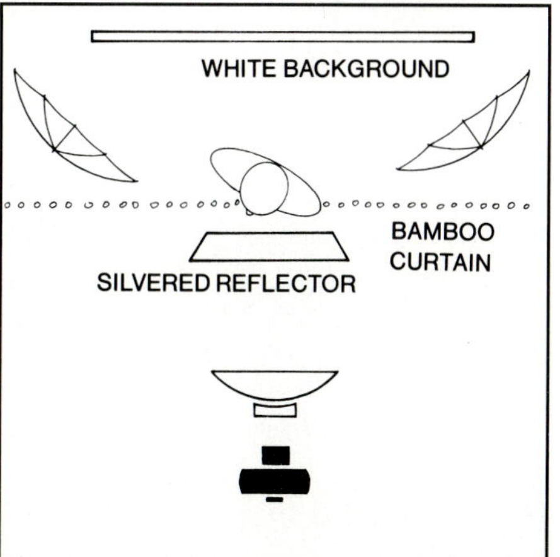

Often, the backgrounds and props used for major ad campaigns are little more than remnants and scraps of fabrics, plastics, or other interesting random materials—used with imagination. When there are no suitable remnants lying around the studio, they can easily be purchased at minimal cost.

In the case of this watch ad, featuring beautiful actress Susan Lucci, the subject's natural exuberance inspired my choice of props. I envisioned Susan entering a room through a beaded bamboo curtain. To feature the client's product, I replaced some of the bamboo strands with strands of watches.

A quick trip to a Manhattan import store provided me with a selection of beaded Oriental curtains in a variety of styles and colors. I chose the plainest in color and design to allow Susan and the colorful watches to steal the show. The watch strands were attached to a portable BD background holder, out of view of the camera.

Two lights in white umbrellas illuminated the background. The single main light was in a pan reflector. I placed a small Photogenic Silfoil reflector below Susan's face to give additional sparkle to her eyes. The exposure on subject and background recorded f-11, giving a perfect subject/background balance. □

Subject: Professional models
Location: Dallas, Texas
Camera: Nikon F3
Lens: 85mm *f*-1.8 Auto-Nikkor
Lighting: Three Photogenic Versatron 800-watt-second electronic flash units in 40-inch umbrellas
Film: Kodachrome 25
Exposure Metering: Minolta Auto-Flash III, incident-light mode
Exposure: *f*-8 (shutter at 1/60 second)

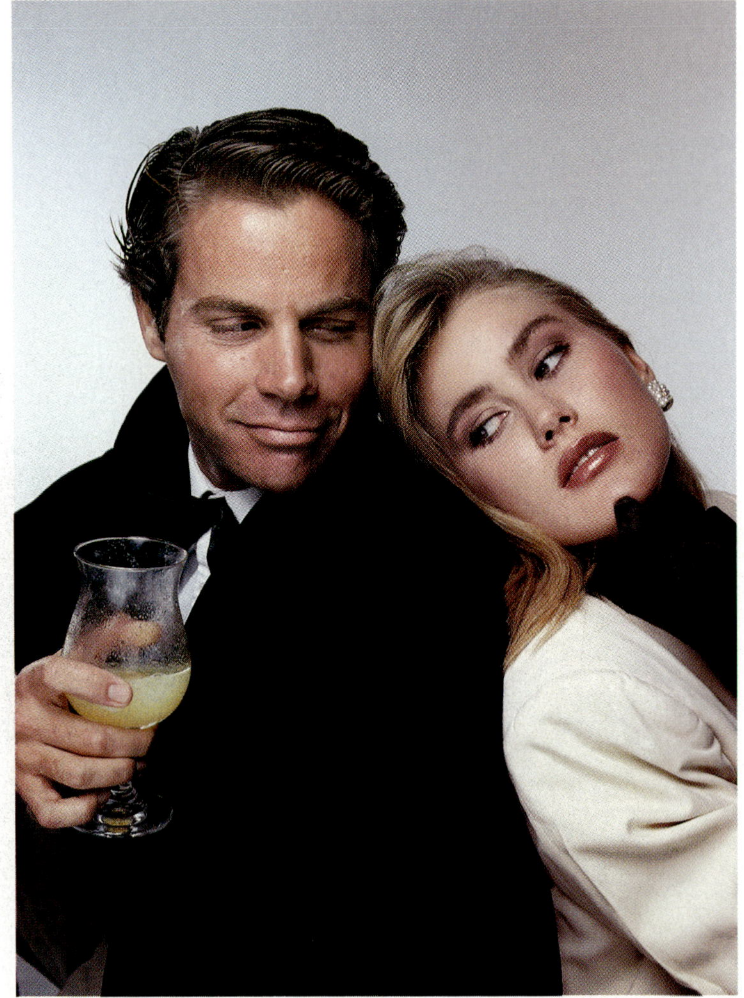

I made these four photos at a photography seminar I conducted in Dallas, Texas. The main-light source was an umbrella light, positioned in front of the two models at a distance of about three feet. Because we didn't have a boom stand, a special "thanks" must go to the gentleman who held the light in perfect position while the series of images were shot. Two background lights—bounced from umbrellas to either side of the models—produced 1-1/2 exposure steps less light than was received by the subjects. Consequently, the background recorded as a medium gray.

A short telephoto lens—such as the 85mm used for this series—is perfect for intimate photographs of couples. The lens is sufficiently long to avoid perspective distortion, yet short enough to give significant depth of field at medium apertures.

First, I posed myself. Then, I asked the models to take my position on the set. I stressed that they should maintain their relative positions, equidistant from the camera, to avoid potential depth-of-field problems.

When the models were in position, I described the series of shots I was looking for: The man glances at his pretty partner; he then gives an overtly confident look toward the camera; his stare returns to his partner—this time with mischief and humor in his glance; finally, he turns toward her and an argument begins. She angrily points her finger and he bites her glove. The models that enacted this series for me were absolutely wonderful.

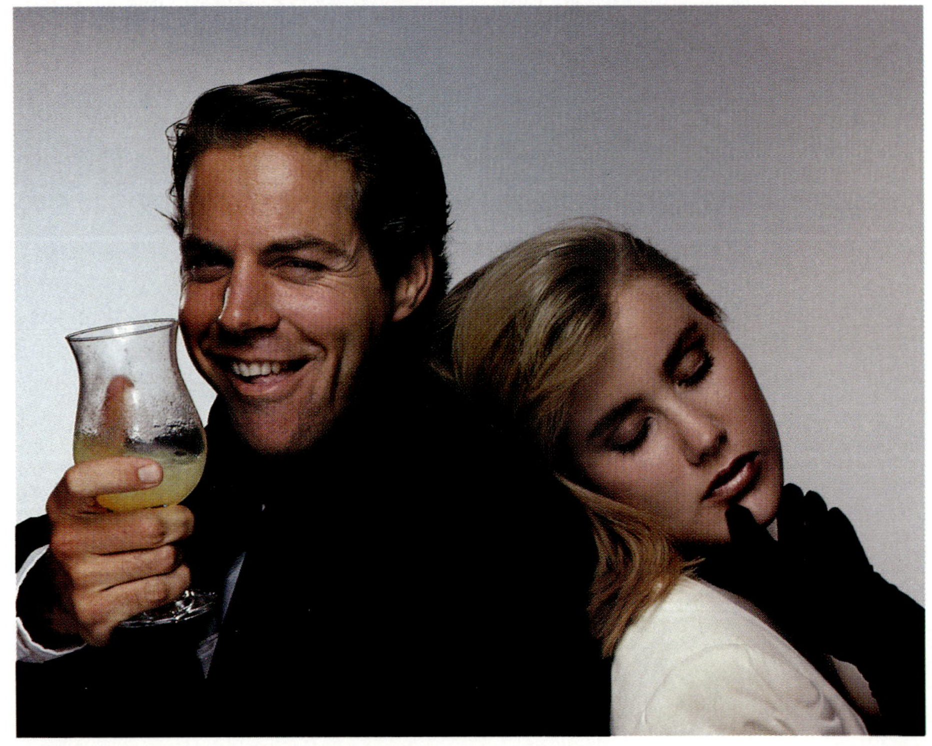

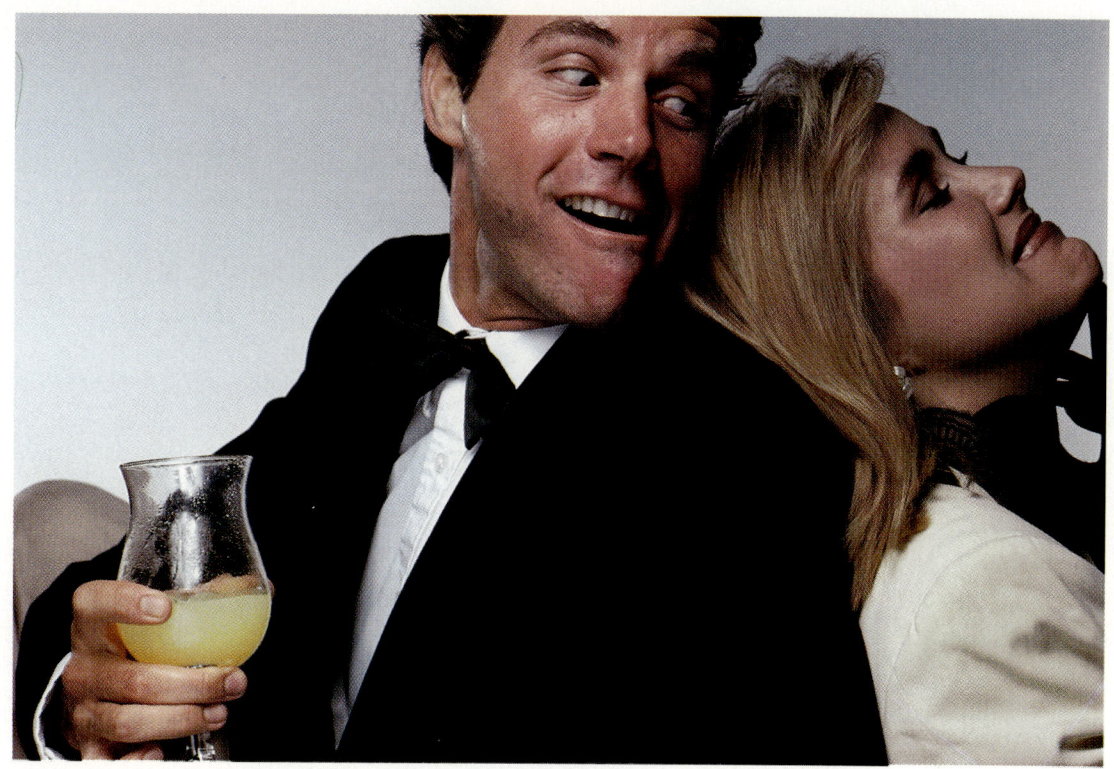

Imagine how a series of shots such as these could service the needs of many potential clients—including, for example, liquor advertisers, clothing companies, perfume manufacturers, and even marketers of orange juice! If private portraiture is your goal, with some subtle variations this same theme could be used for a humorous series with a loving couple. With imagination and enthusiasm, you can do it, too! □

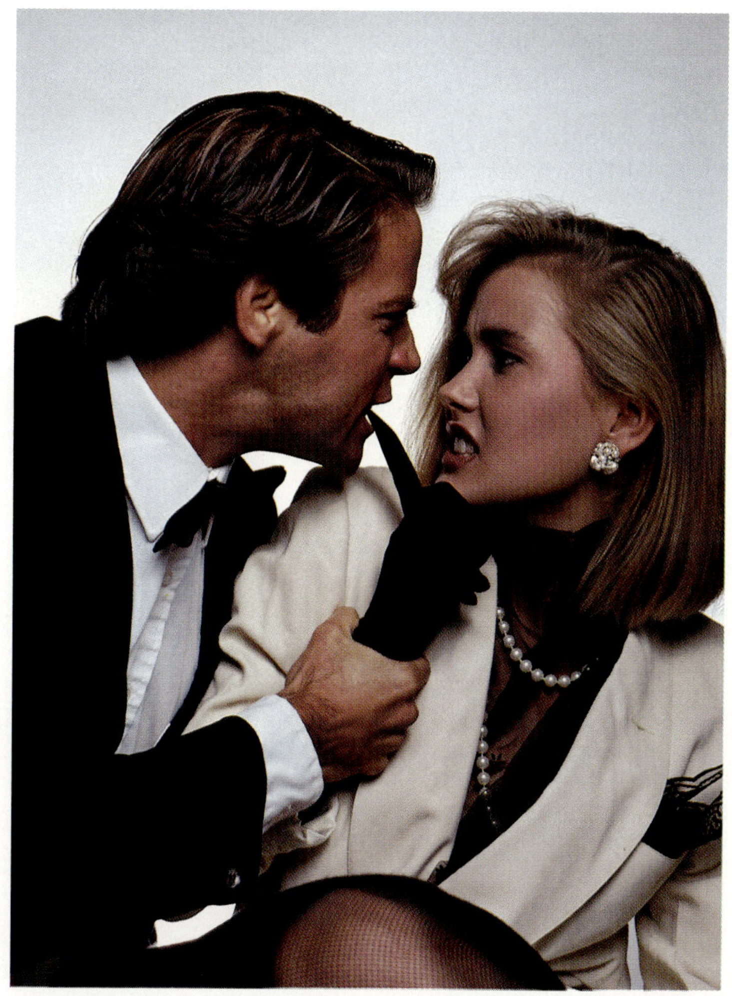

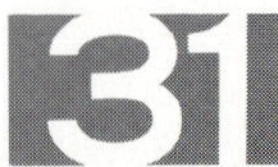

Subject: Professional model
Location: Gary Bernstein Studio, Los Angeles, California
Camera: Nikon F3
Lens: 55mm *f*-3.5 Micro-Nikkor
Lighting: Four 400-watt-second electronic flash units
Light Control: Pan reflector for main light; grid spot for hair light; two wide-angle reflectors for background lights
Film: Kodachrome 25
Filtration: Green filters on background lights; Harrison & Harrison diffuser
Exposure Metering: Minolta Auto-Flash III, incident-light mode
Exposure: *f*-8 (shutter at 1/60 second)

These photos are two of a series taken as a test for a client. I liked the results and wanted to use one of the images in this book. I showed the model my choice for publication—the photo on the opposite page. After viewing all of the shots, she selected the photo on this page. An interesting discussion about the differences between the two images followed.

Although one shot was taken right after the other, two totally different subject personalities are apparent. The image on this page depicts a strong woman. She confronts the camera and viewer with confidence—leaning toward the camera with her weight on the front foot. The strength of her attitude is reflected in her pose and facial expression.

As recorded on the opposite page, the woman is more introspective—perhaps a bit more reserved and shy.

Such is the essence of people photography—the ability to derive a wealth of different character portrayals from a single subject. It's of equal significance that the model and I each envisioned the results differently—in spite of our unity of purpose and direction during the course of the session.

The photos were made with a single main light in a pan reflector. I rated the main light at 1 exposure step less than a hair light with grid spot. Two background lights with green acetate filters were balanced with the subject exposure. □

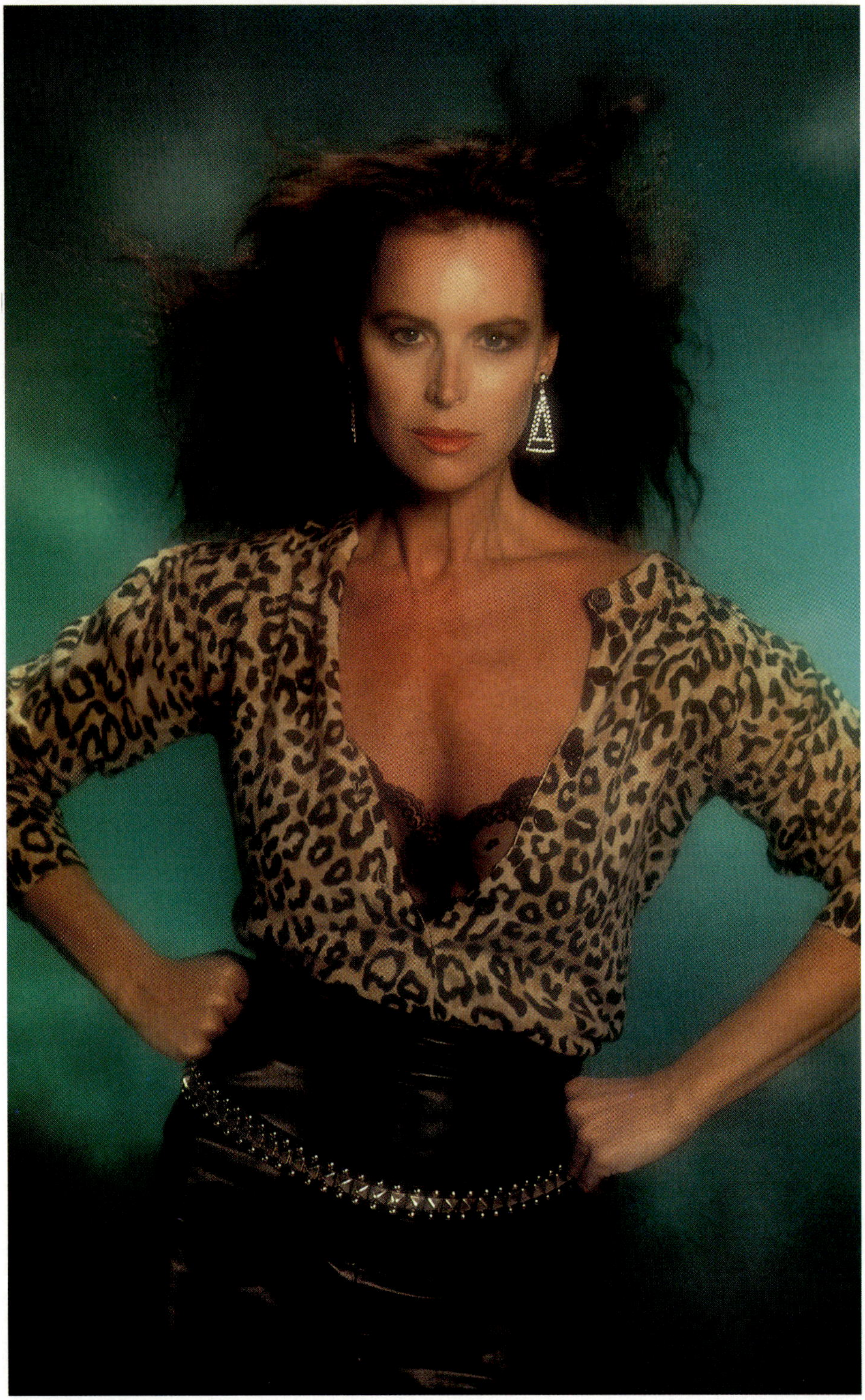

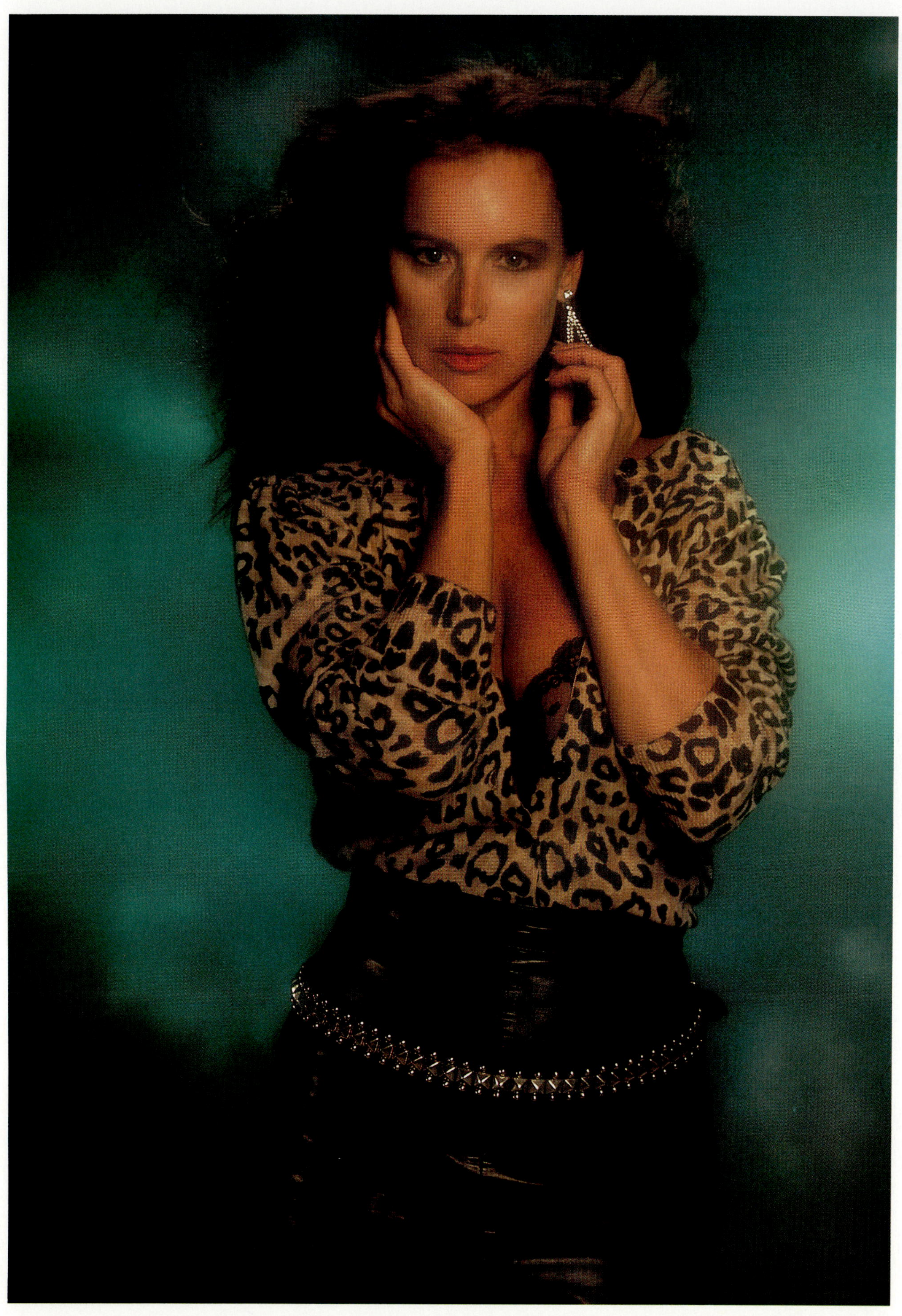

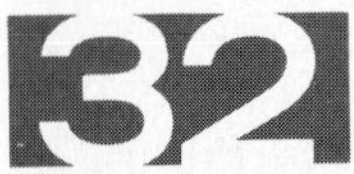

Subject: Billy Dee Williams
Client: Jean-Paul Germain, Ltd.
Art Director: Gary Bernstein
Location: Gary Bernstein Studio, Los Angeles, California
Camera: Nikon F3
Lens: 105mm *f*-2.5 Auto-Nikkor
Lighting: One 1200-watt-second electronic flash unit
Light Control: One 24-inch silvered umbrella
Film: Kodachrome 25
Exposure Metering: Gossen Ultra-Pro, incident-light mode
Exposure: *f*-8 (shutter at 1/60 second)

The great face of Billy Dee Williams and a simple lighting setup enabled me to produce this dynamic image for a Jean-Paul Germain ad campaign. I wanted to emphasize Billy's features and avoid the hand detracting attention from the modeling and specular lighting on the face. I used a small umbrella and brought it within two feet of the actor's face, on his right side. This created sufficient light falloff on the hand—with Billy's face metering at *f*-8 and his hand at *f*-5.6.

Billy was seated on the floor in my white studio cove. A falloff of 2 exposure steps caused the white wall to record as gray on film.

Even in a simple, one-light setup such as this, I meter all critical elements before beginning photography. In this case, I metered the highlight side of Billy's face, his hand, and the white background. □

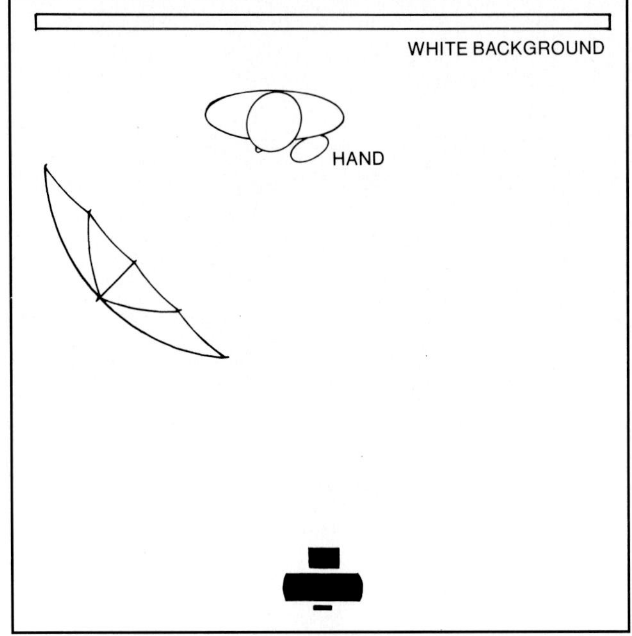

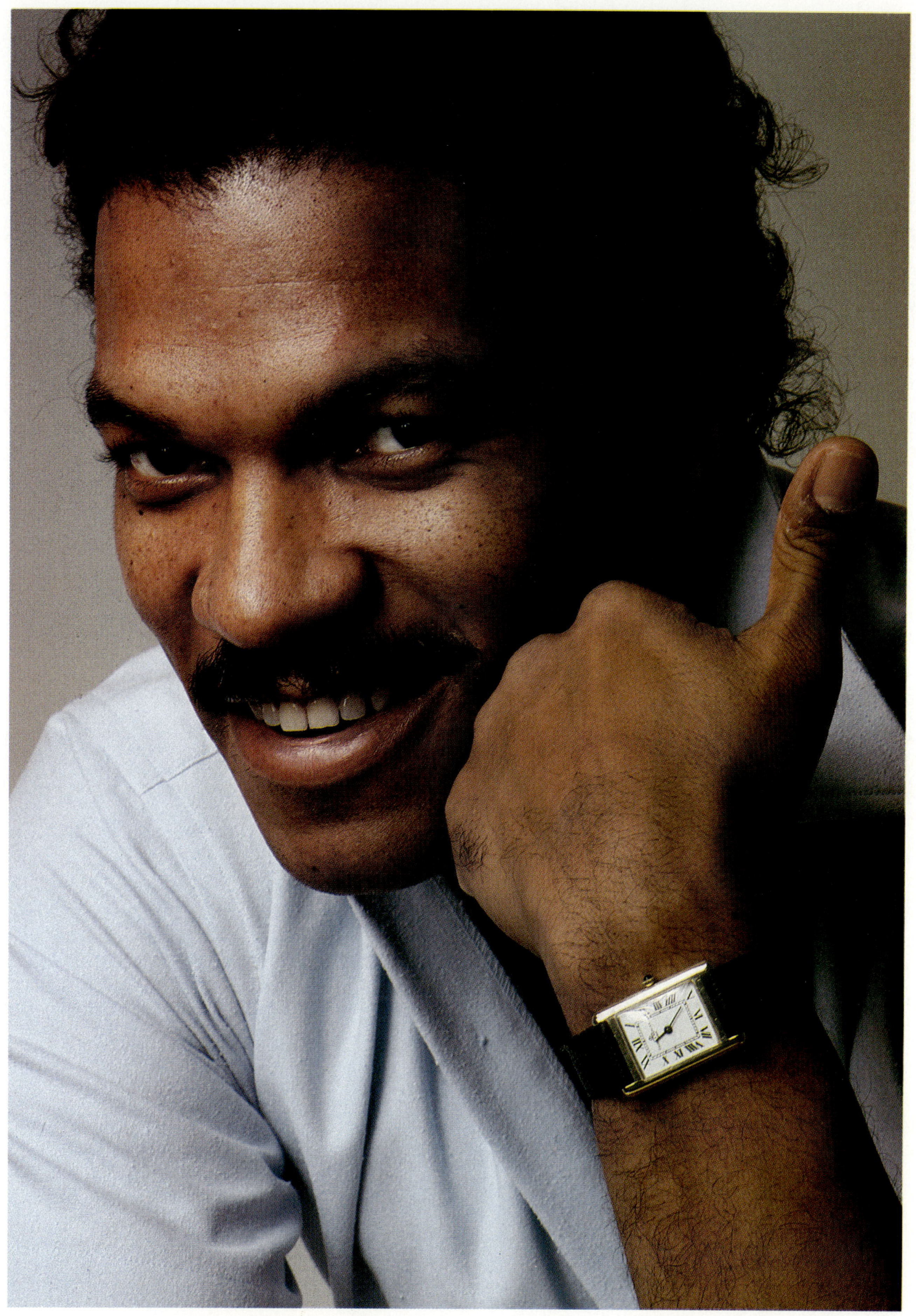

33

Subject: Professional model
Client: Echo Scarves for Woodward and Lothrop, Inc.
Ad Agency: Colopy-Dale, Inc.
Art Director: Bob Sands
Location: Gary Bernstein Studio, New York City
Camera: Nikon F
Lens: 105mm *f*-2.5 Auto-Nikkor
Lighting: Three 1200-watt-second Thomastrobe electronic flash units
Light Control: One 27-inch silver reflector
Film: Kodachrome 25
Exposure Metering: Wein Electronic-Flash Meter, incident-light mode
Exposure: *f*-8 (shutter at 1/60 second)

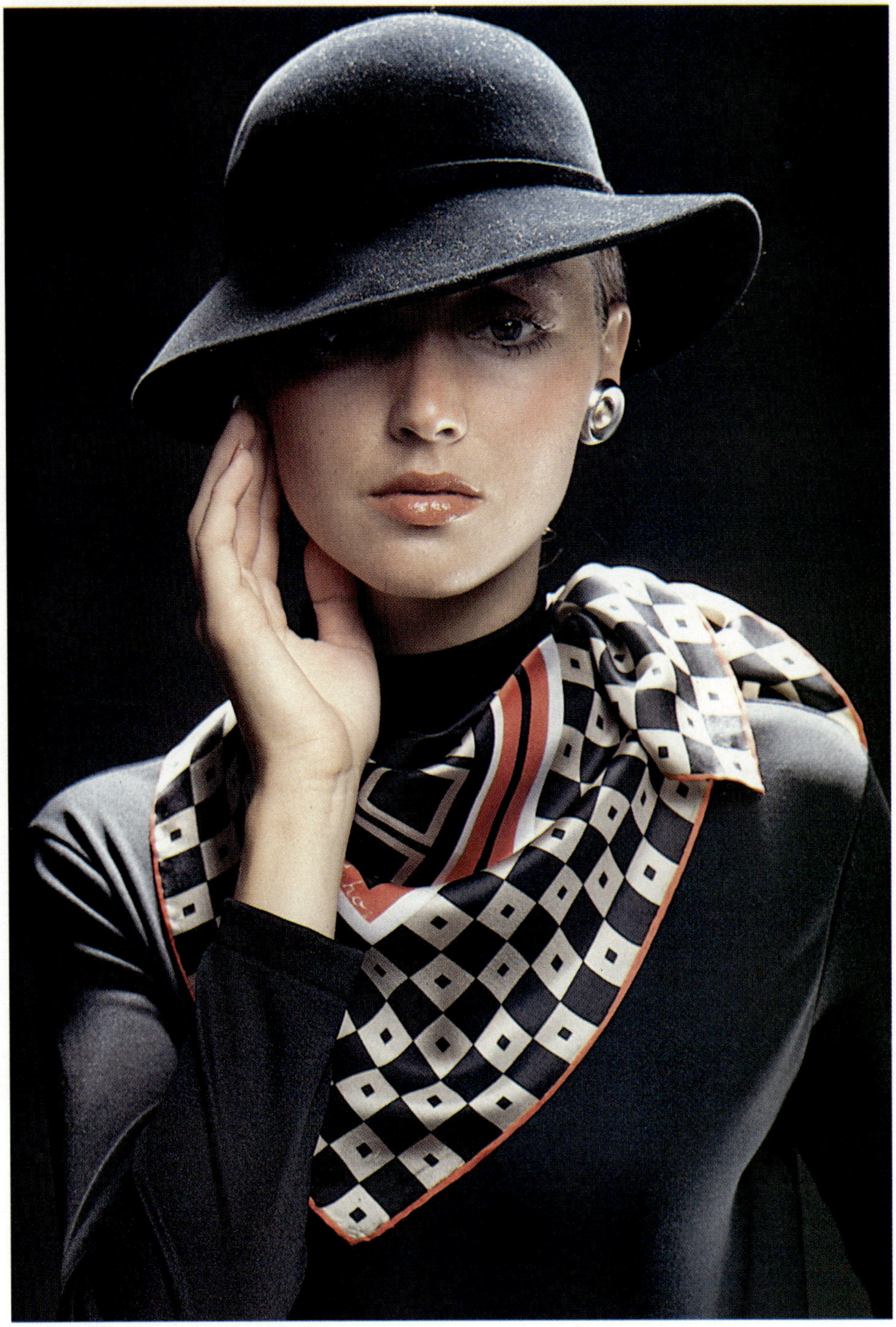

If a dark subject is to stand out from a dark background, a graphic way of separating the two is essential. I used a single, wide-angle light source above and behind the subject to rim light her black hat and the outfit.

The main light—bounced from an umbrella slightly to the right of the camera—was placed low to allow light to reach the face from below the hat brim. To lighten facial shadows, I placed a relatively weak fill light near camera position.

I placed a large silver reflector below the model's face, slightly to the left of camera position. It added a catchlight to the shaded eye.

The metering was done in stages. The fill light recorded *f*-5.6, the main-light reading was *f*-8, and the rim-light metered *f*-11. I made the camera exposure with the aperture set at *f*-8.

Notice the position of the model's hand. It is turned so the edge of the hand faces the camera. This gives the hand a delicate, feminine appearance from camera position. □

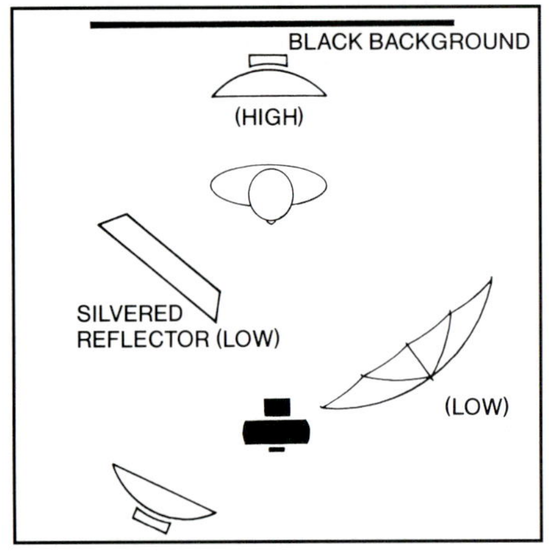

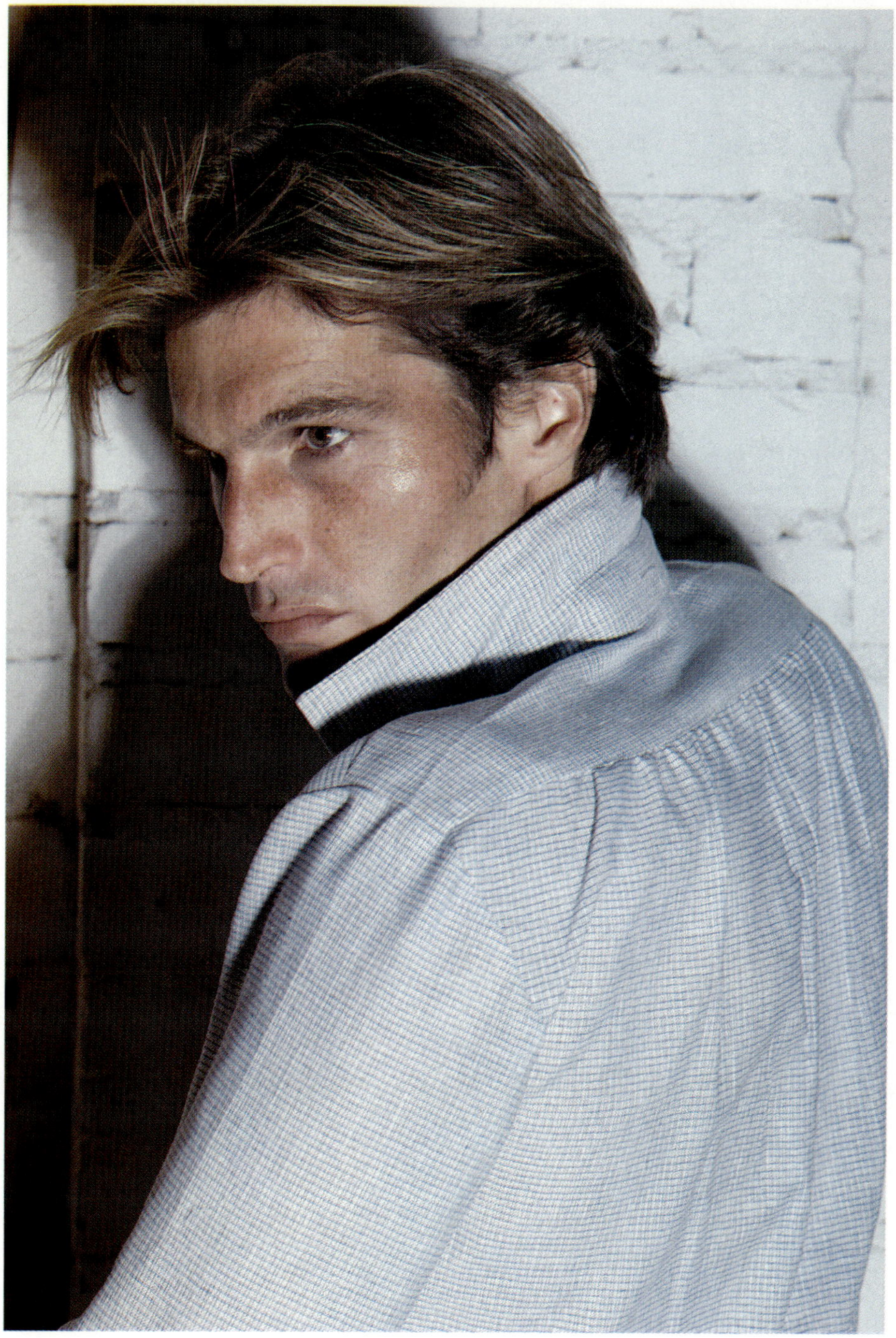

34

Subject: Professional model
Client: Paul Davril, Inc.
Location: Gary Bernstein Studio, Los Angeles, California
Camera: Nikon F2AS
Lens: 85mm *f*-1.8 Auto-Nikkor
Lighting: One 600-watt-second electronic flash unit
Light Control: Focusing grid
Film: Kodachrome 25
Exposure Metering: Minolta Auto-Flash II, incident-light mode
Exposure: *f*-11 (shutter at 1/60 second)

I took this photograph as part of an advertising campaign for a line of French designer shirts. I positioned the model with his back to the camera to show important detail in the back of the shirt.

To emphasize the delicate stitching across the shoulders, I used a spotlight with a focusing grid as the only light source. The angular lighting clearly delineates important detail in the shirt and accentuates the model's strong features.

Because the subject doesn't make eye contact with the viewer, it appears as though he has been photographed without his knowledge. The approach gives the photograph a candid, editorial type of appeal. The lack of eye contact also encourages the viewer to scrutinize the subject without self-consciousness. This technique is often used effectively in advertising photography.

Careful metering is critical when you use a focusing grid. This is because light from a grid falls off sharply outside the immediate area being lit by the focused light. I always take several readings in and around the highlighted area to ensure exposure accuracy. □

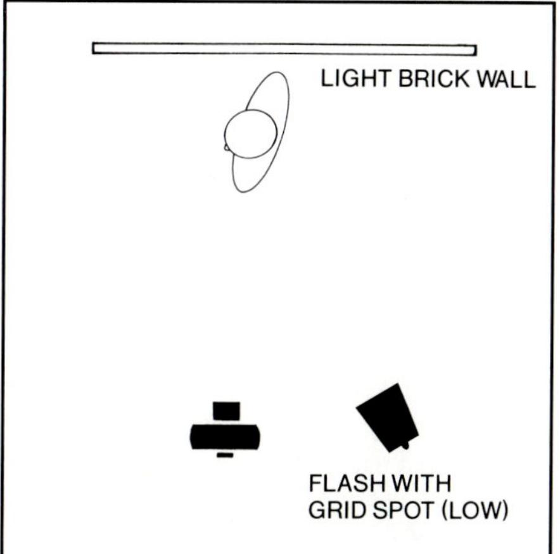

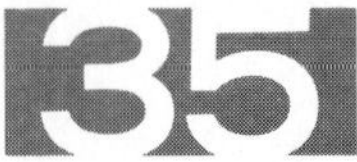

Subject: Professional models (Test session)
Location: Gary Bernstein Studio, New York City
Camera: Hasselblad 500EL/M
Lens: 150mm *f*-4 Zeiss Sonnar
Lighting: One 1250-watt-second Rollei electronic flash in pan reflector
Film: Kodak Plus-X Pan
Exposure Metering: Minolta Auto-Flash II, incident-light mode
Exposure: *f*-5.6 (shutter at 1/250 second)

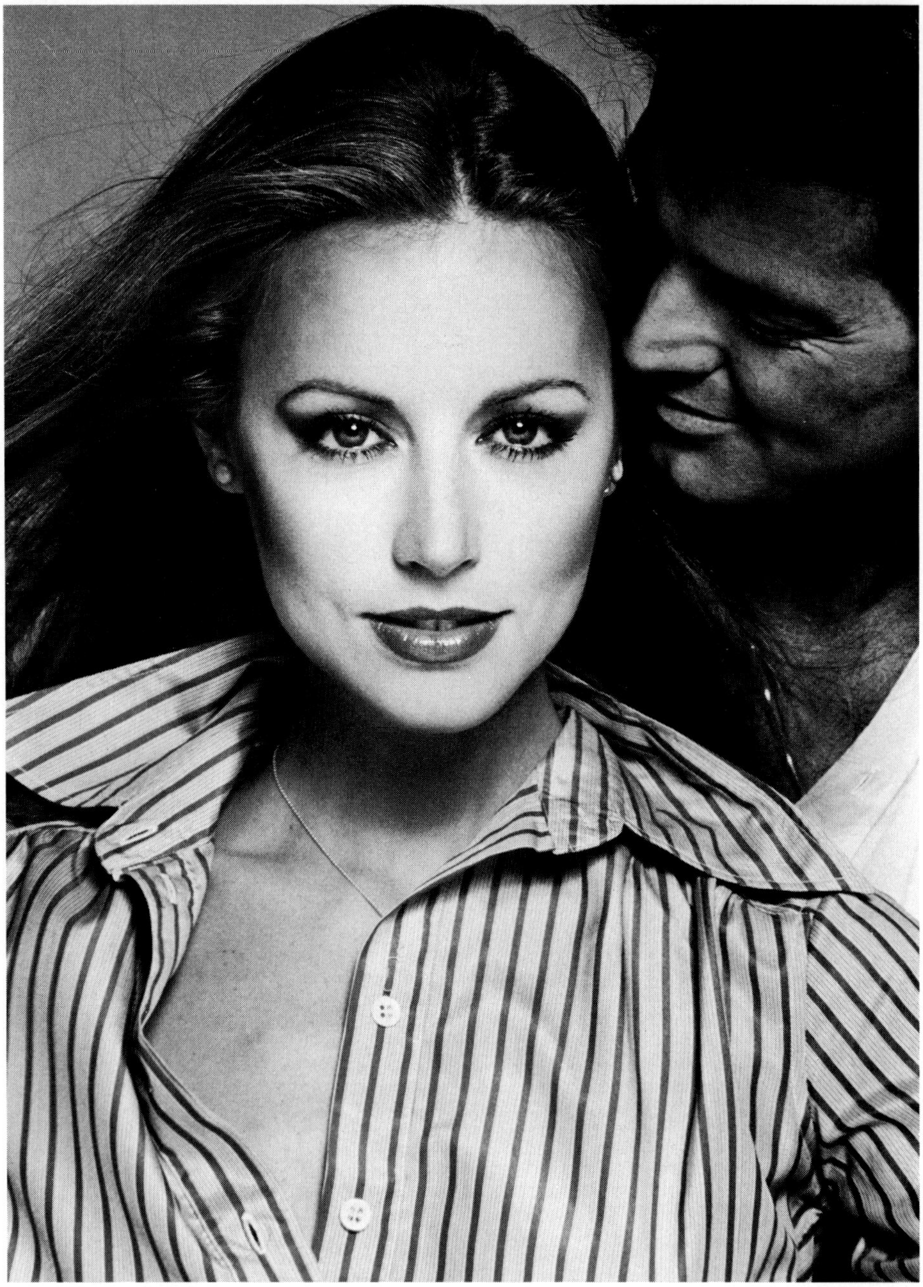

Two of New York's finest models appeared in this series of test photos taken for our respective portfolios. The three images were produced without the help of hair or makeup stylists.

There are important similarities in these images: Each was produced with a single main light, bounced from a flat pan reflector. Each was shot with a medium telephoto lens on a 2-1/4-inch-square camera, giving limited depth of field. Each image exemplifies the ease and simplicity of male/female posing. Each photo uses subject/camera rapport rather than visual communication between the subjects for impact. However, the direction and purpose of each image was totally different.

Because this test session was to satisfy both subjects, each required personal attention. Both had to end up with usable portfolio images.

In the photo on this page, I gave "main billing" to the female model. Her male counterpart merely adds background support to the image. For a tightly cropped head shot of the woman alone, the man could easily be removed from the image. In the left photo, opposite page, I featured the male model. Again, by selective composition, I gave him the option of cropping the photo to produce a single head shot.

The photo on the far right features both models equally. Although the subjects maintain eye contact with the camera, the viewer is aware of the subjects' unity. Subtle elements, such as a hand on a shoulder or a slight tip of a head, as well as the basic position and proximity of bodies, convey a message of oneness.

The man's skin appears darker than the woman's in each of the photos. The darker tone suggests a masculine tan and ruggedness while the lighter tone effectively represents a woman's "porcelain" femininity. This effect can be produced with about 1/2-exposure-step light falloff between the faces. I determined exposure for these photos with an incident-light reading from the woman's face. □

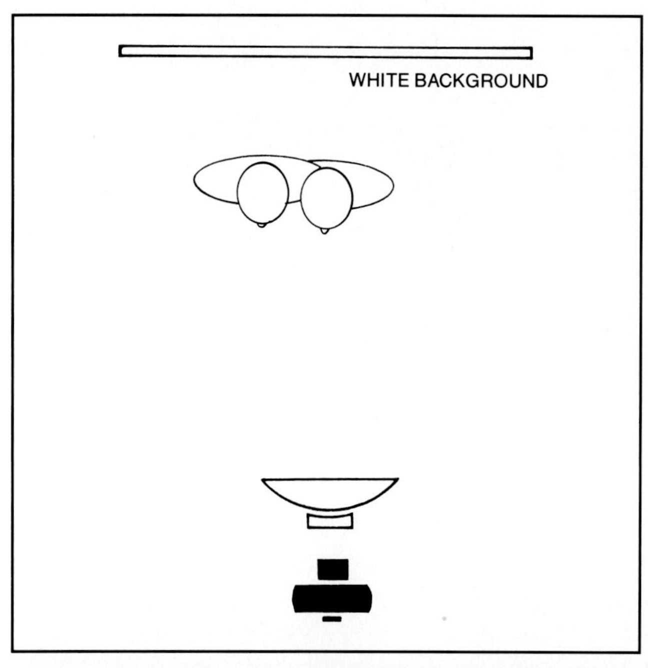
WHITE BACKGROUND

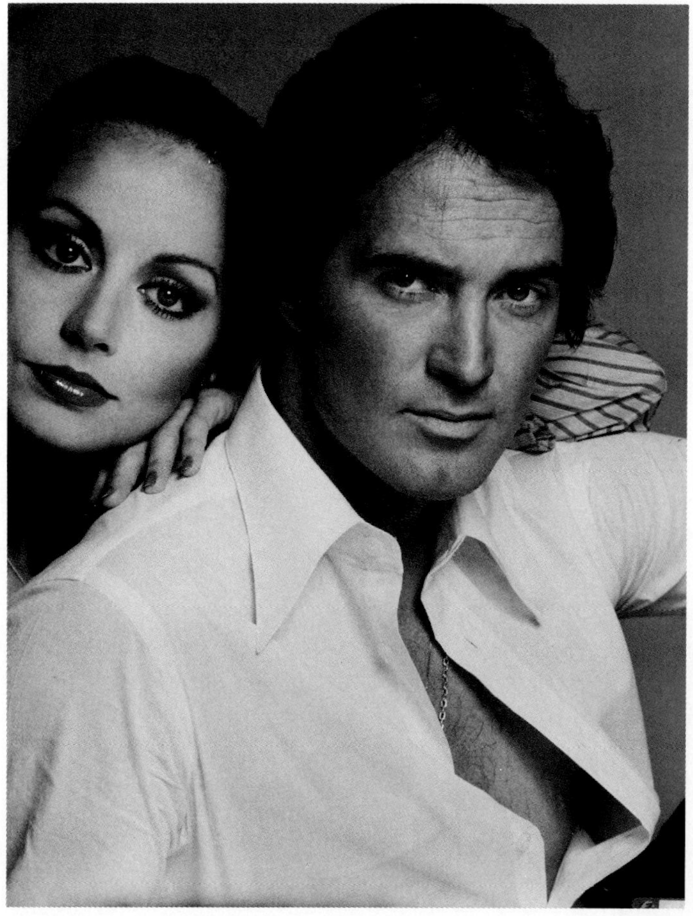

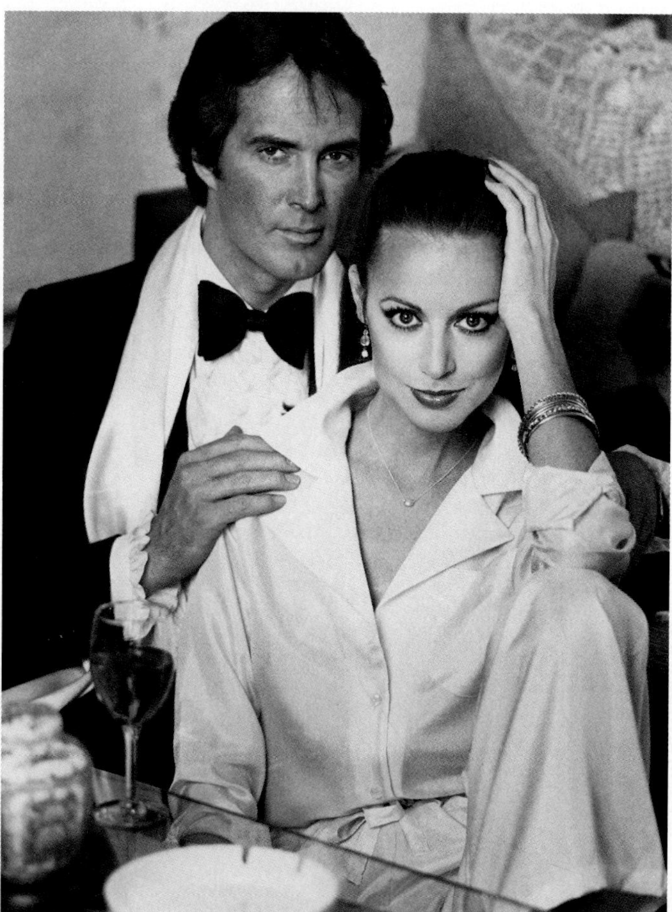

Subject: Professional model
Client: Ski Magazine
Art Director: Pat Doran
Location: New York City
Camera: Nikon F2
Lens: 35mm *f*-2 Auto-Nikkor
Lighting: One 100-watt-second Sunpak electronic flash unit
Light Control: White tissue diffuser
Film: Kodachrome 25
Exposure Metering: Minolta Auto-Flash II, incident-light mode
Exposure: *f*-8 (shutter at 1/60 second)

Taken as part of a 15-page editorial layout for *Ski* magazine, this photo illustrates the beautiful light quality you can get with a small, portable electronic flash unit. The title of the layout was: "Getting Away—To Go Skiing." In this shot, the model departs luxuriously—in the back seat of a Rolls Royce. I was in the front seat with my Nikon.

I was careful to keep the film plane parallel to the car seat and the line of the model's body to avoid any obvious perspective distortion with my wide-angle lens. To give the light a slightly diffused quality, I taped a small piece of tissue to the front of the portable flash.

This shot was taken in a Rolls Royce showroom. An amateur photographer can often receive the same cooperation from a salesperson in exchange for a couple of photographs. □

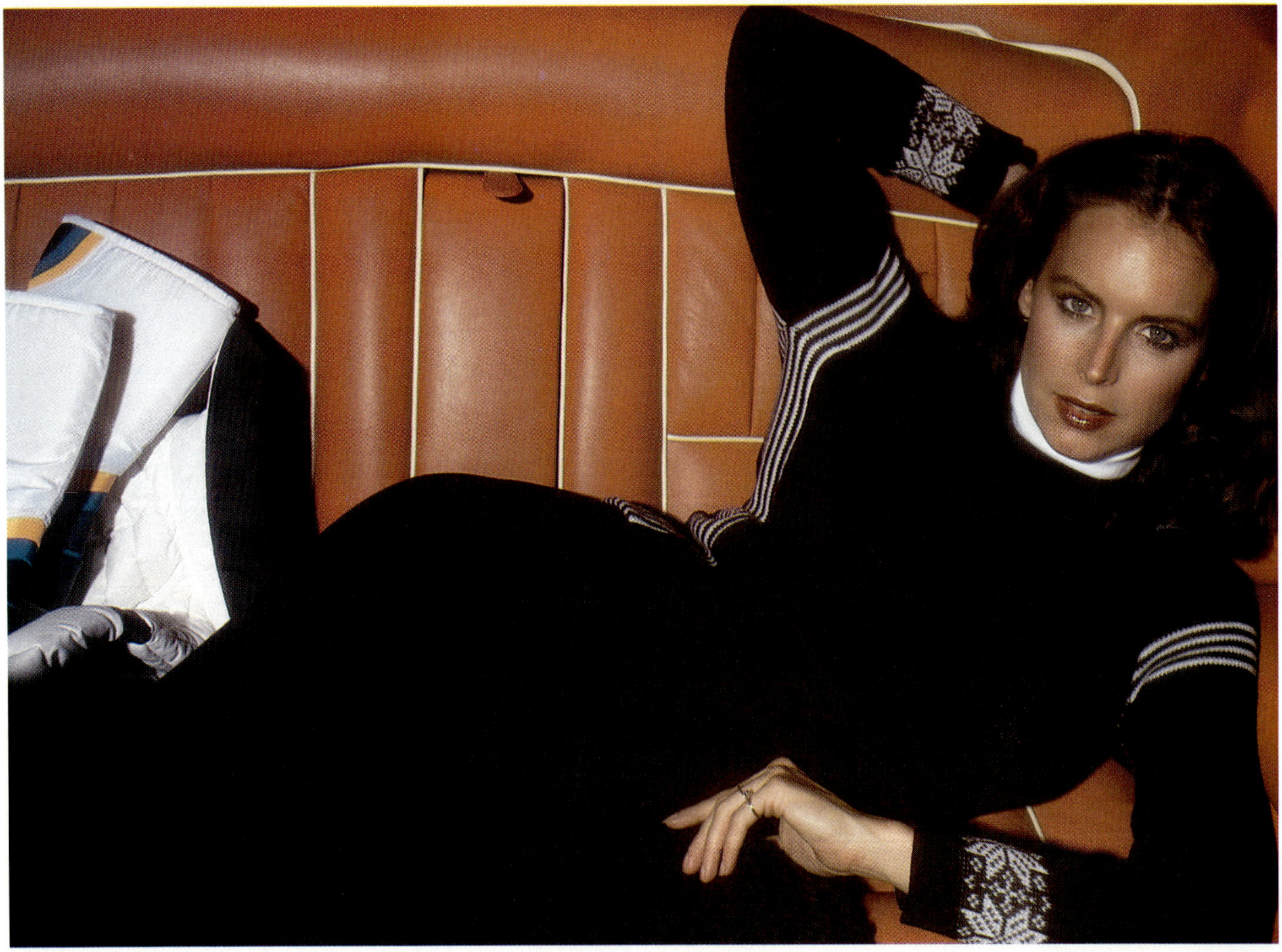

To create the intimate atmosphere of this scene, I deliberately exposed daylight-balanced color film by tungsten lighting. This resulted in the overall reddish tone. This is because the light from a tungsten lamp contains more red than does average daylight. To record this scene "normally" with a 100-watt bulb and daylight-balanced film, I would have needed a combination of blue 80A and 82B filters on the camera lens.

In this scene, I thought the deliberate color shift gave the photo a beautiful "warmth." The lamp was about five feet from the model. I used a handheld incident-light meter at subject position to determine exposure.

For sufficient exposure in the dim light, I rated the Ektachrome 200 film at double its speed (EI 400) and had the lab push-process the film.

You'll notice that I departed from a standard compositional rule—I placed the subject's head in the center of the frame. This added a feeling of peace and tranquility to the scene. You, too, should break rules when it means getting a more effective picture! □

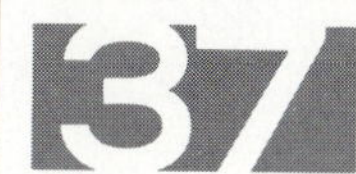

Subject: Professional model
Location: New York City
Camera: Nikon F
Lens: 85mm *f*-1.8 Auto-Nikkor
Lighting: One 100-watt tungsten lamp
Film: Ektachrome 200
Exposure Metering: Gossen Luna Pro, incident-light mode
Exposure: 1/60 second at *f*-4

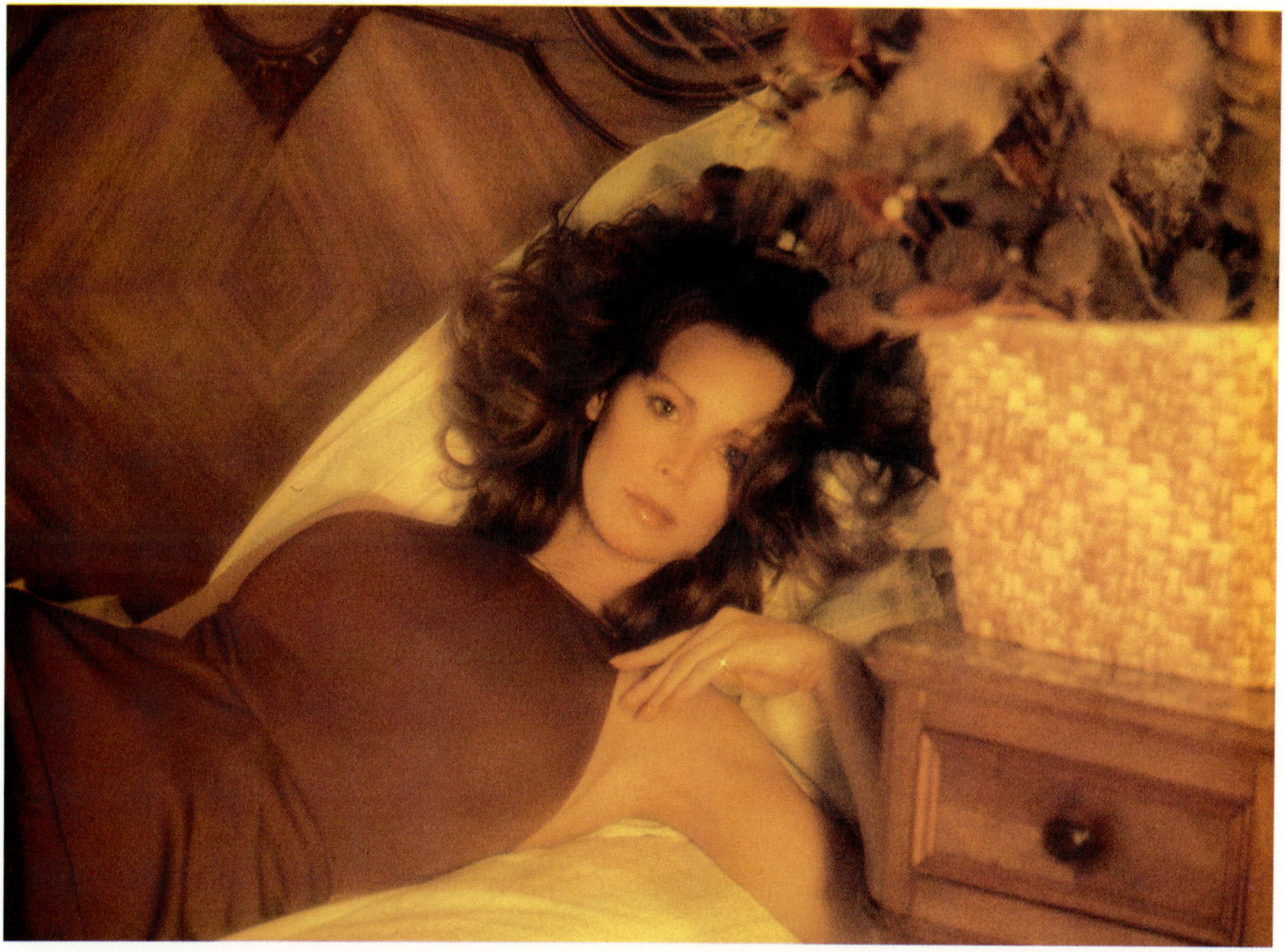

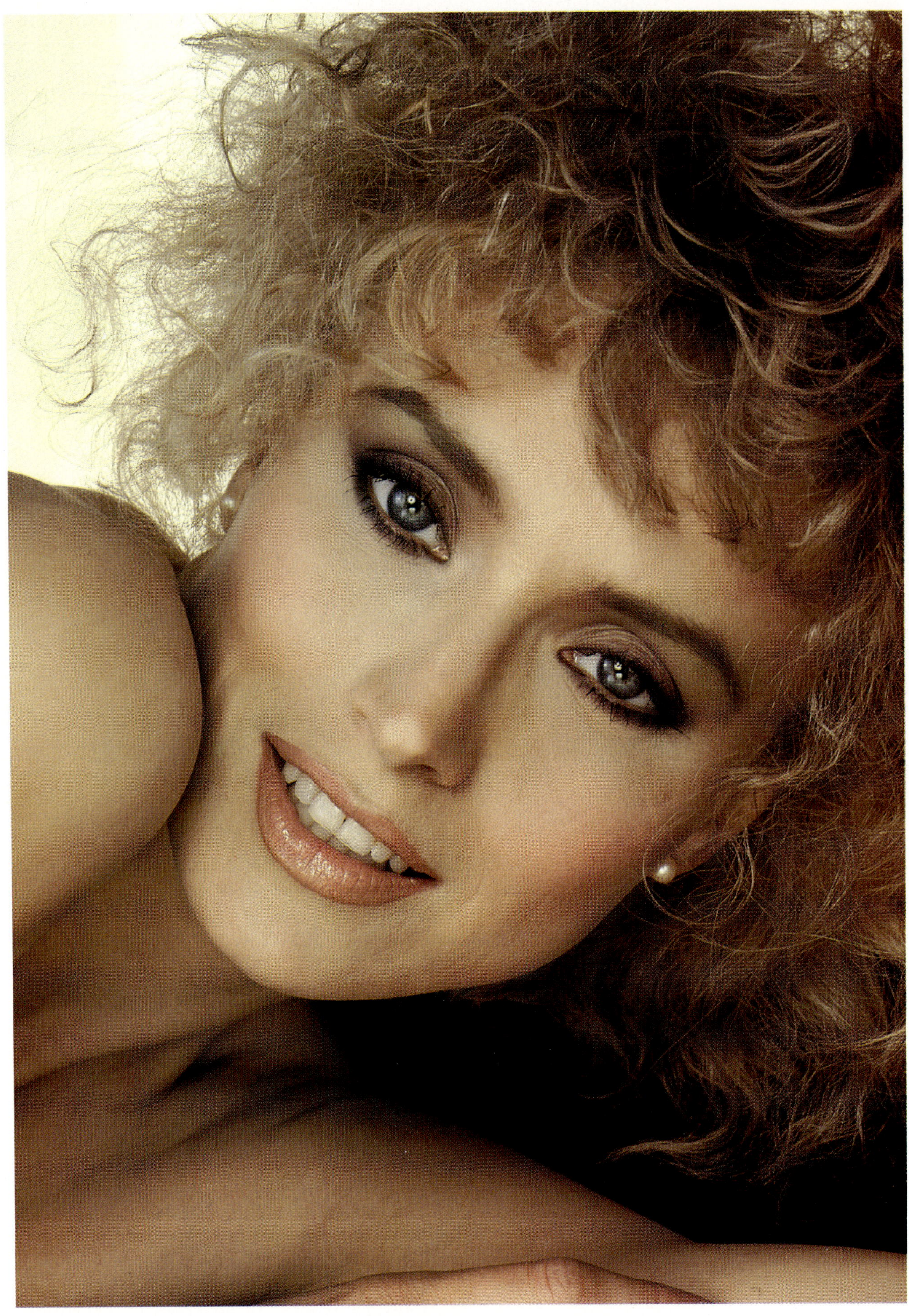

Subject: Professional model
Location: Gary Bernstein Studio, Los Angeles, California
Camera: Nikon F3
Lens: 105mm *f*-3.5 Micro-Nikkor
Lighting: One 1250-watt-second Rollei flash in pan reflector; two 800-watt-second flash heads in softboxes; one 800-watt-second flash in standard reflector
Light Control: One small Photogenic Silfoil silvered reflector
Film: Kodachrome 25
Exposure Metering: Minolta Auto-Flash III, incident-light mode
Exposure: *f*-8 (shutter at 1/60 second)

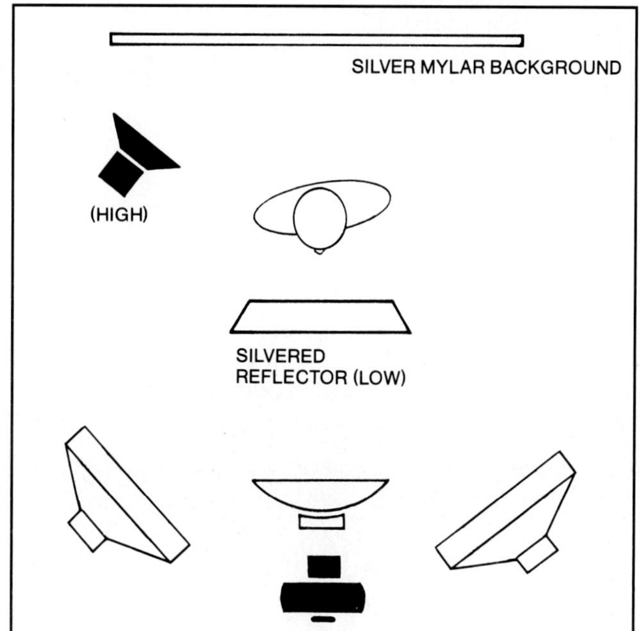

A pretty, talented model and triple main lights accounted for this classic beauty portrait.

To provide fullness to the face and add sparkle to the eyes, I placed a Rollei flash in a pan reflector near the camera position and flanked it by two large softboxes. Main modeling came from the Rollei light, which was positioned for an *f*-8 exposure. Each of the softboxes metered *f*-4 to *f*-5.6—enough light to fill shadows without destroying the modeling.

To add even more sparkle to the eyes, I placed a silvered reflector below the model's face.

I lit the silver mylar background from a high position to avoid a direct reflection back to the camera. The model's head was nearly on the studio floor, and so was my camera position. Close cropping provided a clean, graphic image. □

Subject: Professional models
Client: Chrysler Aviation
Art Directors: John Mercado and Jack Chrysler
Location: Van Nuys Airport, Van Nuys, California
Camera: Nikon F3
Lens: 85mm f-1.8 Auto-Nikkor
Lighting: Three 600-watt-second electronic flash units; three 800-watt-second electronic flash units; two 1200-watt-second electronic flash units
Light Control: Umbrellas and wide-angle reflectors
Film: Kodachrome 25
Exposure Metering: Minolta Auto-Flash III, incident-light mode
Exposure: f-11 (shutter at 1/60 second)

Although I'm generally an advocate of "less is more" where lighting is concerned, there are times when there's no substitute for sheer power. Such was the case in the production of this ad for Chrysler Aviation. I used 6600 watt-seconds of light to illuminate the plane, the two models and the foreground.

The client required an evening shot depicting a chic couple about to leave on a charter jet. Due to the nature of the scene and because I wanted to record the image on high-resolution but slow Kodachrome 25 film, a tremendous amount of light was needed.

First, the Lear Jet was towed into position. Next, a chauffeur brought in the limousine. After choosing approximate camera angle and composition, I mounted my Nikon on a sturdy Gitzo tripod. There was considerable jockeying and shifting of plane and car as I studied the scene through the viewfinder. I envisioned the final ad with the top cropped just above the tail of the plane and dark type running across the bright trunk of the limousine.

We placed seven flash heads parallel to the line of the jet's fuselage at a distance of approximately 30 feet. Each flash had a wide-angle reflector and 52-inch umbrella in overlapping configuration to bathe the plane in even illumination without objectionable reflections.

Next, we wetted the runway to achieve a pleasing reflection of the jet. Great care was taken to keep the water well away from our high-power flash generators. We were now ready to bring the couple into position. Notice that the man's dark hair is against the white background while his partner's blond head is silhouetted against a dark background. Her black dress is subtly outlined against the reflection of the plane.

The light metering along the plane's fuselage indicated an f-8 to f-11 exposure. To illuminate the couple, I used one umbrella light, slightly to the right of my camera. It was set for an f-11 exposure—the exposure I actually used. This caused the jet to be overexposed by 1/2 exposure step. It ensured emphasis of my main subject—the plane.

I used a short telephoto lens, so the plane would appear slightly closer to the couple than it actually was. With the 85mm lens, I needed the small f-11 aperture to get sufficient depth of field. □

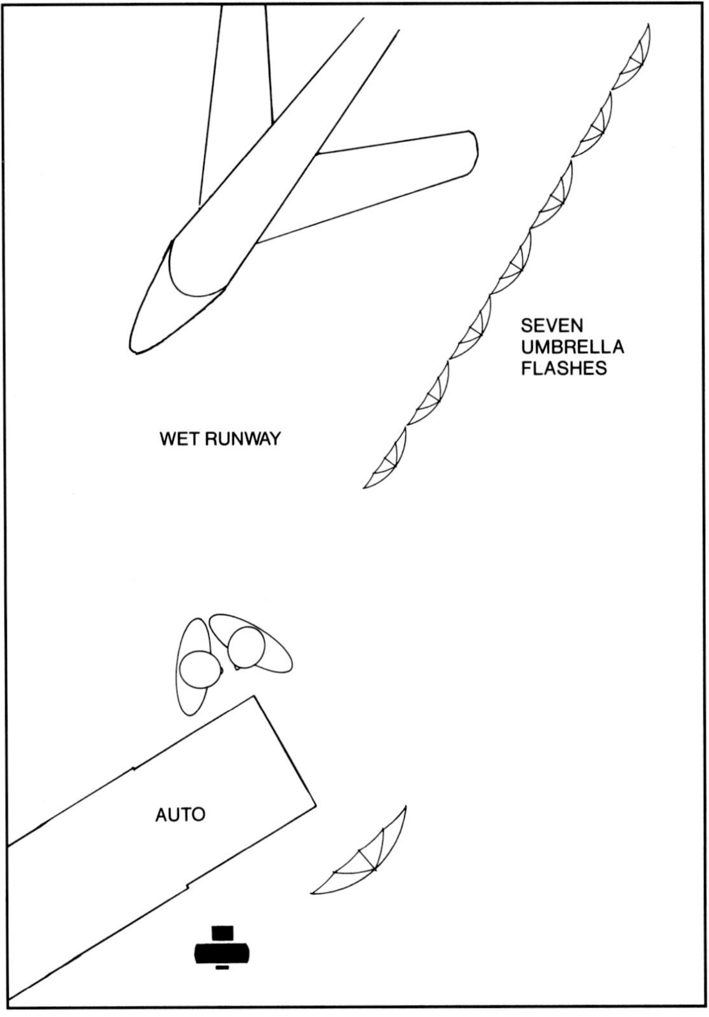

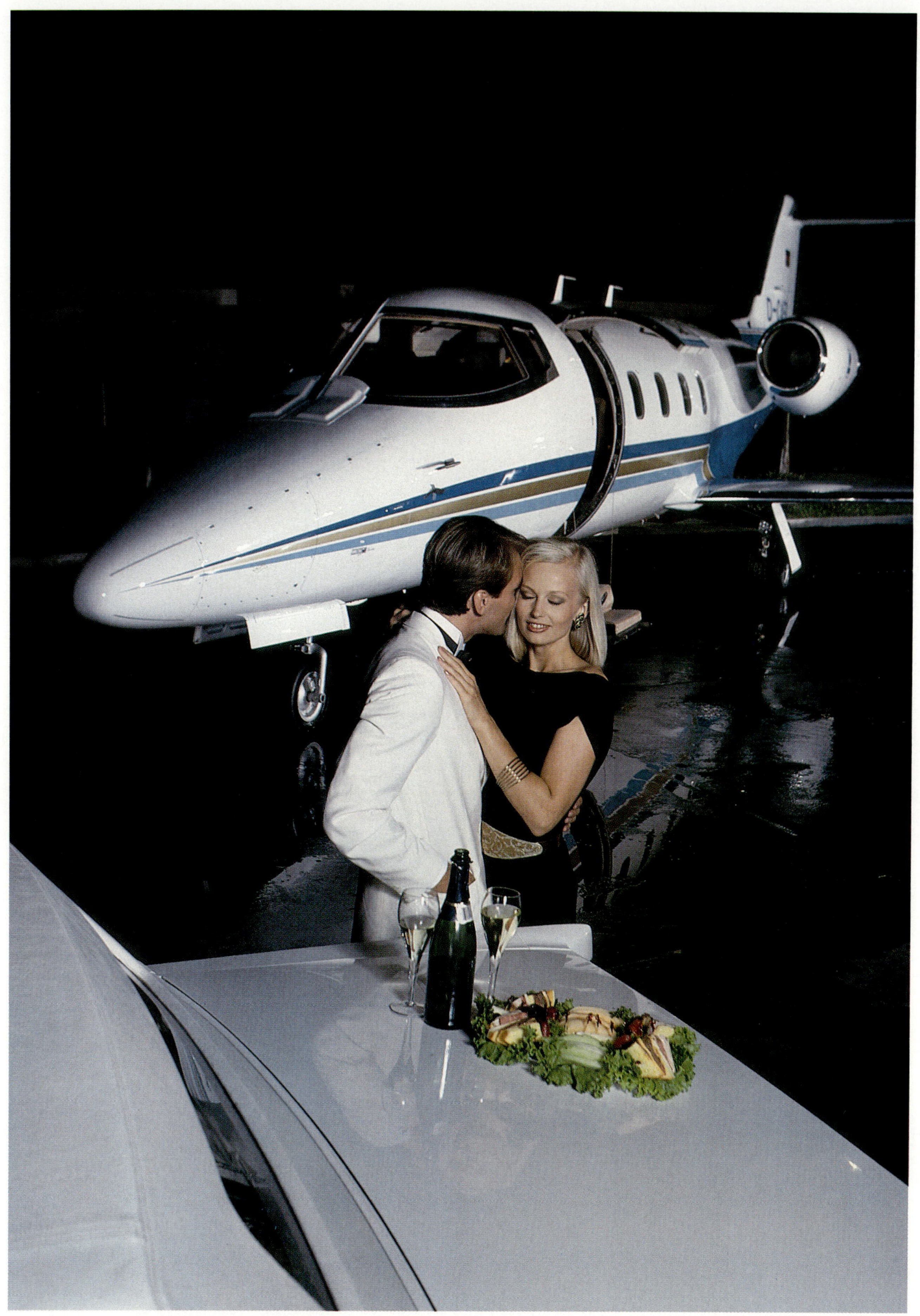

40

Subject: David Brenner
Client: Jean-Paul Germain, Ltd.
Art Director: Gary Bernstein
Location: Gary Bernstein Studio, Los Angeles, California
Camera: Nikon F2AS
Lens: 105mm *f*-2.5 Auto-Nikkor
Lighting: Two 600-watt-second electronic flash units
Film: Kodachrome 25
Exposure Metering: Minolta Auto-Flash III, incident-light mode
Exposure: *f*-8 (shutter at 1/60 second)

As a former east-coast city boy, one of the first things I installed in my Los Angeles studio was a basketball net. It came in handy for this shot of brilliant comedian David Brenner.

I was shooting David for the Jean-Paul Germain *Winners* campaign. David is also a big-city boy—so I decided to photograph him "slam-dunking" a basketball. To get him to the right height, I asked him to stand on a stepladder. I produced the illusion of movement by blowing his hair with an electric fan.

Instead of using a fancy or uniform background, I decided that the shot would look more realistic if I simply shot the studio wall and roof as it is. By using a medium telephoto lens at a medium aperture, I was able to put the background a little out of focus.

To emphasize David's height, I shot from near floor level. To avoid unflattering low lighting, however, I placed the main light at a height of nearly 12 feet. I lit the portion of the background that would appear in the frame with a second light. □

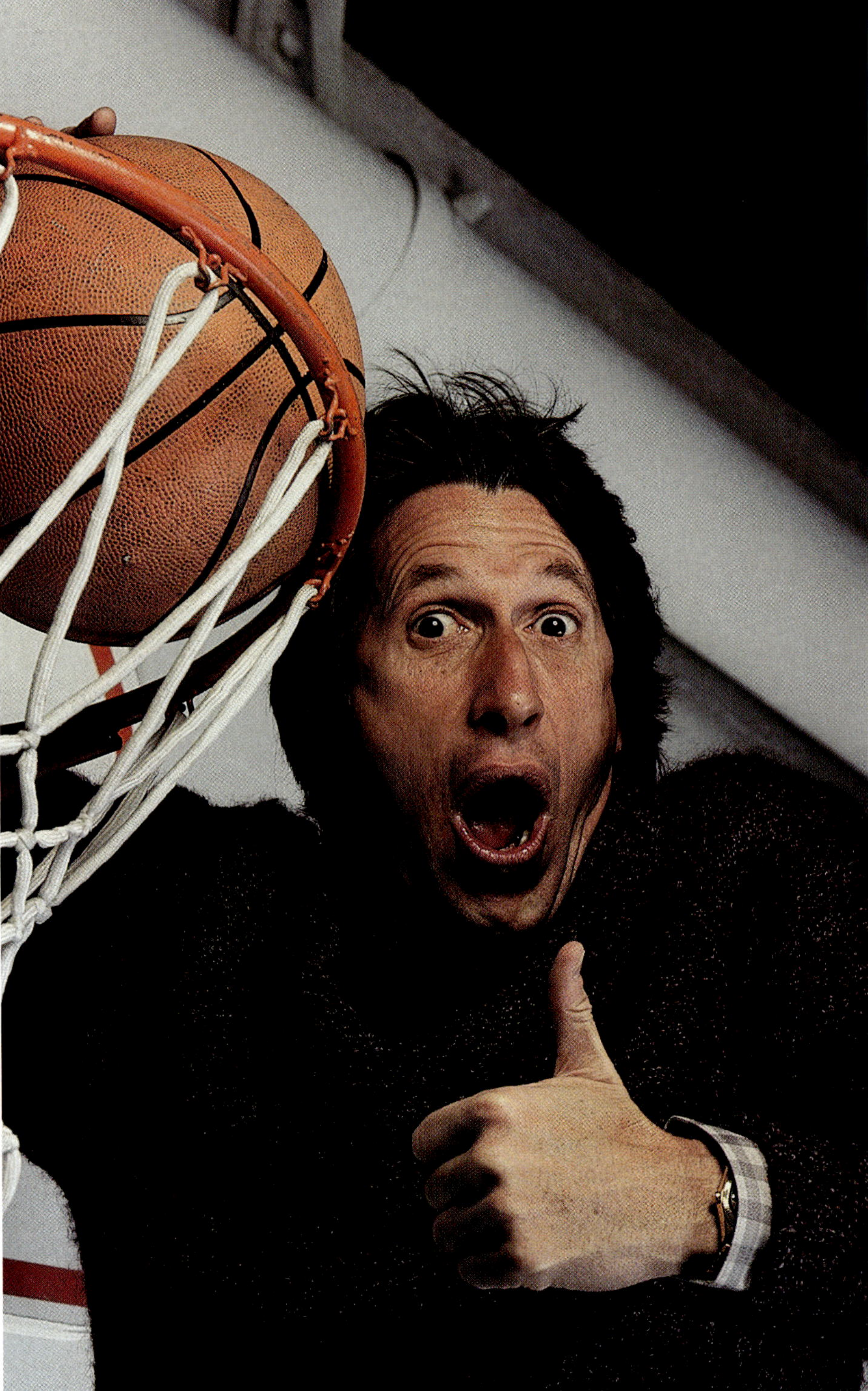

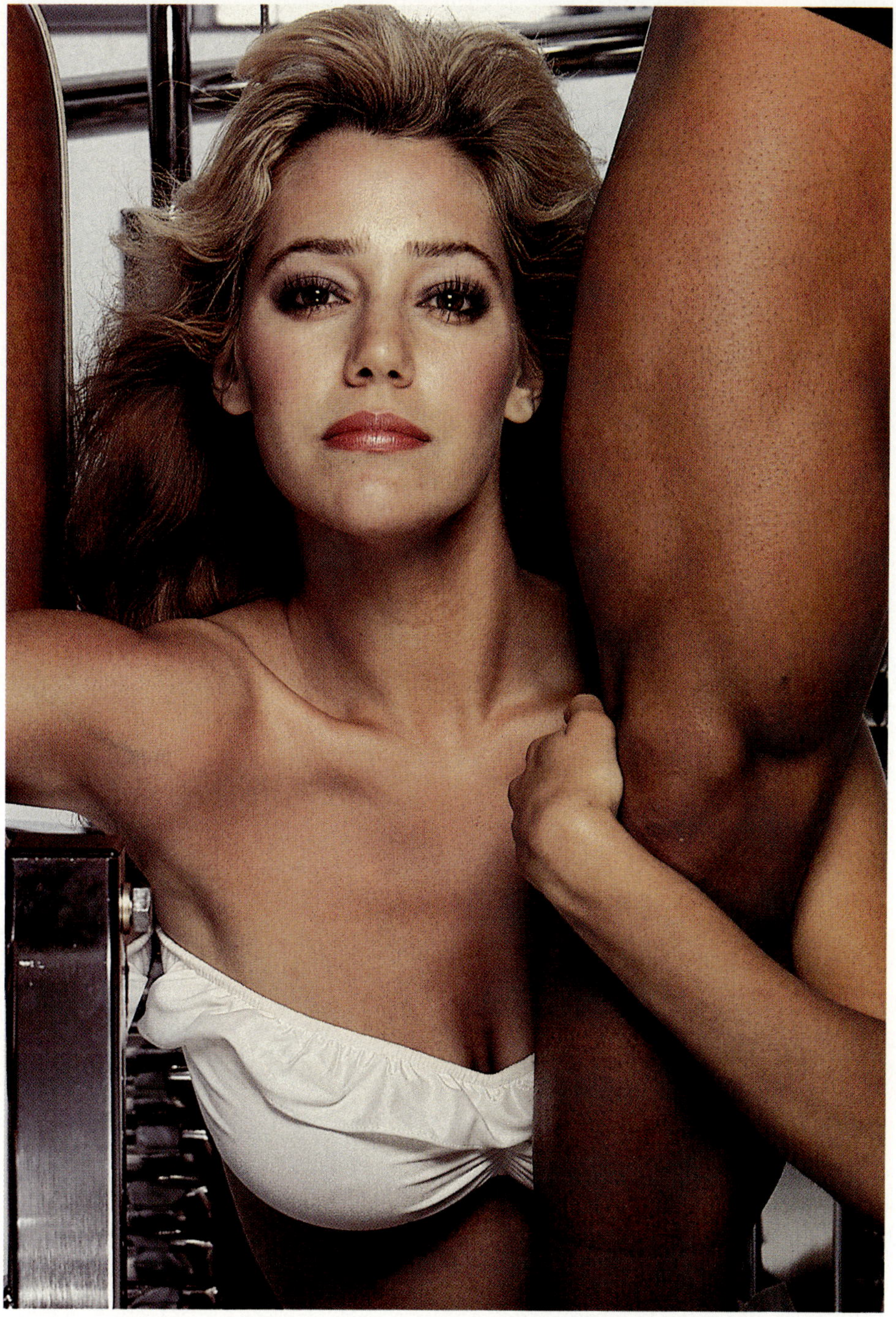

41

Subject: Professional model
Client: Paramount Fitness Equipment Corporation
Art Director: John Nicholson
Location: Gary Bernstein Studio, Los Angeles, California
Camera: Nikon F3
Lens: 85mm *f*-1.4 Auto-Nikkor
Lighting: Three 800-watt-second electronic flash units and umbrellas
Light Control: One Photogenic Silfoil reflector
Film: Kodachrome 25
Exposure Metering: Gossen Ultra Pro, incident-light mode
Exposure: *f*-8 (shutter at 1/60 second)

John Nicholson, Paramount's director of advertising, and I agreed that the best way to sell fitness equipment was by emphasizing well-developed bodies. We wanted to create an image that showed strength and beauty in a clean, uncluttered composition.

The gym equipment was wheeled into the center of a white cove in my studio. The background behind the equipment was lit uniformly by two 800-watt-second flash heads in 52-inch white umbrellas. I used a third 800-watt-second flash, bounced from a 40-inch umbrella, for main lighting. It was positioned approximately four feet in front of the model. I placed a small Photogenic Silfoil reflector below the model's face to give additional sparkle to her eyes.

We selected a male bodybuilder's impressive thigh, with skin tone that nearly matched the color of the leather exercise chair to the model's right. Notice the placement of elements within the composition—how they "contain" and frame the main subject. □

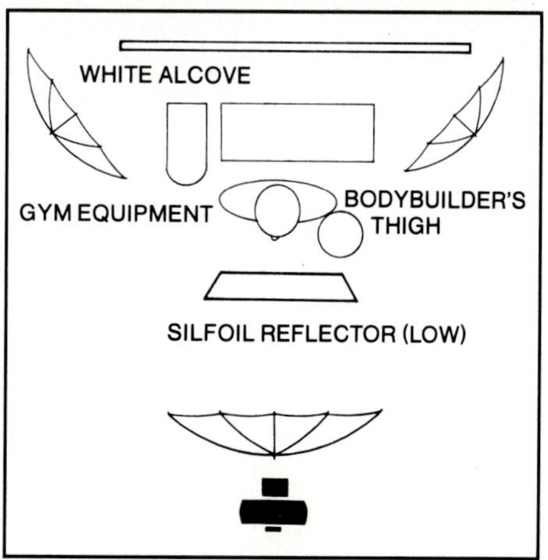

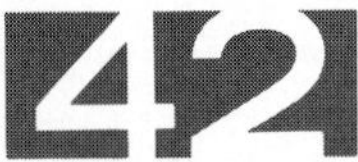

Subject: Tom Berenger (Test session)
Location: Gary Bernstein Studio, New York City
Camera: Hasselblad 500EL/M
Lens: 150mm *f*-4 Zeiss Sonnar
Lighting: One 1200-watt-second Thomastrobe electronic flash unit
Light Control: Grid-spot attachment
Film: Kodak Royal-X Pan
Exposure Metering: Wein Electronic-Flash Meter, incident-light mode
Exposure: *f*-22 (shutter at 1/125 second)

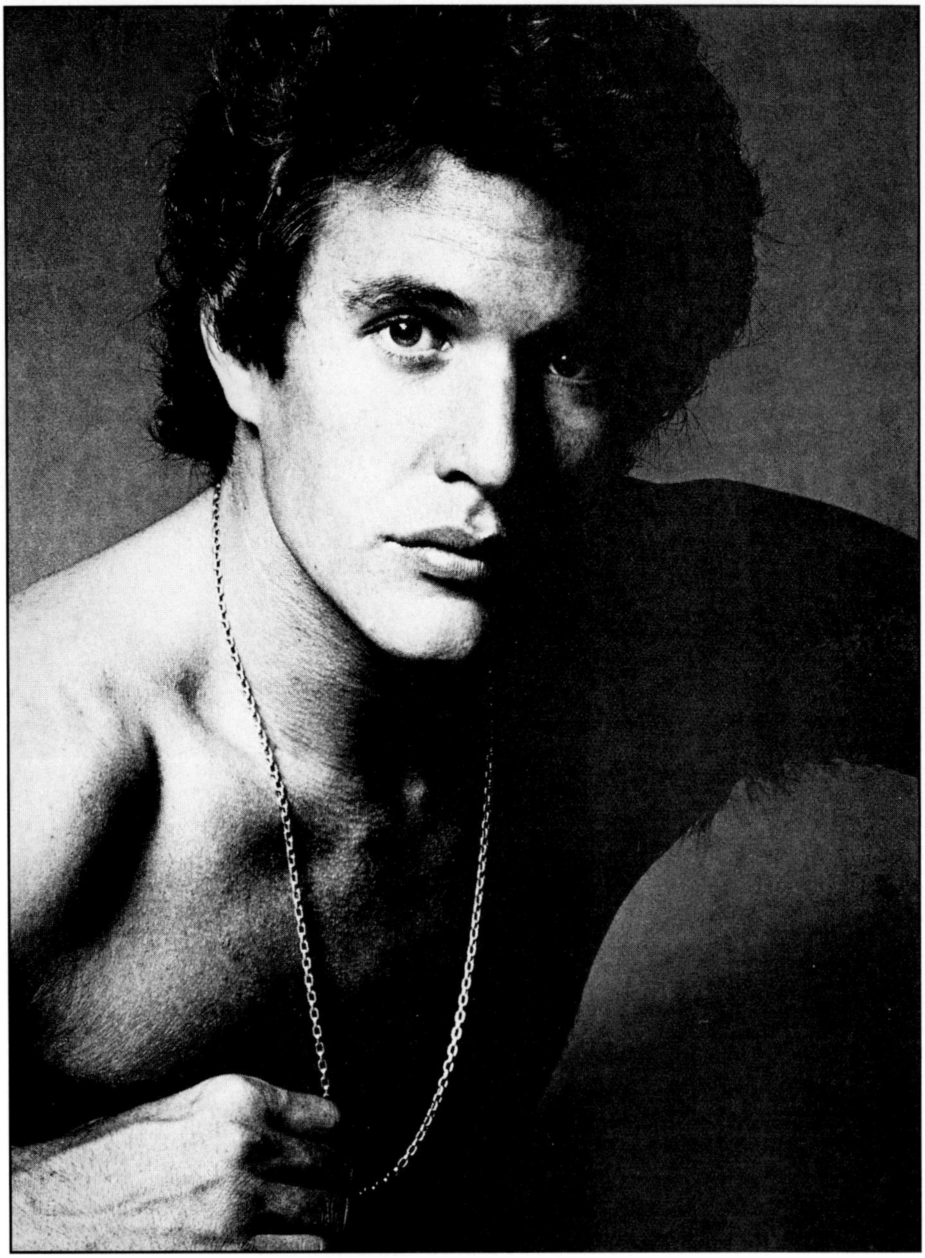

With men, you can take liberties with lighting and camera angles that would be totally unacceptable when photographing most women. In this photograph, I've emphasized the masculine features of actor Tom Berenger with a variety of techniques.

Using a single spot source from far to the left of the camera, I've lit mainly the right side of Tom's face. The shadow on the left side of the face and body lacks detail. Image balance is maintained by ensuring that there is a small area of light on the shaded side of the face. The light placement also ensures a small catchlight in each of Tom's eyes, further strengthening the balance of the image.

I used a coarse-grain b&w film and made a high-contrast print from the negative. This almost gives the appearance of a granite sculpture.

Notice the subject's placement in the composition. His eyes are placed high in the upper third of the composition, lending dominance to the face. The body and neck chain provide a graphically balanced support for the head.

My exposure-meter reading was made for the highlight area. With the high contrast of the scene, this ensured that all shadow detail would be lost. □

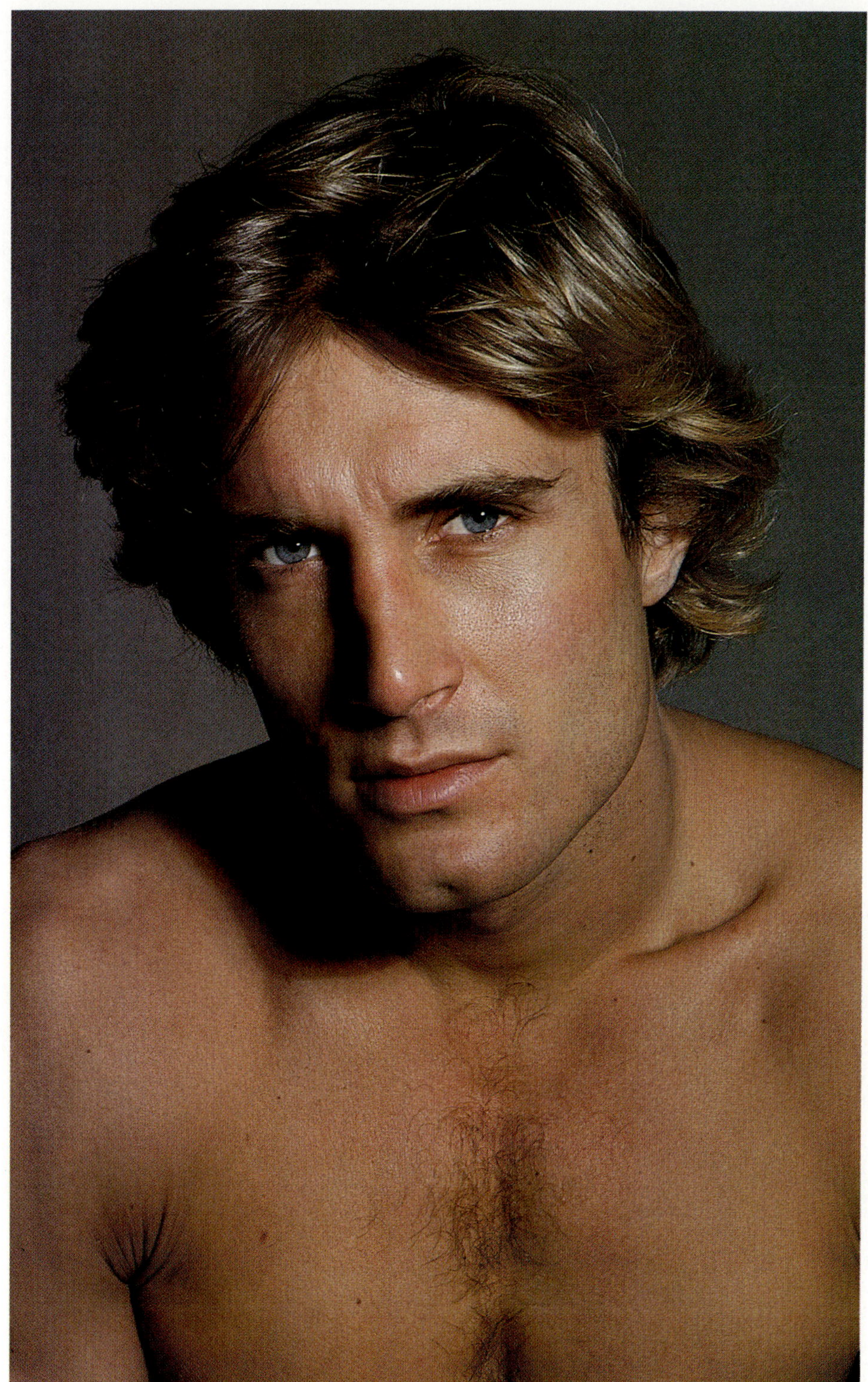

43

Subject: Anthony Hamilton
Location: Gary Bernstein Studio, New York City
Camera: Nikon F2AS
Lens: 105mm f-2.5 Auto-Nikkor
Lighting: One 1200-watt-second Thomastrobe electronic flash unit with narrow-angle reflector
Film: Kodachrome 25
Exposure Metering: Minolta Auto-Flash II, incident-light mode
Exposure: f-11 (shutter at 1/60 second)

Tony Hamilton has always been one of my favorite male models. In addition to his obvious good looks, he has a fine ability to take direction and emote in front of the camera. His subsequent acting success has come as no surprise to me.

In this photograph, I chose to emphasize Hamilton's strong features by using a spot as the only light source. The small source caused dense shadows with little detail. It's an ideal way to bring out classic lines such as are evident in Tony's face.

I emphasized Tony's body and highlighted hair against a dark-gray background—created by underexposing white seamless paper by about 3 steps. With a model having darker hair, I would have added a hair light from the rear to separate the head from the background.

I generated subtle hair movement with an electric fan, set at a slow speed. □

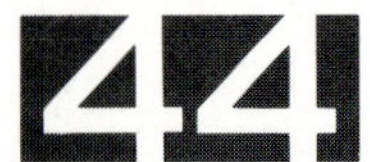

Subject: Natalie Cole
Client: Posner Cosmetics, Inc.
Ad Agency: Hicks and Griest, Inc.
Art Director: Ralph Parenio
Location: Gary Bernstein Studio, Los Angeles, California
Camera: Nikon F2AS
Lens: 55mm *f*-3.5 Micro-Nikkor
Lighting: Four 600-watt-second electronic flash units
Film: Kodachrome 64
Exposure Metering: Minolta Auto-Flash II, incident-light mode
Exposure: *f*-5.6 (shutter at 1/60 second)

This photo of beautiful songstress Natalie Cole was taken for a counter display for a cosmetic company. The clapboard background was built specially for the session and painted to match the color of Natalie's gown.

First I positioned the rim light—a 600-watt-second electronic flash with wide-angle reflector. It was on a 20-foot-high light stand, above and behind the background and aimed to rim Natalie's hair and form. An incident-light reading from the top of Natalie's head recorded between *f*-8 and *f*-11.

Next I placed the main light—another 600-watt-second flash, bounced from a 40-inch white umbrella. The light was set to give an *f*-5.6 meter reading at the subject. This allowed the back light to overpower the main light by 1-1/2 exposure steps. The overexposure created the white halo around Natalie's image.

Finally, the background was lit by two 600-watt-second flash units, placed to either side of Natalie. The background light to the left of the camera gave an average exposure reading of *f*-5.6, balancing with the main-light exposure. The background light to the right of the camera was rated one exposure step higher, at *f*-8. The area it illuminated was purposely overexposed to allow for surprinting of copy on the completed ad.

Natalie and I rehearsed her movement prior to shooting. She perfected it to the point where she could take one step and end up in the right position at will. To be sure to capture the precise correct moment, I exposed every time she *nearly* completed her move. Precision was necessary to ensure that Natalie would be at the right location for best rim lighting and back lighting. Her grace and ease completed an attractive image. □

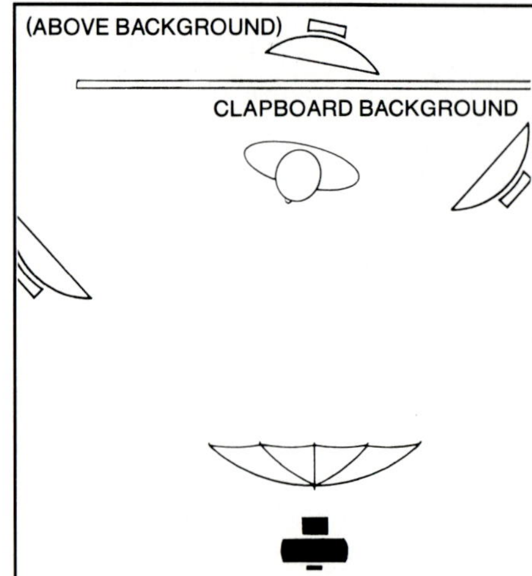

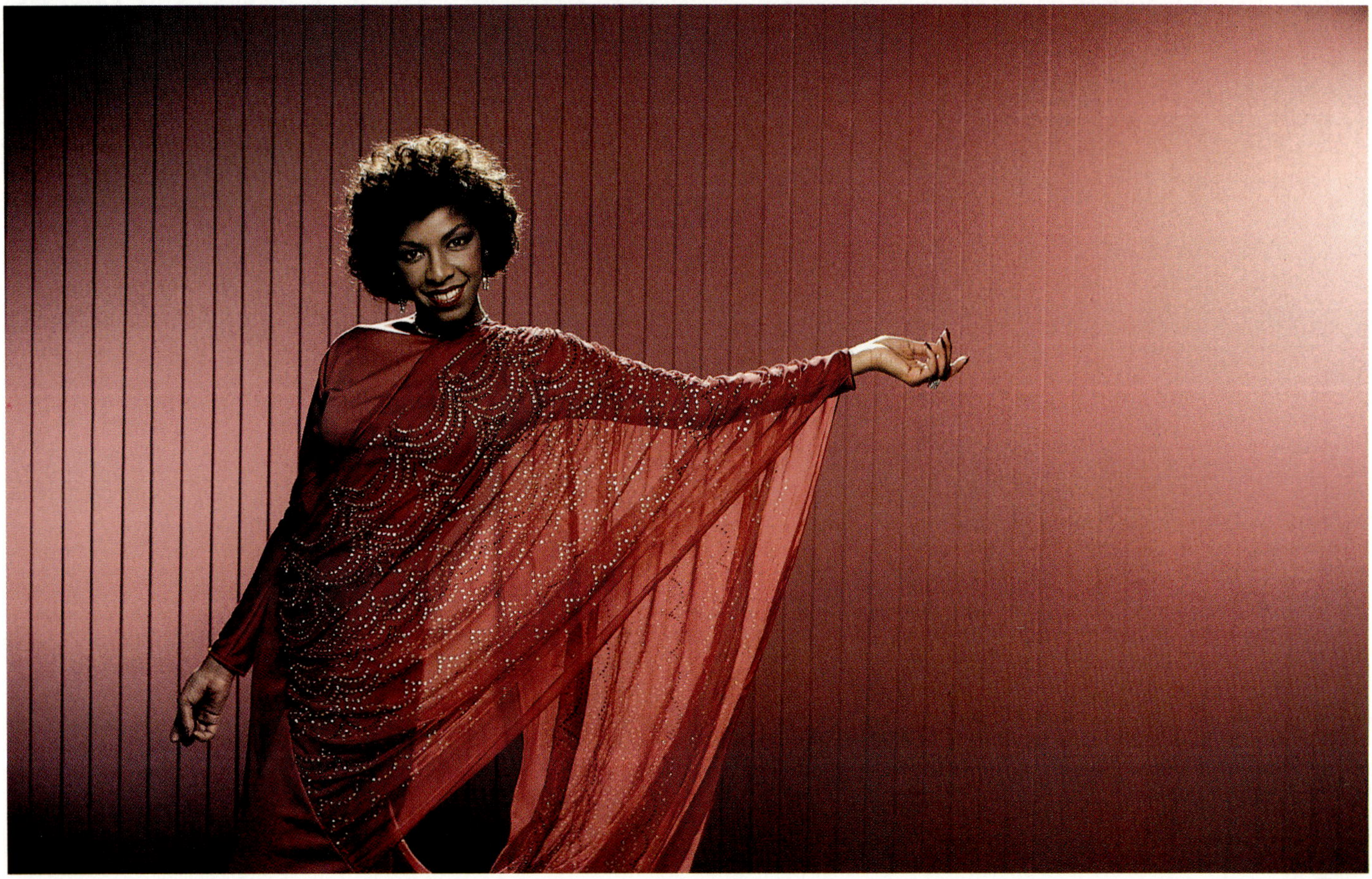

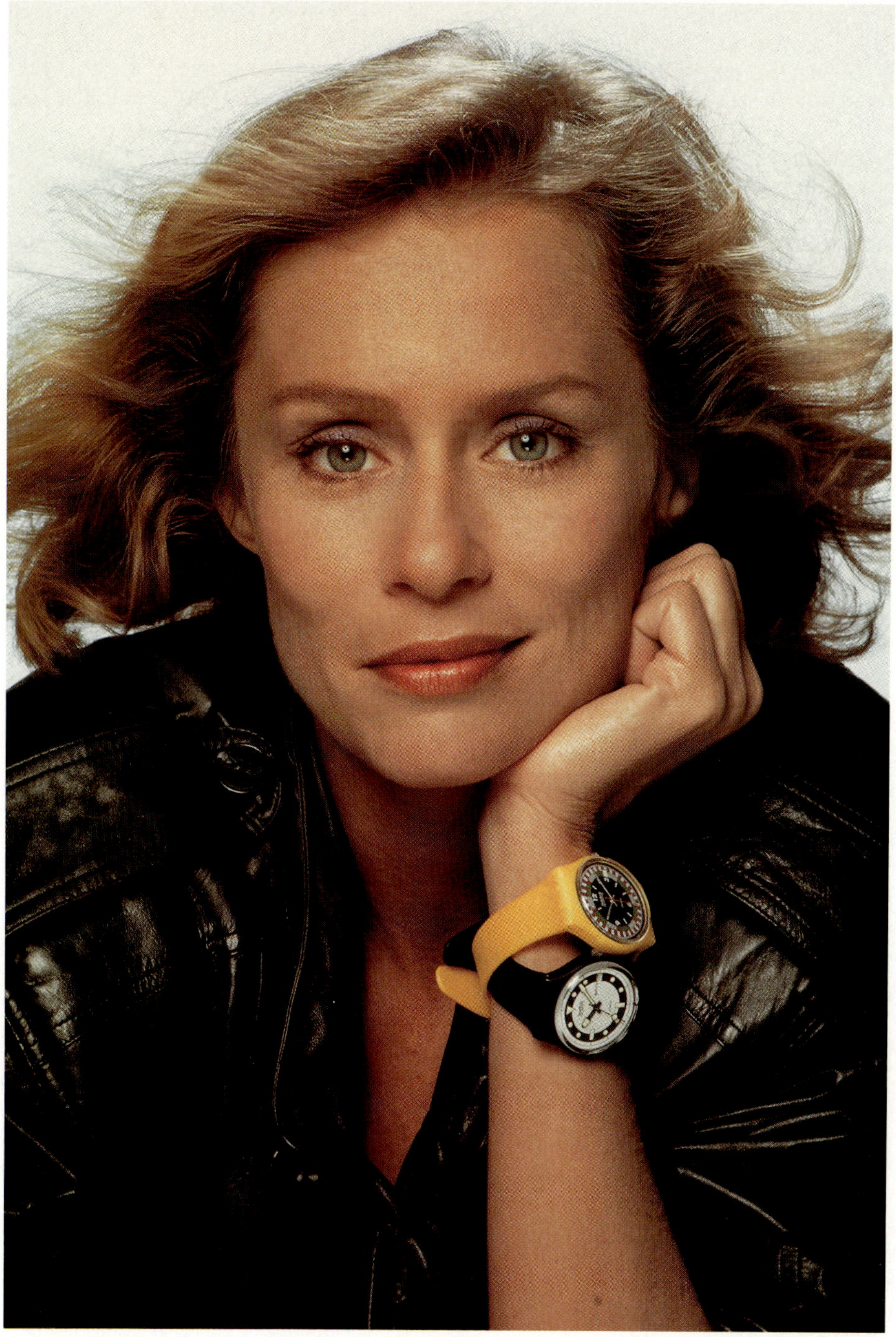

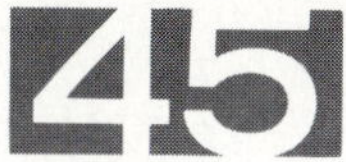

Subject: Lauren Hutton
Client: Swatch Watch U.S.A., Inc.
Location: Gary Bernstein Studio, Los Angeles, California
Camera: Nikon F3
Lens: 105mm *f*-2.5 Auto-Nikkor
Lighting: One Rollei 1250-watt-second electronic flash with pan reflector; two 400-watt-second Photogenic Versatron background lights; one 600-watt-second flash with grid spot on boom stand
Light Control: One 27-inch silvered reflector
Film: Kodachrome 25
Exposure Metering: Gossen Ultra Pro, incident-light mode
Exposure: *f*-11 (shutter at 1/60 second)

It was a pleasure to photograph fabulous Lauren Hutton. As she entered the studio, visions of former *Vogue* covers ran through my mind.

The main light, at 1250-watt-second output, required an exposure of *f*-11 when placed three feet in front of Lauren. The aperture provided adequate depth of field, so I could shoot without worrying about critical focus.

Two Photogenic Versatron background lights, each in an umbrella, were set to deliver an *f*-16 exposure. The one-step overexposure of the white-cove background ensured that it would record as pure white.

A fourth light completed the lighting setup. It was fitted with a focusing grid spot and positioned on a boom stand above and slightly behind Lauren. This light delivered one exposure step more light to the hair than the main light did to the face. It added a highlight to Lauren's fan-blown hair.

As I mentioned earlier in this book, during my early days in New York I learned some useful lighting techniques from top models.

While I answered a phone call, my assistant had placed a reflector to Lauren's left side. She immediately asked, "Gary, does he know what he's doing?" Lauren's doubt was well-founded—the reflector was not positioned properly. I am grateful to Lauren for her professionalism—on *both* sides of the camera! □

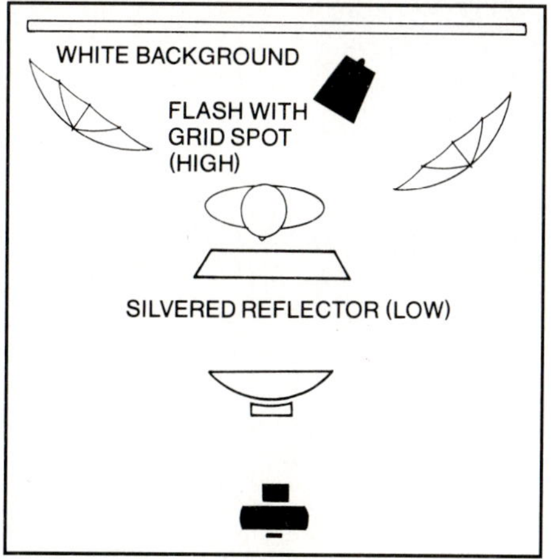

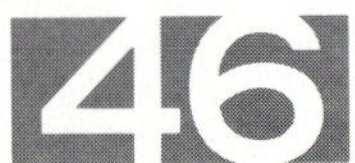

Subject: Pam Dawber
Client: Good Housekeeping
Location: Gary Bernstein Studio, Los Angeles, California
Camera: Nikon F2AS
Lens: 105mm *f*-2.5 Auto-Nikkor
Lighting: Two 600-watt-second electronic flash units
Light Control: 27-inch silver reflector; large, white reflector
Film: Kodachrome 25
Exposure Metering: Minolta Auto-Flash III, incident-light mode
Exposure: *f*-8 (shutter at 1/60 second)

This photograph of pretty, talented Pam Dawber was taken for the cover of *Good Housekeeping* magazine. Pam changed wardrobe, makeup and hairstyle three times during the session. The lighting configuration, however, remained basically the same.

Main light was a 600-watt-second electronic flash, bounced from an umbrella. The light was about four feet from the subject. It provided soft light with delicate facial modeling. Lighting contrast depends on the relationship of light-source size and its distance from the subject. As the light is moved closer, contrast is reduced; as it's moved farther away, contrast increases.

To add extra sparkle to Pam's eyes, I placed a 27-inch silver reflector on the floor below her face.

The background was lit by a 600-watt-second flash. I positioned a large, white reflector in a manner that ensured uniform illumination on the background wall. The light on the wall metered *f*-4—which was 2 exposure steps less light than the *f*-8 registered on the subject's face. Exposing for the face, I got the medium-gray background. □

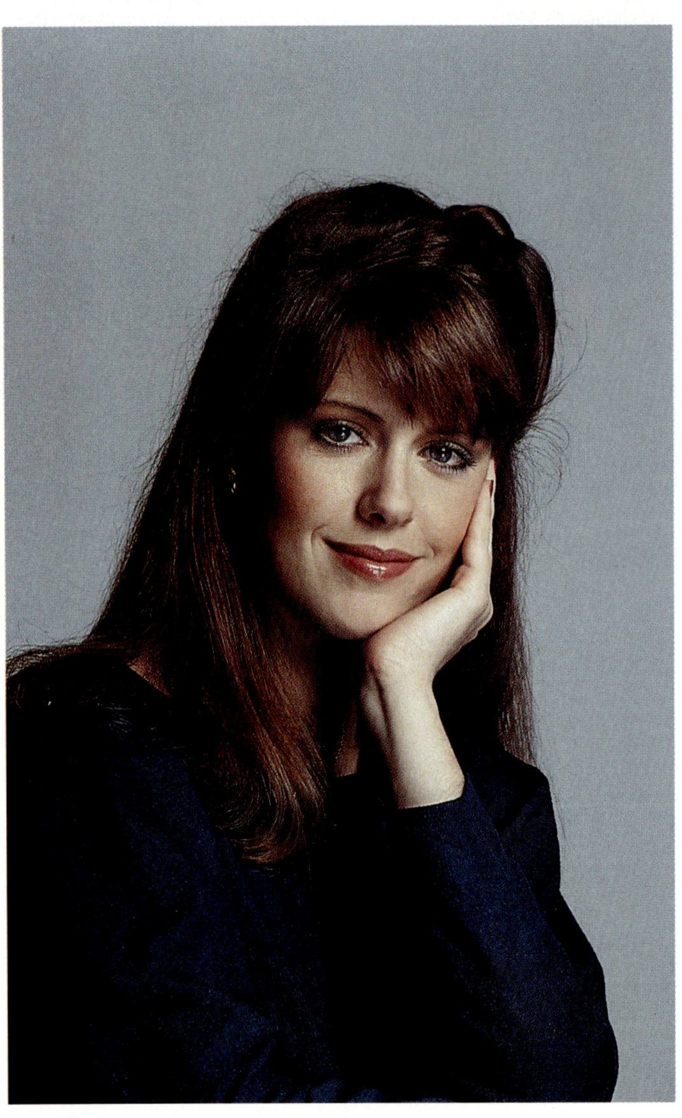

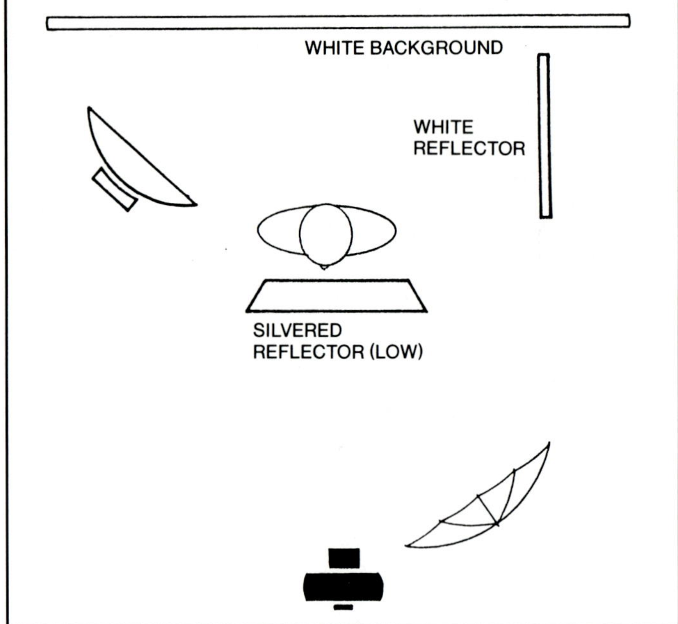

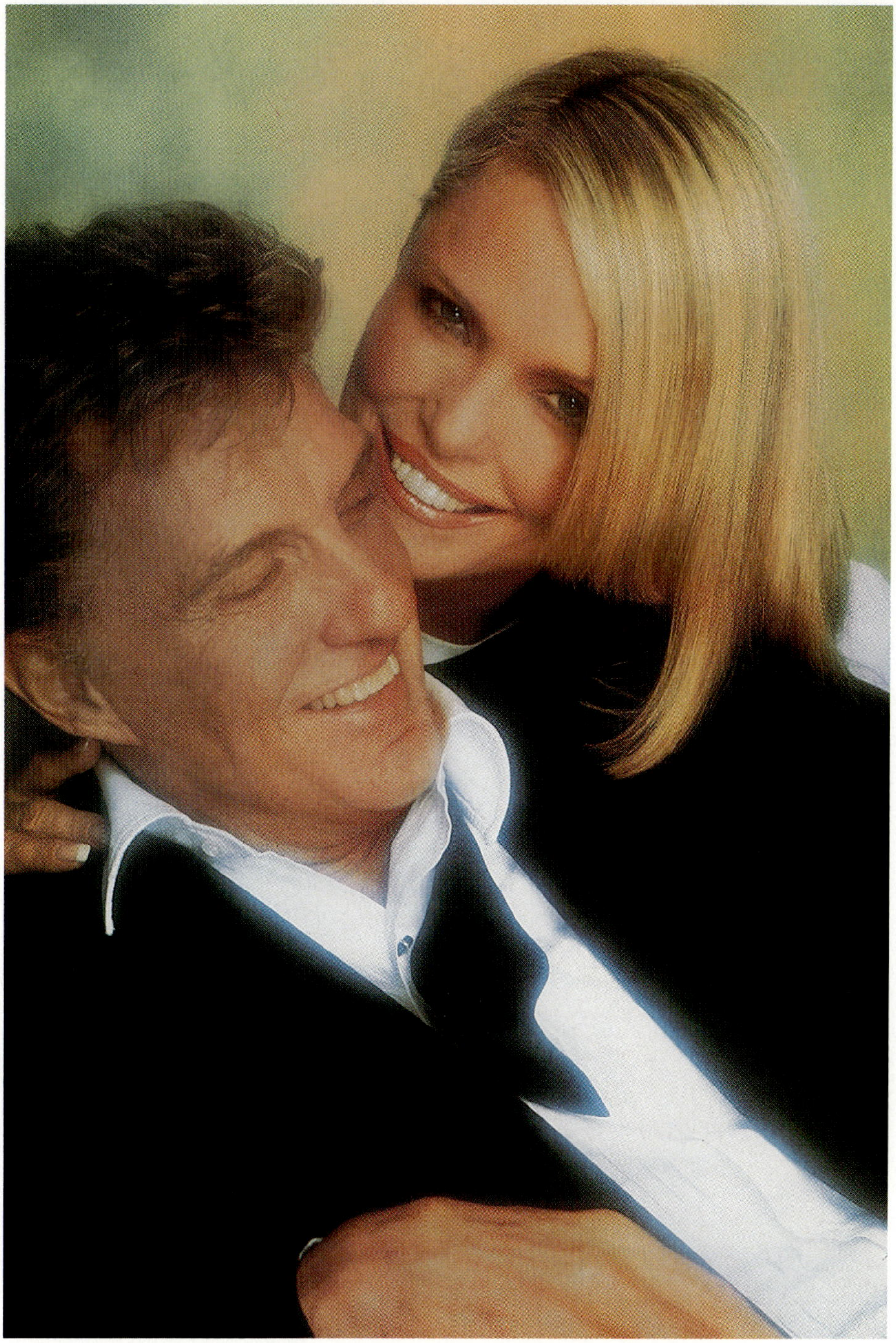

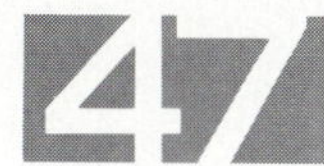

Subject: Robert and Rosemarie Stack
Client: Rosemarie Stack, Ltd. for Les Grains
Art Directors: Rosemarie Stack and Gary Bernstein
Location: The Stack's home, Bel Air, California
Camera: Nikon F3
Lens: 105mm *f*-4 Micro-Nikkor
Lighting: Three electronic flash units
Light Control: 27-inch silver reflector
Film: Kodachrome 64
Filtration: Lens diffuser
Exposure Metering: Minolta Auto-Flash III, incident-light mode
Exposure: *f*-8 (shutter at 1/60 second)

Photographing a beautiful couple like the Robert Stacks is a wonderful occasion. The photo was to promote Rosemarie's new line of romantic French perfumes. What better subjects than a couple who has been romancing for nearly 30 years!

Our initial concept was of "a sophisticated couple returning home after a chic party." Of numerous variations on this theme, this charming, spontaneous shot was the first photo selected for use in the campaign.

I set up a hand-painted background in the Stacks' living room. The background was evenly lit by two flashes in 40-inch umbrellas—one on each side of the subjects. Next, I positioned my main light—another flash bounced from a 40-inch, silvered umbrella. The subject illumination metered at *f*-8 and the background at *f*-11. The additional exposure on the background allowed the colors to record with soft, pastel shades.

The lighting was completed with the addition of a silver reflector, placed below the subjects' faces to lighten shadows. The reflector also added secondary catchlights to Rosemarie's pretty eyes.

The session was candid. I positioned Bob and Rosemarie as I wanted them and then let them talk, cuddle and frolic—which they did with ease! Their spontaneity and believability are evident in the result. The photo truly represents two warm, loving people. □

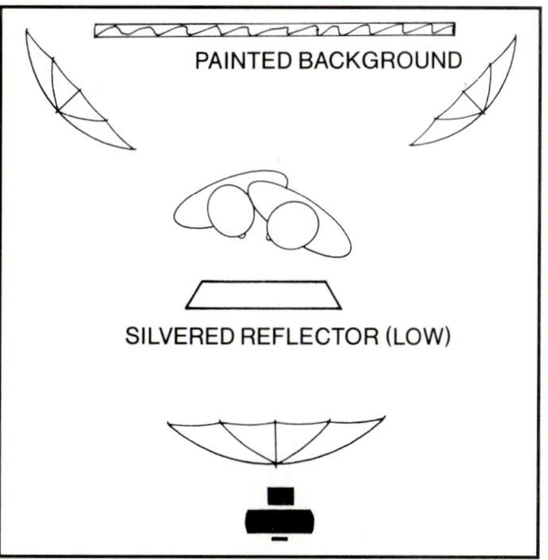

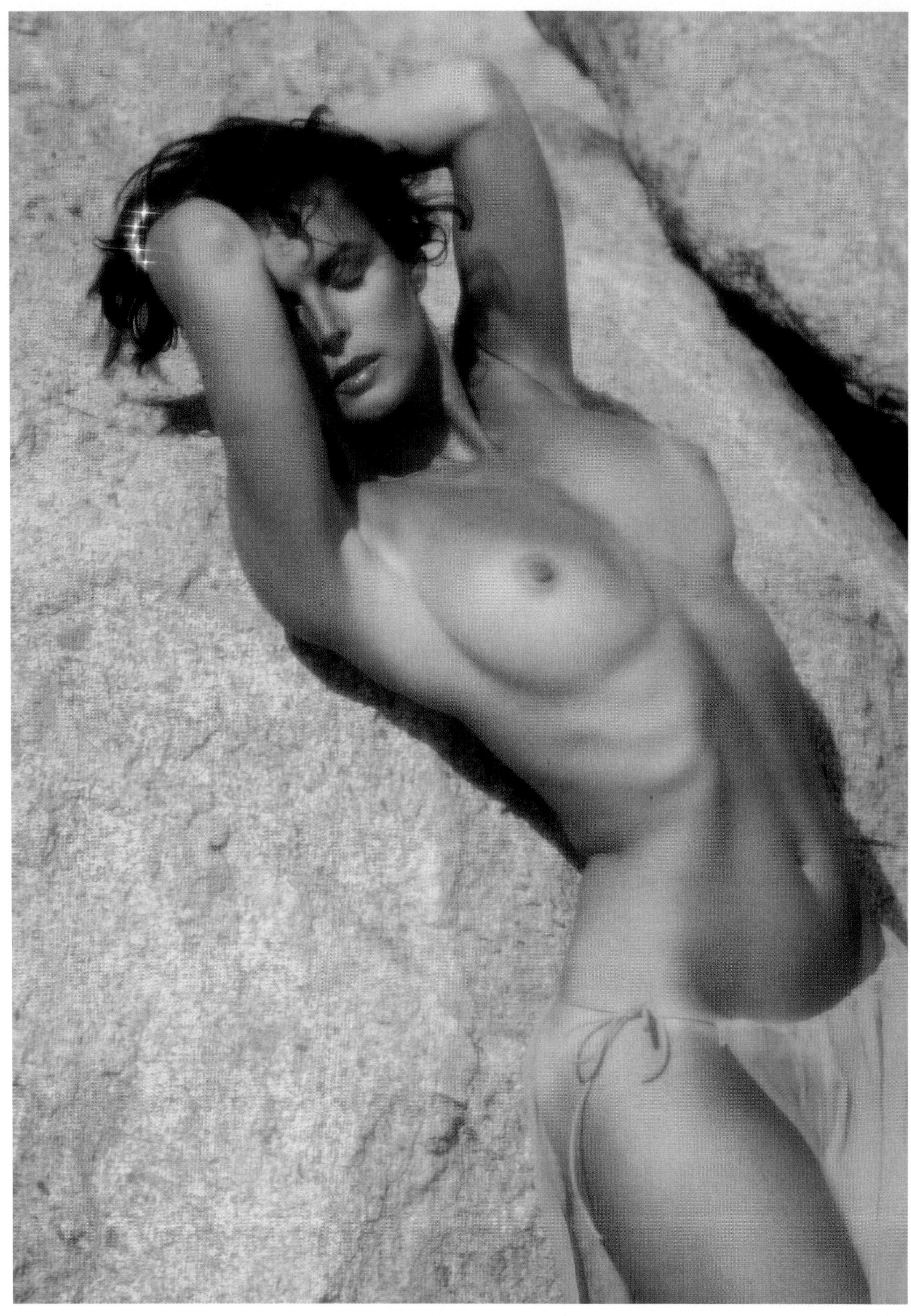

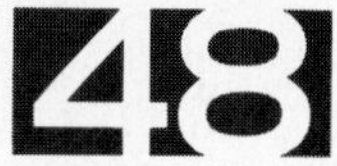

Subject: Professional model
Location: Aruba, Netherland Antilles
Camera: Nikon F2
Lens: 105mm *f*-2.5 Auto-Nikkor
Lighting: Midday sunlight
Film: Kodachrome 25
Filtration: Blue Nikkor B12 filter; star filter; homemade diffuser
Exposure Metering: Nikon through-the-lens, center-weighted
Exposure: 1/250 second at *f*-5.6

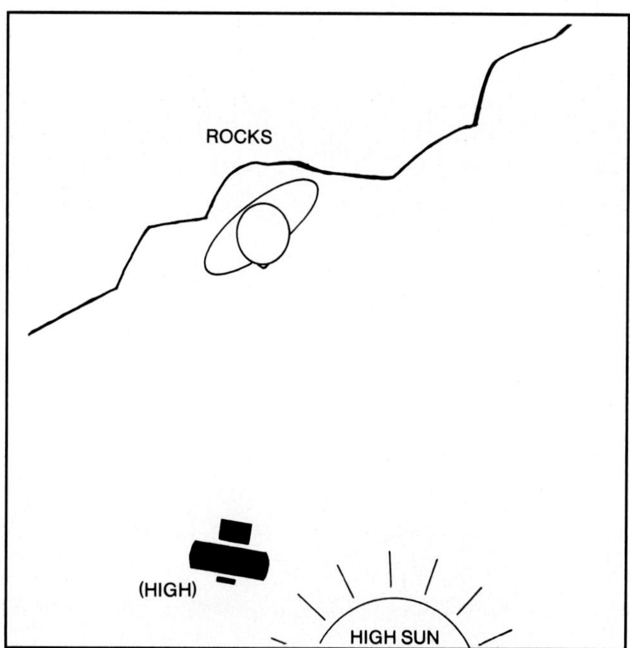

Without modification, direct midday sunlight is too high to be suitable as a main-light source. Normally, its use results in unflattering shadows and deep, dark sockets where the eyes should appear.

For this photo, I wanted to use direct, unmodified sunlight. I could only do this effectively by placing the model so the light struck her from a suitable, flattering angle. I asked the model to arch her back over a large rock.

To get the best camera viewpoint, I stood on a large rock. My back was toward the sun.

I placed a deep blue filter over the lens and bracketed exposures in steps, from the indicated meter reading to four exposure steps less than the reading. By selecting one of the bluish images of appropriate density, I was able to achieve a dreamlike image. □

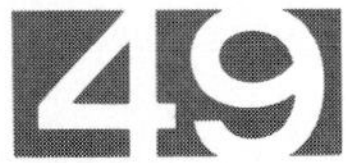

Subject: Professional model
Client: Charles of the Ritz
Ad Agency: Daniel and Charles Advertising, Inc.
Location: Gary Bernstein Studio, New York City
Camera: Hasselblad EL/M
Lens: 80mm *f*-2.8 Zeiss Planar
Lighting: One 1200-watt-second Thomastrobe electronic flash unit
Light Control: Silvered reflector
Film: Kodak Tri-X Pan Professional
Exposure Metering: Wein Electronic-Flash Meter, incident-light mode
Exposure: *f*-16 (shutter at 1/125 second)

These are very different images, yet there are many similarities in how I made them. For both, I used a standard lens on a 2-1/4-inch-square camera. The large image size provides better resolution at high enlargement than the 35mm format. The square format also provides great compositional versatility.

Both images were taken from a low camera viewpoint, adding prominence to the subjects. The viewer of these photos must "look up" to the subjects.

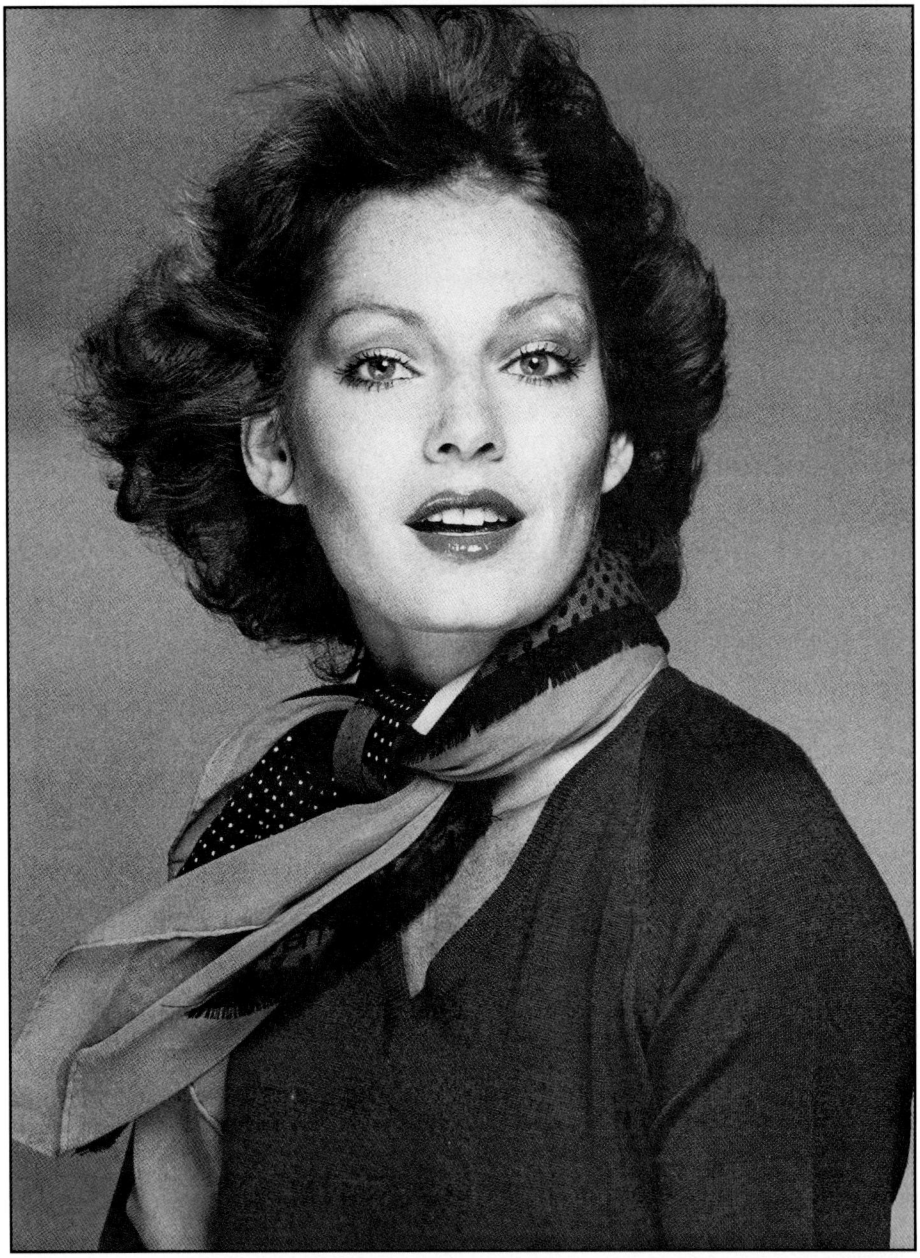

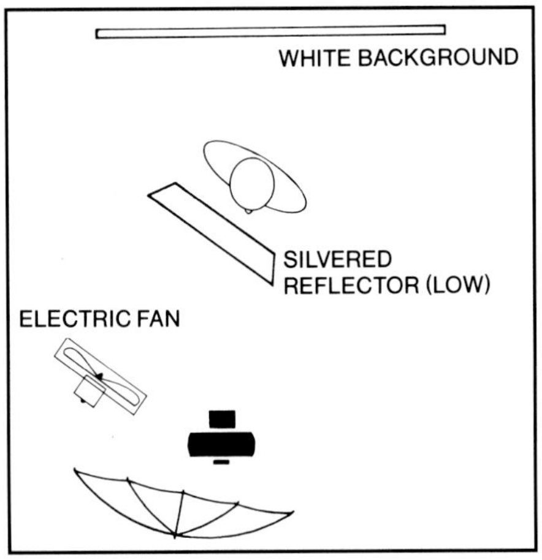

Both photographs were made with a single main light, bounced from a 40-inch white umbrella. The umbrella was approximately eight feet from the subjects. The great flash-to-subject

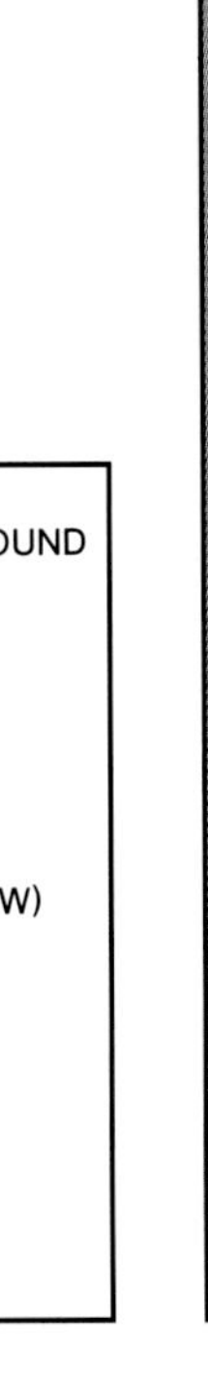

distance allowed the subjects some freedom of movement without excessive exposure fluctuations. It also created a bit of extra contrast. For each photo, I used a silver reflector beneath the faces to soften and fill the shadow areas.

Both images were taken against a white, seamless background that appears gray because it received two exposure steps less light than the subjects.

Notice the hair movement created in each image by an electric fan. It adds graphic excitement. In each photo, the subjects were seated on adjustable stools and asked to position themselves comfortably. The results look totally natural. □

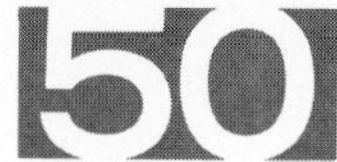

Subject: Couple (Private portrait session)
Location: Gary Bernstein Studio, New York City
Camera: Hasselblad EL/M
Lens: 80mm *f*-2.8 Zeiss Planar
Lighting: One 1200-watt-second Thomastrobe electronic flash unit
Light Control: Silvered reflector
Film: Kodak Tri-X Pan Professional
Exposure Metering: Wein Electronic-Flash Meter, incident-light mode
Exposure: *f*-16 (shutter at 1/125 second)

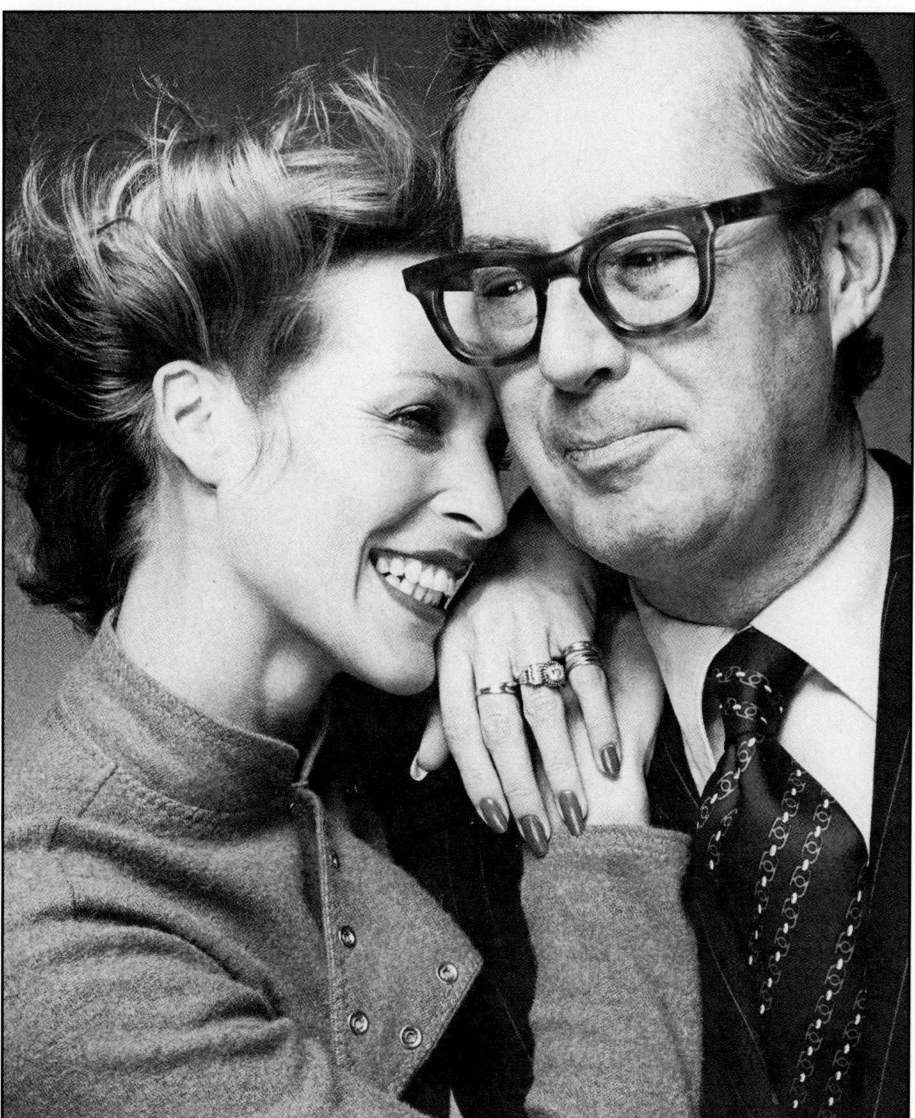

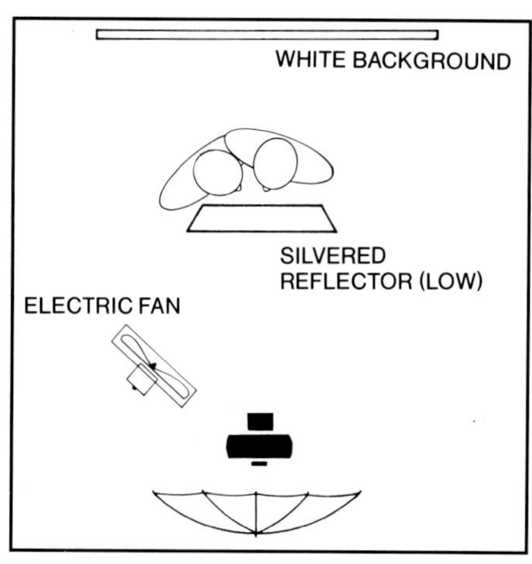

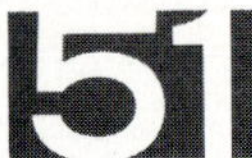

Subject: Professional models
Client: Rainbow Video Corporation, Washington D.C. and Gary Bernstein Productions, Inc. Culver City, California
Executive Producer: Stanley R. Zupnik
Art Director/Producer: Gary Bernstein
Location: Gary Bernstein Studio, Los Angeles, California
Camera: Nikon F3
Lens: 55mm f-3.5 Micro-Nikkor
Lighting: Three 400-watt-second Photogenic Porta-Master electronic flash units
Light Control: Photogenic 32-inch Halo on main light; two 45-inch Halos on background lights; two seven-foot gobo panels
Film: Kodachrome 25
Exposure Metering: Minolta Auto-Flash III, incident-light mode
Exposure: f-5.6 (shutter at 1/60 second)

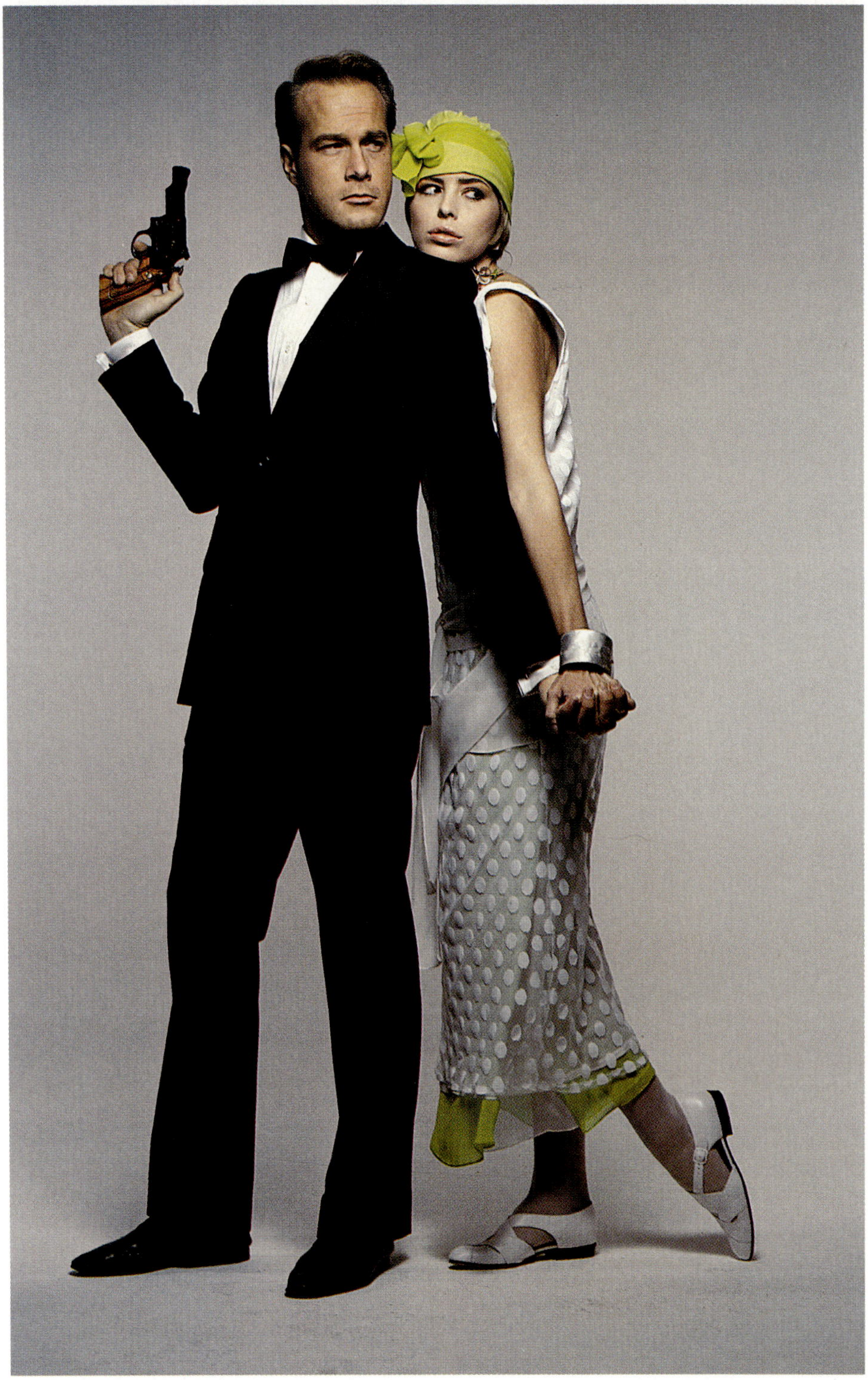

These two images were made for my 40-minute instructional video, *The Magic of Photography.* They were used to demonstrate how a background can be changed from medium gray to pure white.

The light positions were the same for both photographs, The main light, in a 32-inch Halo, was about six feet from the models. Two background lights, in 45-inch Halos, were on either side of the models. To avoid spill light on the subjects from the background lights, I placed a seven-foot gobo panel between each light and the models.

To achieve the gray background, I set the background lights for about 2 steps less exposure than the main light. To achieve the white background, I simply increased the power of the background lights, giving the background about 1/2 step more exposure than the models.

In my video, each of these images is part of a picture sequence, telling a story. Here, they appear singly and out of context. For this reason, the content of the photos may appear somewhat puzzling. □

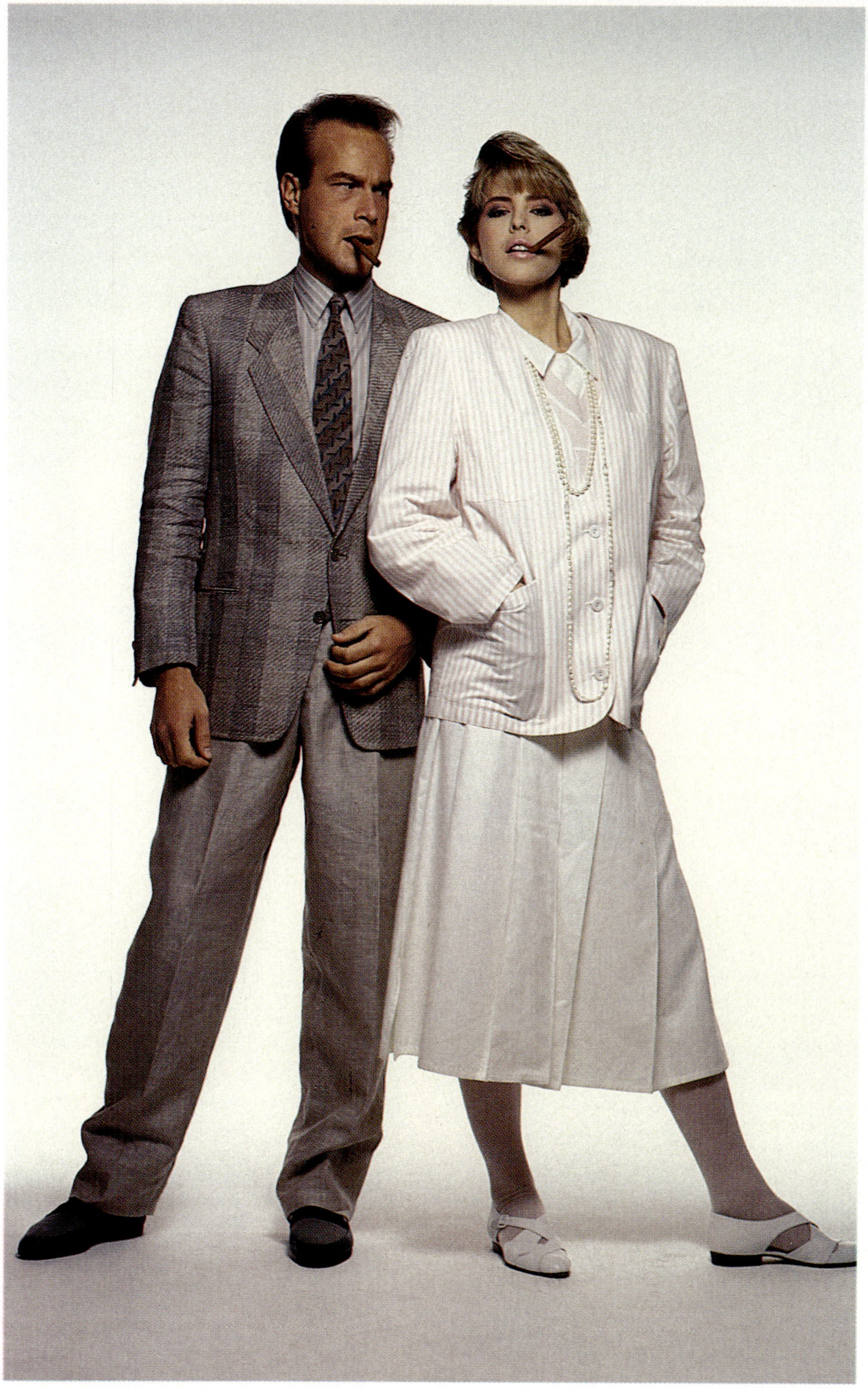

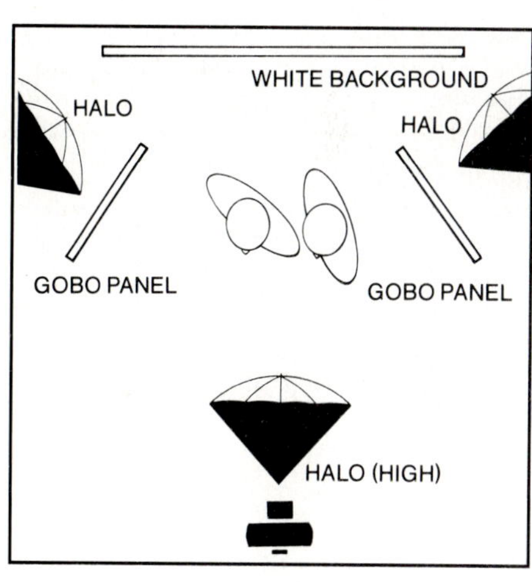
WHITE BACKGROUND
HALO
HALO
GOBO PANEL
GOBO PANEL
HALO (HIGH)

Subject: Professional model
Client: Munich Machine
Ad Agency: Art Hotel, Inc.
Art Director: Chris Whorf
Location: Gary Bernstein Studio, Los Angeles, California
Camera: Nikon F3
Lens: 55mm *f*-3.5 Micro-Nikkor
Lighting: One 1200-watt-second electronic flash unit; two 600-watt-second electronic flash units
Light Control: One 40-inch silvered umbrella; two wide-angle reflectors
Film: Kodachrome 25
Filtration: Harrison & Harrison diffuser
Exposure Metering: Minolta Auto-Flash II, incident-light mode
Exposure: *f*-5.6 (shutter at 1/60 second)

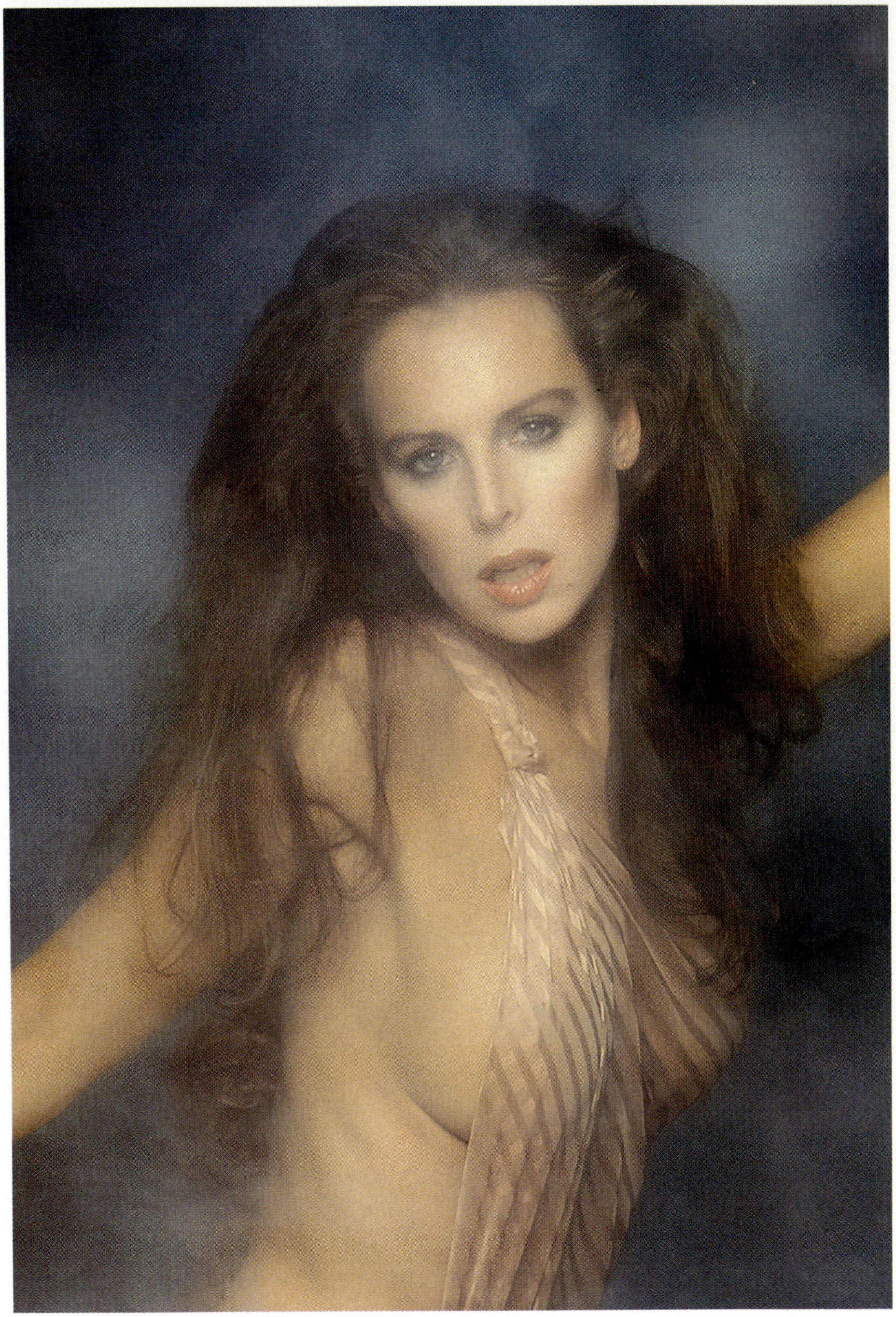

This photo is part of a series made for a record-album cover and accompanying ads and billboards. I painted clouds on sky-blue, seamless background paper. I describe the process in the *Background Variations* essay on page 25.

I rented a CO_2 fog machine from a Hollywood prop house. Unfortunately, I had no way to adequately vent the machine, so I had to halt shooting after each roll of film and manually fan the fumes from the camera room.

The model was on her knees on a pillow. The 1200-watt-second main light, in a silvered umbrella, was on a boom stand approximately four feet in front of the subject. It was set for an *f*-5.6 exposure. I added two background lights with wide-angle reflectors. One was on each side of the subject. Because I wanted the background to record its actual tone, I balanced its light for an *f*-5.6 exposure.

I wanted ample depth of field to clearly record the swirls of "smoke" as well as the painted background. I achieved this by using a 55mm micro lens rather than a short telephoto.

The wild, tousled look of the model's hair adds to the sensuality of the image. Using an electric fan to blow the hair was out of the question because of the "smoke," so the model's hair was teased into its configuration and heavily lacquered with hair spray. □

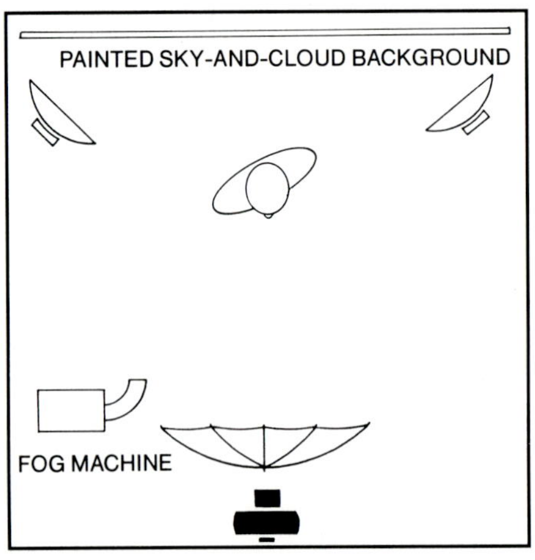

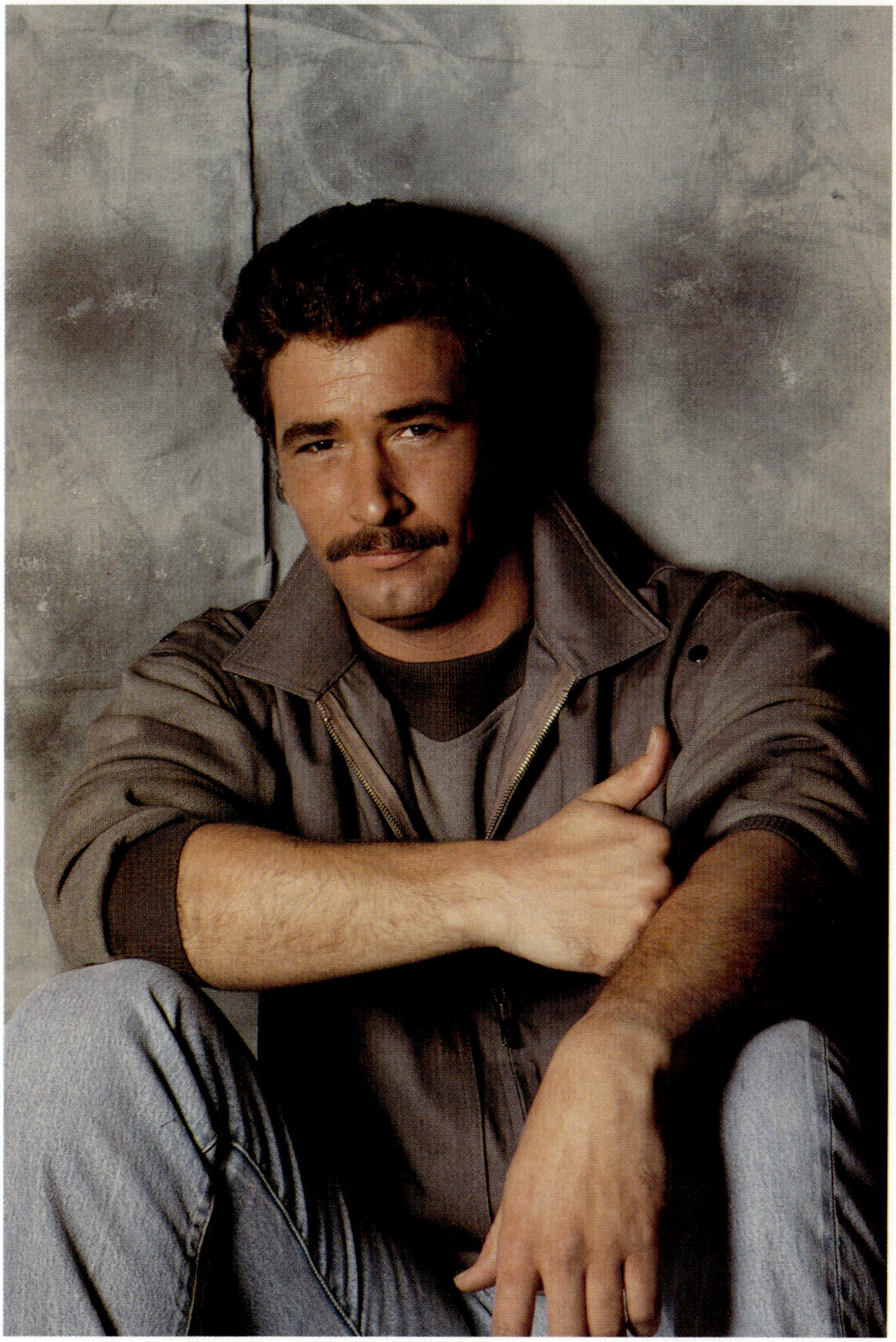

53

Subject: Lee Horsley
Client: Jean-Paul Germain, Ltd.
Location: Gary Bernstein Studio, Los Angeles, California
Camera: Nikon F3
Lens: 85mm *f*-1.8 Auto-Nikkor
Lighting: One 1250-watt-second Rollei flash in 14-inch pan reflector
Film: Kodachrome 25
Exposure Metering: Minolta Auto-Flash III, incident-light mode
Exposure: *f*-8 (shutter at 1/60 second)

I seated actor Lee Horsley against a large piece of painted canvas. The closer a subject is to the background, the more the background dominates the photograph. It basically shares subject illumination and focus. In this case, the rough appearance of the backdrop harmonizes with the rugged look of Lee and his outfit.

Notice that Lee's head and shoulders are squared toward the camera. This body position, confronting the viewer, is best suited for photographs of men.

The single main light at left of the camera created a dark shadow along the left side of Lee's head and shoulder. This adds to the rugged appearance of the photograph.

Background shadows can add to or detract from a photograph. I like using shadows as an obvious design element in a composition. However, random shadows on a clean background often appear like the result of carelessness on the part of the photographer.

I determined exposure by placing the incident-light hemisphere of my flash meter at the right side of Lee's face and pointing it toward the single light source. □

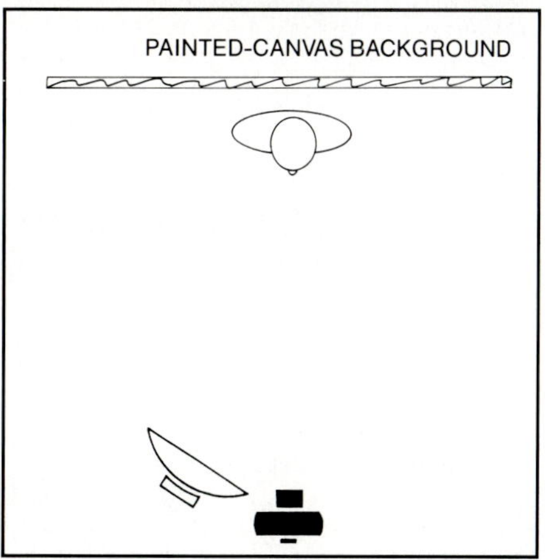

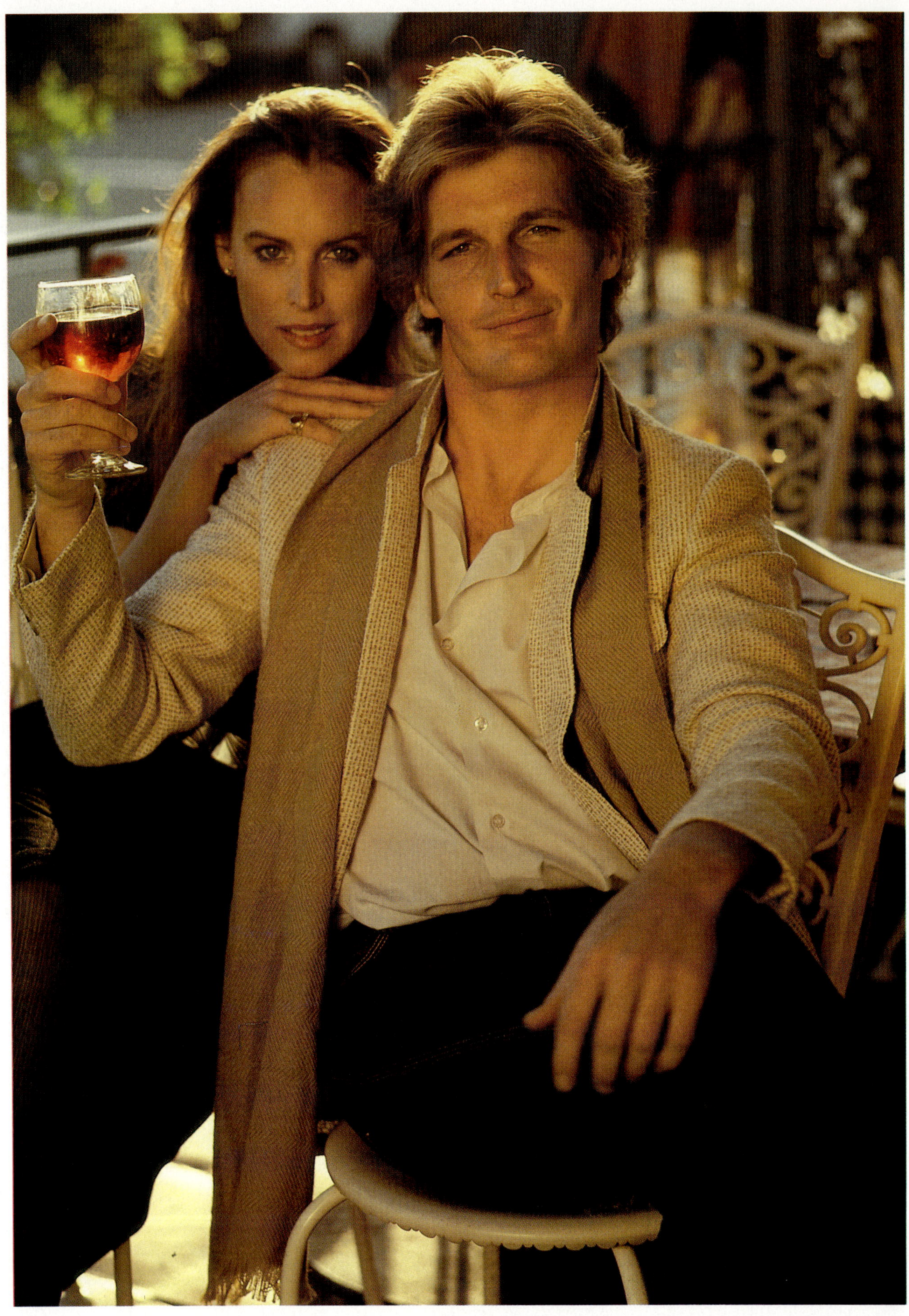

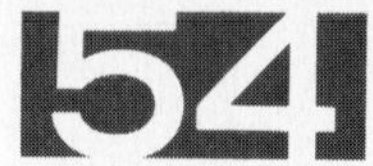

Subject: Professional models
Client: Brittania Jeans
Ad Agency: Wells, Rich and Greene (West), Inc.
Art Director: Bob Grimaldi
Location: Hollywood, California
Camera: Nikon F3
Lens: 105mm *f*-2.5 Auto-Nikkor
Lighting: Late-afternoon sunlight
Light Control: Silver Rocaflector
Film: Kodachrome 25
Exposure Metering: Minolta Auto-Flash II, incident-light mode
Exposure: 1/250 second at *f*-4

To advertise Brittania jeans, the art director wanted a candid-looking photograph of a couple enjoying the "good life." The copy for the ad would read, "My house is in Paris, but I *live* in Brittania." After having my request for three round-trip tickets to Europe emphatically turned down, I searched Hollywood for a suitable alternative location. A small cafe seemed perfect.

We waited until just before sunset to shoot the photograph because I wanted the warm tone of late-afternoon sunlight. With the models' backs to the sun, I placed a silvered reflector in front of the models, to the left of camera position. The reflector bounced the sunlight back into their faces.

Because only the male model was dressed in the product to be advertised, the need for depth of field was minimal. Controlled depth of field is only one way of directing viewer attention to a particular place in the composition. Using a short telephoto lens, I opened the lens to *f*-4. Notice that the female model and the background are recorded with a slight blur.

I metered the scene by placing the hemisphere of my incident-light meter at subject position and pointing it toward the reflector. □

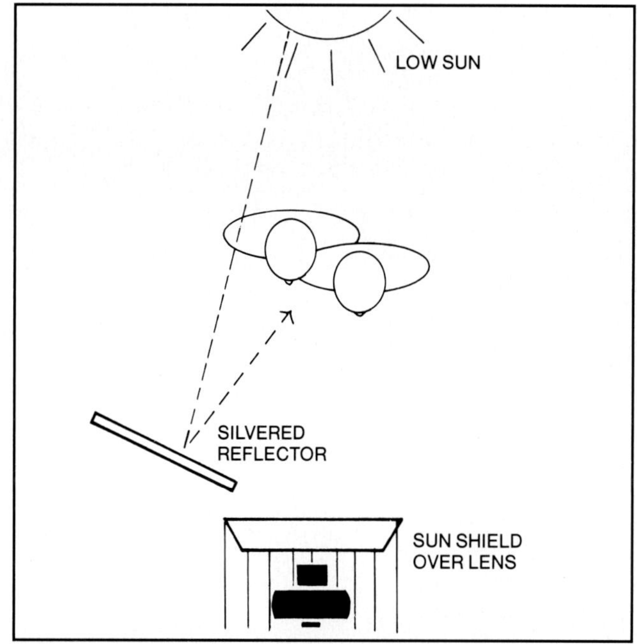

Subject: Joe Montana and professional model
Client: Schick, Inc.
Ad Agency: William Esty Company, Inc.
Art Director: Stan Swensen
Location: Semi Valley, California
Camera: Rolleiflex SLX
Lens: 80mm f-2.8 Zeiss Planar
Lighting: Two 800-watt-second Versatron 800 electronic flash units, powering four flash heads
Film: Ektachrome Professional 64
Exposure Metering: Gossen Ultra Pro, incident-light mode
Exposure: f-8 (shutter at 1/250 second)

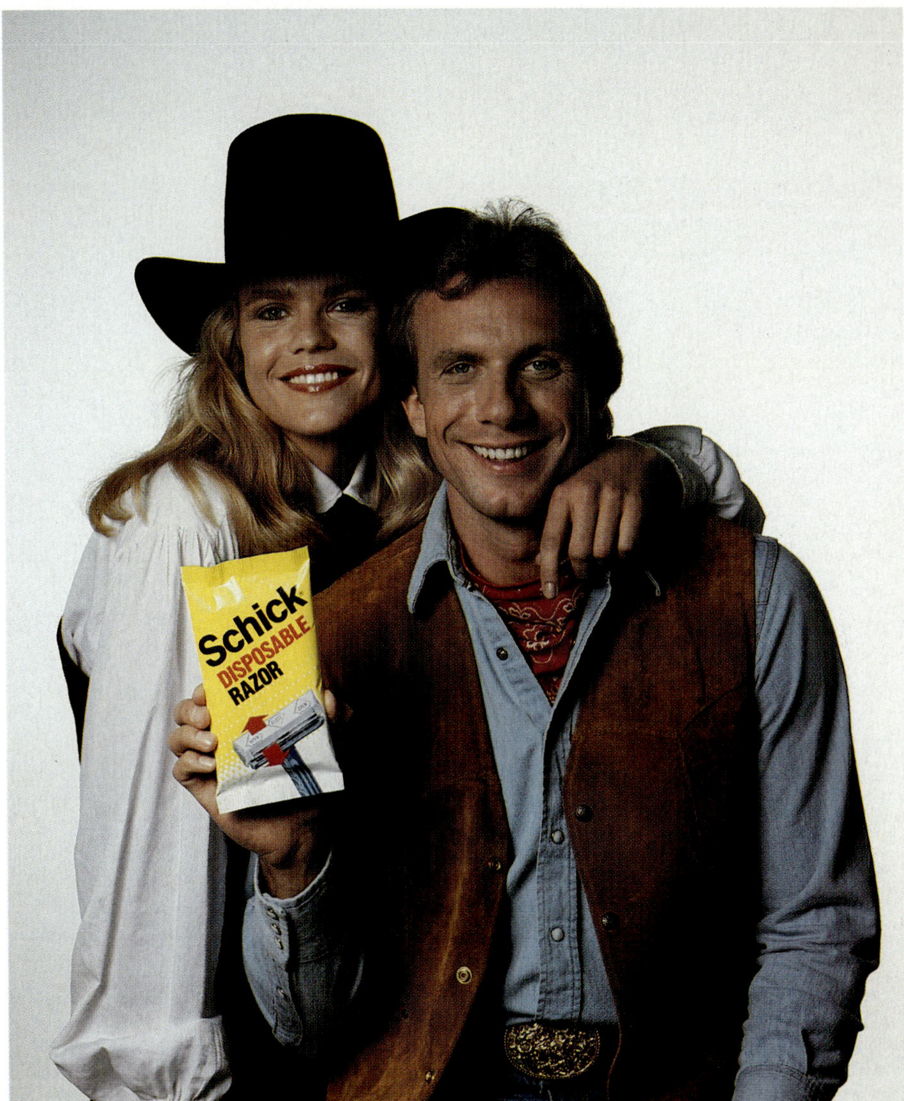

Professional football player Joe Montana has been representing Schick for several years. I took this photo as Joe was finishing a television commercial in an old, dusty ghost town. We set up a small, makeshift studio at the town's saloon. The saloon was very small—barely wide enough to contain my portable nine-foot seamless background and not more much than 12 feet long. I did, however, manage to set up four 400-watt-second lights in the confined space. The two background lights were slightly behind the subjects and placed to avoid light spillage onto the subjects. The two other lights—one on each side of the subjects— provided main lighting. All four lights were in 40-inch umbrellas. The back-light umbrellas were white; the main-light umbrellas, silvered.

Veteran art director Stan Swensen asked for a pure white background to allow for placement of type. I asked Montana to sit on a bar stool and had pretty Jennifer Wallace stand behind him. Montana's position remained stationary throughout our session. Jennifer moved around, providing variations in composition and attitude.

The main lights on each side provided even subject illumination. Uniform lighting was essential to allow for rapid compositional changes and Jennifer's wide-brimmed hat. □

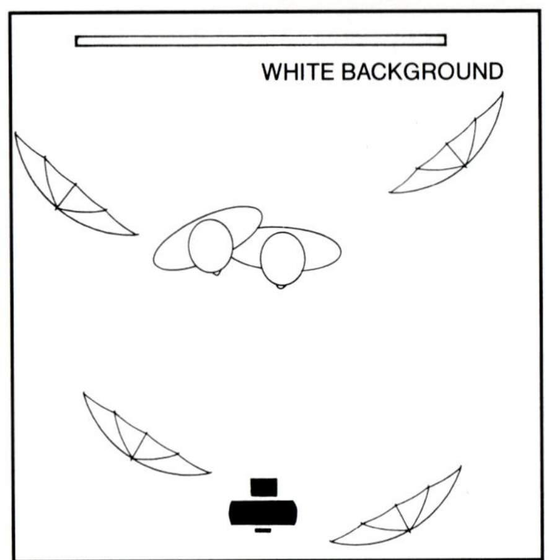

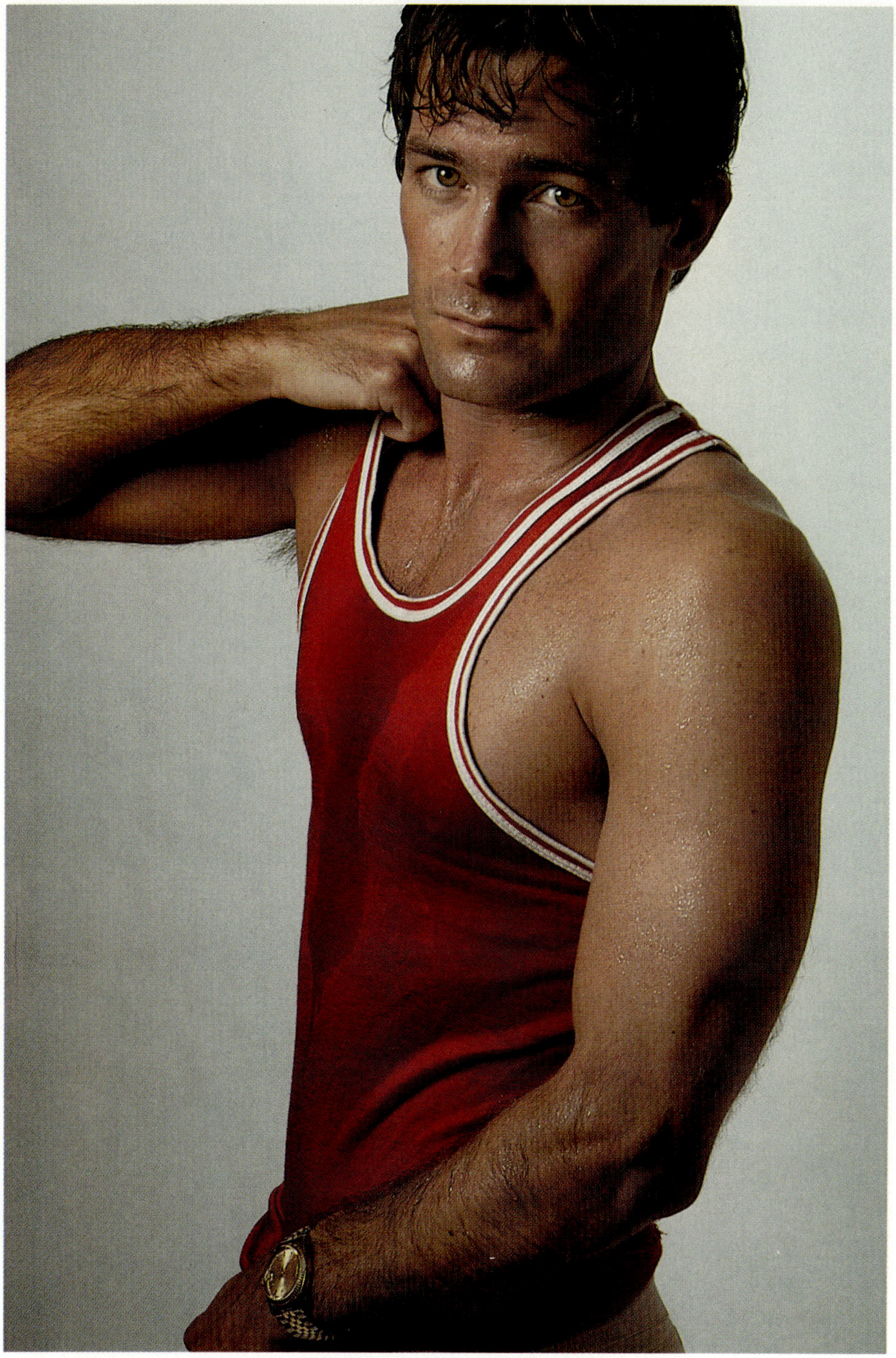

Subject: Professional model
Location: Gary Bernstein Studio, New York City
Camera: Nikon F2
Lens: 50mm *f*-1.4 Auto-Nikkor
Lighting: One 1250-watt-second Rollei electronic flash unit
Film: Kodachrome 25
Exposure Metering: Minolta Auto-Flash II, incident-light mode
Exposure: *f*-8 (shutter at 1/60 second)

Things are not always what they appear to be. To simulate perspiration in this portfolio test shot, we sprayed a mixture of glycerin and water on the model prior to photography.

I asked the subject to lean toward the camera. I elevated my camera angle by standing on a short stepladder. In this way, using a standard camera lens, I achieved the slightly enlarged size of the model's head in relation to his body.

The model's attitude was critically important to the success of the photograph. His haggard "confrontation" with the viewer gives the image its impact and appeal. □

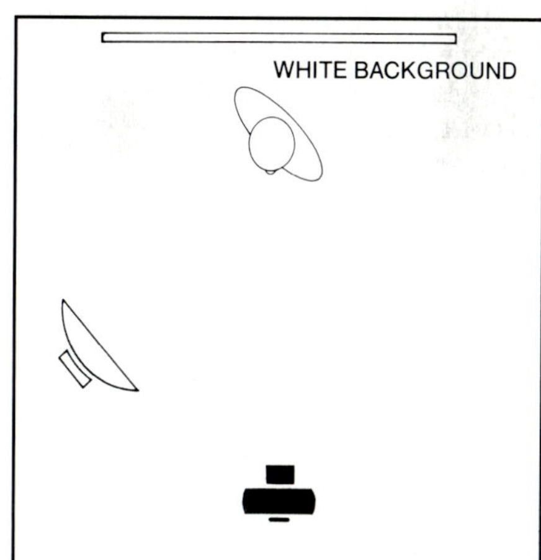

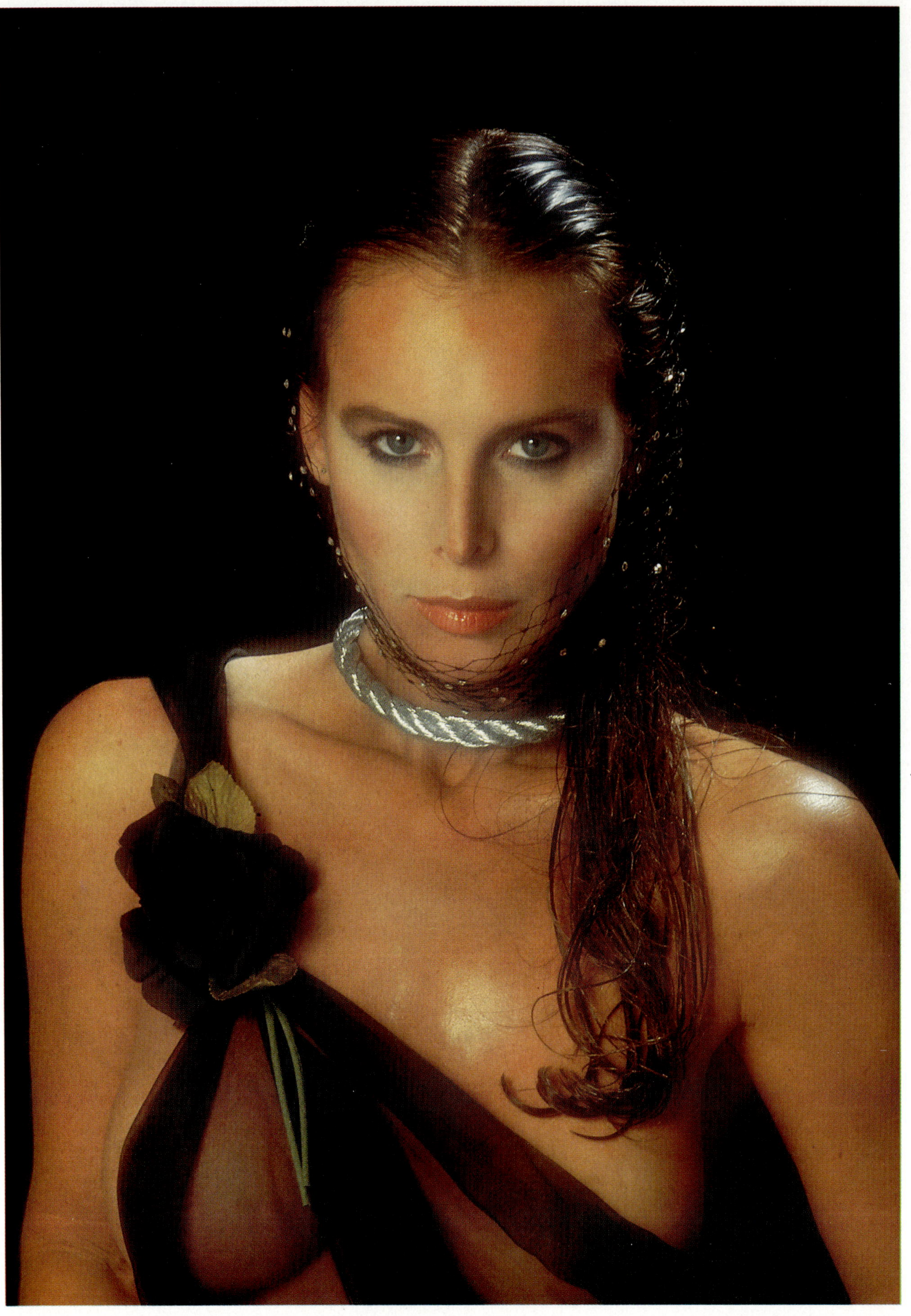

57

Subject: Professional model
Client: Casablanca Record and Filmworks, Inc.
Ad Agency: Art Hotel, Inc.
Art Director: Chris Whorf
Location: Gary Bernstein Studio, Los Angeles, California
Camera: Nikon F2
Lens: 50mm *f*-1.4 Auto-Nikkor
Lighting: Two 600-watt-second electronic flash units
Light Control: One grid spot; one silvered reflector
Film: Kodachrome 25
Exposure Metering: Minolta Auto-Flash II, incident-light mode
Exposure: *f*-8 (shutter at 1/60 second)

This photograph was taken for an album cover for the rock group *Munich Machine.* It dramatizes the impact of skin tone against black. Beautiful model Kay Sutton York designed and styled the outfit she's wearing—a piece of sheer, black fabric, gathered at the flower by her shoulder and taped to her body.

Kay's slick hair is courtesy of Johnson & Johnson baby oil—not water! It's the best way to get a wet look without the problems of dripping water and constantly drying hair.

The main light was reflected from a 40-inch white umbrella, placed about four feet in front of the model and to the left of the camera. The main-light exposure reading was *f*-8.

To avoid Kay's dark tresses blending with the dark background, I used a 600-watt-second flash with grid spot high and behind her. It provided rim lighting to the top of the hair and shoulder to give the needed graphic separation. The rim light metered at *f*-11 at the top of the model's head.

I added extra sparkle to the model's eyes by placing a 27-inch reflector below her face, just out of camera range.

Because I used a standard camera lens relatively close to the subject and because the face is near the image edge, some facial elongation occurred. This deliberate, but subtle, distortion helped create a truly striking image of a face of classic beauty. □

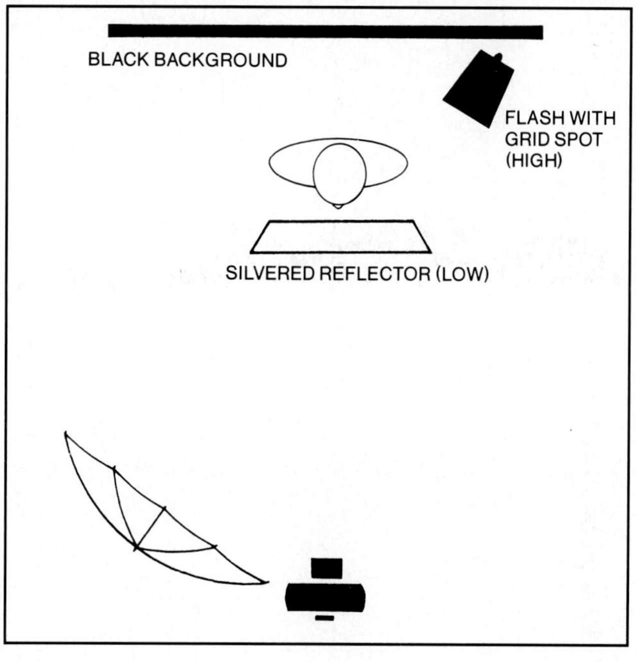

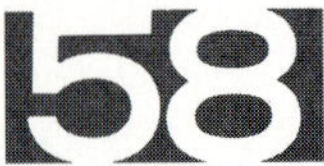

Subject: Professional model
Client: DuPont & Co.
Ad Agency: Ted Bates, New York City
Art Director: Jack Jones
Location: Gary Bernstein Studio, New York City
Camera: Nikon F2
Lens: 105mm *f*-2.5 Auto-Nikkor
Lighting: Three 1200-watt-second electronic flash units
Light Control: One 40-inch silvered umbrella; two wide-angle reflectors
Film: Kodachrome 25
Exposure Metering: Minolta Auto-Flash II, incident-light mode
Exposure: *f*-8 (shutter at 1/60 second)

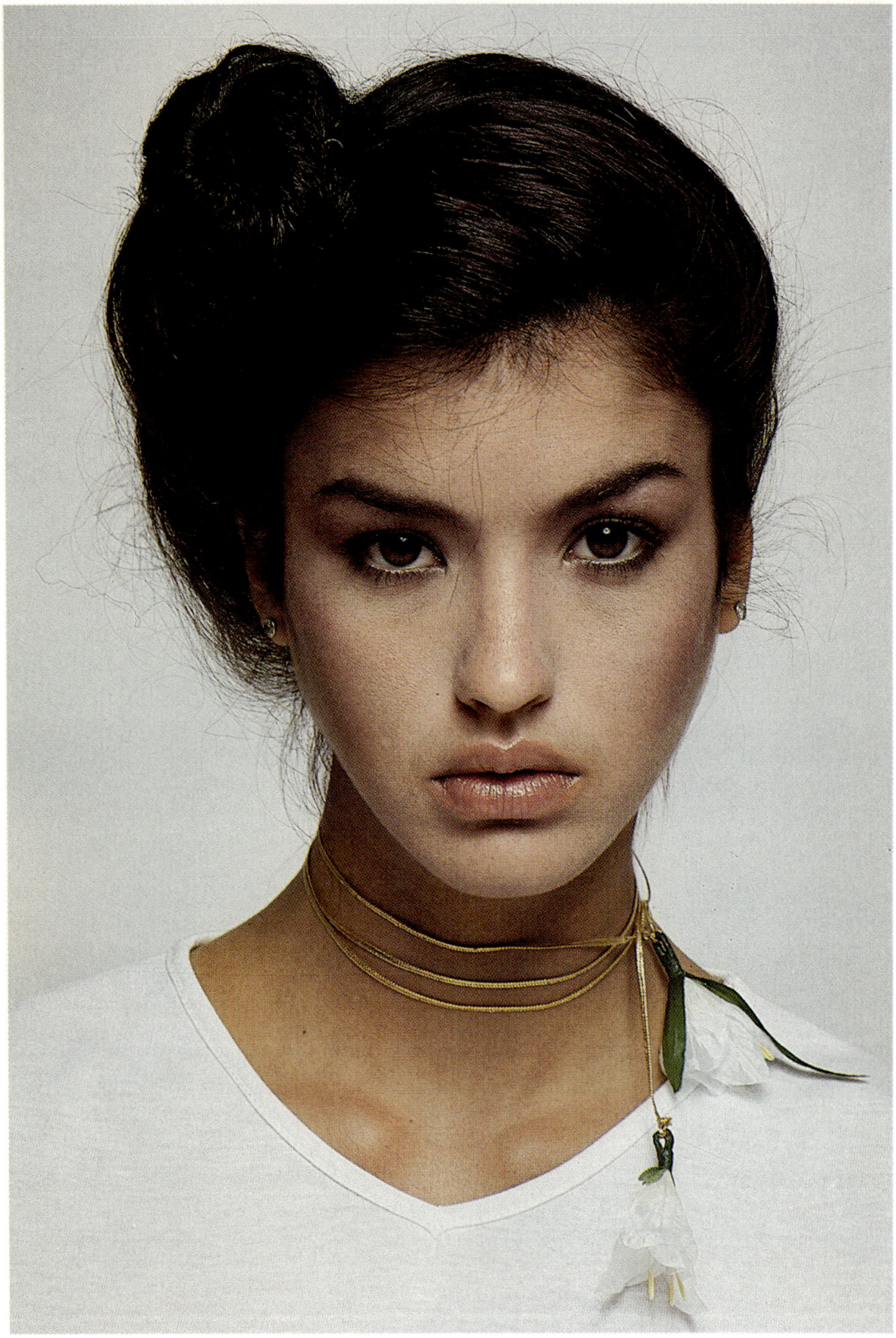

This photograph is part of a series of ads I shot for DuPont. Each ad consisted of a full-length fashion shot, showing a garment made from a Dupont fabric, plus a head shot of the same model to further enhance the appeal of the ad.

The photo represents a basic setup for a high-key portrait against a white background. I used one frontal main light, bounced from a 40-inch silvered umbrella. I also used two background lights, one on each side of the subject. The white background received 1/2 exposure step more light than the subject, ensuring a clean, white background in the photo.

Using a short telephoto lens gave me limited depth of field. This softened the background to eliminate any unevenness that may have existed in it.

Because I use slow Kodachrome 25 film for most of my work and like to work at small apertures for extended depth of field, I require a lot of light.

You could produce similar images with three portable flash units of significantly less power, but you'd have to make some sacrifices. For example, if you used Kodachrome 25, or any other slow film, you would need to shoot at a larger aperture. In doing so, you would lose some depth of field. If you wanted to use a small lens aperture, you would have to use a correspondingly faster film. Another alternative would be to reduce the distances from light to subject and subject to background.

Most of the images in this portfolio could have been produced with significantly less sophisticated and less expensive lighting equipment. The one thing you can't do without, however, is creative thinking and a lot of practice! □

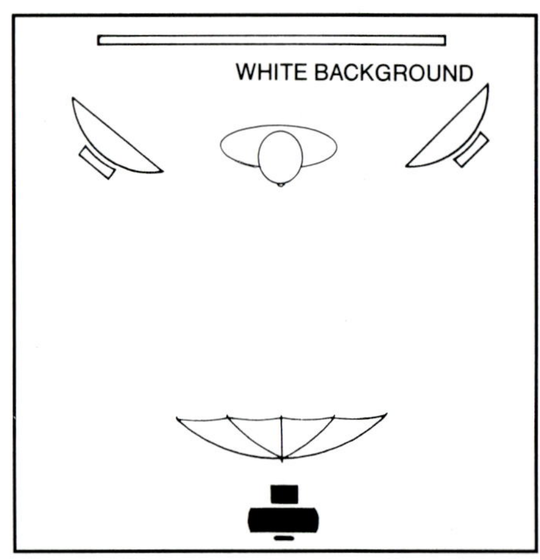

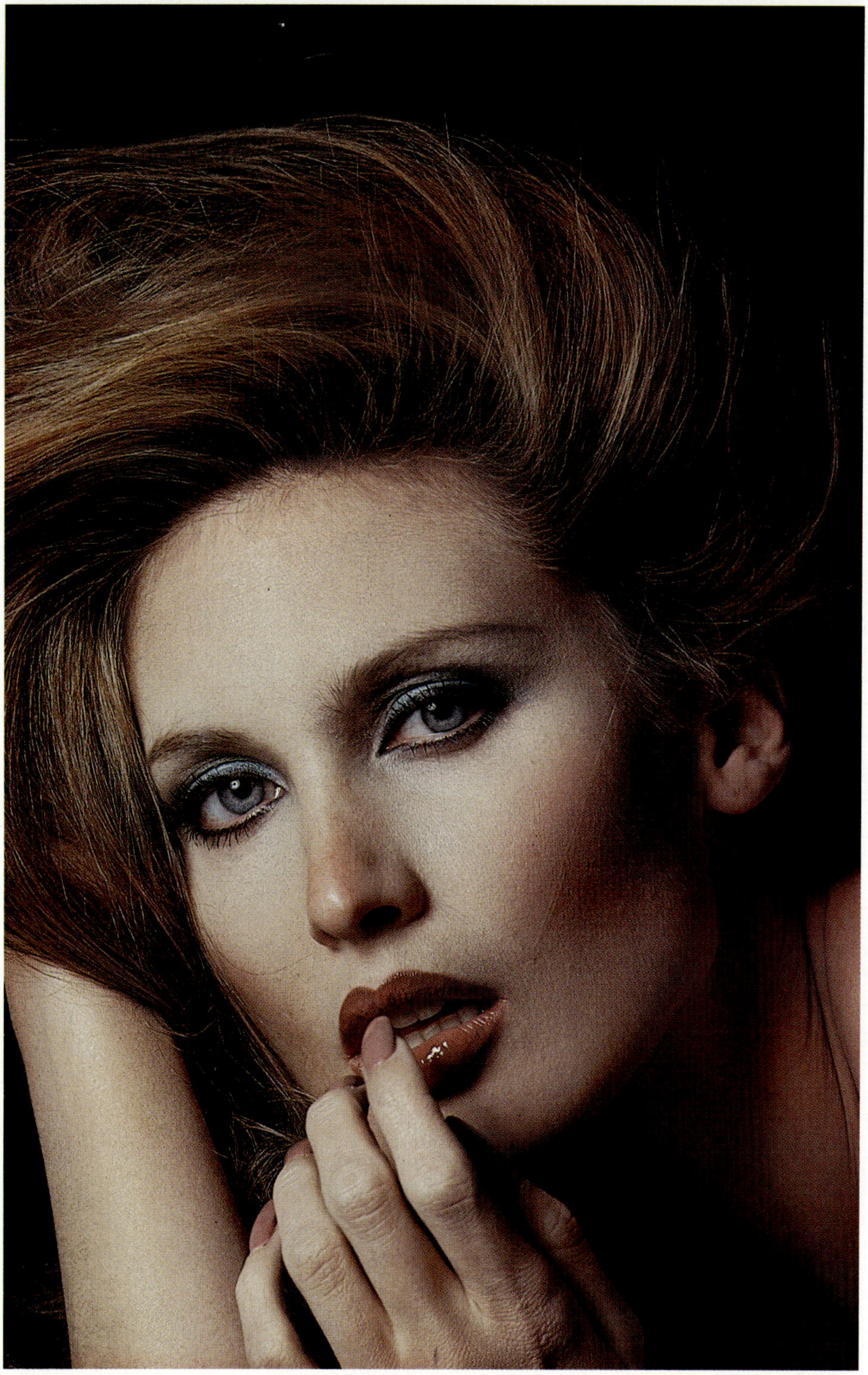

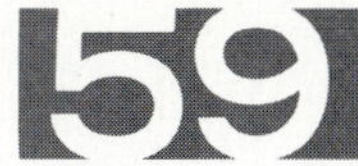

Subject: Professional model
Client: Max Factor, Inc.
Ad Agency: Wells, Rich and Greene (West), Inc.
Art Director: Bob Cole
Location: Gary Bernstein Studio, New York City
Camera: Nikon F2
Lens: 105mm *f*-2.5 Auto-Nikkor
Lighting: One 1250-watt-second Rollei electronic flash unit
Light Control: Two black panels
Film: Kodachrome 25
Exposure Metering: Minolta Auto-Flash II, incident-light mode
Exposure: *f*-22 (shutter at 1/60 second)

This is an outtake from a cosmetic series used by Max Factor. It's an example of *subtractive lighting,* involving the elimination of light to produce the desired modeling and contrast. The main lighting was directional, yet soft. The light "bathed" the surface of the model's skin, producing minimal contrast. Soft lighting reduces the need for retouching.

To add modeling to the face and emphasize the cheekbones, I placed a black seven-foot panel on each side of the model. These black "reflectors" shielded her from side light. This created shadows and yielded greater contrast.

The dark background was created by deliberate light falloff. The actual background surface was white, seamless paper. The fair hair is graphically separated from the dark background. To complete this dramatic shot, I used an electric fan to blow the hair. □

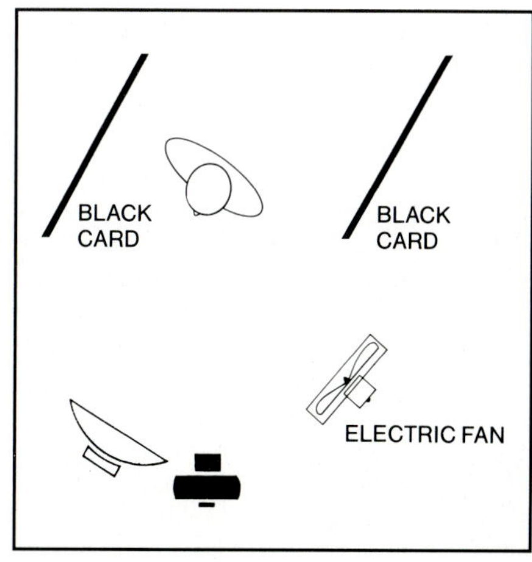

Subject: Professional models
Client: Winona School of Professional Photography
Location: Winona School of Professional Photography, Mt. Prospect, Illinois
Camera: Nikon F3
Lens: 105mm *f*-3.5 Micro-Nikkor
Lighting: One 400-watt-second Photogenic Porta-Master electronic flash unit
Film: Kodachrome 25
Exposure Metering: Minolta Auto-Flash III, incident-light mode
Exposure: *f*-8 (shutter at 1/60 second)

Simple, contrasty lighting, dynamic composition and a viable story are the key elements of these photographs. I provided the models with a simple story line to help them convey the intended attitude: She tells him that the person he's confronting is a threat to her. As they turn to walk away, they give a wary backward glance.

The only light came from a single flash head. Placement of a single spot source, such as was used here, is critical because there is no fill light to compensate for inaccurate placement.

To create a dramatic lighting pattern, I allowed the hard, black shadows to fall on the white background. For further impact, I shielded the tops of the subjects' heads from the light, using a large piece of black cardboard between the light and the subjects. When you partly cut off lighting in this way, take a new meter reading.

These two photos are part of a series that would be appropriate for a perfume, clothing or jewelry ad as well as being fine examples of contemporary portraiture. □

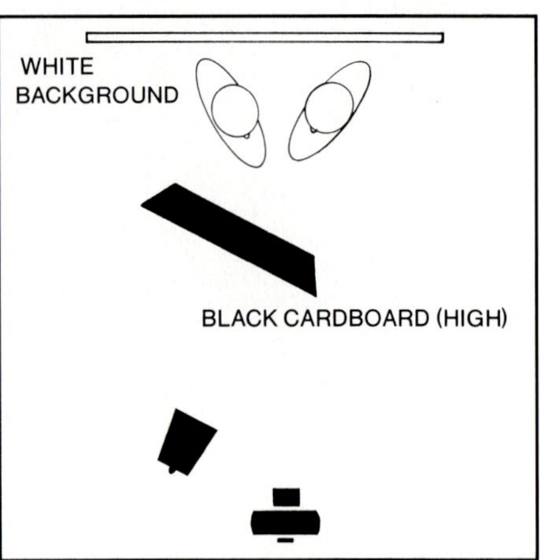

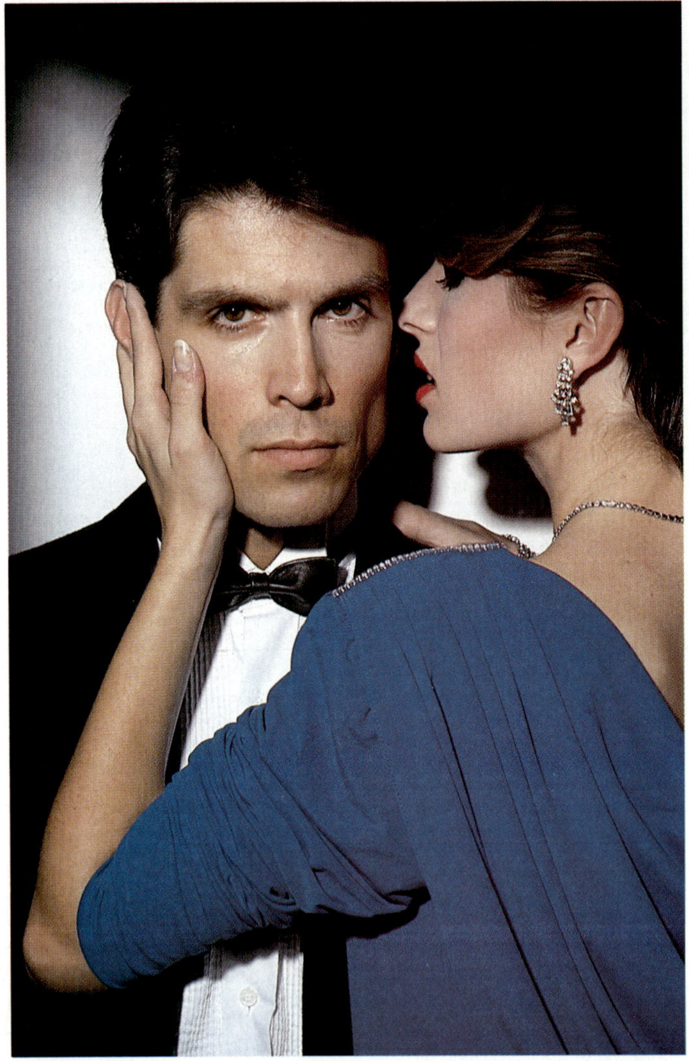

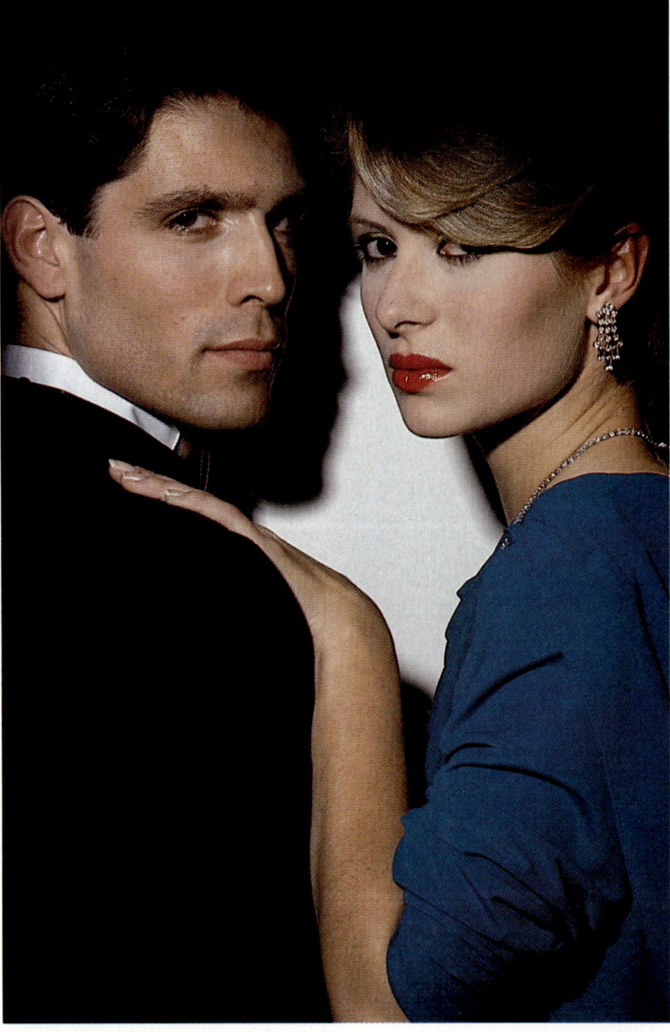

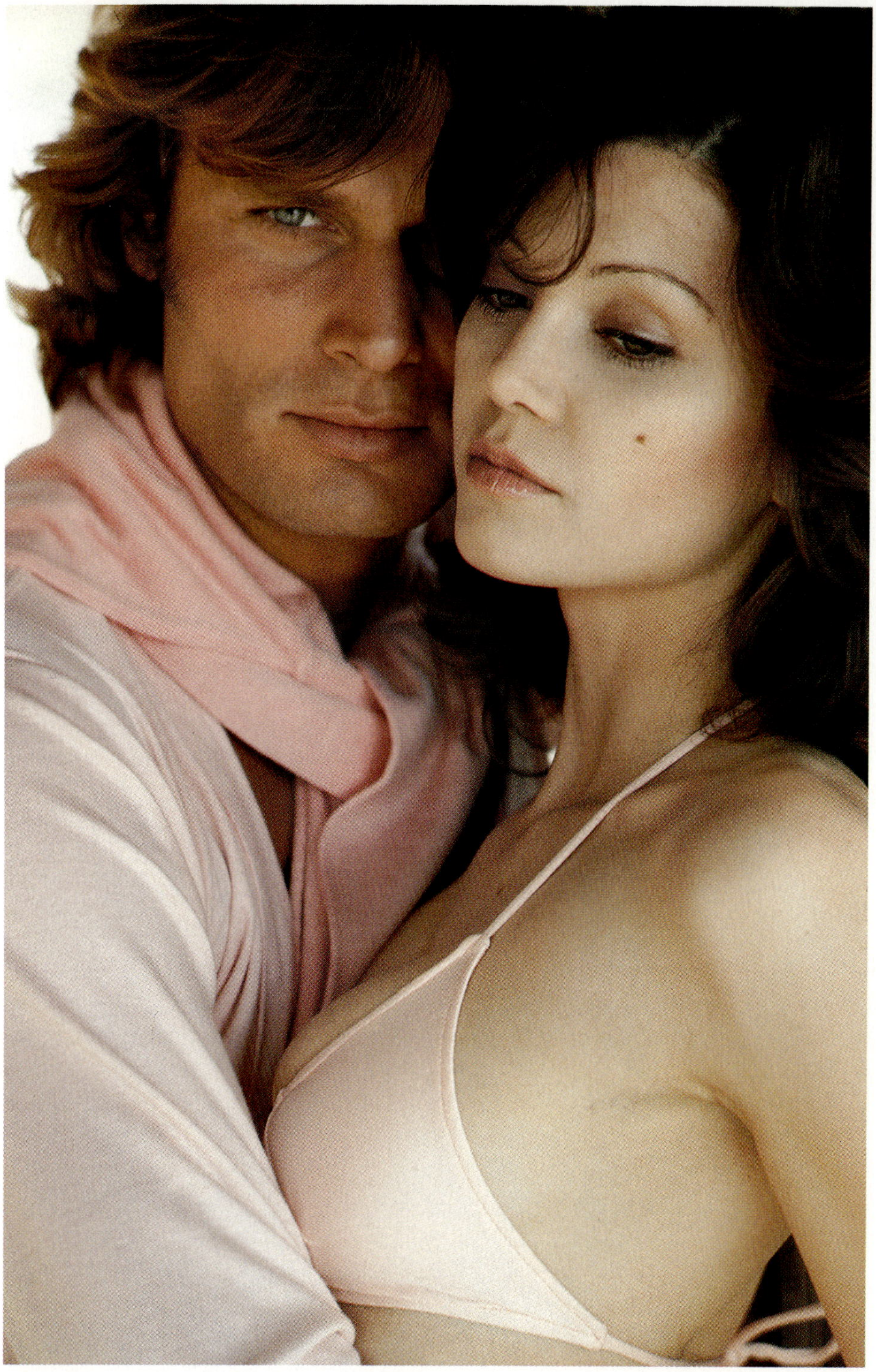

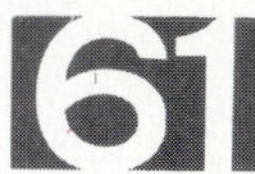

Subject: Victoria Principal and Uva Harden
Client: Esquire
Art Director: Max Evans
Location: Malibu, California
Camera: Nikon F
Lens: 55mm *f*-3.5 Micro-Nikkor
Lighting: Midday sunlight
Light Control: Overhanging pier
Film: Kodachrome 25
Exposure Metering: Gossen Luna Pro, incident-light mode
Exposure: 1/250 second at *f*-8

I photographed top model Uva Harden and beautiful Victoria Principal for a fashion layout for *Esquire* magazine.

Midday sun is suitable as main-light source only when the subject is deliberately positioned to receive the light from the proper angle. For this photo, the subjects were on a sandy beach and I shot from the top of a nearby lifeguard stand. By placing the subjects under an overhanging pier, I shielded them from the direct overhead sun and lit them frontally with skylight. This gave a flattering soft light and good modeling of the features.

The compositional interplay of the two bodies completed the delightful image.

Exposure was based on an incident-light reading, taken with a Gossen meter pointed toward the frontal skylight. □

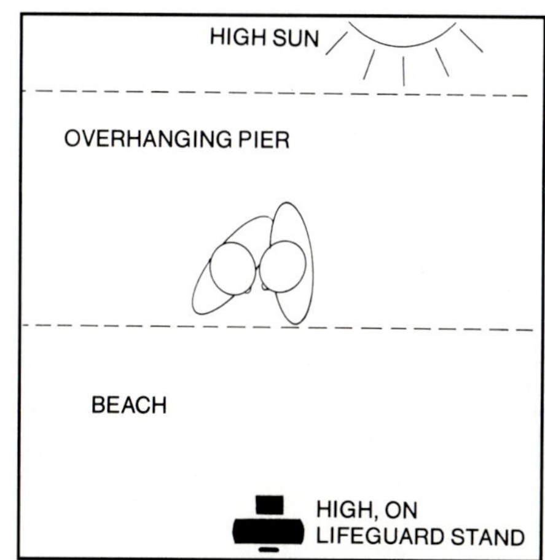

Subject: Professional models
Client: Jean-Paul Germain, Ltd.
Location: Acapulco, Mexico
Camera: Nikon F3
Lens: 85mm *f*-1.8 Auto-Nikkor
Lighting: Late-afternoon sunlight
Film: Kodachrome 25
Exposure Metering: Gossen Luna Pro, incident-light mode
Exposure: 1/125 second at *f*-5.6

The lush tropics surrounding Acapulco were the setting for this dramatic fashion double. The models were lit from the side by the late-afternoon sun. The cross lighting emphasized the texture and folds in the garments and the chiseled features of the faces.

I used a short telephoto lens at medium aperture. The depth of field was sufficient for total sharpness of the subjects, while causing the background to soften to a slight blur.

Some clouds in the sky reflected light into the shadows and lowered subject contrast. The film was able to record detail from the sunlit whites to the deep shadows. I metered the sunlight with my Gossen Luna Pro, placing the incident-light hemisphere at subject position and pointing it toward the sun. □

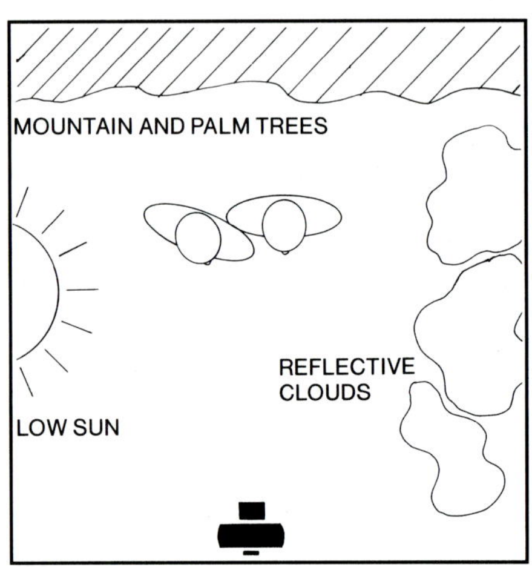

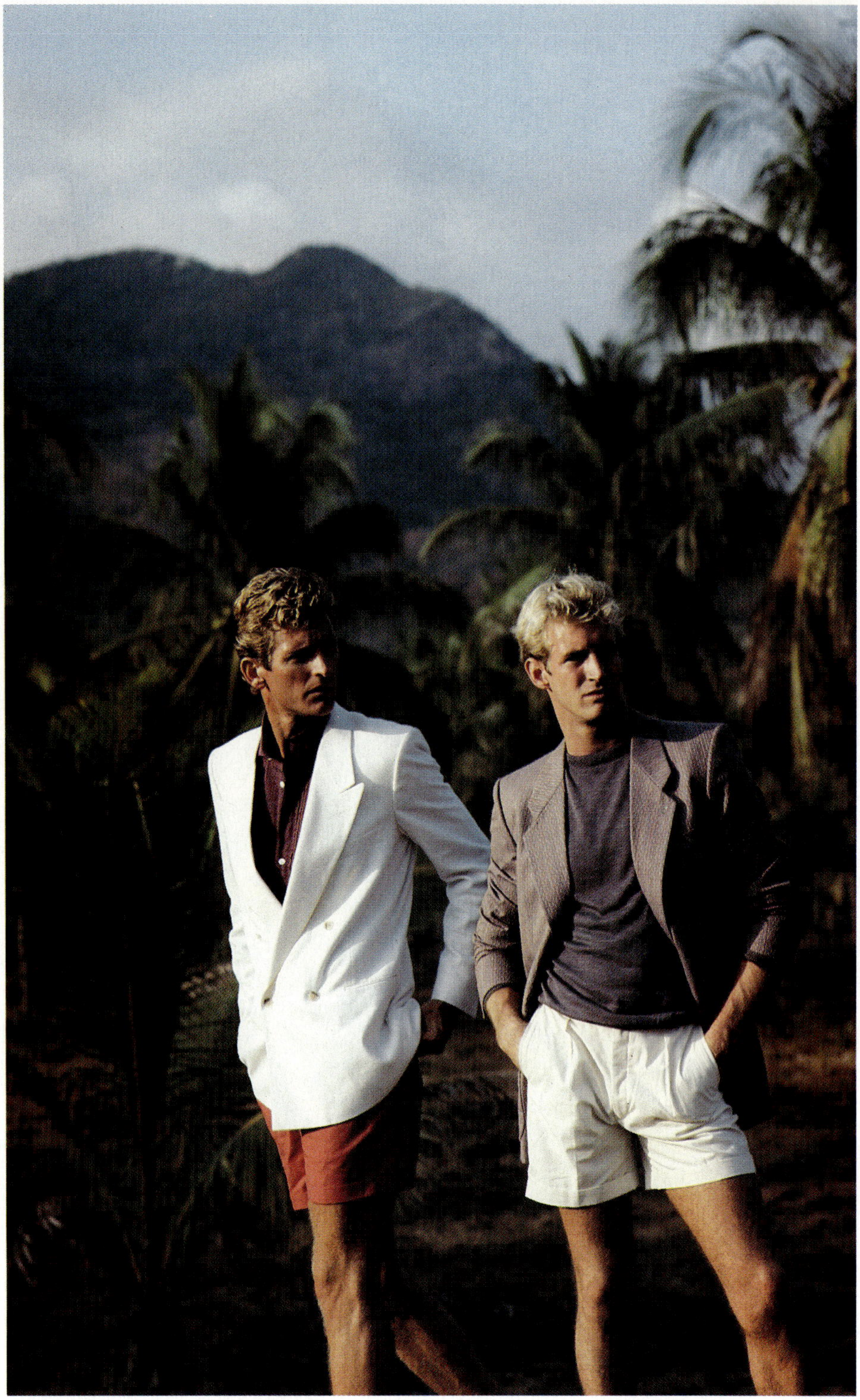

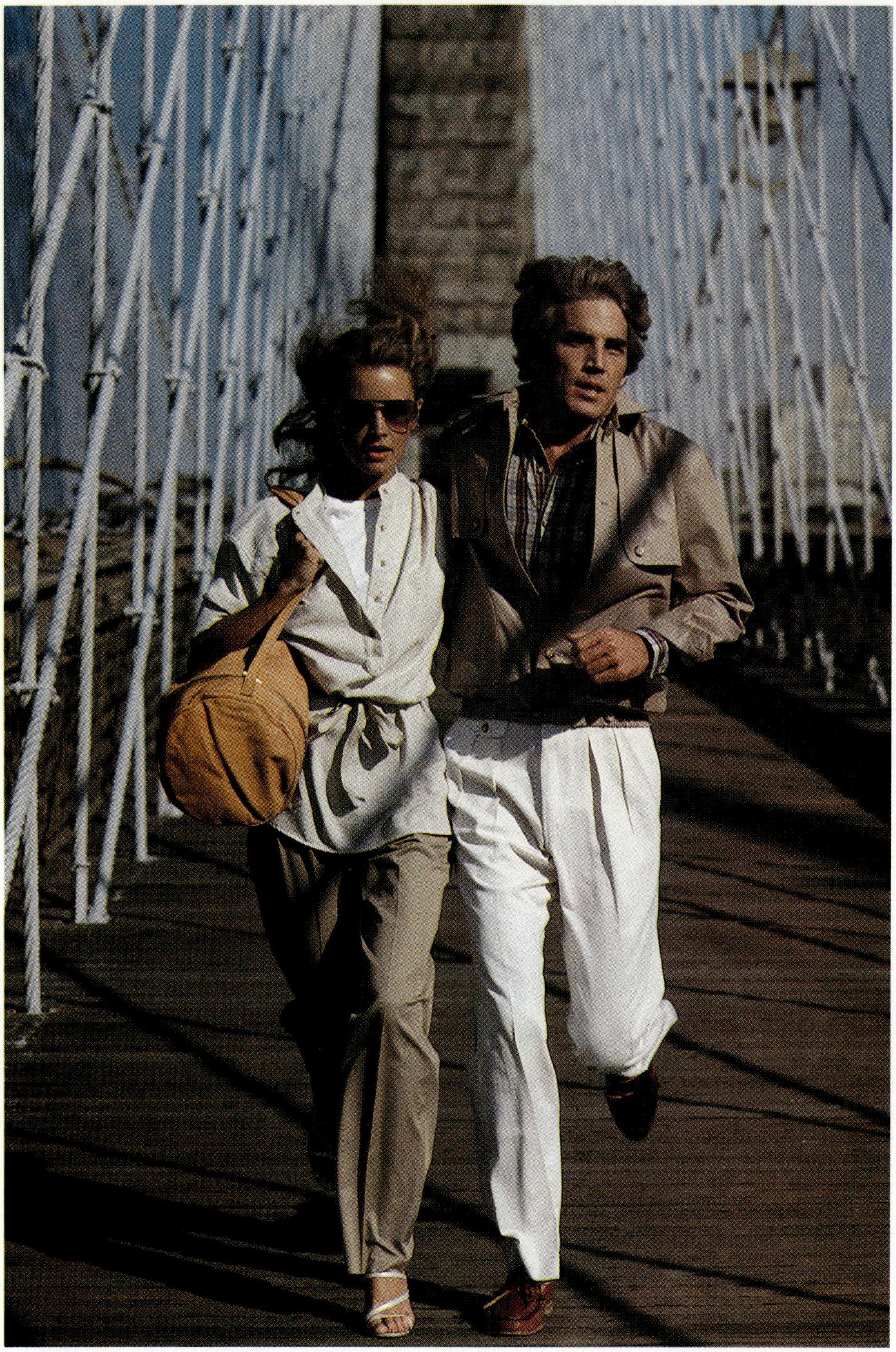

Subject: Professional models
Client: Gant Shirtmakers, Inc.
Ad Agency: Waring and LaRosa, Inc.
Art Director: Howard Title
Location: Brooklyn Bridge, New York City
Camera: Nikon F2AS
Lens: 55mm *f*-3.5 Micro-Nikkor
Lighting: Afternoon sunlight
Film: Kodachrome 25
Exposure Metering: Gossen Luna Pro, incident-light mode
Exposure: 1/250 second at *f*-5.6

This action fashion photo was shot on a hot, humid day in New York City. To avoid unwanted shadows, caused by the cables on the bridge, I had to choose a specific location for photography. I marked the spot with gaffer tape on the ground in front of the models' feet. If the models were slightly in front of or behind the mark, shadows on their faces would render a shot unusable. We rehearsed the models' run several times, slowly building up speed.

My camera was on a Gitzo tripod. I instructed the models to start running about 10 feet behind the mark and to run past the mark by a few feet. An aperture of *f*-5.6 gave me sufficient depth of field to record the runners sharply while allowing the background to retain a softened recognizability.

Because the featured product was on the male model, I placed him closest to the light source. For best facial modeling, I asked him to turn his head slightly toward the light as he approached the point of photography.

I set my motorized Nikon on four frames per second and shot the models as they ran toward me. The first burst of shots was exposed at the meter-indicated exposure of 1/250 second at *f*-5.6. I shot four other sequences, bracketing exposures 1/2 and 1 step over and under *f*-5.6. This assured me of an ideally exposed photo and, unfortunately, a couple of tired models! □

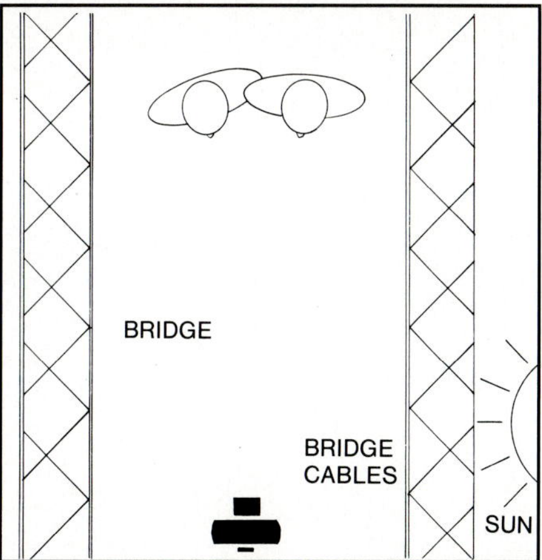

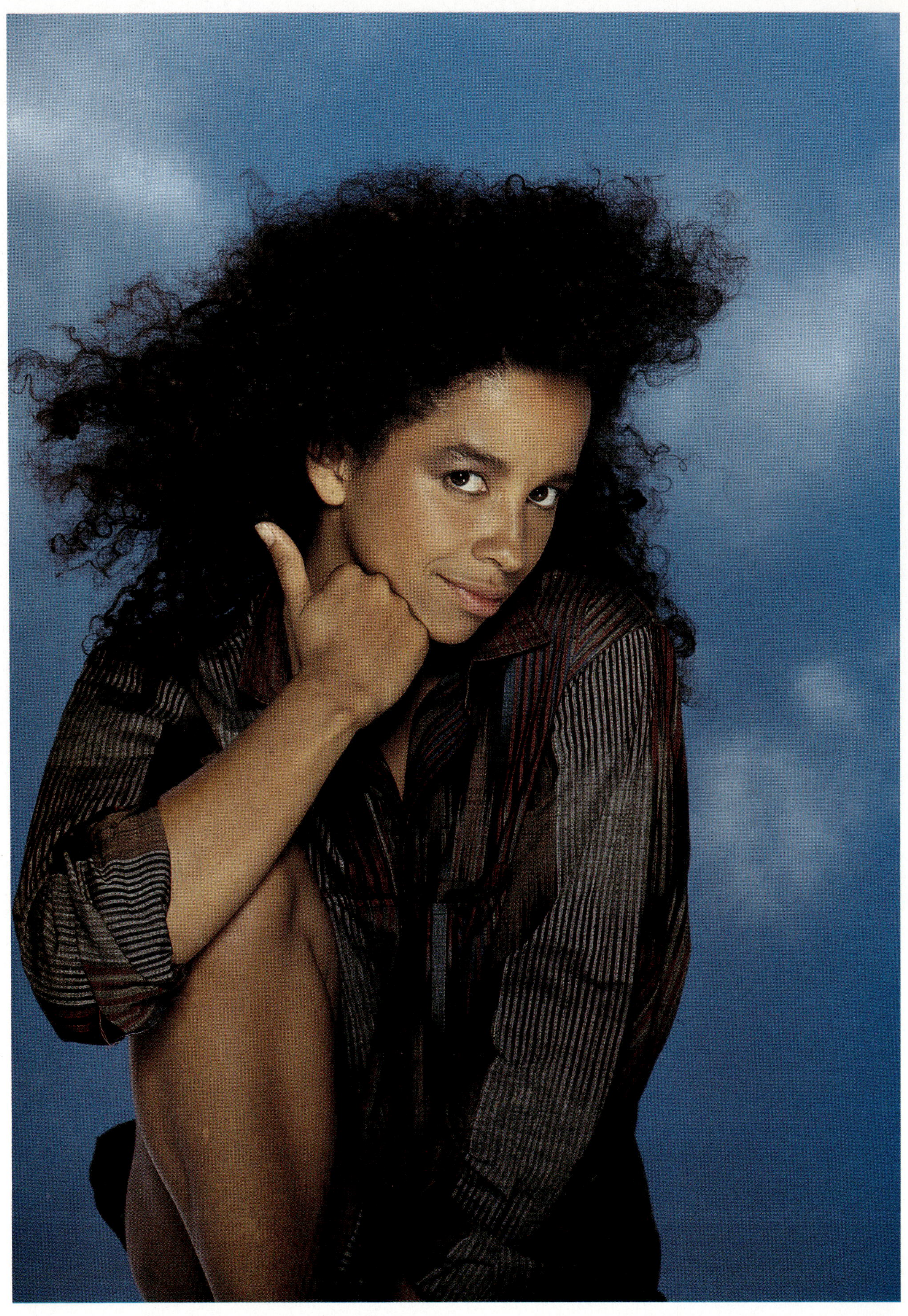

Subject: Rae Dawn Chong
Client: Jean-Paul Germain, Ltd.
Art Director: Paul Winter
Location: Gary Bernstein Studio, Los Angeles, California
Camera: Nikon F3
Lens: 55mm f-3.5 Micro-Nikkor
Lighting: Three 800-watt-second Photogenic Versatron electronic flash units
Light Control: One 32-inch Halo on main light; two 45-inch Halos on background lights; one small Photogenic Silfoil silvered reflector
Film: Kodachrome 25
Exposure Metering: Minolta Auto-Flash III, incident-light mode
Exposure: f-8 (shutter at 1/60 second)

For this photograph of actress Rae Dawn Chong, I painted a cloud background on sky-blue seamless paper, using white spray paint. The method of application is fully described in the *Background Variations* essay, page 25.

I used a 55mm f-3.5 lens. It allowed me to record a relatively large expanse of "sky" and also created an illusion of great distance between subject and background. A longer lens would not have achieved those ends.

To get a realistic sky effect, I balanced the amount of light reaching the background with the light received by the subject. Consequently, the background recorded with its natural color and tonality.

If my subject had been blond, I might have wanted a deeper background tone to provide greater separation between the subject's light hair and the background. In such a case, I would have adjusted the background lighting to deliver less light than the amount of light reaching the subject.

I used the main light in a 32-inch Photogenic Halo and placed a small, silvered Silfoil reflector below Rae's face. □

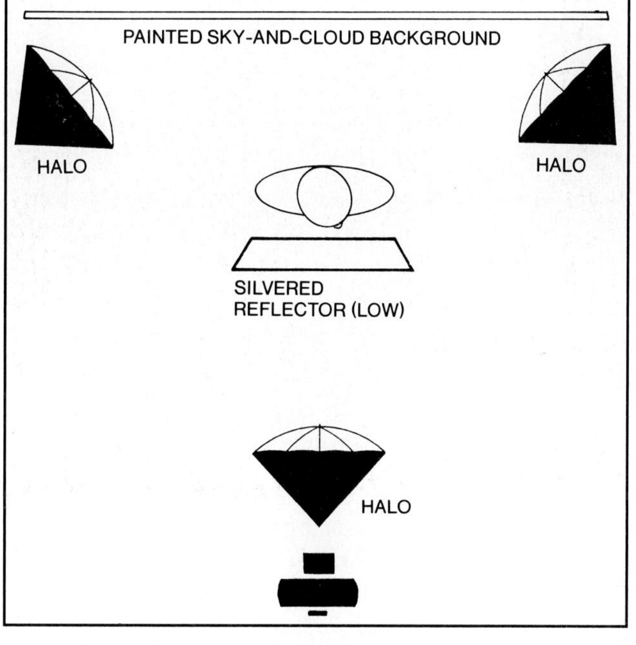

Subject: Diane Lane
Client: Family Weekly
Art Director: Robert Altemus
Location: Gary Bernstein Studio, Los Angeles, California
Camera: Nikon F3
Lens: 105mm *f*-2.5 Auto-Nikkor
Lighting: Three 800-watt-second Photogenic Versatron electronic flash units
Light Control: One six-foot silvered umbrella and one five-foot softbox for main light; two 50-inch white umbrellas for background light
Film: Kodachrome 25
Exposure Metering: Minolta Auto-Flash III, incident-light mode
Exposure: *f*-5.6 (shutter at 1/60 second)

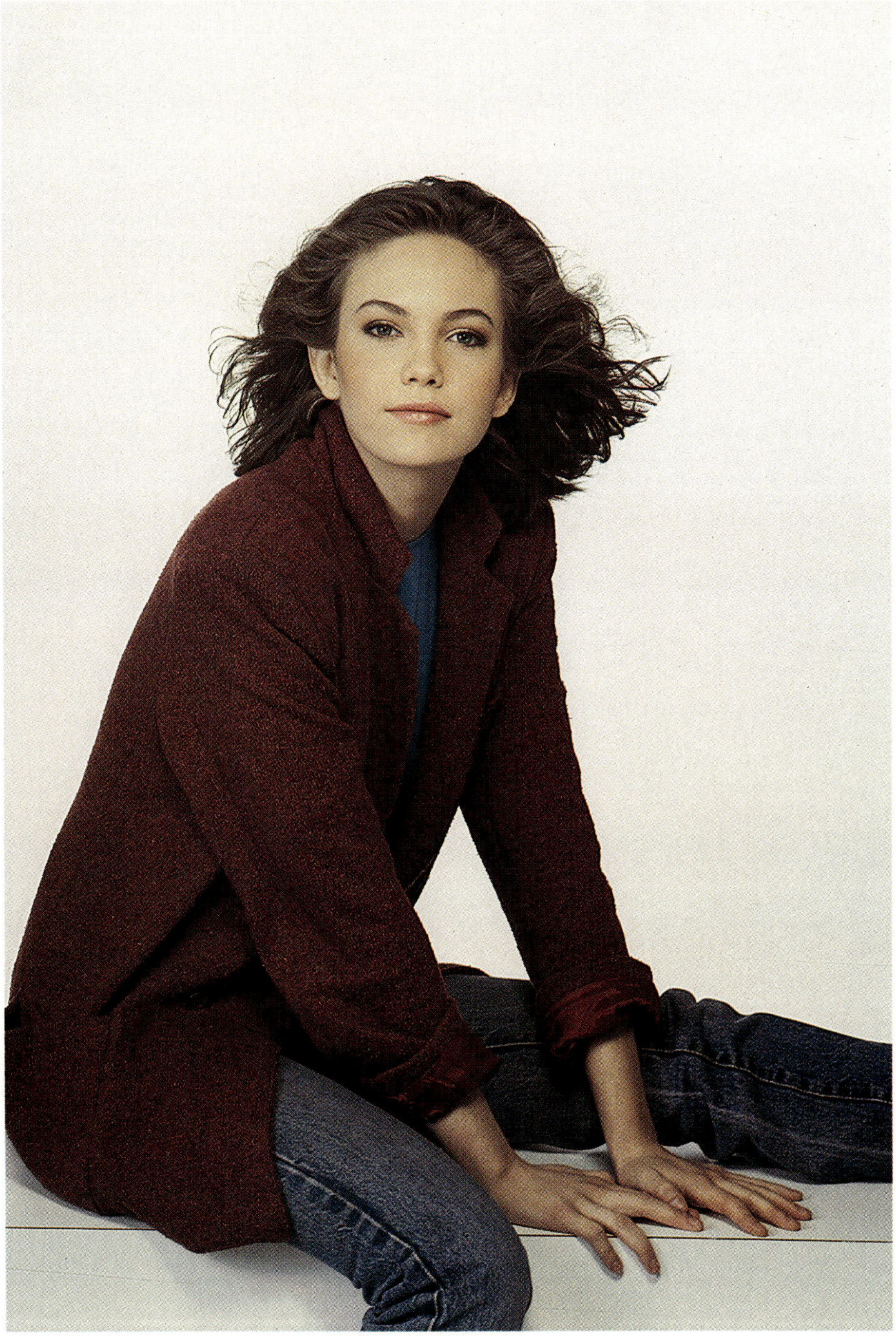

As soon as a subject enters my studio, I begin evaluating potential lighting. In the case of talented actress Diane Lane, I had originally decided to use a single main light of medium to high contrast. The decision was based on two factors—my desire to emphasize Diane's fine features and her flawless, youthful complexion. Both are capable of enduring relatively hard lighting.

I began by asking the actress to assume a relatively static pose, suitable for one specific main-light position. As I began shooting, I noticed a shyness in my young subject and realized that she would be more comfortable in a less constrictive lighting environment.

I replaced the hard, single main light with two softer sources. I placed one light, in a six-foot silvered umbrella, approximately four feet to Diane's right and a five-foot softbox at the same distance from her left. I metered the main lights separately, allowing the umbrella light one exposure step more power, for slight facial modeling.

With this lighting, Diane could move freely in front of the camera without concern on my part for precise modeling because contrast had been reduced dramatically. The change was ideal. Diane moved beautifully, providing my client with a variety of images from which to select.

I lit the background from both sides, using two flash heads in umbrellas. This light was balanced to give a clean, white background. □

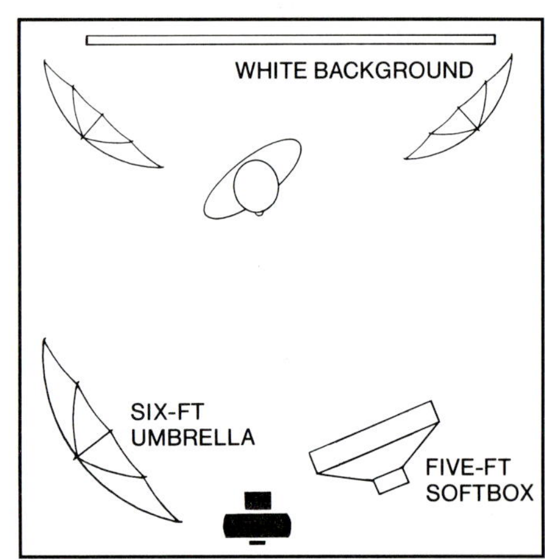

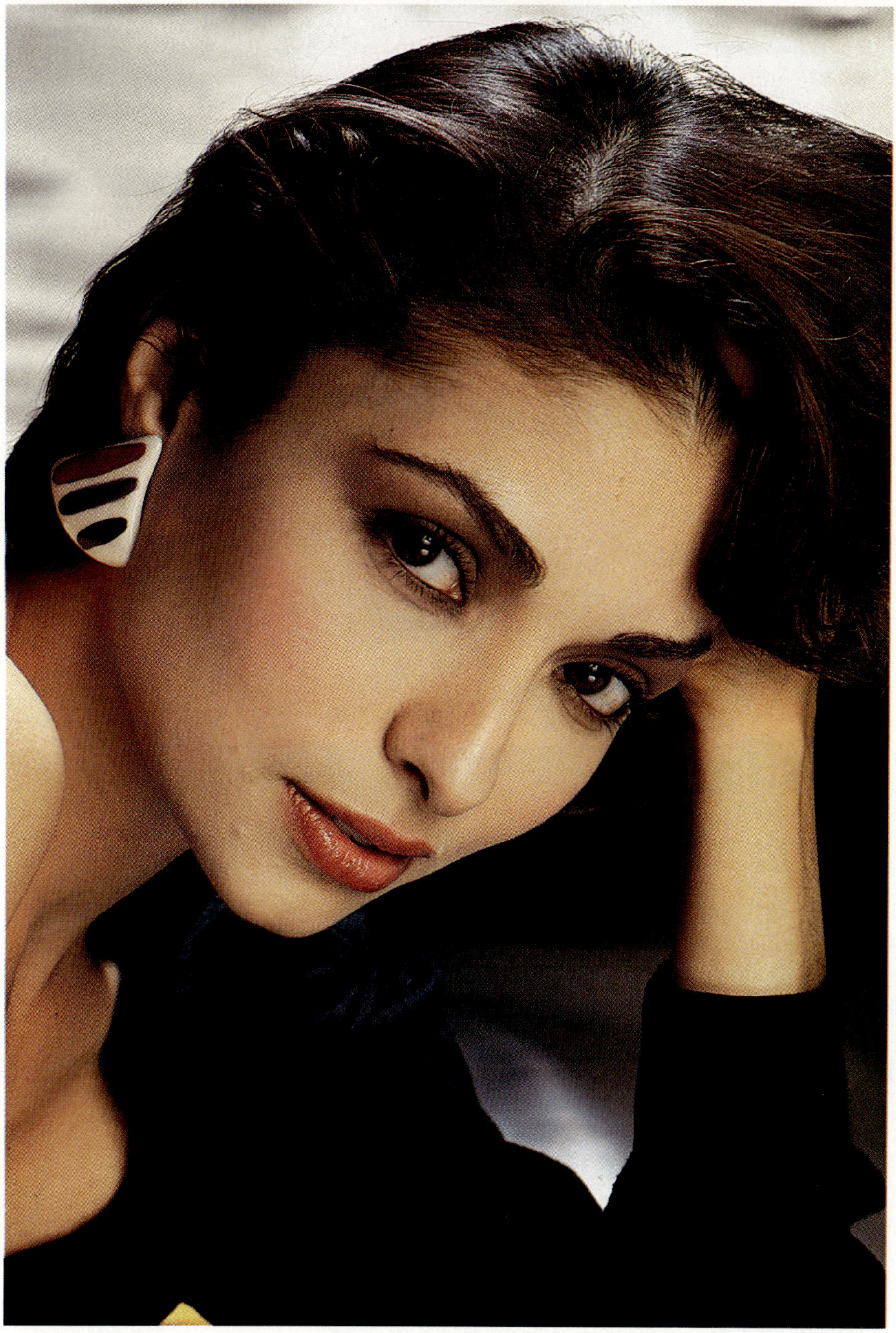

Subject: Professional model
Client: La Costa Products International, Inc.
Location: Gary Bernstein Studio, Los Angeles, California
Camera: Nikon F3
Lens: 105mm *f*-4 Micro-Nikkor
Lighting: Two 400-watt-second electronic flash units
Light Control: One 50-inch silver umbrella; one focusing variable-angle reflector
Film: Kodachrome 25
Exposure Metering: Gossen Ultra Pro meter
Exposure: *f*-5.6 (shutter at 1/60 second)

Two lights and a very simple set enabled me to produce this striking glamour image. A background of silver mylar was suspended behind the model. I used two 400-watt-second flash heads. The main light, approximately four feet from the subject, was bounced from a 50-inch silver umbrella.

The second light was in a variable-angle reflector set for wide-angle coverage. It was on a boom stand, above and slightly behind the subject. It created the rim lighting on the model's hair and shoulder, and added highlight value to the silver mylar. I took care that no unwanted spill light reached the subject's face.

I took an incident-light reading of the model's face. The reading was *f*-5.6. On my 105mm lens, this aperture gave sufficient subject sharpness while allowing the specular mylar to record as a blurred abstraction.

The rim light was metered and adjusted to deliver 1-1/2 exposure steps more light than the main umbrella.

An infinite variety of background configurations and colorations can be achieved with seamless mylar. When working with highly reflective backgrounds, avoid specular reflections back to the camera lens.

It's important to isolate the subject graphically. Notice that the light edge of the model's face is against the darkest part of the mylar while the top of her dark hair falls against a light background area. The only location from which to accurately evaluate the tonal relationship of subject to background is the camera position. □

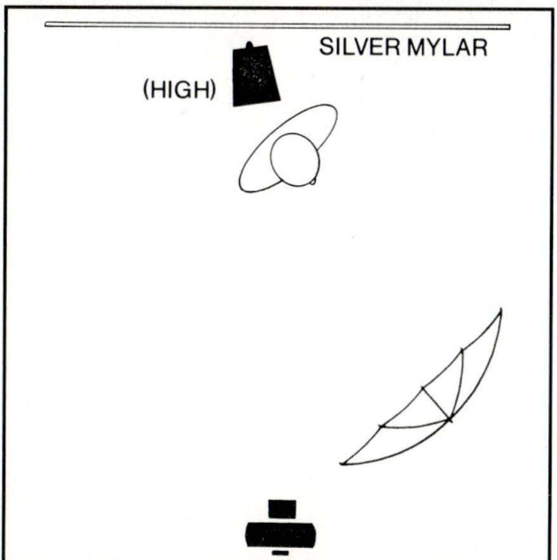

Subject: Professional models
Client: Photogenic Machine Company, Youngstown, Ohio
Art Director: Gary Bernstein
Location: Washington, DC
Camera: Nikon F3
Lens: 85mm *f*-1.4 Auto-Nikkor
Lighting: One 400-watt-second Photogenic Porta-Master electronic flash unit
Light Control: One Photogenic 32-inch Halo
Film: Kodachrome 25
Exposure Metering: Minolta Auto-Flash III, incident-light mode
Exposure: *f*-8 (shutter at 1/60 second)

These two images were purchased as stock photos by the Photogenic Machine Company of Youngstown, Ohio, manufacturers of Photogenic lighting equipment. Both images were shot with one Photogenic Porta-Master 400 flash head in a 32-inch Photogenic Halo. Notice the beautiful light quality produced by the Halo. The light is not as soft and nearly directionless as it would be from a large softbox, and not so hard and specular as to eliminate middle tones.

Both photos were taken against a white, seamless background. For each photo, the Halo was placed slightly closer to the male model than to the female. This lighting position compensated for the man's slightly darker skin tone, producing a more balanced image. The gray tonality of the background was achieved by a 2-step underexposure of the white seamless paper.

These two photos indicate the ease with which a full-length photo may be transformed into a stunning head-and-shoulders portrait. For better composition in the close-up, I asked the female model to stand on some boards to raise her more closely to the height of the male model. The heads are at sufficiently different heights to provide an interesting composition. They are also close enough to each other in height to be viewed as a graphic unit.

The reflection of the Halo in the man's sunglasses is deliberate. □

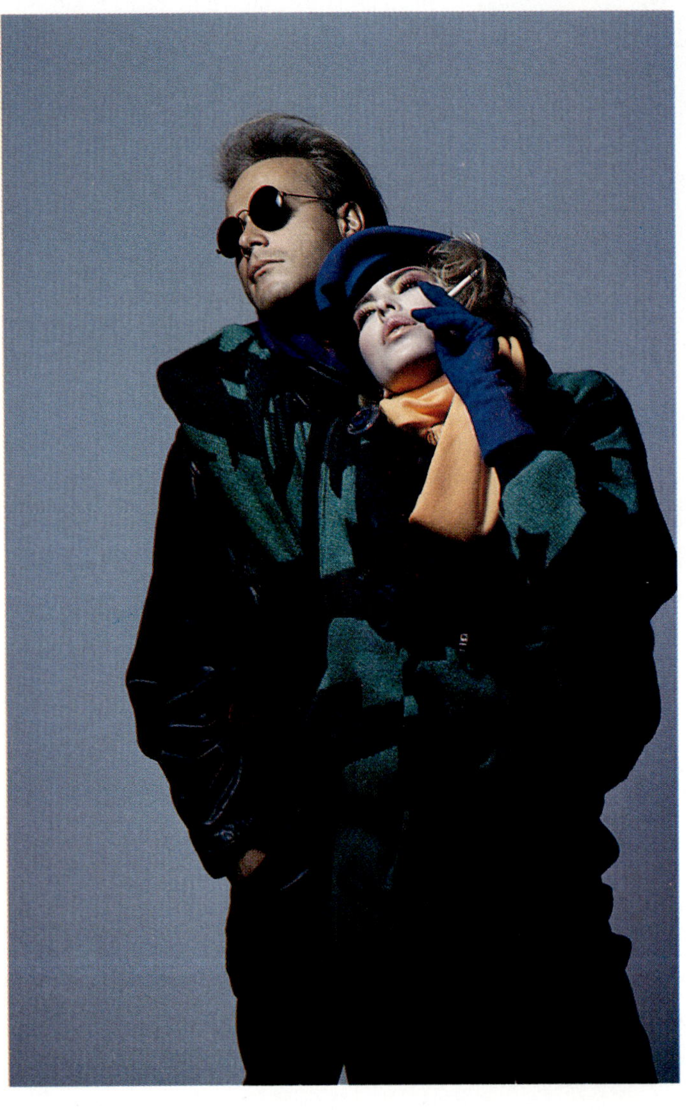

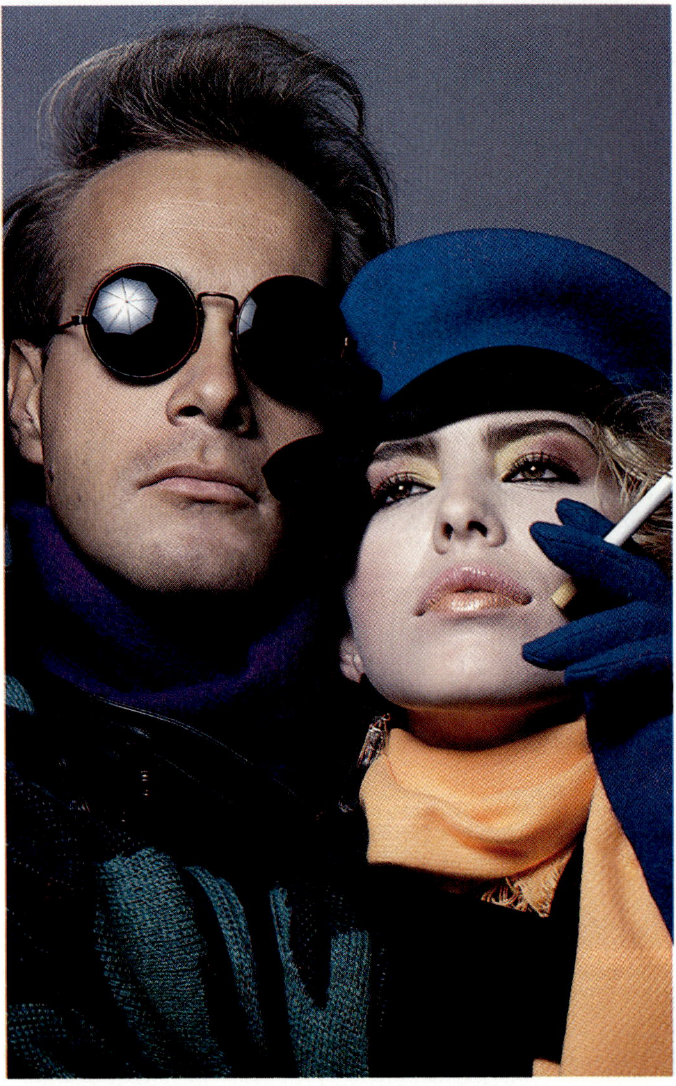

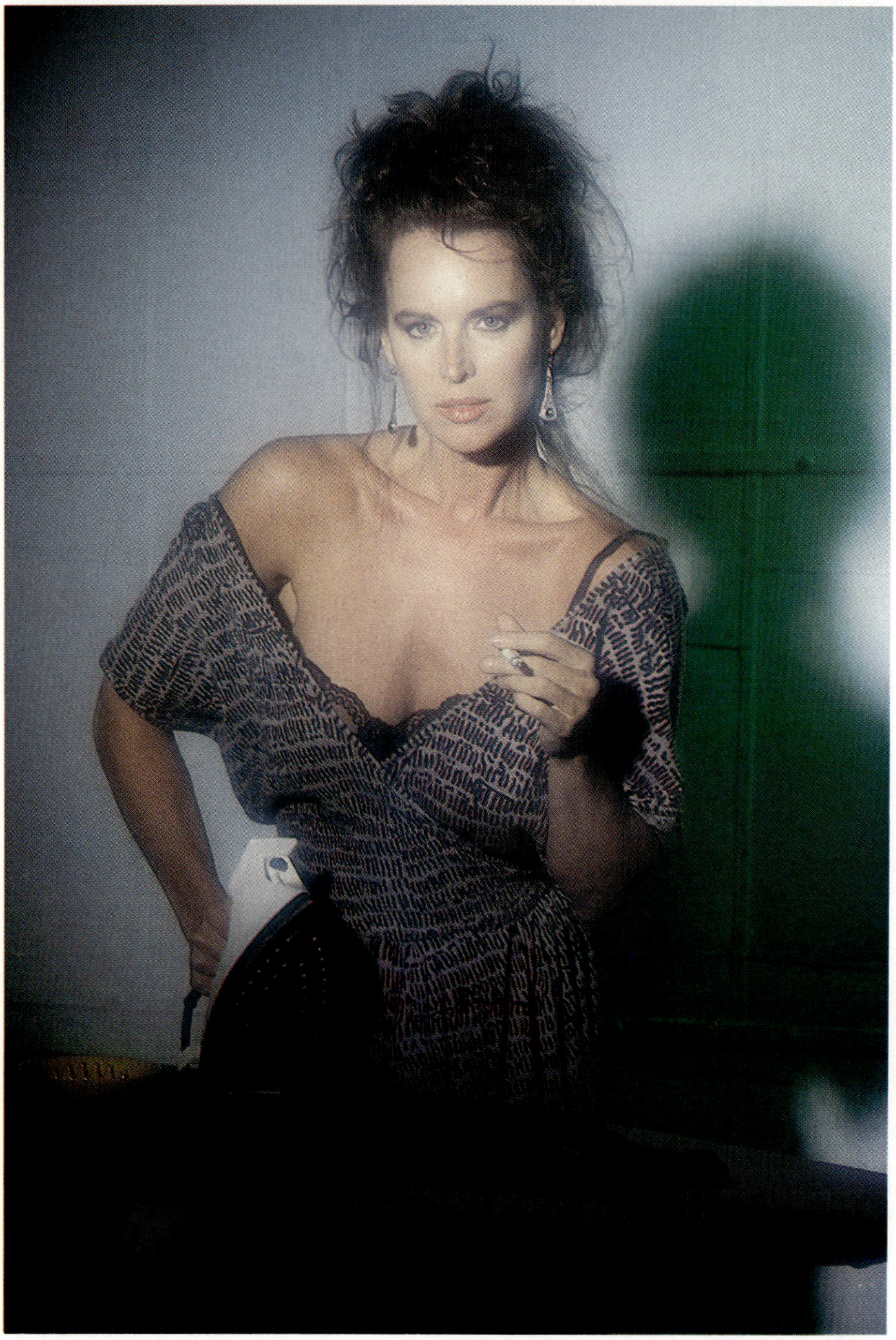

Subject: Professional model
Location: Gary Bernstein Studio, Los Angeles, California
Camera: Nikon F3
Lens: 85mm *f*-1.4 Auto-Nikkor
Lighting: Two 200-watt-second Photogenic Porta-Master flash units
Film: Kodachrome 25
Filtration: Green gelatin filter; Harrison & Harrison diffuser
Exposure Metering: Minolta Auto-Flash III, incident-light mode
Exposure: *f*-5.6 (shutter at 1/60 second)

For this photo, I powered two flash heads from a portable 400-watt-second power supply. Each flash head was in a five-inch reflector. The main light, with barn doors, was slightly to the left of the camera. The barn doors narrowed the light spread, as you can see from the light falloff at the top, bottom and left side.

The subject's shadow on the background added to the pictorial effect. However, as I viewed the image through the viewfinder, it appeared too monochromatic. I altered the lighting to provide a green background shadow. I taped a green gelatin filter to a second flash head and aimed this flash at the background from behind the subject, on her left side.

Main-light exposure was *f*-5.6—determined by placing the incident-light hemisphere of the meter at the subject's face and pointing it toward the main light. Whenever you're using barn doors or grid spots, it's imperative that you take several subject readings. It's the only way to be sure of exposure accuracy in spite of the abrupt falloff of the focused lighting.

I positioned the background light for an exposure of *f*-4. I took the reading by placing the meter's hemisphere at the center of the shadow and pointing it toward the background light. Because the intensity of the background light was less than that of the main light, the shadow on the wall remains. However, the light in the shadow was sufficient to give the shadow a distinct green appearance.

To diffuse and soften the image, I used a diffuser on the camera lens. □

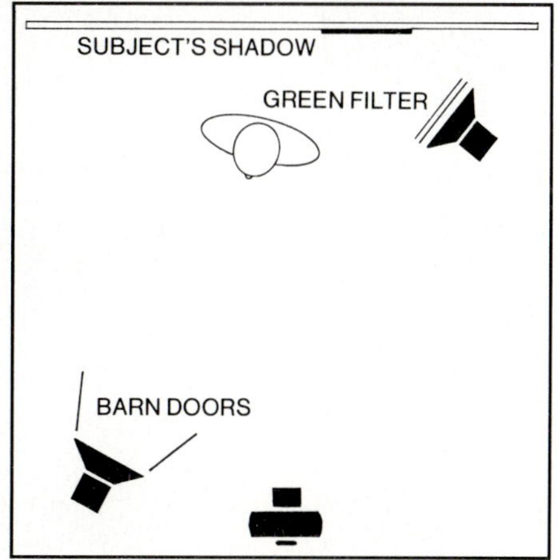

Subject: Professional model
Client: Rainbow Video Corporation, Washington, D.C. and Gary Bernstein Productions, Inc., Culver City, California
Executive Producer: Stanley R. Zupnik
Art Director/Producer: Gary Bernstein
Location: Gary Bernstein Studio, Los Angeles, California
Camera: Nikon F3
Lens: 105mm *f*-1.8 Auto-Nikkor
Lighting: Seven 400-watt-second Photogenic Porta-Master flash units
Film: Kodachrome 25
Filtration: Red acetate filters on lights
Exposure Metering: Minolta Auto-Flash III, incident-light mode
Exposure: *f*-5.6 (shutter at 1/60 second)

I made this series of photos for the opening sequence of my 40-minute instructional videotape, *The Magic of Photography.* The images are accompanied by an audio track of *I Put a Spell on You,* recorded by Screamin' Jay Hawkins (CBS Records). The images complement the music. The leather outfit and background of smoke and fire are ideal for the heavy blues rendition.

The diagram shows the set. There were three layers of cut silver and gold mylar strips, supported on portable BD stands. Behind them was a black background. On each side, facing the mylar layers, I placed 400-watt-second Photogenic Porta-Master flash heads—six lights in all. Each light had a red gelatin filter.

The subject was lit by a single 400-watt-second flash spotlight on a boom stand. All lights were balanced for an *f*-5.6 exposure. I took incident-light background readings from the center of the mylar curtains, pointing the meter toward the side lights. I took an incident-light subject reading from the model's face, pointing the meter toward the main spotlight.

A large electric fan blew the strips of mylar and the model's hair. Therefore, each image has a different background and subject appearance. Each image reflects the reddish light differently from the constantly moving gold and silver mylar. □

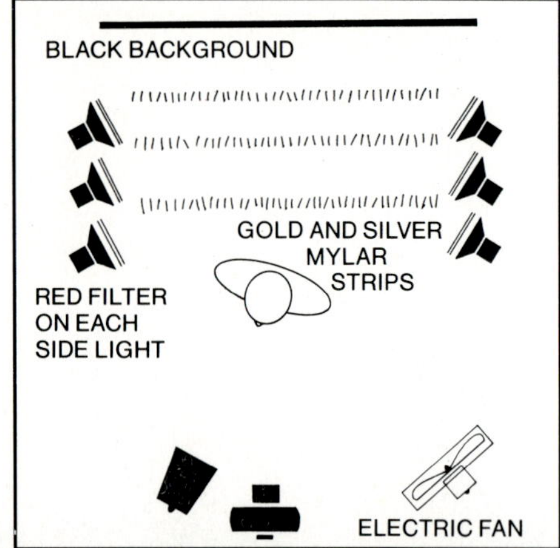

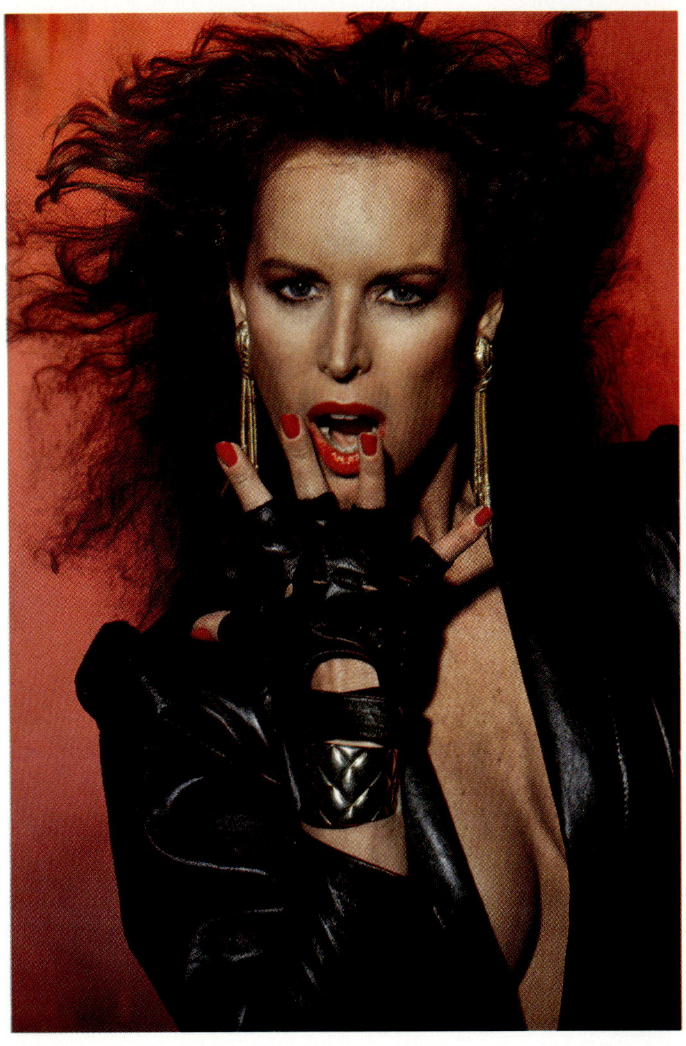

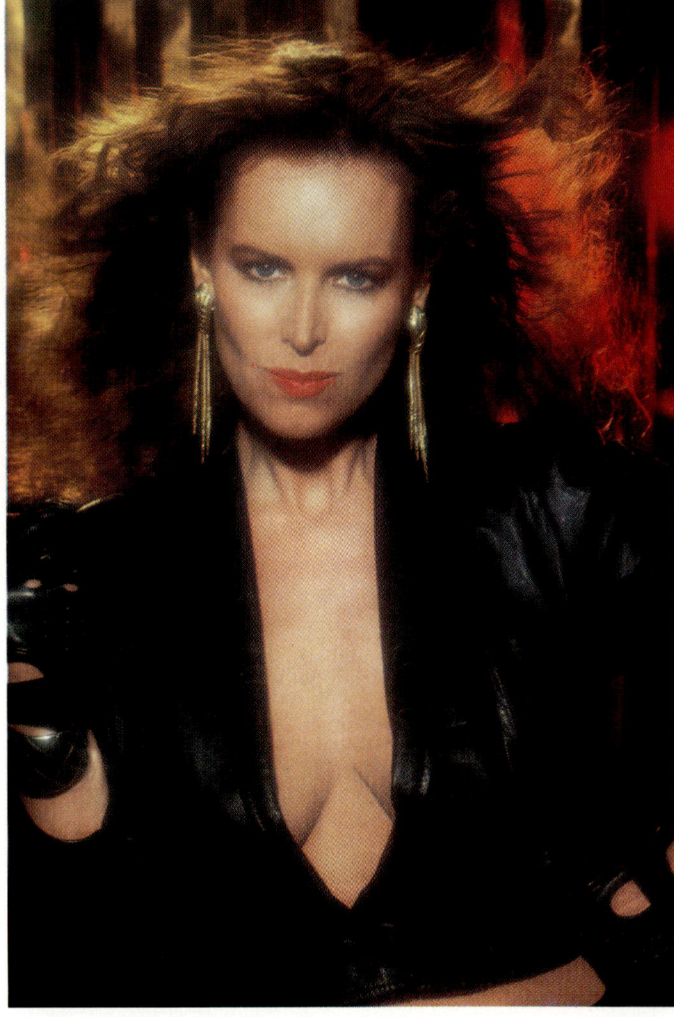

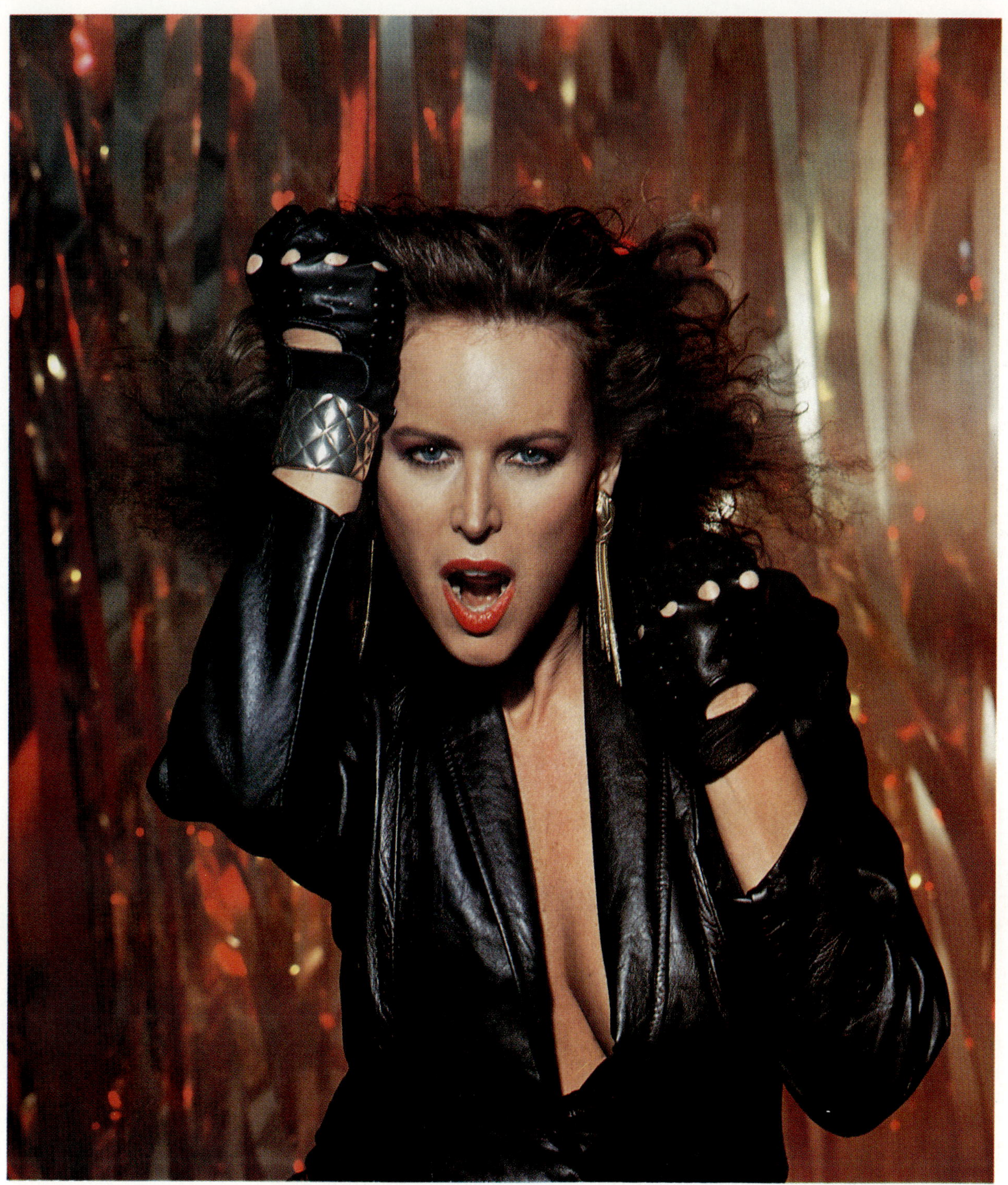

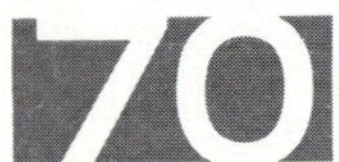

Subject: Professional models
Location: San Diego, California
Camera: Nikon F2AS
Lens: 105mm ƒ-2.5 Auto-Nikkor
Lighting: Two Balcar 600-watt-second electronic flash units
Film: Kodachrome 25
Exposure Metering: Minolta Auto-Flash III, incident-light mode
Exposure: ƒ-8 (shutter at 1/60 second)

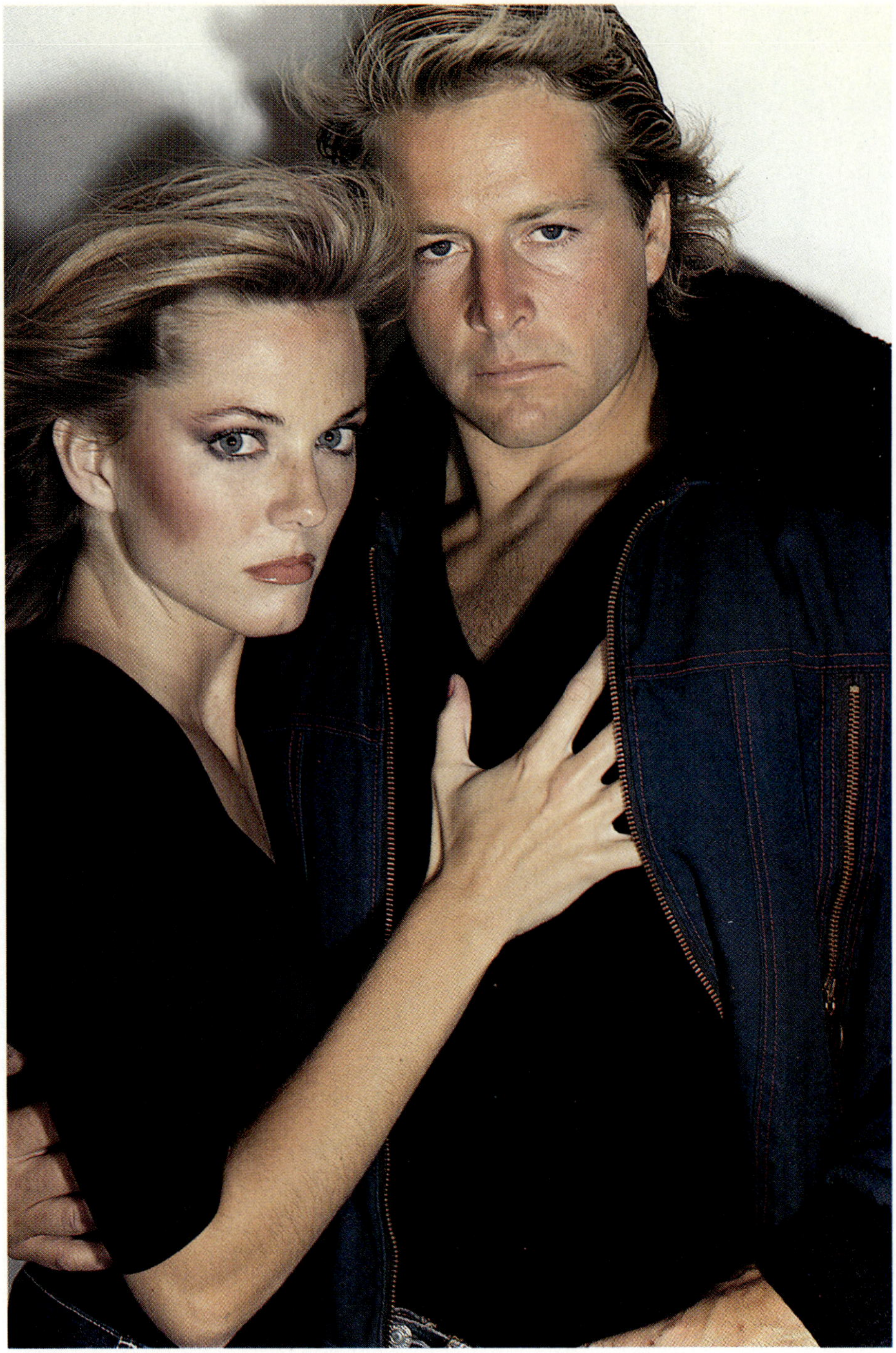

This was the first shot taken during a two-day photo seminar I gave in San Diego, California. I wanted serious subject attitudes, appropriate for the harsh, directional main lighting. The models, who had only met each other moments earlier, responded perfectly.

I began by posing the man with his head and shoulders facing the camera. In classical portraiture, this body position is regarded as a *masculine* pose. Next, I directed the woman to turn her body toward the man while looking toward the camera. This created a typically *feminine* body position. By tilting her head slightly toward her partner she effectively enabled the couple to record as a unit—graphically and emotionally.

The photo was lit with two spotlights—one to either side of my camera. The multiple background shadows are an intended part of the graphics and composition. The two conflicting shadows on the wall add a sense of movement to the image—an effect I enhanced with the addition of a small fan to blow the subjects' hair.

I metered the shot by placing my incident-light meter between the two subjects and pointing it between the two main-light sources.

All individuals—not only professional actors and models—possess some acting potential. Getting the desired response for the moment of photography is the photographer's responsibility. The effectiveness of the attitudes of these models is largely attributable to the rapport and communication between us. At the moment this photograph was taken, they were aware only of our relationship. □

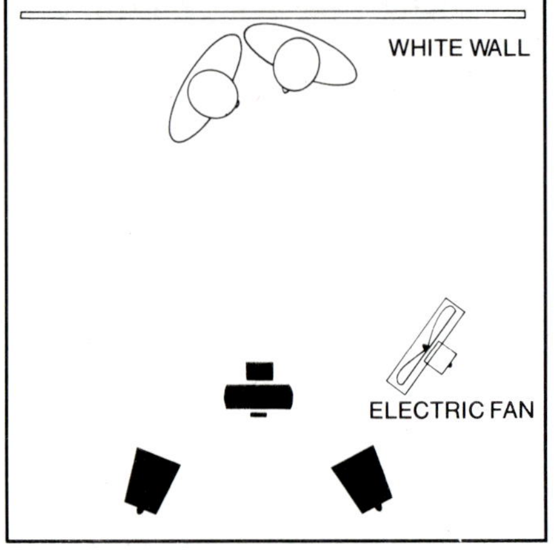

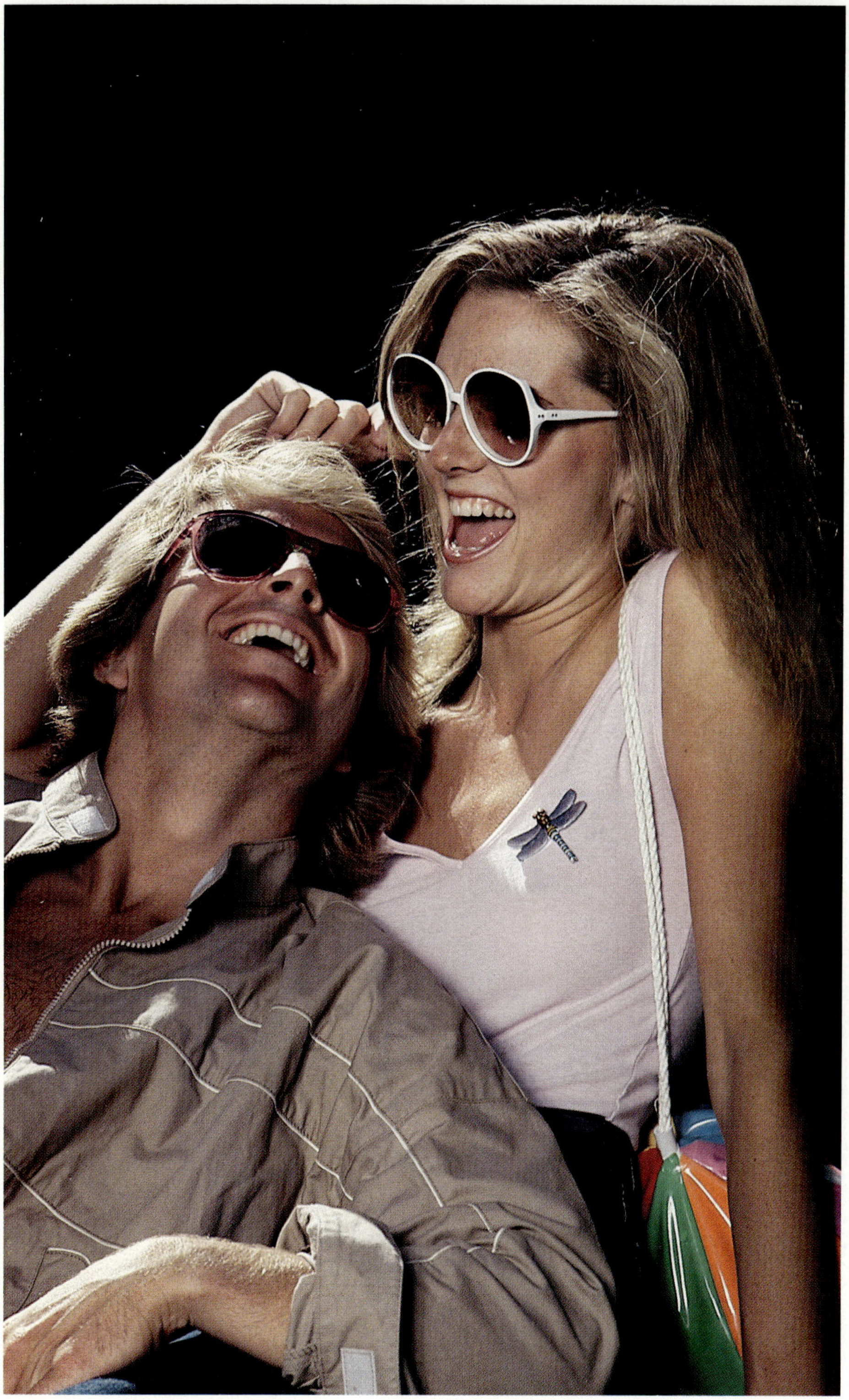

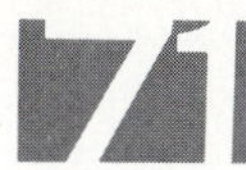

Subject: Professional models
Location: San Diego, California
Camera: Nikon F2AS
Lens: 85mm ƒ-1.8 Auto-Nikkor
Lighting: Midday sunlight
Light Control: Silver Rocaflector
Film: Kodachrome 25
Exposure Metering: Minolta Auto-Flash II, incident-light mode
Exposure: 1/250 second at ƒ-11

This natural-light photo was taken at the same San Diego seminar as the photo on the opposite page. Not only do I enjoy teaching photography seminars, but they also provide the opportunity to produce new images for my portfolio.

This photograph illustrates the control of midday sun afforded by an efficient reflector. The shot was for a make-believe ad for sunglasses. The ad depicted a guy and his lady having fun in the sun.

The black background consisted of a group of palm trees in deep shade. I asked my models to sit in the sun, immediately in front of the palms. Direct sunlight rim lighted the subjects, accentuating their forms against the dark background.

The sun, reflected by a large silver reflector just to the left of my camera, was the main-light source. I metered the shot through the lens of my Nikon camera, bracketing a full exposure step in either direction.

I asked the models to play and have fun, without concern for lighting or camera angle. As they played, I made a series of shots. The result reproduced here is a "planned candid" with believability and impact. □

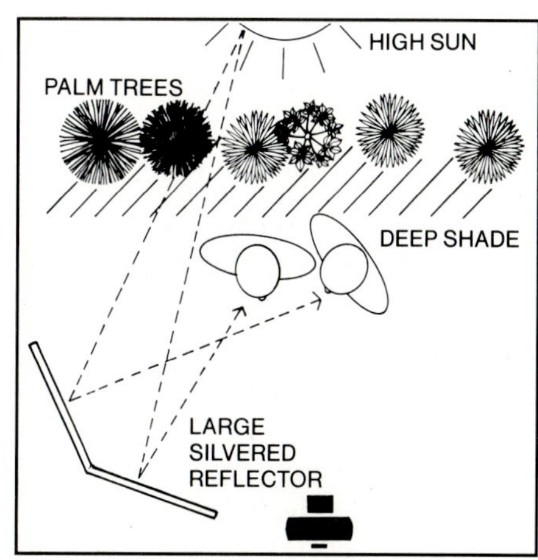

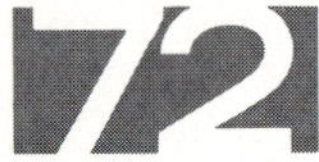

Subject: Professional model
Client: La Costa Products International, Inc.
Art Directors: William Randall and Russ Heinze
Location: Carlsbad, California
Camera: Nikon F3
Lens: 50mm *f*-1.4 Auto-Nikkor
Lighting: Daylight and one 600-watt-second electronic flash unit
Film: Kodachrome 64
Exposure Metering: Minolta Auto-Flash III, incident-light mode
Exposure: 1/8 second at *f*-4.5

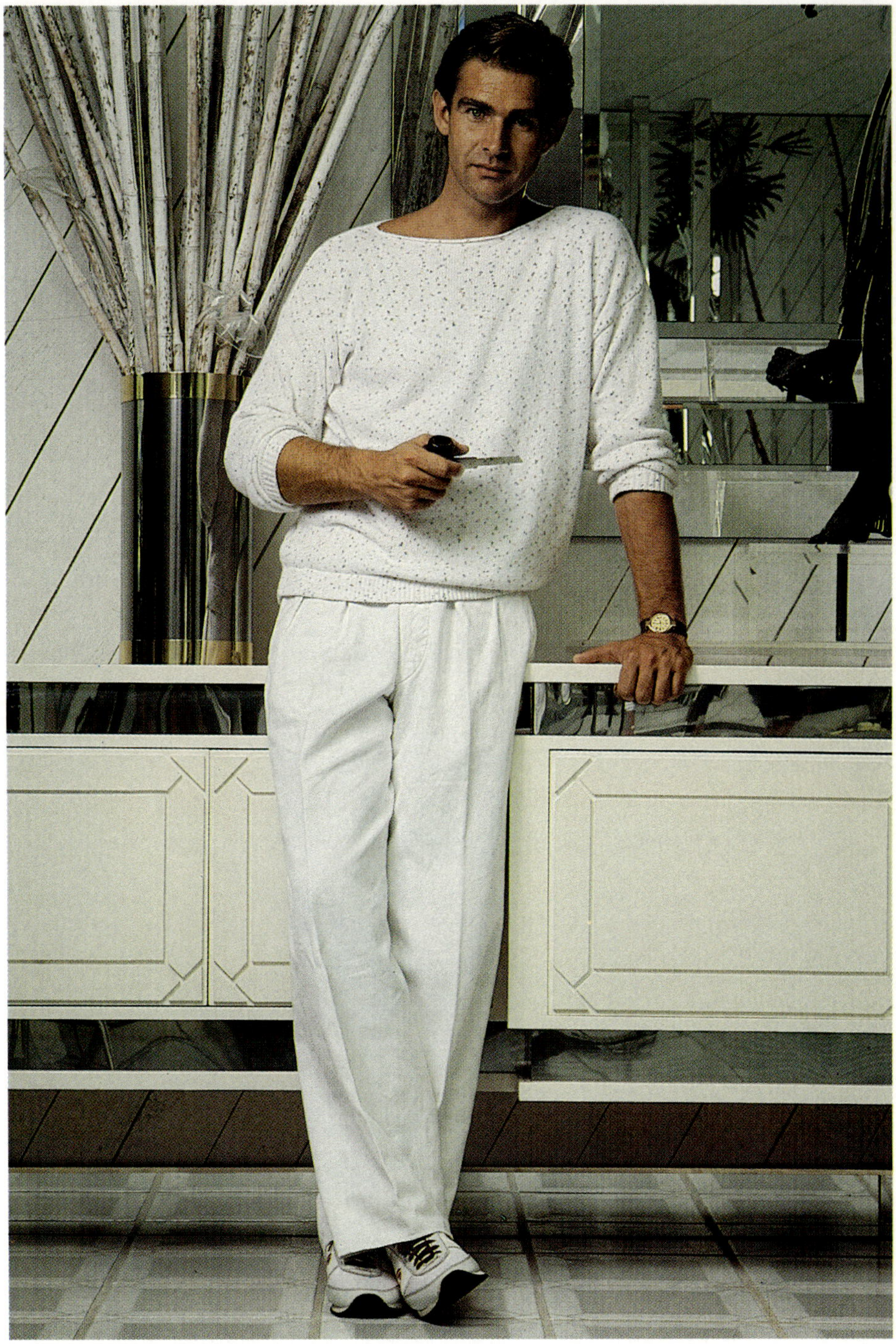

Synchro-sunlight photography combines electronic flash with daylight. It is commonly used outdoors when the sun is high in the sky, giving poor facial modeling to a subject's face. At such times, a subject's eyes fall into shadow, devoid of catchlights or detail. Adding electronic flash from a lower angle brightens the eye sockets, adds catchlights to the eyes, and creates more pleasing facial modeling.

For this photo, I used synchro-sunlight indoors. The ambient light in the scene came from large skylights in the ceiling above the model. This light served as fill light. I used a hand-held incident-light exposure meter to determine the amount of available light falling on the subject. Holding my meter at waist level and pointing the incident-light hemisphere at the ceiling, I got a reading of 1/8 second at *f*-4 for Kodachrome 64 film.

For main light, I placed a 600-watt-second electronic flash, bounced from a white umbrella, to the left of the camera. The resultant light on the right side of the subject's face was adjusted for a highlight exposure of *f*-4.5. The background was underexposed slightly to lend additional emphasis to the subject.

In synchro-sunlight photography, the flash can serve either as fill light or, as in this example, as main light.

When you photograph a structural setting such as this one, including walls, mirrors and cabinets, try to keep vertical elements parallel to the vertical borders of the image. You achieve this by aiming your SLR in a true horizontal direction, or by using a special perspective-control lens. □

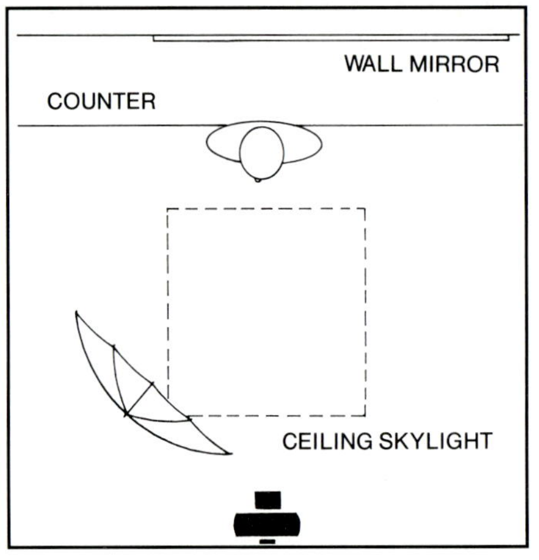

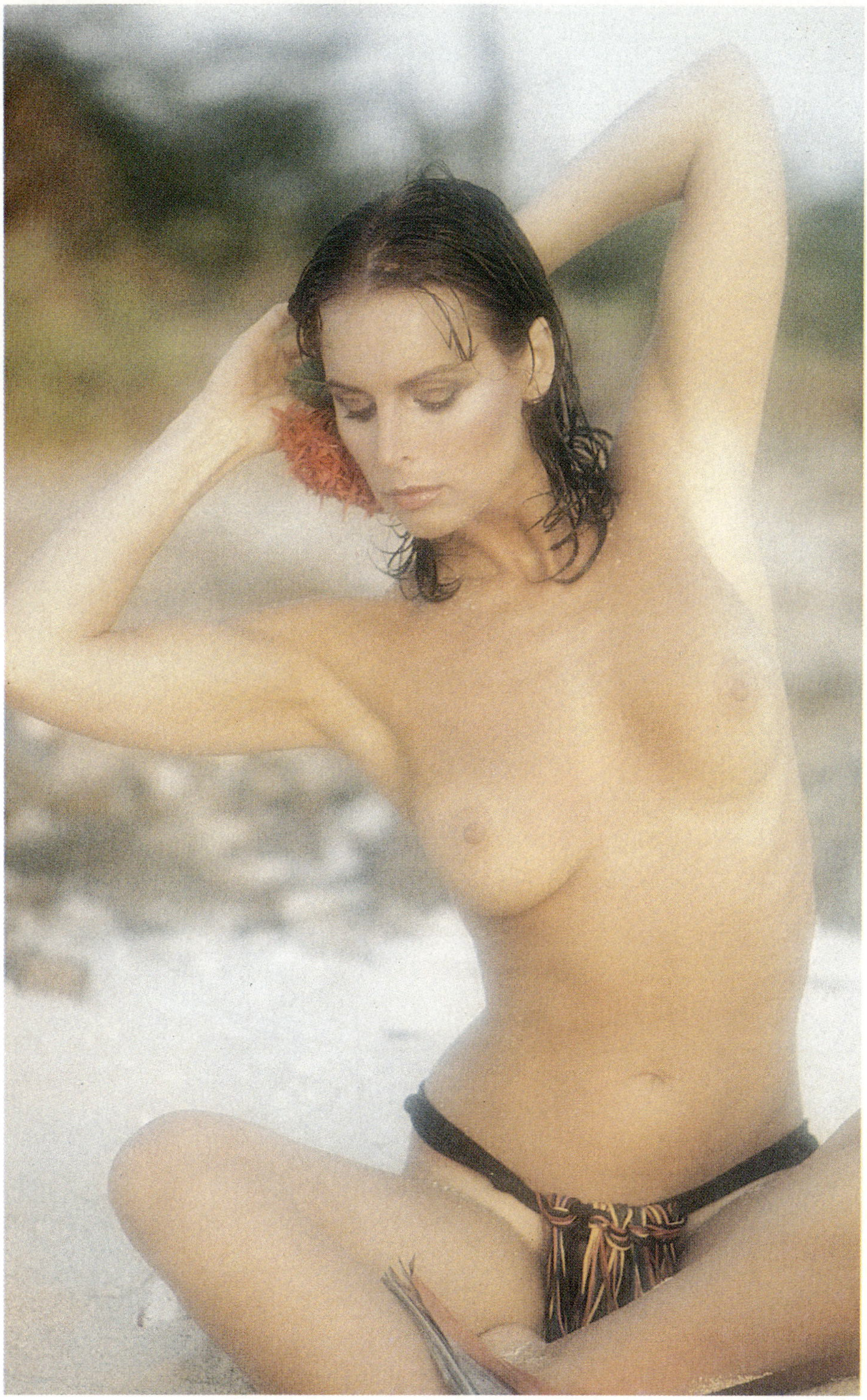

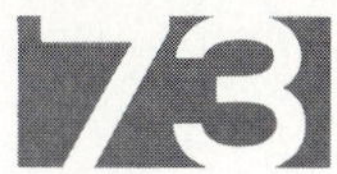

Subject: Professional model
Location: Aruba, Netherland Antilles
Camera: Nikon F3
Lens: 105mm *f*-2.5 Auto-Nikkor
Lighting: Overcast daylight
Film: High-Speed Ektachrome 160
Exposure Metering: Nikon through-the-lens, center-weighted
Exposure: 1/500 second at *f*-4

Pictorial continuity in a photo sequence is important, whether you're preparing an editorial layout, a catalog, or a picture story. This continuity involves maintaining the same basic atmosphere and light quality throughout.

This photo is from a series I produced for my first book, *Burning Cold.* I maintained pictorial continuity in several ways. I used a homemade lens diffuser, prepared by spraying a skylight filter with plastic fixative. To ensure limited depth of field, I used a short telephoto lens at a large aperture setting. I maintained a continuity in styling and a similarity in subject attitudes.

I took this photo at midday, using natural overcast daylight as the only source of illumination. Light from above, even when diffused, can throw a subject's eyes into shadow and yield unflattering facial modeling. By seating my subject on the highly reflective white sand on the beach, I was able to bounce a lot of overhead light up into her face to lighten shadows.

As a final touch, I selected a fast film of relatively coarse grain and low contrast. □

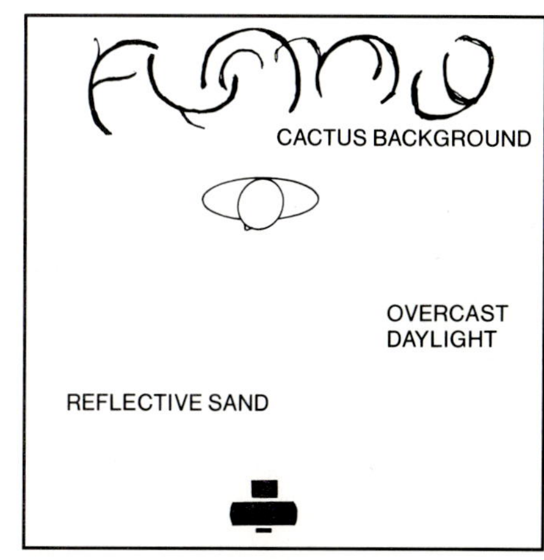

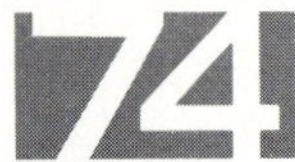

Subject: Stacy Keach
Client: Jean-Paul Germain, Ltd.
Art Director: Gary Bernstein
Location: Burbank Studios, Burbank, California
Camera: Nikon F3
Lens: 85mm *f*-1.8 Auto-Nikkor
Lighting: Two 600-watt-second electronic flash units
Light Control: 40-inch silvered umbrella on main light; wide-angle reflector on background light
Film: Kodachrome 25
Exposure Metering: Minolta Auto-Flash III, incident-light mode
Exposure: *f*-8 (shutter at 1/60 second)

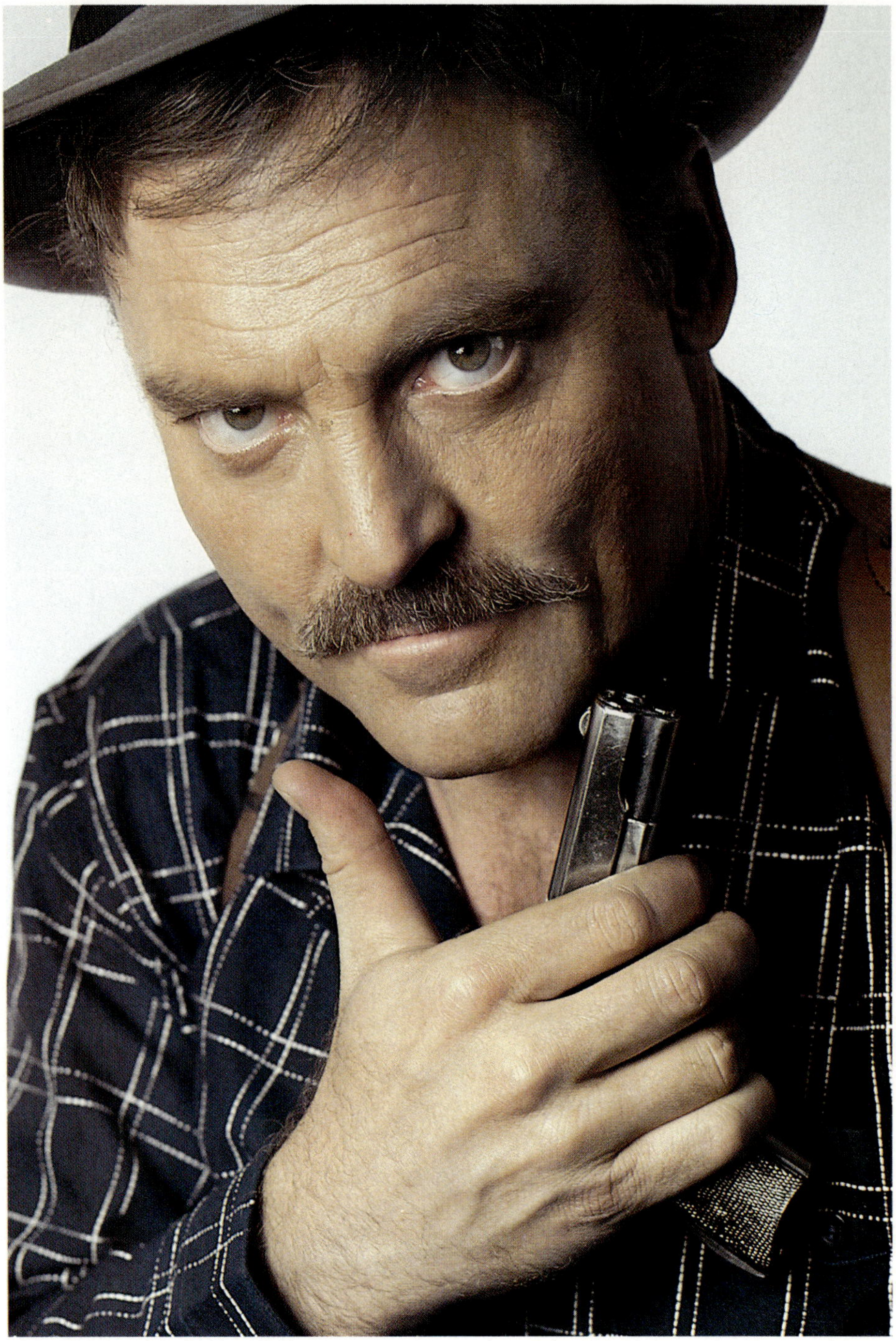

My client desperately needed a photograph of Stacy Keach for a magazine-ad deadline. Keach was in the middle of shooting an episode of the TV series, *Mike Hammer.* After discussing several options, all of which would have caused us to miss the dealine, I opted to photograph him in a very small office at Burbank Studios. I was allowed a maximum of 15 minutes to get the shot before Stacy would have to return to the set.

We quickly set up a white, seamless background on a portable BD background stand behind a desk. Next, we placed a 600-watt-second flash head with wide-angle reflector on the floor between the seamless and the desk. The flash was pointed at the background. We set up a 600-watt-second main light in a silvered umbrella. By the time Stacy arrived, everything was set. I asked him to sit on the edge of the desk. He couldn't have been more cooperative or better in front of the camera. It made the rushed session much easier for me.

I decided to shoot Stacy as his T.V. character, Mike Hammer, and asked him to don his hat and shoulder holster. When I asked for the gun, he realized it had been left on the set. We found a cigarette lighter in the shape of a small automatic pistol. Stacy's hand carefully covered the "giveaway" parts of the lighter.

After just five minutes, we had recorded a series of wonderful images with that classic Keach look. □

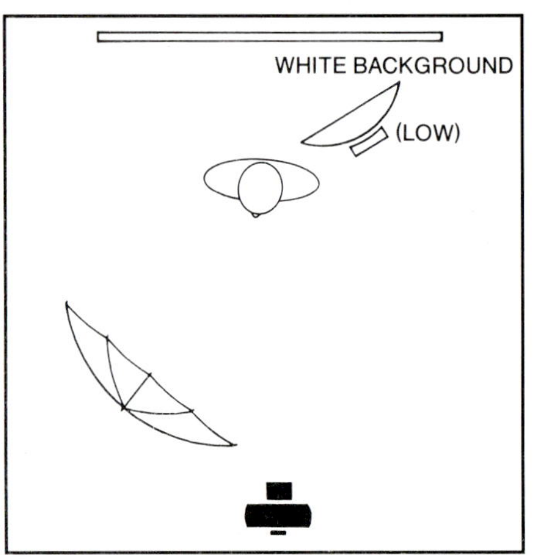

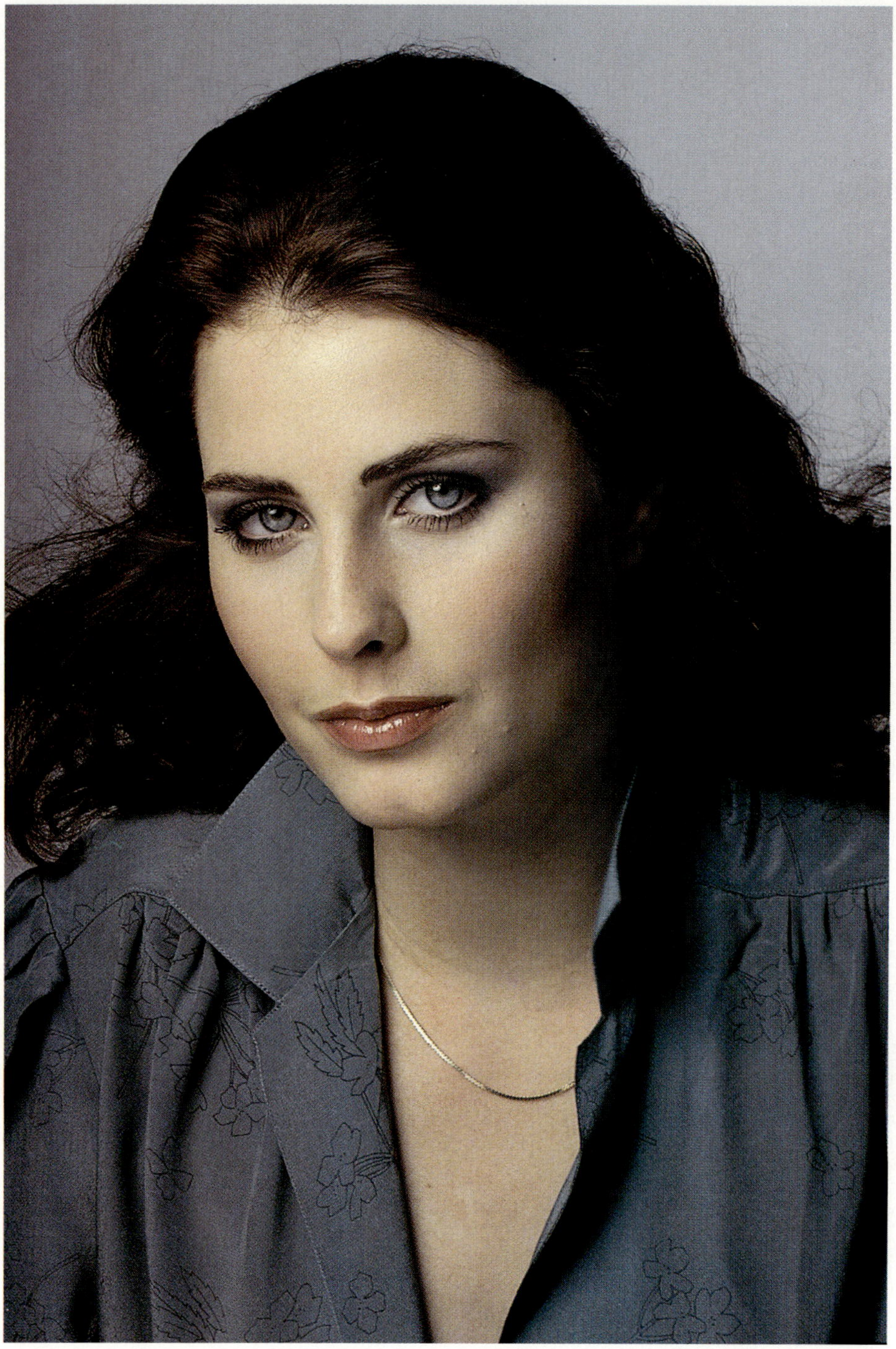

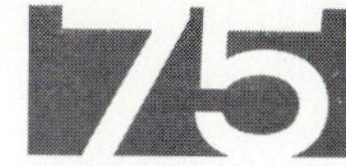

Subject: Professional model
Client: Max Factor, Inc.
Ad Agency: Wells, Rich and Greene (West), Inc.
Art Director: Bob Cole
Location: Gary Bernstein Studio, Los Angeles, California
Camera: Nikon F2
Lens: 105mm *f*-4 Micro-Nikkor
Lighting: One 1250-watt-second Rollei electronic flash in pan reflector
Film: Kodachrome 25
Exposure Metering: Minolta Auto-Flash II, incident-light mode
Exposure: *f*-11 (shutter at 1/60 second)

Posing for pictures is an everyday occurrence for this top New York model. However, most subjects are nervous during a photo session. Use every means possible to relax the subject and build his or her confidence. Background music and the availability of beverages are a "must."

It helps the subject if you start with basic and simple poses. I begin most sessions by having the subject seated on my studio floor. Regardless of a subject's age, this seems to give lots of support—both physically and emotionally.

As a further posing aid, I have a couple of stools that can easily be raised or lowered. The stools, made by The Adjustrite Company, Bowling Green, Ohio, work in unison, one providing a seat and the other a resting surface for hands, elbows, or even the head.

The posing-stool system provides a lot of versatility. For example, you can tape a pillow to the front stool and cover it with a variety of fabrics, from silk to burlap. This can provide a perfect head and forearm support for tight headshots. The stools are compact and easily stored.

To make this beauty shot advertising a cosmetics product, I taped a Photogenic Silfoil reflector to the top of a stool in front of the model. It bounced the main light back into the model's face, reducing contrast and lightening her blue eyes. The single light recorded *f*-11 on the subject, with a falloff of 2 exposure steps on the white background to produce the gray tone. □

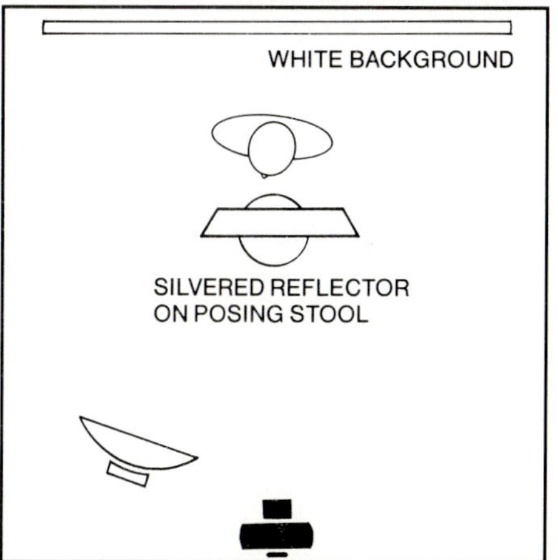

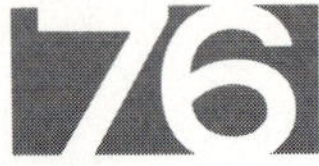

Subject: Professional model
Client: Bullock's Department Store
Ad Agency: Harrison Services, Inc.
Location: Los Angeles, California
Camera: Nikon FM
Lens: 35mm *f*-2 Auto-Nikkor
Lighting: Two 1200-watt-second electronic flash units
Light Control: Two seven-foot V-shaped reflectors
Film: Kodachrome 64
Filtration: Homemade diffuser
Exposure Metering: Minolta Auto-Flash III, incident-light mode
Exposure: *f*-5.6 (shutter at 1/60 second)

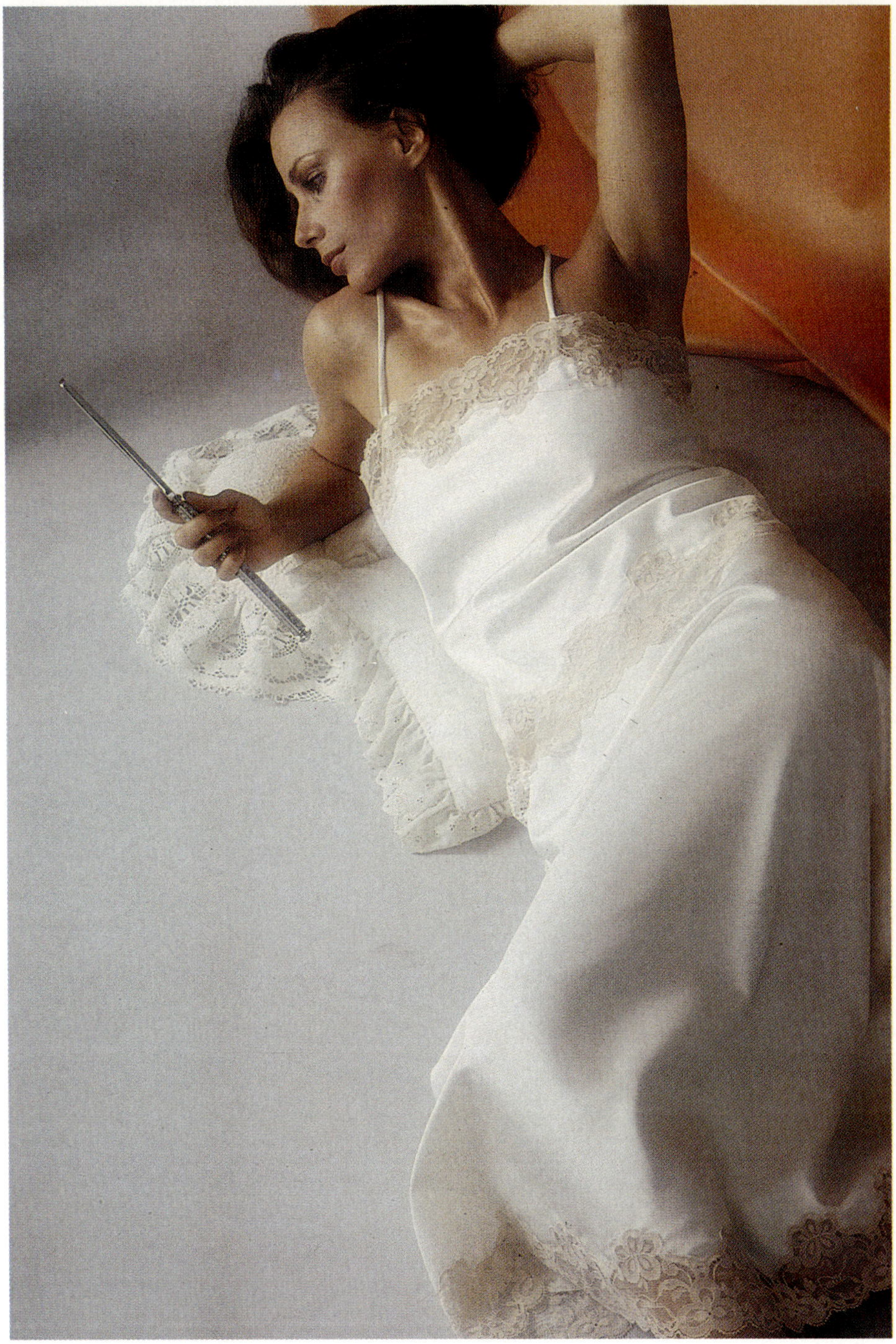

This photo is one of a series I made for a lingerie catalog for a department store. To subdue subject detail in these "intimate" photographs, the client wanted to avoid the super sharpness possible with modern lenses. To satisfy this requirement, I used a lens diffuser, which I made by spraying acrylic fixative on a haze filter. Toward the same end, I also used soft lighting.

I placed a bare flash head close to each of two seven-foot-high V-shaped reflector cards. One reflector was approximately five feet from the model, to the left of the camera. The second reflector and light were behind the model and directed toward the melon-colored fabric. Each light source indicated an exposure of *f*-5.6.

I posed the model on the studio floor, allowing her body to curve toward the camera position in a long S-shape. I exaggerated the composition by using a 35mm wide-angle lens. This gave me the graphic effect I wanted and also provided depth of field over the entire garment featured.

Although this image was taken for advertising purposes, it would be just as appropriate as part of a personal portrait series. It's to your advantage to try many photographic variations with your subjects—especially in professional portraiture. Even a subject who originally wanted only a head-and-shoulders portrait would find it difficult to turn down a soft and beautiful full-figure rendition such as this one. □

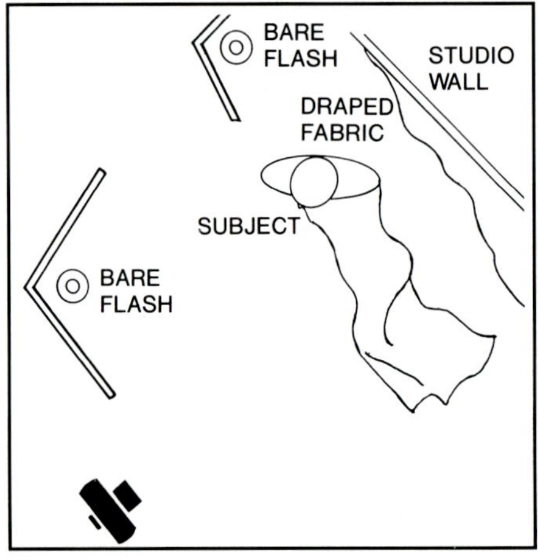

Models Appearing in this Book

The professional models and other subjects not named on the picture pages are listed below. I want to express to each of them my sincere gratitude.

COVER:

Kay Sutton York

ESSAYS:

3-2 Mary Maciukas for Truform
3-3 (left to right) Heidi Lane, Thed Ostindien, Bob Pitard, Joe MacDonald, Dennis LaMarsh for Rich's/Atlanta
3-4 Linea Hogan
3-5 Matt Collins for Paul Davril
3-6 Kay Sutton York
3-7 Darlene Fluegel
3-9 Scott MacKenzie
3-12 Ted Dawson
3-13 Paul Garcia, Joseyann for *Esquire*
3-14 Matt Collins for *Esquire*
3-16 Greg Seton
3-17 Cynthia Cypert for La Costa Products
3-18 Cynthia Cypert for La Costa Products
3-20 Bill Looke, Lynn Hollbrook for The Horchow Collection
3-21 Pamela Hensley for Hart, Schaffner & Marx
3-23 Lynn Brooks, Scott MacKenzie for Gant
3-24 Kay Sutton York for Virgin Islands Rum
3-26 Roy Sumerset for J.P. Stevens
3-27 Bob Pitard for J.P. Stevens
3-28 Kay Sutton York for Max Factor
4-1 to 4-12 Kay Sutton York
6-1 Kay Sutton York
6-2 Kathy Speirs
6-3 Kathy Speirs

PORTFOLIO:

2 Liz Miller, Bill Simpkins
3 Kay Sutton York
5 Susan Scott, Frank Telfer
6 Jeff Henry, Linda Karecki
7 Romé Bernstein
8 Kay Sutton York
10 Bob Menna
11 Donna Keegan, Paul Rich
12 Romé Bernstein
13 Patty McGuire
14 David Connell
15 Ron Hays
16 Nancy Pianta
17 Pam Miller
18 Scott MacKenzie
19 (clockwise from top left) Kim Goodwin, Allan Elsmo, Sherry Bahr, Kerrie Clark, David Monroe, Pamela Miller
20 Susan Scott
23 Patty Roseman
25 Kay Sutton York
28 Kay Sutton York
30 David Cullinane, Johanna Weiting
31 Kay Sutton York
33 Nancy Dutiel
34 Matt Collins
35 Lynn Brooks, David Olander
36 Kay Sutton York
37 Kay Sutton York
38 Darlene Fluegel
39 Gunnar Magg, Kate Nyberg
41 Debbie Fares
48 Kay Sutton York
49 Linda Kelly
51 John Rusnak, Kristina Kincaid
52 Kay Sutton York
54 Kay Sutton York, Matt Collins
55 Jennifer Wallace (w/Joe Montana)
56 Kalani Durdan
57 Kay Sutton York
58 Janice Dickenson
59 Kathy Speirs
60 Alan Elsmo, Pamela Miller
62 John McMurray, Jiles Kirkland
63 Lynn Brooks, Scott MacKenzie
66 Diane Marie Manzo
67 John Rusnak, Kristina Kincaid
68 Kay Sutton York
69 Kay Sutton York
70 Brenda McKinley, Terry More
71 Brenda McKinley, Terry More
72 Giles Kohler
73 Kay Sutton York
75 Will Russell
76 Nancy Bleir

Equipment

Listed below is equipment I have found useful in my beauty and glamour photography. I recommend these quality items. For information, write to the addresses supplied. Or, see your local photo dealer.

Gossen Light Meters
Rolleiflex Medium-Format Cameras and Lenses
Rollei Lighting Equipment
Sunpak Flash Units
Berkey Marketing Companies
25-20 Brooklyn-Queens Expressway West
Woodside, NY 11377

Minolta Light Meters
Minolta Corporation
101 Williams Drive
Ramsey, NJ 07446

Nikon Cameras and Lenses
Nikon, Inc.
623 Stewart Avenue
Garden City, NY 11530

Gitzo Tripods and Ball Heads
Karl Heitz, Inc.
34-11 62nd Street
Woodside, NY 11377

Hasselblad Cameras and Lenses
Victor Hasselblad, Inc.
10 Madison Road
Fairfield, NJ 07006

Photogenic Porta-Master 400 and Versatron 800 Lighting
Halo Light-Control Systems
Silfoil Reflectors
Sibern International
419 Main Street
Rochester, IN 46975

Balcar Lighting Equipment
Balcar-Tekno, Inc.
221 West Erie Street
Chicago, IL 60610

Thomastrobe Lighting Equipment
Thomas Instrument Co., Inc.
1313 Belleview Avenue
Charlottesville, VA 22901

Bannister Stand Clamp
Bannister Enterprises, Inc.
Temple City, CA 91780

BD Seamless Background Paper
BD Background Supports
The BD Co.
P.O. Box 3057
2011 West 12th Street
Erie, PA 16512
